Also by Jeremy Treglown

Franco's Crypt: Spanish Culture and Memory Since 1936

V. S. Pritchett: A Working Life

Romancing: The Life and Work of Henry Green

Roald Dahl: A Biography

MR. STRAIGHT ARROW

MR. STRAIGHT ARROW

The Career of
JOHN HERSEY,
Author of
HIROSHIMA

JEREMY TREGLOWN

FARRAR, STRAUS AND GIROUX
New York

Farrar, Straus and Giroux
175 Varick Street, New York 10014

Printed in the United States of America
First edition, 2019

Library of Congress Cataloging-in-Publication Data
Names: Treglown, Jeremy, author.
Title: Mr. Straight Arrow : the career of John Hersey, author of Hiroshima / Jeremy Treglown.
Description: First edition. | New York : Farrar, Straus and Giroux, 2019. | Includes
    bibliographical references and index.
Identifiers: LCCN 2018041575 | ISBN 9780374280260 (hardcover)
Subjects: LCSH: Hersey, John, 1914–1993. | Authors, American—Biography. | Journalists—
    United States—Biography.
Classification: LCC PS3515.E7715 Z89 2019 | DDC 813/.52 [B] —dc23
LC record available at https://lccn.loc.gov/2018041575

Designed by Abby Kagan

Our books may be purchased in bulk for promotional, educational, or business use. Please
contact your local bookseller or the Macmillan Corporate and Premium Sales Department at
1-800-221-7945, extension 5442, or by e-mail at MacmillanSpecialMarkets@macmillan.com.

www.fsgbooks.com
www.twitter.com/fsgbooks • www.facebook.com/fsgbooks

1   3   5   7   9   10   8   6   4   2

To Maria

Contents

Preface: Civic Virtue and Our Present Difficulties

PUBLIC SERVICE: It has a quaint ring, along with modesty, truthfulness, decency. John Hersey didn't so much sign up to those values as live them—not always flawlessly but inherently, by birth, upbringing, and determination. A fellow journalist called him "Mr. Straight Arrow," and the fact that this wasn't meant kindly suggests that by the mid-twentieth century, for all the moral anger of those years, the phenomenon was already going out of style. Although often praised as a progenitor of the New Journalism, Hersey was unrepresentative of the genre in his dislike of publicity and also his insistence that reporters shouldn't make things up. A long puritan inheritance was involved in this, so much so that even when he wrote fiction, he almost always gave it what used to be called a "moral," as well as a cargo of historical fact. His respect for truth, along with his belief that human beings as a species are capable of improvement, matters more than ever in an age that doesn't just tolerate lies, corruption, greed, cruelty, and sheer shallowness, but votes for them.

Hersey dreaded such a state of affairs. He saw versions of it in wartime Moscow and in the Washington of Richard M. Nixon and knew how vul-

nerable the qualities he thought essential were, how easy it could be to accept their opposites. As a child of U.S. missionaries living in what was
then Tientsin, China, in the late 1910s, he had ridden to school in a rickshaw, paying "a human being a very few coppers for pulling me there."
For a boy to be able, simply by virtue of being a foreigner, to wield power
over adults in their home country was bewildering, disturbing, and imaginatively formative. Among the complexities of his upbringing was the
fact that when the family returned from China to the United States in 1924,
the ten-year-old and his elder brothers felt like immigrants. They lived in
Briarcliff Manor, a small town in Westchester County, where initially he
attended the local public school and where for many years his mother,
Grace, ran the public library. She remained in the village until her death
in 1965.

Standing on wooded slopes by the Hudson River between and a little
inshore from Sleepy Hollow and Ossining, Briarcliff gradually became a
suburb of New York City. In 1952, when it celebrated its fiftieth anniversary, a committee of nine people was set up to write a history. Grace Hersey
was the only woman on it. The resulting booklet is proudly communitar-
ian. A section called "The Park and Pool," for example, begins, "No person ever passes through the Village without noticing these centrally-located
and ever-popular possessions of all residents." Today, Briarcliff also has a
rather less inclusive golf course, built by and named after Donald Trump.

When I first visited Briarcliff, Mr. Trump was already a candidate for
the presidency, but few people I met there took seriously the idea that he
might be elected. He had made himself unpopular in the neighborhood.
His ostentatious Trump National Golf Club doesn't fit the town's low-key,
rustic image. More objectively, a lack of environmental sensitivity (and of
sheer neighborly consideration) was evident in the fact that drainage measures and ornamental water features introduced there seemed to be the
cause of the flooding in 2011 of more modest public facilities down the
hill: library, school, recreation ground, and all.[1] There were taxation issues, too. Whereas for some purposes Trump boasted that the finished
project was "worth" $50 million, when it came to tax assessment he val-
ued it at $1.5 million. He also argued that local taxes on the private houses
on the club grounds should be drastically reduced. The roads they stood
on were Trump roads, after all, and their occupants were unlikely to send

their kids to the town's tax-funded public schools or to borrow books from the public library.

Everything John Hersey learned as he grew up—from his missionary parents, from the Congregational church in Briarcliff, from his interwar education in the town and subsequently as a scholarship student at Hotchkiss and Yale—is the opposite of what the forty-fifth president stands for. With intelligence, passion, and sheer hard work, Hersey applied his values through half a century of celebrated journalism and fiction. And while his writing was crucial, he also served pro bono in organizations devoted to helping people who needed help, particularly those who had suffered, or might suffer in the future, as a result of belligerence, exploitation, prejudice, or passive neglect. Public education, civil rights, arms control, and the natural environment were among the causes he fought for, and though repeatedly faced with the fact that the ameliorations he helped bring about were both inadequate and fragile, he was fortunate enough to live in a period when, roughly speaking and bit by bit, things did seem to be getting better. That this is no longer the case is one of the reasons why reading Hersey matters.

MR. STRAIGHT ARROW

1. A Sentimental Journey

WHEN JOHN HERSEY WAS IN HIS SIXTIES he made what he called "a sentimental journey" to Tientsin, now Tianjin, the east China port where he and his brothers had been born and where he had lived until he was ten. He wrote about the trip in a series of four articles published, like the majority of the nonfiction he had written since the mid-1940s, in *The New Yorker*.[1] He was at an age when it's common for people to look back over their lives and their family histories. He was researching a big novel about the YMCA in China, where his parents had been missionaries. His own life, too, offered plenty to review with pride, though that wasn't the topic of this fifty-thousand-word analysis, or not directly.

More than forty intensely busy, satisfying, at some points glamorous years had passed since the appearance in 1942 of his first book, *Men on Bataan*, which used journalistic sources to give a ringside view of the United States' earliest efforts to fight back against Japan while those efforts were still going on and it was far from certain that they would succeed. For reasons we'll come to, Hersey would be embarrassed by *Men on*

Bataan, but, together with *Into the Valley*—a directly personal account of another, smaller but similarly unsuccessful military episode—the book made his name as a war writer, one who understood the popular appetite for heroes but didn't shy away from awkward facts like fear, retreat, or defeat. As early as July 1942, the young correspondent already himself made news. "Well, yesterday evening I had quite an exciting time," an army medic wrote home from a station hospital. "John Hersey was here."[2]

Hersey's globally translated account of the immediate impact on people in Hiroshima of the 1945 bomb has never gone out of print. First published in *The New Yorker* soon after the first anniversary of the bombing, and filling an entire issue—an unprecedented move for the magazine— *Hiroshima* was the earliest, arguably the only, work on its subject to have such an impact. Four years later the author also became the first American to publish a novel about the Shoah, and it's hard to imagine, today, just how extraordinary, how huge, how problematic-seeming that achievement was. It's called *The Wall*. Around the same time, Anne Frank's *Diary of a Young Girl* was rejected by ten English-language publishers[3] and Primo Levi had difficulty finding a substantial Italian outlet for *If This Is a Man*.

Novels by Hersey based on other aspects of the Second World War won prizes and were made into films. *A Bell for Adano*, set in Sicily in 1943, was published while the Italian campaign was still being fought and despite the fact that it hinges on a strongly critical portrait of the American commander, General Patton. *The War Lover* (1959), set on a U.S. air base near Cambridge, England, is what it says it is: an attempt to depict a man who, not unlike Patton, really enjoys war. Sufficiently trusted to be given unprecedented personal access to serving presidents Truman (in 1950–51) and, in the early 1970s, Ford, to write day-by-day accounts of the workings of the U.S. government, Hersey was nevertheless a forthright critic of many national policies and actions, particularly the Vietnam War, to which he objected publicly even within the White House itself.[4] His participation in the Freedom Summer of 1964, staying with an African American family and writing for a mass-circulation magazine about attempts by people like his hosts to register for the vote was part of a series of battles by him to affect people's attitudes toward race: the attitudes of lawmakers and law keepers, administrators, and politicians, as well as private individuals. This was the heyday of the New Journalism, which Hersey's *Hiroshima* is sometimes said to have prefigured,[5] and while younger writers were making the genre their own—Joan Didion, Michael Herr, Norman Mailer, George Plimpton, Hunter S. Thompson, and Nicholas Tomalin, as well as their anthologist Tom Wolfe—Hersey went on contributing to it in his own way. His furious, self-castigating, procedurally controversial exposé of the torture and killing of a group of young people, mainly black, by white police and National Guardsmen in Detroit during the riots of 1967 still resonates all too loudly today,[6] as does his defense of the radical actions of Yale students during the Black Panthers trials, held within shouting distance of the campus two years later—actions that had led wealthy alumni to threaten to withdraw funding from the university.[7]

Hersey himself was a Yalie. Not only that, he was a member of the elite fraternity Skull and Bones and, by the time of these radical interventions, master of one of the university's residential colleges.[8] Unlike many of the New Journalists (or many famous war correspondents), he was a reserved, sometimes aloof-seeming man, "not exactly an Abbie Hoffman type," as one contemporary joked, referring to the anarchist countercultural founder of the yippies.[9] Moderate in his habits except in his devotion to work, physically fit, devoted to his family, a bit formal in dress and manner, he worked from inside the conventional establishment. In his day the youngest-ever fellow of the American Academy of Arts and Letters, and soon one of the academy's officers, he served on advisory bodies and commissions of inquiry large and small and was in constant demand as a speaker. The need to keep these activities under control, along with the complexities of his literary affairs—film and stage rights, radio adaptations, translations, paperback reprints—would have persuaded anyone else to employ a small office of assistants, but Hersey had begun his career as an individual with a notebook, and all his life he managed most of his business affairs himself. Again there was something of his parents in this. As a child, he had watched them doing their best for other human beings, within and sometimes despite a massive international organization, in the vast, complexly divided, and rapidly changing China of the early twentieth century.

His 1982 New Yorker series was more, though, than a meditation on origins. "The House on New China Road" contemplates then-new cultural, political, and economic developments against a geologically long history, putting Western privileges and Eastern political upheavals into revelatory contexts. Even the title is rich in meanings. The street the Herseys' home stood on had been known as Recreation Road, after the sports ground that it ran alongside. The language used for place-names, like for everything else in the British concession, was English. Now the street is called Xinhua—New China. To most Western readers in 1982, "New China" meant something unclearly situated between Mao's failed Cultural Revolution and the more outward-looking but still imperfect and unproven reforms of Deng Xiaoping. There's a paradox, too, in the idea of newness in so ancient a setting. Hersey's lens is sometimes long, sometimes wide, but he had learned his trade at Time-Life, so there's also an acutely sympathetic if unsystematic focus on people's domestic circumstances, their ambitions, their compromises and refusals to compromise, above all their individuality. In the course of the weekly installments, he steadily drew away from autobiographical preoccupations—from a stage-setting, disappointable kind of nostalgia—toward optimism about China's present and future. In its emphasis on resilience, enterprise, and the power of education, the approach is characteristic of him: despite everything he had seen by then, and despite an underlying puritan strain of melancholy, he was still hopeful about human beings. Typical, too, is his journalistic knack for being a bit ahead of others on any big story. For all the reforms the country was making and the détente heralded by President Nixon's visit a decade earlier, not all commentators saw in Deng's China an impressively diverse, sophisticated, adaptable, and—in relation to the region's own history and beliefs—surprisingly free culture.

Still, in his return Hersey was also investigating a personal question: whether, as he bluntly phrased it, "my parents' lives had been worth living."[10] There's no way to ask that without also, and perhaps first, wondering about the value of one's own existence. The premises of Hersey's career were moral to an extent that went beyond the engagements he had in common with many of the cultural idols of his time. The period he lived through confronted everyone with questions about whether the world could truly be made a better place—questions or hopes or doubts that, however perennial, are sharpest when they occur, as these did, at times of widespread material growth. Hersey's parents were his first ethical models and, in being determined to emulate them, he was prompted by two extra pressures. He thought he had discarded the religious beliefs they taught him.[11] Whether or not that was true, he thought it and was eager for a purely rational support system for the humanitarianism that, in the elder Herseys, was nourished by Christianity. At the same time he had watched as illness caused his father and therefore his mother, too, to give up their work in China, to settle for the comforts but also the limitations of the Hudson River suburbs of New York and, in his father's case, to die relatively young. The death of fathers, as Hamlet knew, is nature's common theme, but it only happens to anyone once, and for the young man to see his idealized father-hero brought low was a testing experience.[12]

Hersey publicly confronted his childhood's intensest moments in his 1982 series—or as much of them as anyone so uncommunicative about himself could have been expected to. That uncommunicativeness was itself a bit of an illusion, but how Hersey begins is with the classic story of a certain kind of American past:

> My father grew up on a small farm in Red Creek, New York, not far from the eastern end of Lake Ontario. He and his brothers worked hard on the farm from an early age, most years going to the local district school only in winter. They had a Methodist upbringing. By prodigies of application . . . my father somehow managed to get up the Latin and Greek needed to get into Syracuse University.

The last decades of the nineteenth century were, as he wrote, a time of exceptional American optimism and idealism—or, according to your point of view, of arrogant national self-delusion. Hersey had seen at close quarters some problems endemic in global expansionism and in its often hypocritical-seeming relationship with political and, especially, religious ideals, and these conflicts were among his main themes as a writer. In 1905, Roscoe Hersey had gone to China on behalf of the YMCA, "he thought, for the rest of his life."[13]

> At that stage he didn't know a word of Mandarin. He was a gentle, kindly, bookish, unprepossessing person, still and always a hard worker. My mother, besides being good-looking, was quietly strong and serene. She and my father teamed well together in their work . . . They were as much interested in the quality of life of the people they served as they were in converting them. They brought medicine, education, science, agronomy, conservation, and ideas for social planning.

The secular emphases here are given a stronger religious context in the book version, Hersey's long biographical novel *The Call*, published three years later. His parents' work went on through famine, flood, and sometimes violent political change for twenty years.

These recollections weren't uncontested. Disagreements arose between him and Arthur, the eldest brother, over matters of fact and interpretation to do with their upbringing, and also about ways in which—if at all—their story should be told. Still, some memories were uncontroversial, if only because in their particular form they were unique to the teller. John described their house and its surroundings, the recreation ground opposite with its bulbous pavilion, the local church, their schools (first a traditional English establishment close to their home, then its new American equivalent, farther off), and was delighted to find some of these buildings still standing in 1981, as some remain today. The former British concession has been sub-segmented by the "Five Roads"—hectic multilane urban thoroughfares—that now give the area its name, but tree-lined avenues and residential streets between them are being preserved and, in some cases, restored as part of China's new urban conservationism. It's more common than not, as in the case of what was 5 Recreation Road, for them to be in scruffy multi-occupation and for apartments within them to be jostling between uses as family housing, cafés, and motor-repair workshops, but plaques bearing the words "Historical and Stylistic Architecture of Tianjin: General Protection" have sprung up everywhere. Meanwhile, even when what existed has been torn down and built over, there are continuities. The former recreation ground is now home to a gym and a state-of-the-art tennis school.

Townscape apart, Hersey wrote, too, about family, pets, and boyhood friends. Among the latter was an eclectic mix of colonial immigrant and national neighbors and friends. The contrasts were not all between rich Westerners and poor Chinese. As one of the "concessions" ports, Tientsin was full of outsiders who preserved what they could of their past within their national ghettoes, little tax havens that were also separate jurisdictions as well as conservation areas for cultural beliefs and practices. Some people were there of their own volition, others by force of circumstance. The violinist Paul Federovsky was in the second category. John was musically gifted and was taught to play the violin by this "terribly poor and starkly thin" Russian who had fled the recent revolution with his wife, Olga

Averino, a soprano later well known in the West. In 1924 the couple managed to get from Tientsin to Boston, Massachusetts. They flourished as professional musicians in the United States, where the adult Hersey saw them from time to time,[14] but in Tientsin the boy "tortured that sensitive man with my first tentative strokes of the bow. Once he actually screamed and threw his hands over his ears."[15] Other local exiles included a Socialist German Jewish family whose clever son Israel Epstein, having broken a leg when he was nine years old, impressed Johnny by embarking on an attempt to write a two-volume history of the world. "Eppy" was to spend most of his life in China and was among several of the Herseys' former acquaintances imprisoned during the Cultural Revolution. But in the intricate cosmopolis of the 1910s and early '20s John also regularly slipped into the servants' quarters. They were, he wrote, "used to having me around and often forgot I was there, for I used to sit still, watching the old cook lazily lift and put down his rose-water pipe, punctuating his puffs of the pale smoke with sage sayings." This cook was the source, too, of an impressive range of Chinese swear words,[16] and at the same time as the boy learned demotic Chinese (though never, Arthur later reminded him, quite as well as he himself had done), he discovered how strange Western customs seemed to his kitchen friends. Why, at Christmas, did the Herseys worship a tree? Worse, why was so well-brought-up a boy unable to explain the practice?[17]

In retrospect it was the cosmopolitanism that struck him most: the distinctiveness of each foreign quarter of Tientsin—a segregated mêlée epitomized now as then by Wilhelm Kiessling's famous international restaurant: not so much fusion as compartmentalization.[18] More intimately, the musician manqué remembered sounds: "A servant . . . singing a passage from a Chinese opera in a high falsetto . . . men in this dusty city clearing their throats, like lions roaring; the thrifty clicks of an abacus in an open fruit stall" and the noises, too, of the family making music, Grace on the piano, Roscoe Senior on the cornet, or just listening to records on their wind-up Victrola gramophone. There were also the less rarified oddities of any childhood. The rubbish bins of nearby colonial clubs enabled John to make a very full collection of corks and bottle caps. He won a prize for it, handed out with other awards by the American commander in chief William Durward Connor, who understandably assumed that these relics had been procured from the boy's father. "Envious congratulations" were due, he joked, to (the, in fact, deeply temperate) Mr. Hersey, for "making this remarkable accumulation possible." John acted as servant and messenger for his elder brothers, Arthur and Roscoe Junior, especially in connection with a secret society that met in an attic hideout constructed by the latter, and did his fierce bit as a foot soldier in their gang wars.

He was a tall boy and competed on his own terms in more formal sports, of which there were plenty—for example, the annual Tientsin Rowing Club Regatta. There were amateur theatricals to take part in and watch, including a version of *Through the Looking Glass* staged in the all-purpose Victorian-Gothic Gordon Hall, in which, he said, "I saw my brother Roscoe maltreat oysters as the Walrus"; and summer holidays in Peitaiho, a "sparkling place" by the sea.[19] He also read a lot, with an appetite for nonfiction—*The Book of Knowledge*, an encyclopedia aimed at children, and, more ambitiously, the family's set of *Encyclopedia Britannica*. And with his father's typewriter, John produced an intermittent bulletin, "The Hersey Family News," which incorporated "ads offering my older brothers for various kinds of hard labor at very low wages."[20]

The house was modest by the standards of avenues closer to the river but seemed impressive to a small boy and was surrounded by a walled garden, which their mother also enjoyed; she was pleased with the rapid growth of her morning glories. But Grace had work to do, and not just as her husband's close colleague. Independently, she was a teacher. The 1904 founders of the school where she taught English went on to set up Tianjin's Nankai University while the Herseys were still in the city. Among the people the writer met on his 1981 trip was a former dean of the university, Huang Yusheng, by then in his eighties. Huang had been taught by Grace Hersey—as had, he believed, the Communist leader Zhou Enlai, whom Hersey interviewed in 1939.[21] Certainly Zhou attended the school, and the classroom in which he studied and Grace taught has been preserved in a museum dedicated to his and his wife's careers.[22] But there was also the routine missionary work Grace described in a circular letter home: teaching "Bible" to one small group and English to others, "including 2 hrs with the daughter of Ex-Pres Li" and a Mothers' Club "of about 100 kids whose mothers . . . [work for] but a few coppers per day." At this day care center, she explained, "each child receives a good 'feed,' a toy, a bag of nuts & sweets, a coloured ball, a ten cent piece, and cotton and cloth."[23]

After he was eleven, Hersey returned just three times: as a war correspondent in 1939 and 1945 and now, at last, after a long period in which he was refused a visa, in 1981. Imaginatively, though, he had been there much more often. Reporting and intelligence gathering apart, China gave him settings for two novels and some short stories in addition to his 1985 hybrid of history, family annals, and fiction, *The Call*. Because he saw them in a long perspective he wasn't excessively alarmed by what he regarded as temporary political phenomena, taken by other Western observers to be not only harmful—which they were—but permanently so. Some Asian analysts thought he was soft on Deng's regime: "Your rather positive impressions," one editor at a specialist journal wrote, "seem somewhat at variance with things we've recently been hearing and reading"[24]—a line confirmed seven years later by the massacre in Tiananmen Square, and again by developments in the mid- to late 2010s. Apart from long-view tolerance (and, with that, potential complacency or at least boosterism), Hersey's position was a matter of loyalty—in fact of patriotism. China was, he liked to say, "my natal country." Equally important was his resistance to Manichaeanism, an attitude similar in practice to his tendency to search for unfamiliar angles of vision. There was a danger here of a reflex, which is a form of bipolarity in itself, though in reverse; *White Lotus* (1965) is the most conscious, systematic example, an allegorical fantasy in which China has won a war against the United States and taken large numbers of Americans into slavery.

Privacies

In composing the *New Yorker* series, if Hersey found himself loyal to his country of origin, there was something revealingly atavistic, too, about his attitude to a few long-buried memories that the process of excavation exposed. Among his notes are half a dozen typed, undated, apparently free-associative memory-prompts, very close in content to more personal elements included in the first two articles but striking for what he eventually chose not to use.[25] He writes there about how his violin teacher Mr. Federovsky scared him by impetuously cutting his fingernails, as if he were about to stab him (you can't do the fingering on the strings of a violin if your nails are too long). Still more vividly he recalls sexually charged moments from childhood—playing "doctor" with a girl, seeing his father's genitalia, becoming aware of the smell of his mother's menstruation. While most of the other notes, again filled out and in a changed order, are worked into the deftly shaped mix of personal and public, past and present, American and Chinese, of the published articles, these are practically the only things he eventually chose to omit.

Much of his writing shows a related ambivalence between efforts at a modern frankness about sexuality and an old-fashioned avoidance of it; more broadly, between self-examination, however oblique, and privacy. Yet Hersey's reticence often also yields delicate forms of autobiography, though not exactly—to adopt a distinction used by the critic Dan Chiasson about Susan Howe's poetry—of personal candor.[26]

While these China articles contain the most sustained, overt attempt he ever made at a memoir, he is personally present, too, in a great deal of his other nonfictional writing, particularly the large proportion of it that consists, one way or another, of portraits of others: fabulous pieces of human observation, insight, revelation. What's fascinating is how many of them are about modern saints and heroes, and that this is the kind of person Hersey, with his childhood sense of destiny, wanted to be. In late adulthood such wishes can express disappointment as well as idealism: meditating on greatness and goodness may be a result (but also a cause) of thinking one hasn't lived up to one's best hopes. To a severe conscience of this kind, outside attention is unwelcome, less because there's something especially bad to hide than because—or so it can feel—there's nothing all that good to be found. The dilemma is intense for a writer. To publish one's work is, literally and inevitably—at some level deliberately—to attract publicity. And the care a writer lavishes on his work, because it is verbal, tends to be more evidently personal, more overtly (if often misinterpretably) a communication of his private, individual concerns, than that involved in art of any other kind. So a paradoxical, even viciously circular situation can arise in which the author fends off biographical attention while seeking to control it; and, partly in pursuit of control, produces autobiographical utterances that themselves attract supposedly unwanted attention. Late in life, Hersey wrote self-reprovingly about what he called "strains of ambition and vanity in my makeup."[27] Guilt, this might suggest, was another element.

The changes in his most sustainedly autobiographical text aren't easy to assess. William Shawn, who edited the China articles, was exceptionally fastidious, and some of what Hersey didn't include may have been a result of his editor's influence. But it's interesting to compare what happened here with the author's dealings with his publisher, Alfred A. Knopf, about publicity for this or that book, which show his privateness in a less burdened, more superficial, yet still nagging form. He repeatedly dismissed publicists' concerns as being on a par with those of magazine writers who (if only in the literary world's mythology) are always asking what kind of cereal their subject likes for breakfast.[28] His dealings over his midcareer novel *White Lotus* are typical. In August 1964, Hersey's longtime editor at Knopf, Harold Strauss, asked him whether the firm might use the same biographical note on the book's jacket as on his previous one, a 1962 nonfiction collection called *Here to Stay*. Busy with the civil rights actions in Mississippi,[29] Hersey didn't at first respond, but at the end of the month he told Strauss he would prefer to take the first paragraph from the author biography he had prepared for another recent work, *The Child Buyer* (1960), saying he would adjust it in proof. Two weeks later, however, he offered something supposedly quite new but in fact barely distinguishable—and then changed his mind yet again.[30] Words, though, weren't all that the book jacket involved. While these refinements were going to and fro, Strauss's assistant asked Hersey more than once what photograph of him they should use on the back.[31] Strauss himself had taken one that everyone liked; maybe it would do. But Hersey now produced another, taken by his wife, Barbara, explaining apologetically and at length why he preferred it. Two weeks later, he sent some new pictures, the result of a professional shoot, correspondence about which continued into November. Still another image, however, was being used in a newspaper ad for the book, and Hersey was worried about it ("fire seems to be coming . . . out of my nose!").[32] And so it went on. Most people care, of course, about how they look in photographs and how they are described to others, and in any case Hersey was a perfectionist about all aspects of the physical form his books took.[33] He was also anxious about how *White Lotus*—a sustained allegory about U.S. race relations—would be received.[34] Still, for an issue about which he professed scorn, and for a writer so well established, he gave a lot of attention to it.

Around this time, when he was in his early fifties, he broke precedent by agreeing to be interviewed. A liberal-arts-college teacher, David Sanders, was writing a short book about Hersey's work for an academic series and for some time had been trying to get access to him.[35] Responding to the concern of his loyal publishers about the intrusion, Hersey made a familiar but, in the terms in which he expressed it, highly debatable distinction between being helpful about his books while discouraging Sanders from writing about him personally, "except as I appear in them."[36] What is this exception, really? On the one hand, Hersey could have meant that he "appears" very little in his work, but we'll see that this is untrue. If, on the other, he was implying that the Hersey-like observer-narrator-commentator common in his writing is an imaginative construct (or a collection of such constructs), then that figure is surely open to interpretation and evaluation like any other aspect of how the books are written.[37]

But if the question was open to argument, it wasn't to logic. Biographical interpretation reminded him of the vanity he was always trying to suppress: he liked attention but disapproved of himself for doing so. This was a family preoccupation, a puritan hangover that struck again in confrontations between him and his brother Arthur over "The House on New China Road." Just as there's a strong overt personal tension in the narrative between the intimacy of John Hersey's return to his birthplace and the scale of what he is forced up against there, it also, at the time, involved a no-less-strong but, as far as the reader is concerned, hidden tension between John and Arthur about how the family should be presented.

Author

When the writing and editing were at a late stage, Hersey sent the text to both brothers, Rob and Arthur. Rob—artistic, clever, but more relaxed than his brothers, his own life increasingly disheveled—said he was happy with it. Arthur, by contrast, a Washington economist, while generally admiring, made a lot of criticisms.

Arthur carefully read two separate versions, including galley proofs, and made detailed notes on them.[38] He found some aspects of how their parents were presented sentimental. (Was it strictly true that their father had sacrificed his life for China? And wasn't the evidence that their mother had taught Zhou Enlai tenuous?) The strength of his reaction may have come in part from the fact that other matters were at stake, feelings that chime with worries of John's in other contexts. Arthur found the depiction of himself superficial and embarrassing, and he wanted his name removed from passages describing the boys' upbringing—parts where he is mentioned with nothing but affection and admiration. In fact he wanted Rob's name removed, too.

For siblings of different ages reflecting on their childhood, few things are stranger than the differences between what they separately remember of their parents. To the eldest, the views of the younger are inevitably shallow, arriviste. And even when experiences were shared, or just overlapped, the memories of the eldest must surely be shrewder, deeper. For the youngest, other forms of rivalry and possessiveness are involved, among them envy of the older sibling's earlier experiences—envy of his or her sheer priority in every sense. Whether or not this situation, shared by all except solitary offspring, engenders feelings that go on being hard to manage in adulthood, the issues are hugely amplified when one of the siblings has more of a "voice." Current psychological language having learned from literary criticism, there's no ready way of summarizing the argument between Arthur Hersey and John other than saying it was about control of the narrative.

Several matters were at stake here, one of them being privacy. Arthur respected his brother's journalism and found the more objective reportage "topnotch." But he hated being part of the family story—especially, it seems, though he didn't put it this way, so small a part of it. He used various avenues of attack, all difficult for John to deal with, because what Arthur disliked included aspects of the story that, in its own terms, were distinctly successful, but also because, while John himself was writing a frank and in some ways painful kind of autobiography, his feelings about doing so, as expressed in other contexts, were so similar to Arthur's.

Among his many gifts, John Hersey could be diplomatic as well as meticulous. His long replies to Arthur express gratitude for his care, deal with each objection, draw on feelings and beliefs common to both men. Wisely, the first of these letters—sent on April 17, 1982, three days after Arthur returned the proofs—makes no reference to the pressure of deadlines, though the first article was due to appear within weeks. John did, though, call in aid the views of other readers, potential and actual; in the latter case, the by then legendary *New Yorker* editor William Shawn. As far as sentimentality was concerned, the matters Arthur objected to were among those Shawn most admired—in part because he liked what John called "the author's investment of feeling in the question" of how successful or otherwise his parents' lives had been. (How can Arthur have felt about John's ostensibly neutral yet surely rank-pulling reference to himself as "the author"?)

Then there was Arthur's complaint that he and others came across as two-dimensional. Scores of people were mentioned in the articles, John pointed out, not just family members but servants, friends, colleagues, survivors, descendants, and new people he had met on successive visits. He could do little more than sketch them. This was a matter of practicality but also of literary economy. In such a process, names have power. Not to name the servants, he pointed out, would be to diminish them, while to name them but not the brothers would make the latter even more insubstantial than they already were: "For 'a brother' to play 'The Happy Farmer' is not nearly so visible as for Roscoe to play it; the same with a brother [Arthur] appearing in a doorway to console."

Besides, Roscoe himself was unbothered by being named, and here John's letter co-opted Arthur into a loyal conspiracy, a coauthorship team: "Obviously we'll have to treat both brothers in the same way, but I respect both brothers and I think the choice you've made for both may be unfair to one." Whatever the rhetoric, however, Arthur was not John Hersey's coauthor and, having thanked him, debated with him, pleaded with him ("Would you be kind enough to give this some further thought . . . ?"), the younger brother closed this letter with an assertion of his independence: "The essential point is that as a writer I have to be true to my own voice, or everything's lost."

If this wasn't clear enough, John's next communication was sent after the magazine had gone to press. By then, Arthur had given way over names, and John in turn had conceded most of Arthur's more objective points. As far as the representation of family members was concerned, though, he said that his editor had consulted four other people at *The New Yorker* who had read the articles and everyone had supported his approach.

Something not mentioned in this friendly if tough exchange, but that must surely have grated on Arthur, was that one person does come through the articles in considerable complexity: the author himself, both as a child in China and as a writer whose return visits have had a cumulative impact on him. The intensity of his most recent trip, in fact, his frustration over the years of delay before he was given a visa; the upsetting mix of familiarity and utter change in Tientsin/Tianjin; the difficulties he encountered over hotel accommodation and access to certain individuals, and his unexpectedly thin-skinned reactions to these setbacks; the flood of emotion he felt, by contrast, when one of the poor families living in the Herseys' former home invited him to stay; and his own recognition of his selfishness, his slowness, for example, to allow for the implications of the fact that Tianjin had recently suffered an earthquake—all this contributes to what is, however "objective" the story increasingly becomes, unmistakably a high-caliber form of autobiography. There's nothing "sketchy" about it. While emphases shift from one installment to the next, the running theme is John Hersey and his "sentimental journey."

Within this, the author confronts a single issue that implicitly lay behind the argument with Arthur. How can a writer communicate the experiences of others? How can anyone know what they are? (It is a main theme of his 1967 novel *Under the Eye of the Storm*.)[39] We're used to the attempt, but if we stand back from it, surely it is doomed. Subjectivity, cultural differences, historical change, varieties of political interpretation, the sheer number of other people there are to consider individually, let alone together—all these frustrate the effort. In more than one way, then, "The House on New China Road" is an assessment of the writer's lifework. The criteria were ultimately quite simple: Had his career served a moral purpose? Had anyone or anything been significantly improved by it? Had Hersey himself, through the efforts involved in it all, become a better person? In short, had his life been worth living?

Archives

While these questions absorbed the writer, he felt sure that they were no one else's business. Yet there's one stubborn piece of evidence that he hoped his life would be studied and that at some level his heirs have hoped the same; in fact, many thousands of pieces of evidence: the contents of his

and his family's archives, acquired in installments and painstakingly preserved by Yale University.

The first of these, a packet of drafts of his novel *A Bell for Adano*, was
given at the request of Yale's librarian in 1944, when the book had just become a bestseller. It was followed by other donations, at first purely literary as distinct from biographical in character: the manuscript[40] of
Hiroshima, given in 1947; manuscripts and typed drafts of *The Wall* in
1951; a succession of similar materials related to other books in the 1960s.[41]
Then there was a gap, but in the spring of 1992, when Hersey was still alive,
the library acquired the largest and in biographico-historical ways most
valuable tranche of material. It includes personal correspondence with his
parents and his first wife, and from his second wife to her mother-in-law,
as well as boxes and boxes of other letters, arranged alphabetically by name
of correspondent and in date tranches of at first fifteen years, then twelve,
then, as he got ever busier, four years at a time. These items are a mix of
personal and professional, and there are also separate boxes of dealings
with his American and British publishers, and again of drafts of stories
and articles, as distinct from book-form writings.

They take up seventy-one feet of shelving, but there is still more. For
his historical novel about Christian aid missions in China during the period of his father's career, Hersey had made exhaustive notes not only on
books but also on the contents of relevant archives. These were given to the
Yale Divinity School. They might sound dry but for the alphabetical head-
ings under which an early cataloger described some of them: "Chinese
Renaissance; Chinese religions; . . . Diseases . . . Famine; Foot-binding . . .
Japanese attack . . . Martyrs . . . Prostitution. Queue [male pigtail] cutting . . .
Westernization . . . Yangchow riot . . ." Beyond these materials there are
the archives of Yale University itself and of Pierson College, recording tumultuous events in which the place and its teachers and students were
involved during Hersey's career: a career that made a big mark in this
respect as in others. Again, the rich collections of Hersey's publisher,
Alfred A. Knopf, in Austin, Texas, and of *The New Yorker* at the New
York Public Library contain a great deal of material about his work and
about his personal dealings with editors and others.

Yet even at the most private-seeming level still more was to come. In
1994, after Hersey's death, the family passed to Yale some materials that
he had previously held back: papers and photograph albums concerning

the family's life in China in the first decades of the twentieth century, plus three caches that between them give an even closer impression of their author. They contain, first, letters he wrote home from Clare College, Cambridge, during his year as a student there, 1936–37. Second, there's a file of diary-form letters, each of them tens of thousands of words in length, written during his trip to Japan and China in 1939, when his birthplace was under military attack. And then there are copies of articles and briefing cables sent back to Time-Life from the Pacific War in the second half of 1942. These weren't the only episodes that made Hersey who he was, but if he thought them especially significant, he was right. And although the papers touch on many of the concerns you'd expect from a man in his twenties, as well as from anyone else living through that period, one of the main things about them is their sheer quantity: that and the fact that they were so carefully kept and handed on. "Did William Hersey go to America in 1735 or 1635?" John wrote to his parents about an ancestor when he was in his early twenties. "It doesn't matter! For we live for the present and future, don't we?"[42] Whatever his reasons for this youthful impatience with family history and legend, he soon grew out of it. If anyone other than himself was going to take an interest in whether John Hersey's life had been worth living, he gradually, paradoxically, and perhaps entirely unconsciously made sure there was plenty of material to work with.

2. To Be a Hersey

WHEN ROSCOE AND GRACE HERSEY FIRST ARRIVED in China, they couldn't have imagined the changes they would later see there. Weakened by the commercial inroads of European powers and by internal anti-foreign resistance of various kinds, the imperial regime collapsed in 1912. Japan took advantage of the situation by exacting new trade concessions from the warlord government. When the First World War began, while Japan committed itself against Germany and Russia soon did the same—its ensuing military failures contributing to the discontents that came to a head in its revolutions of 1917—China's new leaders held back. In 1917, however, calculating on Germany's defeat, they belatedly backed the eventual victors in the hope of being rewarded by the repatriation of Germany's former possessions in China. (Instead, these had already been promised to Japan.) As a token of its newfound allegiance, China shipped out around 100,000 "volunteers" to do manual labor in the ports of France and Belgium, where they replaced Western laborers needed on the battlefield. The Herseys had a period of home leave around this time, and their voyage itself brought home to the impressionable Johnny something of what current displacements meant to those affected. For instead of staying with them in Montclair, New Jersey, his father continued eastward to Europe.

After the armistice, the coolies were kept on to help clear battlefields. Housed in what were little different from prison camps, under the orders of Western officers impatient to retire from one or other colonial army, they became understandably mutinous. Roscoe Hersey and other YMCA volunteers did their best to negotiate improvements in the men's material conditions and help organize their repatriation at the end of the war. Later, John Hersey often drew on the intricacies symbolized by this episode, most directly in *The Call*. The novel shows how important it was to him that his father had a role not just in helping these men, valuable though that was, but in a wider historical process. Classes run by the YMCA in the camps in France overlapped with and were reinforced by moves toward cultural modernization back in China, themselves often led by Western-educated Chinese. There was a literary dimension to this. Imperial China's discouragement of mass literacy had been part of its elitist culture. While some works of fiction were written in the vernacular, the only books to achieve critical esteem were in classical Mandarin: a language officially as current as Latin had been in medieval Europe but similarly inaccessible to most of the population. In postimperial China, pressure toward the vernacular came from various quarters: from radical intellectuals but also missionaries and other educationalists, and from Communism. *The Call* gives detailed attention to the matter: for example, one of Roscoe's colleagues, the Yale-educated Jimmy Yen (Johnny Wu in the novel), went on from teaching members of the Chinese Labour Corps to become head of a mass education movement in mainland China. Emphasizing how the United States paid some of its colonial debts through educating the colonized, Hersey focuses on an article titled "Some Tentative Suggestions for the Reform of Chinese Literature," written by a Cornell graduate and published first in America and subsequently in the popular modernizing Chinese magazine *Youth*. The magazine's editor, he points out, was Chen Duxiu, soon to be one of the founders of the Chinese Communist Party along with another young campaigning educator, Mao Tse-tung.

China's post–World War I humiliation, both by the West and increasingly by Japan, inevitably brought unrest. Once again, what became of the Chinese Labour Corps symbolized what was happening elsewhere. Many of the corps' survivors, having been taken back to China, were dumped in poverty in Shanghai, then the most "Western," most cosmopolitan, and superficially most prosperous of East Asian cities, where they lived in a ghetto that became sardonically known as "Little France." It's not difficult to imagine how these ex-slaves saw their liberation or what they thought of their recent European masters—not difficult, but also too easy. China's situation was immensely complex, and so were the relations of the Chinese both with one another and with foreigners. What John Hersey experienced as a boy was an earlier version of J. G. Ballard's Shanghai childhood fictionalized in *Empire of the Sun*—domestically and politically less catastrophic but full of bitter ironies of its own, and still benefiting from a degree of multiculturalism encouraged by the best missionaries.

Roscoe and Grace Hersey were devout Christians whose attitude to other belief systems was essentially that they were not bad or deluded but were differently refracted versions of a truth to which everyone was moving, in a journey on which Christians were fortunate in having a head start. Personal endurance, for example, combined with a belief in the family as a nucleus of value, was something both cultures—indeed, all the cultures present in early-twentieth-century Tientsin—subscribed to. The ego, on the other hand, had little status there, and this absence helped constitute John's character in a way that set him apart from others of his generation in the West, for whom psychoanalysis developed alongside the machine gun. In his upbringing, the main elements were "muscular Christianity"; the traditional values of Chinese peasants; and, in due course, a classical education involving Latin and Greek. Something all three had in common was admiration for stoicism. His father's work with the Chinese slaves in France fed the boy's sense of what this meant, but so, too, did the older puritan strain in the family. As he was to phrase it later, echoing John Bunyan's famous pilgrim hymn, he would labor night and day "to be a Hersey."[1]

It was by these standards that, returning to China in 1981, Hersey measured what he depicted as his own self-centered, impatient Western nostalgia by contrast with the courage of the local people, some of whom had lost their homes and livelihoods, whether recently to the earthquake or earlier as a result of wars, invasions, and internal political change. When he met the many occupants of his old family home, what moved him most—more, even, than their offer of hospitality—were "the patience, the endurance, of these Chinese, their calmness as they talked, their acceptance of their hard circumstances, the many signs of their industry, frugality, and aspiration." These were values inculcated in him by his parents and his other earliest encounters. In the prosperous but still intensely idealistic education system of early-1920s New England, he found them continuing by other means.

Westchester County

Briarcliff Manor became Cheever Country. The writer John Cheever bought a house on Cedar Avenue in 1961 and lived and worked there until the inner rebellions he tried to master or conceal in those conformist surroundings were multiplied by them and overwhelmed him. To current residents of the "tree streets" (Oak Road, Larch Road, etc.), their rural-suburban comforts, combined as they always were with close proximity to the city, remain precious and can seem timeless. They were an enterprise of William Law, an English magnate born in 1837 who developed the community on eighty thousand acres of land he had previously farmed, and who died in 1924, the year the Herseys arrived. With the Macys and Vanderlips he had been among a handful of big landowners in the area. They included descendants of Frederick Philipse, whose property had stretched from upper Manhattan to Croton-on-Hudson. Earlier still, of course, the lands had been home to the Wiechquaeskeck and Singsink tribes, the latter immortalized in the names of the town Ossining and its maximum-security prison, Sing Sing.

Manhattan, just visible thirty miles downstream, had been brought closer by railroads—the New York & Putnam and New York Central—and then by the automobile. Construction of the Saw Mill River Parkway began soon after the Herseys' arrival. Westchester County still had—still has—atavistic allegiances northward to the forests and lakes, and these meant more to Roscoe Hersey, with his farming background, than they did at first to the local developer. Back in England, William Law's father had supplied floor coverings to much of Birmingham. William continued the family trade in Yonkers, going into partnership with the manufacturers of Axminster carpets. He prospered and in the process discovered rural dreams of his own, developing a farming business on the hilly land he bought beside the river and building a mansion on it. Soon, New Yorkers bought milk that had come from his cattle; later, he supplied the rich with roses grown in his hothouses. He even sold them bottled water from his own streams.[2] When citizens less well off than Law but secure in their own ways began—individually, so they felt, but in practice as a class—to be attracted to rural suburbs, Law profitably built a community for them on the fields he had acquired: villas with gardens looking over the river; parks, schools, and the public library where Grace Hersey soon went to work to help support the family.[3]

Like most of their neighbors, the Herseys shared Law's confidence that schooling and physical recreation combined with spiritual zeal could bring human beings as close to perfection as was possible in a fallen world. Law was a devout Congregationalist (when a Canadian prime minister wanted to visit Briarcliff Farms and his schedulers suggested he might come one Sunday at 11:00 a.m., Law replied that he had a regular engagement at that time).[3] He built a fine little stone Congregational church at the village's center, its floor Axminster-carpeted from his own factories, the interior brightened by fashionable Tiffany windows. In 1927, Hersey was baptized there, just after his thirteenth birthday.

To secular liberal Western readers now, the Christian social practices of a century ago—the culture everyone in New England breathed—can seem more remote than modern Islam. The same is true of past educational assumptions, tied as they were into a network of ideals and hopes so close to people that few analyzed them. Not that our own time has seen a triumph of the examined life, but general knowledge today of other societies, however superficial, is so much richer and more immediate than that of our counterparts a century ago that we too easily patronize what can seem the unquestioning, insular self-confidence of our forebears. Hersey's upbringing in China, combined later with international experiences of very different kinds in the Second World War, made him feel detached from American beliefs, yet he was still formed by them and accepted some of them on their own terms. As a foreigner, he easily saw through Western complacency; but it was as a foreigner, too, that, like other immigrants, he embraced the ideals of the country in which he now lived. For him, those ideals had always been Christian.

Originally a branch of radical nonconformist Protestantism, the Congregational Church had paradoxically become the established creed of those whose pilgrim forebears identified themselves as rebels. By the twentieth century it was much modified, opened up to Christian beliefs beyond its own (though not much to Catholicism), and weakened in social power. Even so, the European immigrants who had worshipped in the open air of seventeenth-century Connecticut while the first churches were still being built there drew allegiance and pride from their descendants. They had broken away from state-dominated religion. Like other Protestants, they believed that the individual could deal directly with God, while, as the name of their church suggests, they placed special importance on the value and power of human groups. Congregationalism supplied the broad foundation of Americanness. If this is a huge generalization, what underlies it is a no-less-huge, albeit partly submerged, element in a communal identity.

For children, daily Christian worship and some formal, unicultural religious instruction were built into the school curriculum. How history and literature were taught was consistent with, indeed designed to sustain, Christian belief. Science might raise difficult questions and mathematics might conveniently ignore them, but the National Educational Association's decisions about public education, made in 1894 by a "Committee of Ten" under the Harvard president Charles W. Eliot, ensured that the basis of every American child's schooling (that is, the schooling of every American child who had access to a schoolteacher: an important caveat, as Hersey would learn) lay in the liberal arts as seen from a Christian perspective. Even sports, which from the 1920s on found a role in the life of public schools as dominant as the one they had long held in private education, were interpreted and defended by means of Christian, though in some cases also more ancient, moral metaphors: running the race that is set before us, fighting the good fight, the healthy body necessary to house a healthy mind.

John Hersey fitted in excellently. He was growing up tall, big-shouldered and strong-necked, dark-haired, dark-eyed, a bit serious, very keen on sports, and academically successful, though not to an extent that divided him socially from other boys. The generally favorable early school reports he took home in Briarcliff Manor speak of occasional carelessness. When he first applied to a private school, his Latin and Greek let him down. Still, after a couple of years in the Briarcliff community school, he was awarded a scholarship by Hotchkiss, an elite boarding establishment planted forty years earlier amid woods and fields and lakes, with the aim of protecting and forming the sons of the ever-growing upper-middle class. Like similar schools, Hotchkiss—which took its name from its founding benefactor, Maria Hotchkiss, whose fortune derived from arms manufacture—made generous provision for children of clergy. Hersey quickly earned his place. At the end of the first year, in 1929, he won the Upson Prize for "the freshman who is most distinguished in scholarship, athletics and citizenship combined."[4]

Traditional boarding schools, with their quaint customs, their supposedly beneficial cruelties, their conformism nowhere deeper than in acts of minor nonconformity, their teachers so toweringly eccentric and brilliant in the minds of former pupils,[5] can be a little hard for outsiders to appreciate. Hersey, we're told by the official history of Hotchkiss, was not only on the school's football, hockey, and baseball teams and president of his class and of the student council, but head, too, "of St. Luke's . . . chairman of the *Mischianza*, Ivy Orator, and winner of the Treadway Prize." Keen students of the book will have gathered that St. Luke's was a school organization for promoting Christian values, the *Mischianza* a magazine miscellany. For Ivy Orator and the Treadway Prize, we're left to guess, but they were clearly momentous.

The boy wrote regularly to his parents, eighty miles away in Briarcliff, about swimming, tennis, baseball, football, ice hockey, outings to waterfalls, tobogganing, and skiing. There was also the Glee Club and, important to him, classical music: he played the violin ever more seriously, including in a quartet with an older friend, the future record producer John Hammond.[6] In his erratically punctuated and spelled earlier letters ("We are reading Dicken's *Our Mutual Friend*, and I hope that I can thereby become acclamated to Dicken's, whose works I have never liked"), literature comes across as an afterthought,[7] but Hotchkiss had an exceptional English teacher in John McChesney. A year or two on, McChesney encouraged the boy to read Faulkner's new novel *The Sound and the Fury* when, as Hersey later recalled, "I was wasting my eyes on Galsworthy."[8] Another of his teachers was Gordon S. Haight, later a Yale professor of English and an authority on George Eliot. He, too, saw promise in the young Hersey and, when he bought a new typewriter, gave his pupil the old one, a large "standard" (i.e., nonportable) Woodstock with a defective line-spacing mechanism but otherwise in good working order. In his junior and senior years, the boy wrote a couple of stories that were published in the school magazine.[9] Both are set in China, the first of them, "Sea-Dragon," on the night of a lunar eclipse vividly depicted in the present tense through the reactions of a rural money changer and, after he has given the alarm, the rest of a village community. The second, "Why?," is Hersey's account of the family's Tientsin servants' bemused reactions to their Christmas celebrations. Both are plainly written, with a strong sense of narrative impact and shaping. In different ways they are about cultural and religious differences and affectionate toward Chinese characters like the money changer, "long black hair wound into a prided pigtail," his fingers "sneaking out now from long threadbare sleeves, tawny from handling coppers."

Epistulatory Matters

John often apologized for slackness in what one of his early letters calls "epistulatory matters," but few parents can have received fuller accounts of their offspring's day-to-day existence. From Hotchkiss, or from one of the Congregationalist summer camps where the young deacon was a hit with his sunset homilies and violin playing;[10] and later from Yale, from sailing holidays, from Cambridge (England), from the house of the novelist Sinclair Lewis, whose secretary he briefly became, and from the offices of *Time* and *Life*, Hersey continued to send home typed or neatly handwritten letters and postcards, always once or twice a week, sometimes every day. They naturally tend to be about what he thought would interest his parents—the content of school sermons, for example, is passed on with sometimes comical dutifulness. (On the text "well done thou good and faithful servant," a visiting preacher at Hotchkiss claimed "that the root of 'well' is 'we' and that to do anything *well* we must have a *we* spirit.") There's news about his grades, his acne, and his outings from school to football games, including at Yale, where in due course Rob was on the team and grown-up Arthur joined them for lunch. By the time John is seventeen there's also his fast-expanding social life: a dance organized jointly with Miss Hall's School for Girls in Pittsfield, Massachusetts, or an invitation to go with the family of a friend, Bob Noble, to the Yale-Harvard regatta at New London. In the latter case, John mentioned that Bob's father was a wealthy man, "high in the 'Life Saver' corporation." Candy-manufacturing evidently didn't seem enough of a recommendation to Grace Hersey, whom John soon had to assure that he wasn't "getting millionaire ideas," and who wanted full details of the trip. "Q. no 1," the teenager patiently answered. "The Nobles live at Greenwich, Conn. Bob will drive up to get me. He is sane and a licensed driver."[11]

The corrupting tendencies of a puritan-rooted society that had flowered into wealth (when John went to a Congregationalist camp, it was held at Blair Academy, a school less distinguished than either Hotchkiss or Miss Hall's but at least as expensive) were no less clear to John Hersey than to his parents. As "mishkids"—children of missionaries—he and his brothers were most of the time educated on scholarships.[12] Once at university and obliged to take more responsibility for their own upkeep, they often had money worries. Hersey paid his way, as he later described, by "waiting on tables, tending telephones, working as a librarian, and by working, in summertimes, as a life guard, an electrician's assistant, and a tutor."[13] In terms of religion, although he later lost his faith, he became a deacon in Yale University's church, Battell Chapel—again, a Congregationalist foundation, as was Yale itself. The most important lesson his parents had taught him, John told them, was "to walk humbly." This was in a letter about one of his major student achievements, being elected to the elite Yale secret society Skull and Bones, which came in May 1935, soon after he had been chosen to chair the committee for the junior prom. He had already made his mark at sports and was on the staff of the *Yale Daily News*. Walking humbly can't have been the easiest response for so gifted and popular a young man.[14]

Yale and John Hersey, like Hotchkiss and John Hersey, were a perfect fit. (In many respects the one was simply a continuation of the other: forty Hotchkiss boys went to Yale in the same year he did.)[15] His admiring contemporary and sparring-partner-in-argument August Heckscher communicated the impression he made and the mild solemnity of the world in which he made it: "A tall thin youth, meditative, firm of purpose; an aesthete but also an athlete. He became one of a firmly cemented small circle of friends, but his influence spread until he was a member of almost every group in the class where judgment and good advice were sought."[16] Judgment and good advice—they aren't what we tend to look for now in the formation, let alone the successes, of important writers, but they're among the classic virtues Hersey's friends and colleagues always valued in him and tried to describe. To the Yale historian Howard R. Lamar they were part of a moral conscience he particularly associated with Yale writers: Sinclair Lewis, Archibald MacLeish, Thornton Wilder, and others.[17]

Without any thought of becoming a scholar in the narrow sense, he shone as a student of a combined major, "History, Arts, and Letters,"[18] adding his own cultural encounters to what he was taught, working solidly through the curriculum while going to the cinema and the theater with friends: the "Four Lunatic Marx Brothers" in *Duck Soup* ("one of the craziest movies I have seen in ages"),[19] Charles Laughton in *The Private Life of Henry VIII*, Gertrude Stein's *Four Saints in Three Acts*, Garbo in *Queen Christina*. He had reluctantly dropped playing the violin[20] but went to concerts and recitals (Myra Hess, Lotte Lehmann, the young Yehudi Menuhin) and wrote about music for the *Yale Daily News*. He also showed an interest in contemporary art, making a trip with a girlfriend at Sarah Lawrence College, Sarah Key, to see the controversial, soon-to-be-destroyed Diego Rivera murals at Rockefeller Center in 1933 and going on with her to the Waldorf Astoria, where "there are some things in the great dining room by a man called Sert."[21] These were the moderately advanced, respectably unconventional enthusiasms of the time, and he shared them with a lively, soon-to-be-famous social set that included Brendan Gill, son of a wealthy physician, and, from one of the more ancien régime New York families, Douglas Auchincloss and his younger brother Louis, as well as Jack Bingham, whose father, Hiram, a U.S. senator, had "discovered" Machu Picchu; Dillon Ripley, great-grandson of a president of the Union Pacific railroad; and Hugh Chisholm, whose father's 244-foot yacht, *Aras*, was so serious that it was later turned over to President Truman for official use.[22]

This was the 1930s, not the Jazz Age. The Depression changed how people thought about wealth, and at Yale, with its ethos of citizenship, attention to social inequality was linked to prosperity and expansiveness. The university goes back to 1701, and because the most conspicuous of its buildings, along with their monastic-collegiate arrangement, recall the Middle Ages, it takes an effort to register how new a place much of it was. When Hersey arrived, it had only recently stopped being a construction site. James Gamble Rogers's massive Sterling Library, the result of what was in its day the biggest bequest ever received by an American university, was opened in 1931. It formed the center of, in effect, a new campus to the north of the original group of buildings. The clean, Dutch-gabled lines of Connecticut Hall had been complemented on the older site by the nineteenth-century brick Gothic of Russell Sturgis's Henry Farnam Hall, but Rogers's architectural ambitions were more aggressive.[23] He announced them, as well as the tastes of his patron, with the soaring Harkness Tower, finished in 1922, to the west of the Old Campus. After an interval the Sterling Library followed—from the outside a kind of readers' prison, though the interior is more accommodating—along with the Sterling Law Building (also 1931), the Hall of Graduate Studies (1932), Trumbull and Calhoun Colleges (1933), and Berkeley College (1934). All these are Rogers's with the exception of Calhoun College,[24] which benefited from the lighter touch of a different architect, John Russell Pope. Also Rogers's are several other, only slightly outlying colleges of the same busy period, among them the ersatz-eighteenth-century Pierson, where Hersey would later serve as master.

Colleges were being tried out at Yale not just as buildings, but as an Oxbridge-modeled social system instituted at Yale at the behest of the Standard Oil heir Edward Harkness. Hersey and other students of Trumbull College were watched over by the redoubtable first master, the medical researcher, soldier, and academic politician Brigadier-General Stanhope Bayne-Jones, and still more by his hospitable and appropriately named wife, Nannie.[25] Not that Hersey needed moral guardianship. He kept his distance from the "football scrimmage," choosing the company of those he called "the clean livers," or so he emphasized in his letters home. He was no killjoy, but his status at Yale never depended on acting up. There he was, on the masthead of the *Yale Daily News*, and a deacon of Battell Chapel and a member of Skull and Bones, and on the Yale Bulldogs football roster coached, toward the end of his time, by the future U.S. president Gerald Ford (Hersey spent most of his time on the bench but won his "Y," being brought on for the last two minutes of the Harvard game):[26] pretty much whatever counted.

It would be surprising if his contemporaries didn't notice the rare moments when luck abandoned him. His roommate Chester Kerr, later one of the best academic publishers of his generation, described how in a home game against Brown, Hersey "punted the ball so high into a fierce wind that it landed 20 yards behind him, where he just managed to fall on it before six onrushing Brown players could do so."[27] But luck wasn't what was involved. Hersey worked at it all—and by working, not by sucking up to people or showing off. In the process he was becoming part of the last generation of the East Coast ruling class, albeit one who didn't feel any special entitlement and who was frequently reminded by his parents of the need to avoid expensive distractions. A small battle was going on between the young man and the values of a father against whom, because of the latter's infirmity, John could not actively rebel. The struggle was partly internalized. When he wrote "Sarah [Key] has invited me to a freshman dance at Sarah Lawrence, and I, in turn, have asked her down here to our dance," he felt bound to reassure his parents but perhaps also himself that "the expense will be practically nil for the following reasons: my ticket to the dance will be free, as I am a committeeman; Sarah is getting a ride down (I am getting one home on the 3rd, by the way); and she will be put up in a New Haven home. Whether I wanted a girl down or not, I would be somewhat obliged, in my position, to have one, because I have to spend half my time booming [advertising] the dance idea."

Daily News

His news remained for the most part compatible with muscular Christianity, reports of chapel attendance mingling with accounts of his efforts to improve his tennis or learn to ride. July 1935 found him sailing on the East River in his capacity as a family tutor: "Oh, this life is glorious. If only I could coast along all year 'round with the same carefree attitude! Nothing but sunlight, air, exercise, food, sleep, reading—nourishment to brain, body, and spirit. It is quite wonderful." Term time was just as good. The following November he wrote from Yale, "Another week: how fast they go, these busy, happy days."[28] Still, Grace must have been concerned, at a time when U.S. unemployment was running at 25 percent, that in the spring of his senior year her son joined a glitzy sailing trip to the Bahamas on the Chisholms' yacht. The party included Sarah Key and her mother. He flew down to Nassau, where Sarah and Hugh met him. "Mr. Chisholm was waiting in one of the three power launches," he told his parents with frank excitement. "After a quick change on the boat, we went for a swim in the warm waters and a bask on the hot beach of the Porcupine Club, an exclusive organization of which Mr. Chisholm seems to be a charter member. We had lunch there, too. After lunch Sarah and I crossed the harbor to the town of Nassau, which is steeped in a native charm which whisked me back to the days at Peitaiho."[29] That afternoon, he airily continued, "We expected the Duke of Kent and his wife to come out for tea"—these were Prince George, the youngest son of the British king George V, and Princess Marina of Greece, who had just married—"but he sent a message saying that he was having to shake the hands of a great number of natives and so would be unable to come." The trip was a success: "Sarah and I have been treated wonderfully, separately and together, and of course it has been a beautiful adventure for us."

In articles for the university paper he had meanwhile been learning to be a writer. The process was gradual but unmistakable, and quietly self-aware. In February 1933, halfway through his freshman year, Hersey joined the editorial board of the *Yale Daily News*—the oldest college daily paper in the United States. It provided a serious training. A team of a couple of dozen student editors and associate editors worked three at a time in rotation to bring out the four-page mix of Yale news—particularly of sport and other competitive activities—humorous gossip, reviews (the only signed items), and interviews, stiffened by a digest of international stories and articles by or about public figures. Advertising, which at the beginning and end of the college year pushed the paper up to eight or even sixteen pages, brought in revenue out of which staff received small amounts of pay. Fellow staffers of Hersey's included future journalists, of course, but also policy makers, businessmen, and a Bletchley code breaker.[30] His own interests were soon reflected in the paper, partly through interviews with musicians and other cultural personalities[31] but especially in pieces on China, among them a front-page interview with an American Asia expert, George Sokolsky, about the recent collision between the League of Nations and Japan over the latter's incursions into Manchuria. Sokolsky had gone to Russia to cover the revolution but was forced to flee to China, where he lived in Tientsin from 1918, working for a number of American and British papers. When Japanese hostilities against China heated up in 1931, he returned to the States.[32] The *News* interviewed him immediately after the Japanese walkout, which occurred early in Hersey's career on the paper. From a Southeast Asian perspective, the Second World War was about to begin.

Hersey wasn't neglecting his studies, which included the visual arts. For the subject of his "senior essay," a long final-year research project, he chose the historical painter John Trumbull, who designed the original Yale art gallery; the largest collection of his work is there. The choice of subject was dutiful—Trumbull was the son of a governor of Connecticut after whom Hersey's college was named—and his research was thorough. As a recent Yale student has established, it involved, among other things, reading Trumbull's voluminous letters: "1,500 pages . . . at the New York Historical Society, 600 pages at the Library of Congress, 500 pages at the Connecticut State Library at Hartford, 300 pages that one of Trumbull's relatives donated to Yale in 1929, 100 pages at the New York Public Library, 100 pages at the Connecticut Historical Society, and 25 pages at Harvard."[33] The diligence was typical, as were Hersey's high expectations. In the end he decided that Trumbull's achievement was limited to a "few paintings that are true gems" and that he therefore didn't warrant the biography the student had originally intended to write. What he submitted instead was an annotated selection of the letters.

England

Again, it was to his parents that he sent this account of his decision. His letters home were increasingly style-conscious. "Rain is driving down so thick and fast that it looks like snow," he wrote in November 1934: "little flurries chase each other up the bare street."[34] Within a few years, such phrases grew into paragraphs, set pieces. In October 1936, after spending part of the summer tutoring for and sailing with a family called Ingraham in Buffalo Bay on Lake Ontario, he went to Clare College, Cambridge, on a Mellon scholarship. He had, or thought he had, been promised a job at *Time*, having declined one with Procter and Gamble,[35] so continuing his studies felt initially like a chore. The Oxbridge system of those days required American graduates, however distinguished their home university, to take an abbreviated version of the Oxbridge first degree—in effect, to remain as undergraduates—which in his case meant repeating some work he had already done. Cambridge was damp, cold, and lonely at first; London, to which he occasionally escaped, little better. His letters exclaim about the weather as if New England were California. Most of his initial sadness, though, was a matter of missing Sarah Key, and if anyone could alleviate that in those days before transatlantic flights, it was the

Chisholms, whose son Hugh was also at the university. The Chisholm parents popped over on the boat so often that Grace called them "the commuters."

In any case, there was plenty to involve John in his new surroundings, and he took to them soon enough, writing amusingly about the differences between American and British academic customs:

> In America, arriving students are hurried into a great room together, given schedules, put to work immediately on definite projects. Here, when one gets around to it, he goes, entirely on his own, to see the Tutor of his college; finds that "when he gets around to it" was much to[o] early; is told to come around tomorrow, when he . . . talks to such a one as Mr. Thirkill, large, genial, vague, who . . . tells you to see your "moral tutor" when the spirit moves you; you find it impossible to see your "moral tutor" before noon the following day; you find him, then, far vaguer, completely unable to organise himself or you, rushing nervously about the room looking for vital papers . . . terribly sorry to have forgotten what you are "reading," and, withal, very kind-hearted, most anxious to please; he assigns you to a Supervisor, who is, actually, the one who is to direct your studies.[36]

He seems to have met most of his numerous American contemporaries at Cambridge—encounters vivid enough at the time and in some cases made more so by what history has added to them: a "canoe-jaunt" up the Cam toward Grantchester, for example, jolted out of cliché by the fact that Hersey's companion was the as-yet-unknown poet John Berryman.[37] Even his supervisor was American: Andrew Chiappe, at the time finishing his graduate studies, later a distinguished Shakespearean at Columbia. The closest Chiappe came, initially, to giving his new pupil "definite projects" was to tell him to "read some Greek tragedy . . . and go to hear some lectures."

For all the quaintness, it's noticeable, given that we tend to look back to the first half of the twentieth century as a time when the communications revolution had not yet diminished the world, how much had already changed. Watching a rugby match in mid-November, Hersey and a Princeton friend realized that the Princeton-Yale game was going on at home, rushed back to college, and listened to it on shortwave radio.[38] The telephone, too, already both shortened distances and increased them, as he found when Sarah called him from the States at New Year. He satirized the resulting conversation:

> "Hello!"
> "Hello!"
> "How are you?"
> "What?"
> "How are you?"
> "Oh, I'm fine, thanks. Isn't this exciting?"
> "What?"
> "I say, isn't this exciting?"
> "I should say it is. I can hear you as plain as day."
> "What?"[39]

He even saw a demonstration of television.[40]

Hersey was becoming an alert observer, which in his case increasingly meant a moral as well as a behavioral sort of observation. A certain kind of Englishman, he found, "talks too well to be entirely convincing; he says things he does not believe just so he may defend what he has said by watertight logic."[41] There was an unfamiliar flippancy also in some English political attitudes: "They laugh, for instance, at the horribly stark Russian trials."[42] But he was also meeting other foreigners, among them an expansive, aristocratic Basque, Ramón de la Sota, who had seen action in Spain's new civil war. What struck Hersey immediately from their conversations was how much the Basque situation complicated the war's polarities, and the differences between what he had been reading in the papers—"an attack, a town captured, an air raid"—and the human situations recounted by Ramón, who became a friend. Another unexpected factor was Ramón's sheer relish of the conflict: "He has loved every minute of it"—so much so that he used the six-week Christmas vacation to get back into action.[43] It was clearer to Hersey than to many of those he talked to that, however covertly, the British government supported Franco, but also that outside intervention would accelerate a larger war.[44] In general, it surprised him how far European fascism had weakened non-fascists' confidence in the League of Nations, and how carelessly confident some of his European fellow students were that war was the inevitable settler of differences.

Between his studies and cultural pursuits, at both of which he worked hard, and sports (he took up golf, played rugby for the Clare College "Unemployed" XV, and, when the summer came, was on the college's tennis team), he traveled: exploring the fens on a bike, visiting Oxford, driving north via the Lake District to his mother's ancestral home in "a dismal little back street of connected houses" in Annan, Dumfriesshire, where he was made welcome by an elderly distant cousin and felt ashamed of his tailored clothes and borrowed car. And of course there was London, with its art exhibitions and concerts (Artur Schnabel at the Guildhall—"He puffed and blew and stormed and talked to the piano!"),[45] and visits to and from the Chisholm family, including for a whole week in February. In their company and far from familiar territory, he seems to have been unconscious—Dumfriesshire notwithstanding—of how rich a world he was now moving in. The dollar went a long way. He wrote home from Claridges, where Sarah Key was staying with the Chisholms.[46] Quaglino's, Boulestin, the Café de Paris, "a lovely sherry party . . . for the Marchioness of Reading": he rattled the names onto his typewriter with innocent zest. A train journey down through France to Italy during the Easter vacation was transformed into a sailing holiday along the Ligurian coast on someone's hundred-foot schooner when acquaintances obligingly chartered the boat and its crew. And there were country-house weekends, dinner dances, birthday parties, in the course of which he met a covey of upper-class Englishmen and Englishwomen, among them Laura Bonham Carter ("very London, very bright"), granddaughter of Herbert Asquith and soon to be married to the liberal politician Jo Grimond; the writer Robin (2nd Viscount) Maugham;[47] and the picturesque Myles Thoroton Hildyard, who within a few years was to be captured by and escape from the German army in Crete.[48] Under such influences his letters home, particularly to his left-leaning brother Arthur, are conservatively defensive of the British class system. He told his parents he was getting so English that "I *affect* Americanisms!"[49]

He took a keen interest in the abdication crisis. King George V died at the beginning of 1936. His dapper but not very bright eldest son and immediate heir, Edward, was in a relationship with a married (and previously divorced) American, Wallis Simpson. This mattered constitutionally, but in any case the social taboos involved were still widespread and many people were vicariously touched by what happened. During Hersey's first term at Cambridge, the uncrowned Edward VIII, having refused to give up Mrs. Simpson, was forced to abdicate.

The planned coronation went ahead on the intended date the following spring, but with Edward's nervous younger brother George on the throne and George's spirited Scottish wife as queen. Hersey's journalistic instincts drove him out of his college bed well before dawn on May 12, 1937, to travel to Liverpool Street with another American student and join the crowds watching—or, rather, mainly waiting for—the coronation procession. In a typed, single-spaced ten-page letter home the next day, he conveyed the occasion through how people around him talked about it— far more revealing than anything directly to do with history or protocol. One garrulous bystander told him, "We loved our Edward and we couldn't be expected to love our George yet. It'll take time. We'll love him before long but we don't yet. It'll take time."[50] Hersey's feeling for how he and the other spectators interacted with one another and with all that was going on was combined with a literary experiment in how to convey external events and sensations while being true also to his subjective state. In the hours he spent standing and sitting on the pavement outside Liberty on Regent Street, he was intermittently reading the second volume of *À la recherche du temps perdu*, and Proust's influence, as well as that of other modernist writers, can be seen in the narrative. Helped by them, Hersey was responsive to the new synesthesia of public events: the simultaneity of the conversations of people around him, the words on the pages he was reading, and the service at Westminster Abbey coming over loudspeakers in the street, their different registers as discordant as if the episode were a late prose addition to Eliot's *The Waste Land*:

> Swann in love with his hard-hearted Odette, being treated miserably, behaving as badly himself . . . She spoke to Swann about a friend to whose house she had been invited, and had found everything in it was "of the period." Swann could not get her to tell him what "period" it was . . .
>
> Great lorries rumbled up the street, doling out lunches to the troops, and the people near us who had not had the sense to bring any lunch with them groaned with envy. The soldiers were very neat and orderly now,

standing in line at either side of the road, with the white paper bags of lunch at their feet . . .

Oh Lord, Holy Father, who by anointing with oil didst of old make and consecrate Kings, said the Archbishop's voice through the metallic speaker . . .

"Blimey," said the schoolteacher, who was following the service in the official program, "We've only gotten through one page, and we've got eight to go. Blimey!"

It was a young writer's mimicry.[51] His future style, like that of most people who grew up with modernism but became adults in the 1930s, would be simpler.

He had already more or less decided to put formal study behind him and get a job. New anxieties about his father's health may have been an element;[52] Sarah was another, though she crops up less and less in his correspondence. At any rate, having gone home at the beginning of the summer vacation of 1937, he turned up at *Time*'s office to find that the expected vacancy no longer existed. It was only a brief setback. Through a Yale friend, almost certainly Brendan Gill,[53] he heard that the novelist Sinclair Lewis was looking for a secretary. In July, he wrote punctiliously to the Mellon Foundation and to his Cambridge tutor, thanking them for the opportunity he had been given but resigning his award.

A Man Totally Given Over to Writing

Both commercially and critically, Sinclair Lewis was the most successful American writer ever. *Main Street* and *Babbitt* had huge sales, and in 1930 he became the first U.S. novelist to win the Nobel Prize in Literature. By the time Hersey met him, he was in his fifties and, though Hersey didn't yet know this, an intermittently unmanageable drunk. With hindsight Hersey said that the Lewis he knew "was past his best work—this was a couple of years after *It Can't Happen Here*." But that powerful, sardonic novel, in which the United States is imagined as having become a fascist dictatorship, was another of Lewis's major successes—a stage version had opened in eighteen cities simultaneously while Hersey was at Cambridge— and neither reputations nor ambitions die that fast. Creatively, as well as in his obsessions and impersonations and practical jokes, Lewis was still a force to be reckoned with.

In the early summer of 1937 Lewis had gone on a binge with his minder-accomplice Louis Florey. It seems that he was trying in a confused way to estrange himself from his wife, the celebrated political columnist Dorothy Thompson, of whose successes and political clear-headedness he was jealous and whose efforts to get him to control his behavior he resented still more. If that's true—and Hersey didn't detect anything of the kind[54]—it can't have helped that it was Dorothy who rescued him, and that she took it on herself to fire Florey. Still, "Red," as he was called, went back on the wagon, arranged to interview potential replacements for Florey, and in an oblique fashion chose Hersey.[55] It may have been part of Hersey's appeal to Lewis that he was clearly overqualified: If there had to be a minder, better that he shouldn't stay too long. Soon Lewis was in touch with a friendly editor at *Time*, pressing for Hersey to be tried out at the magazine.[56] For now, the novelist told his new assistant to learn shorthand and touch-typing and installed himself for the summer at a cottage in Stockbridge, Massachusetts, where he would be close to the most recent of his hospitals if he needed help.

Hersey joined him a month later. His duties consisted chiefly of typing drafts of a new play and a novel, dealing with correspondence, driving, and buying chocolates: "no nougat in the fillings, no nuts, Louis Sherry creams—to appease a liver which, to my unknowing, had been mightily revved up by his years of drinking."[57] The house was soon full of actors from the local theater, whose youthful, lively, unintellectual company Lewis enjoyed and for whom Hersey, in turn, played the role of bartender. He did some writing of his own[58] and naturally became part of the artistic, intellectual, and journalistic life Dorothy brought to her table, where he met, among others, the feminist Betty Swing, the French correspondent Raoul de Roussy de Sales, Alexander Woollcott of *The New Yorker*, the young Joseph Alsop, and—a particularly useful contact—the political thinker and strategist C. D. Jackson, then Henry Luce's special assistant at Time Inc. This social side of his life with the Lewises helped him through his and Sarah Key's drifting apart: "Things do look rather dark for S and self," he confided in a letter home.[59]

Lewis's work was all-consuming. Often writing at night, he finished his play and then what Hersey later described as a "shockingly bad," feebly conformist novel, *The Prodigal Parents*, which his new factotum was obliged to type. Parties were one thing, but Lewis was still and only a writer. Years later, in 1954, Hersey had a brief correspondence with his former employer's first wife, Grace Hegger Lewis. She had sent him her newly published memoir, affectionate about Lewis and especially about their son, Wells, killed in the Second World War. Hersey's thoughtful reply says he had no idea "in those brief weeks" he spent with them "how much I was learning, not just about my craft but about being alive."[60] He subsequently expanded on the craft aspect in a conversation with one of his students, the novelist Jonathan Dee:

> I was able to see the life of a man totally given over to writing. Even though he was not producing important novels anymore, he was so gripped by what he was doing . . . He would get up in the middle of the night, cook up some coffee, and work for two or three hours and then go back to bed. He led an irregular life, but a life that was passionately devoted to his work. I was exposed to someone who lived for his writing, lived in his writing, in a way.[61]

As for "being alive," the serious, circumspect Hersey may have meant Lewis's antic energy, or his vulnerability, or the imaginative engagement of his writing at its best, or all three. At the time he was in no doubt that he was "amazed, stimulated, amused, delighted, by this man. He talks and talks and talks, about anything that comes into his head, and many things do."[62] They were very different from each other both in character and, once Hersey had become established as a writer, in their work, but in ways that produced mutual affection and admiration. Lewis took more paternal interest in his "wise, gentle" young protégé than in his own sons.[63] After the Second World War, and after Hersey's early successes with *A Bell for Adano* and *Hiroshima*, the older man disclaimed having had any influence on him: "You did not learn anything from me except the slightest tricks of how to keep the saw & chisel free from rust. You had the instinct for work from the beginning, & I've always been extremely proud—& boastful!—about knowing you!" For his own part, however, Hersey was "constantly amazed" at how much he owed Lewis. "He was a much bigger, a much greater person than his latest books let people believe."

For all the differences, Hersey's work shares some broad preoccupations with Lewis's. A century and a half after independence, at the end of the main era of immigration from Europe, and at a point where U.S. economic and military power in the world was being exerted ever more strongly, both writers asked what it was to be American, what the core American values were, and how far Americans lived up to them. Consciously or not, Hersey was influenced by Lewis in several novels that dramatize these questions. The younger man's *Too Far to Walk* is more psychological, more "serious" than *The Prodigal Parents*, but it touches on similar issues in the relationships between rebellious young and the older generation, and both novels were successful with parent-readers facing similar problems. The position of a bright, attractive, educated woman in a provincial, still semirural society is the topic of many novels apart from Lewis's *Main Street* and Hersey's *The Marmot Drive*, but there are other resemblances between the two. And when Hersey translated U.S. slavery to a Chinese setting in *White Lotus*, the metamorphosis had something in common with what Lewis's *It Can't Happen Here* had brought about by imagining Nazism in power in America (an echo that can also be heard in Hersey's much later *Manzanar*).[64] Lewis's sense of the vulnerability of liberal values gradually became Hersey's predominant concern.

Time passed before these affinities showed. The biggest resemblance between the men, though—sheer hard work—was immediately apparent to Lewis. In Hersey's case, it was soon put to use at *Time* magazine. At 11:00 a.m. on Thursday, October 7, 1937, he reported to one of the business editors, Ralph Paine, soon to become Luce's PA, who had promised to "find you a desk, give you a typewriter, and put your name on the payroll."[65]

Headquarters of Lying

As if to atone for the rising dominance of film and photography, American magazines were hiring some of the best writers on the market and giving them extraordinary freedom. The boom had begun back in the 1890s, when new printing technology and the growth of display advertising combined to make magazine publishing exceptionally profitable, but it was arguably the development of sophisticated fashion magazines containing good writing—the relaunched *Vogue* and *Vanity Fair* especially—that made journalism seem a smart career choice in every sense. In *Vanity Fair*'s 1920s heyday, its offices next to Grand Central Terminal seemed from the outside a party venue as much as a place of work, models and photographers mingling with Dorothy Parker, Robert Benchley, and P. G. Wodehouse. The scruffier, quirkier *New Yorker*, begun just down the street in 1925 as a primarily humorous and imaginative as well as self-consciously non-provincial form of entertainment, soon began publishing serious nonfiction, including profiles (a new term for an old genre) and long articles in the section "Behind the News" (the original title of the department that became "Reporter at Large"). Also nearby, the advertisement-packed *Time* magazine had been started a couple of years before *The New Yorker* by an ambitious pair of recent Yale graduates who had worked together on the *Yale Daily News*. One of them, Briton Hadden, died young, leaving his restless partner, Henry Luce, in sole charge. Luce, whose formation was identical to Hersey's—the China mission field followed by Hotchkiss, Yale, and Skull and Bones—soon married one of *Vanity Fair*'s staffers, Clare Boothe. He added a business title, *Fortune*, in 1930, under the management of a *New Yorker* dissident, Ralph Ingersoll, and in 1936 started the mass-circulation picture magazine *Life*.

In this fluid world, most participants were at home in more than one midtown office. *The New York Times* and what was then the *New York Herald Tribune* were both in the neighborhood, as were some key publishing houses. Harper and Brothers was downtown on remote Franklin Square, but Alfred A. Knopf was on Madison Avenue between Fifty-Second and Fifty-Third Streets, Scribner around the corner on Fifth Avenue between Forty-Eighth and Forty-Ninth. For some writers daily life was centered on the New York Public Library, for others on the Algonquin Hotel or "Bleeck's"—the Artist and Writers' Club on West Fortieth—but wherever you were and whatever group you were most at ease in, you couldn't step outside without bumping into someone whose work you knew, and sometimes even respected. The poet and translator from classical Greek Robert Fitzgerald—later a close friend of Hersey's—was on the staff of *Time*. At *Fortune* the writer-editors included another poet, Archibald MacLeish, who had spent most of the 1920s among the American exiliocracy in France. Katharine White, a steadying force behind the impulsive Harold Ross at *The New Yorker*, had been at the most intellectual of women's colleges, Bryn Mawr. Even the austere Edmund Wilson served a period at *Vanity Fair* as business manager.

So it was a sellers' market for authors.[66] But by the mid-1930s, while the tone of the "smart magazines" was still light, hard questions had become hard to avoid, and for some writers—and photographers—the allure of magazine publication was not only that it was well paid and happened in a stimulating part of town, but also that you might be able to get away with something that would open people's minds or soften their hearts. Henry Luce himself, almost a generation older than Hersey, was self-parodically high-principled about politics, education, and innovation, and surrounded himself with clever people with similar feelings, though not always the same views. The brilliant, uncompromising, then unknown James Agee, for example, was commissioned by *Time* to write a text to accompany a photographic feature by Walker Evans on the lives of poor southern blacks. The process was so agonizing to him that what started as a magazine feature took him four years to complete, and when it finally appeared in 1941, and then in the form of a book, it was crowded out by world events. *Let Us Now Praise Famous Men* survived to become a transformative text for a later generation of readers.[67]

Agee's impetus, in Hersey's later words, was "to try to set the truth free in what he saw as the headquarters of lying."[68] Others at Time-Life, among them Dwight Macdonald, had different kinds of truth they wanted to communicate. A Yale graduate, like so many of Luce's early recruits, and later one of the founding members of the radical group tendentiously known as "the" New York Intellectuals, the as-yet-apolitical Macdonald joined *Fortune* when it began in 1929 and also wrote about business for *Time*. He described *Fortune* accurately as "a *de luxe* mag, in format like *Vanity Fair*... devoted to glorifying the American businessman." The more businessmen he got to know, though, and the more he saw of the consequences of the Wall Street crash, the more uneasy he became about unfettered capitalism and the more drawn to its opponents. His research into the American Federation of Labor led to a long article on the American Communist Party published in September 1934, and to his own temporary conversion—despite a fervent dislike of Communists en masse—to broadly Communist views. It was in this context that *Fortune* boldly sent him forth to investigate the steel industry, whose captains wined him and dined him but failed to win him over. His resulting long article on Republic Steel, though rewritten at Luce's request by Archibald MacLeish, met with objections from the company's management that it was "socialism."[69]

Dwight Macdonald was among the first of Luce's journalists to complain that his magazines were moving to the right. Media magnates in their role as literary patrons are too little praised, and the comical aspects of Luce—his vanity and touchiness—have encouraged a notion that in the early days of *Time*, rather than wanting to encourage his journalists to communicate what they found, he simply failed to control them. But while Luce's intelligence was of an unusual kind, he knew, though he later often forgot, that readers didn't want papers that told only one story. Hiring brilliant if wayward writers and giving them scope wasn't inconsistent with firing them if and when it became clear that they were really determined to get fired. The 1930s were a time of what today seems culpable credulity and crudely polarized views. Collisions between Luce and individuals on his staff were to become one of the journalistic battle-training grounds of the Cold War, and in Hersey's case his eventual break with Luce would be both tough and career-determining. For now, however, he was far too busy to think much.

He was put through the departments at *Time*, covering business, religion, radio, music, books, news, and was writing articles often and fast. In an exuberant letter to his parents from "the fiftieth floor, with a view uptown, over what proves to be a glorious and thrilling city" ("I am having *such* fun!"), he described "a gradual process of absorption and imitation" by which he was mastering "the intricacies and hidden mysteries of *Time* style"—intricacies whose absolute correctness in the eyes of his elders he already found irksome.[70] One day he had to file something quickly about T. S. Eliot ("the most gift-stricken poet of his time," Hersey memorably called him),[71] because Eliot's portrait by Wyndham Lewis, submitted in May 1938 for the Royal Academy's summer show, had been rejected. Or there was a dinner for Vincent Sheean, of the *Herald Tribune*, just back from the Spanish Civil War. (Among the guests was W. H. Auden.) Because of their shared background as well as his talent and professional commitment, Hersey was becoming a protégé of Luce's. At any point he might be called upstairs by the boss to discuss a story involving China. World events were moving very fast, and by March 1939 he was freed from his apprenticeship and given a regular job in the Foreign News section. Within a month Luce wanted him to bring himself up to speed on Japan. Why not make a trip there, and remind himself of China while he was about it?

We Are So Sorry to Be Giving You Lots of Trouble

There could scarcely have been a more important journalistic assignment. It's often said that Pearl Harbor came as a complete surprise to the United States, but from the mid-1930s on, newspapers and magazines were full of stories about Japanese militarism and the threat from the Pacific.[72] China and Japan had been at war for two years officially and in practice a good deal longer. In October 1938, encouraged by the weakness the British government showed at Munich toward Nazism, Japan landed thirty thousand troops at Bias Bay (Daya Bay) north of Hong Kong, captured Canton city (Guangzhou), cut off the rail line between it and Kowloon, and then took Hankow. Almost immediately, the Japanese government published its plan for a "New Order" in Asia. The United States, like Britain, protested but remained passive, opinion split between appeasing (or indeed actively befriending) Japan[73] and supporting China; and, in the latter case, between enthusiasm for the nationalist leader Chiang Kai-shek—which was, and remained, Henry Luce's position—and a widespread sentiment, much encouraged by Edgar Snow's 1937 bestseller *Red Star over China*, for Mao Zedong and Communism.

By mid-May 1939, Hersey was in the Imperial Hotel, Tokyo. A month short of his twenty-fifth birthday he wrote home with an easy zest far removed from the studied artistry of his letter about the coronation of George VI two years earlier:

> Here's a typical day: up at 8, breakfast and a few notes on the previous day's interviews. At 10:30, interview with a very young man in the Foreign Office, who gives me the orthodox imperial views; at 11:30, a talk with the military attaché of the U.S. Embassy about the relative strengths of the Chinese and Japanese Armies; lunch with the youngest [member of the] Saionji [family], the last of the Elder Statesmen (Genro) of the Meiji Era; after lunch a talk with the press bureau chief at the War Office, to get military views; tea with a man named Matsuoka, recently retired President

of the huge Southern Manchuria Railway; dinner Japanese style with a professor of the Imperial University; then either to bed or to kabuki (Japanese theater, classical plays & dances), or a chat with an American newspaperman in the lobby of the Imperial Hotel . . . I'm getting a lot (not much that makes me happy) out of these talks, and I hope I can write more sensibly about the Far East when I get back.[74]

He wrote pretty sensibly while he was there, in fact. The situation was extremely complicated, not least by Western constitutional and especially financial interests in Hong Kong and Shanghai. Military aid to China accompanied efforts to bolster the Chinese dollar against the yen, moves that increased Japanese determination to capture Western assets while their owners were preoccupied by events in Europe. We can't be sure how much of *Time*'s reportage from the region during those weeks used Hersey's words, but the magazine's summary of events over the past months is clear enough:

Russia, riddled by the purges of the Trotskyite dissenters, was in no mood to fight a Far Eastern war on behalf of the Chinese. Great Britain, strongest European power in the Far East, was hampered by fears lest the year-old Civil War in Spain leap its national boundaries and rage through the Mediterranean and along the Rhine. The French Popular Front Government, bedeviled by fiscal troubles, was in no position to take part of the White Man's Burden in Asia on its sagging shoulders. The U.S., meanwhile . . . had signaled its desire to grant independence to the Philippines, leading Japan to conjecture that the U.S. might be abdicating its role in the Far East forever.[75]

Reporting apart, his professionally typed diary-letters home to his parents amount in length and substance to a book.[76] The details are telling—a tight bomber formation going toward China as his ship arrives in Yokohama; an immigration official's close scrutiny of Hersey's copy of Auden and Isherwood's new book *Journey to a War*—and even more so is the innocent air of entitlement among his fellow travelers, recorded without comment by Hersey, who at this stage evidently felt something similar himself: entitlement to be there, or anywhere; entitlement not to be inconvenienced personally by what was going on. This soon gives way in

Hersey's case to a more intimate set of responses as he gets closer to his birthplace. In Hong Kong he met his boyhood friend Israel Epstein, as well as powerful new contacts and informants such as Edgar Snow. From there he flew to China's wartime capital, Chungking (Chongqing), and talked to Britain's unorthodox ambassador Archibald Clark Kerr—soon to be posted to Moscow, where in 1944–45 he and Hersey became good friends. At a press conference given by Chiang Kai-shek and his wife, Hersey formed impressions that would help him assess changes in the couple's outlook when they met again in the same room seven years later.[77] He also got his first sight of bomb damage, still a new phenomenon, and part of his letter about this gives a sense of the war correspondent he was in the process of becoming:

> Not a single military or political objective has been bombed—only homes, banks, shops and parks. The whole banking district has been destroyed, one large section of the business district is completely ruined but worst of all was a huge swath of the crowded homes nearby the hill on which stand various foreign embassies (except the American, which is across the river) . . . In this section fire followed the bombs. Five hundred Chinese were caught by the fire and forced to move up the hill toward the embassies. A high stone wall separates their part of the town from the Embassies' and gradually they were forced flat against that wall. No help was forthcoming from the German embassy just above—all five hundred were roasted to death against that wall . . . One of the greatest difficulties in the bombings is the superstition of the people. They think, for instance, that if they get under a tree they will be perfectly safe.[78]

At last, after various delays and extensions, and despite a warning from Jardine, Matheson, his travel organizers, that they couldn't guarantee his arrangements and believed the last leg of his route to Tientsin to be impracticable,[79] he reached the Japanese-controlled city in late June 1939.

As is often said, good journalists are identifiable in part by their good luck. While it would have been hard for a reporter to go anywhere in the world just then without finding something newsworthy to write about, it's remarkable that Hersey made his first return visit to his birthplace just at the outbreak of what became known as the Tientsin Crisis. Two months before, the manager there of the Japanese bank in China, who had recently also been put in charge of customs, had been assassinated in the British concession. In the immediate aftermath the British adopted what again seemed to be a conciliatory attitude to Japan, though one that vacillated according to which official the Japanese were dealing with.[80] In May, Japan bombed Chungking and arrested the British military attaché to China. On June 14, it began a full-scale blockade of Tientsin. Again, *Time*'s reportage showed the benefits of its international staff, but only Hersey was in a position to provide on-the-spot "color":

> Small comfort it was to the British that outside their Tientsin Concession the Japanese military set up a loudspeaker system to "explain" their action to English-speaking passers-by. Said the plaintive voice through the loudspeaker: "We are so sorry to be giving you lots of trouble."[81]

The British concession became in effect a prison camp, and a diplomatic storm was caused when people going in or out were strip-searched. Hersey was present at a lavish but only mildly apologetic press conference given by Major-General Masaharu Homma at his Tientsin headquarters, where guests were treated to "liquor, caviar, plates of ice cream, and other goodies now scarce in the British Concession. The general blithely lamented that some of his sentries were 'simple peasants who do not understand European standards of modesty.' His countrymen, he explained, do not mind disrobing in public . . . To prove his good faith, the General offered to take his own clothes off then & there for the correspondents." Hersey remembered this occasion a couple of years later, when U.S. general Douglas MacArthur faced Homma and his army in Bataan.[82]

While his reportage remained ironic, his letters home are full of a sense of dispossession doubled by current events. The more what he remembers has changed, the more reminiscences pour onto the page. At the former family house, an embattled new servant of a new owner wouldn't let him in. "It was my house," Hersey wrote in frustration. "It is my house. He had no right to keep me out."[83] The letters from Tientsin, pages of minutely detailed recall addressed to his parents, are a childhood autobiography written in a headlong rage of loss:

> The Empire [Theatre]. How new it was when we left, and how tumbledown now . . . You took me to *Aida* there . . . I was so impressed by the set

for the last act—the huge hall above, the dungeon below, all in one scene, like a Charlie Chaplin cutaway house—that even now I cannot enjoy Metropolitan [Opera] *Aidas* for my disappointment.

The little park across the way, where we used to swing by the hour. How much time we wasted![84]

He had been busy talking to officials, diplomats, and journalists and keeping an eye open for new stringers. Two of the contacts he made were to be of lasting importance to him. One was Archie Kerr. The other was a journalistic recruit, Theodore H. White, a young Harvard graduate who had studied with the sinologist John K. Fairbank and was now working for the Chinese propaganda office in Chungking while looking for something better. White came to idolize Hersey, the "blithe, handsome, tall . . . Yale varsity football player" who gave him his start in journalism together with the good advice that he should "try to tell not what had *happened*, but what was *happening*."[85] He meant, among other things, noticing what went on at the edge of the frame. There's an example in Hersey's description of his slow thirty-mile boat journey through the flatlands between Tangku (Tanggu) and Tientsin. At the center of attention lay the Japanese-controlled town he was heading toward. Traveling in the opposite direction was a boat crammed with women and children being evacuated to Peitaiho (Beidaihe), the summer resort of his childhood, on the coast to the north. But he noticed a couple of other things. The deck of the Victorian tender was reinforced with sheet steel, some on the afterdeck, some on the bridge, concealed in part by canvas and cloth coverings, among them a British flag. "Here was another of the symbols I have been meeting all the way; the Union Jack, which used to be enough, backed up by a steel shield. The implications were not reassuring."[86] The other was a timeless rural scenario: "For fifteen minutes, around one bend, I watched one man trying to catch a donkey, which stayed just ten feet away from him the whole time."[87] Emblems, visual parables, would always catch his eye.

Having returned to New York by the end of July, by which time, among other heated exchanges, the United States had terminated its 1911 commercial treaty with Japan, Hersey prepared a report for the paper's editors and took part in a series of working lunches with Far East specialists as well as with Luce himself.[88] A couple of months later, Teddy White sent him an impassioned eyewitness account of a Sino-Japanese engagement in the mountain-bordered Ch'in (Qin) River plateau in northern China. Judging the geographical and tactical specifics of the article too remote from readers' interests, Hersey tackled the problem drastically by working the material into a story initially about White himself. Shansi Province, he wrote, was so rugged, so vague to foreigners, that little news came out about what was happening there. White's discoveries, though, were "enough to make any parlor warrior drop his teacup."[89] Who was this intrepid adventurer? "A 24-year-old Harvard graduate with short legs, freckled face, cocky eyes, indomitable spirit, a compassion for suffering people, and a curiosity which could cost a cat all nine of its lives at the same time," White had gone to see for himself. Having built up his reporter as the immediate focus, Hersey then worked in background material of his own while using—but in the third person—White's description of the hazards of his journey and then of the hellish battleground he found. Only then did the article straightforwardly quote paragraphs of White's own, about the desperate fate of combatants in the region, Chinese and Japanese, and their mutual cruelties. The result is a model combination of brave reportage and skilled, knowledgeable editing for a mass readership.

By now Hersey was listed among *Time*'s associate editors and was one of those putting together the Foreign News section. They did so from material sent in by a large staff of correspondents, three of whom, in addition to White, had been newly signed up by Hersey on his travels. What any of them delivered was regarded as part of the raw material from which a story would be compiled, the other parts including reports sent in by others, the independent expertise of the section editors, "house style," and the paper's political line. Stories were generally unsigned and were regarded as belonging—in every sense, including copyright—to the paper itself, which, one way or another, had paid for them. Though this was standard journalistic practice to a degree that would before long cause some awkwardness for Hersey,[90] it inevitably grated on writers who cared about their expertise, their take on events, and their style. Tensions ran high at *Time* between journalists who were among the best in their fields and a proprietor who, as he gained confidence, became more eager to see his own worldview reflected in his newspapers. Luce knew, at least at first, that he couldn't be on top of everything, but the more he was fêted by potentates and diplomats, the more he came to believe what they told him about himself. He spent much of his time on fact-finding journeys in different parts of the world (not excluding parts of the United States), often coming to conclusions at odds with what his assiduous, skeptical, locally based correspondents were telling him.

They were themselves fallible, of course, as were the editors immediately responsible for what appeared in the magazines. More than a decade before Hersey's arrival at *Time*, the foreign editors had included Laird Goldsborough, whose hatred of Communism was equaled by his admiration of Mussolini and underestimation of the dangers posed by Hitler. Among Goldsborough's successors was a former Soviet agent turned proto–Cold Warrior, Whittaker Chambers, who devoted himself to correcting the generally softer line of any overseas correspondents who, like White, combined socialist sympathies with, as the war went on, recognition of the military importance of America's Soviet allies as well as of the rising Communist powers in China. "I read the incoming cables," one indignant staffer wrote to Luce, "and am amazed to see how they are either misinterpreted, left unprinted or weaseled around to one man's way of thinking."[91]

Disagreements like these weren't confined to *Time*. The magazine reflected, as well as steering an irregular course through, the controversies of its period, which were particularly intense in relation to China. Luce liked and believed in Chiang Kai-shek, his family, and the ruling republican Kuomintang party that he led, and deplored the United States' reluctance to divert resources—however badly needed elsewhere—in support of what was in practice a corrupt and badly managed regime. His views before and in the early stages of the Second World War were more nuanced than they were later on, but he grew increasingly cut off from his staff, so the arrival of someone as eager as Hersey, as yet unconnected with office politics and so similar in background to Luce himself, was particularly welcome to him, and their relationship was cordial. "Working hard on the China story today," the young journalist wrote to his parents in the middle of August 1939, "trying to dope out what the lineup would be in the South China Sea if a general war breaks out." That was early in a week that had begun with his spending Sunday on eight Far Eastern stories, the gist of which he relayed to his parents, ever interested both in the region and in what Johnny was doing. The shorthand of his daily postcards suggests how well informed they were:

The Tokyo parleys seem to have broken down pretty thoroughly as everyone expected they would. Other stories were on anti-foreignism, the state of Wang Ching-wei and Wang Keh-min (the Peking puppet governor), a proposed Soviet loan to China of $133,000,000 which would certainly be a tremendous boon, the second anniversary of the outbreak of hostilities in Shanghai, a piece on the state of women in wartime based on Tokyo research, and a small one on factory fires in Japan.[92]

The following Friday he had lunch with Luce. There was still hope that world war could be averted, so Hersey took a short break in the Adirondacks. On September 1, though, Hitler's invasion of Poland meant that war was "no longer something to worry about and fear. It is an actuality"—albeit one that meant less in the United States than it did in Europe. "We are still endlessly remote from its realities," Hersey lectured his parents in the cadences of his employer.[93] "Geography is good fortune. We have no gasmasks, dugouts, evacuations. But we have terrific responsibilities which we ought to be assuming. We've got to save what we can of the little bit of good in us." Just one month later he was put in charge of the magazine's new section, War.

3. On Top of the Hill

INTERNATIONAL POLITICS weren't quite everything. A year earlier, the still-new *Life* magazine had run a photo feature celebrating the tenth anniversary of Sarah Lawrence College, the women's private liberal-arts institution in Bronxville where Sarah Key had been a student.[1] The college presented itself as being ahead of its day in taking its students into workplaces—the stock exchange, the law courts, and, for those concerned with social issues, the poorer neighborhoods of Manhattan. *Life* treated all this in the manner of a fond but skeptical uncle, patronizingly faux-respectful, its eyes mainly turned on the fathers, many of whom, directly or indirectly, were important to the magazine as purchasers of advertising space. A typical caption read, "On an 'El' platform, Betty Blanchard, daughter of a manufacturer, and Helen Larmon, daughter of an advertising executive, converse briefly with a toothless derelict." The pictures were by Alfred Eisenstaedt, and a full page was given to his image of a creative writing class in "the New York apartment of Genevieve Taggard, poet, editor, critic and Sarah Lawrence faculty member." Seven young women in skirts, blouses, and cashmere jerseys are tastefully grouped around their tutor, who—though this isn't mentioned—was a socialist civil-rights campaigner from a missionary family. One of the students sitting literally at Miss Taggard's feet is identified as "Frances Ann Cannon, whose father makes Cannon towels."

To be precise, her father, Martin Luther Cannon, was one of the sons of James William Cannon, who had built up a prosperous cloth-manufacturing business in the South. By the standards of the time and region, Cannon was enlightened in his self-interest, providing decent accommodation and leisure facilities for his employees and encouraging the growth of the YMCA in what became the considerable-sized town of Kannapolis (originally Cannon-opolis), North Carolina. The family lived some distance away on the Blue Ridge, in Blowing Rock. By the 1930s the business, now in the hands of James's sons, was a household name.

Hot Pursuit

James's granddaughter Frances Ann was intelligent, attractive, sociable, passionate, and talented. After Sarah Lawrence, where she overlapped with Sarah Key, she spent time in London and was among the American young women selected to be presented at court in the English debutante "season." She then took a business administration course at the Webber Business College in Boston. It may have been in Massachusetts that she met John F. Kennedy, whose father, the U.S. ambassador in London, was best known among rich, settled Protestant Southerners like her parents for three alarming things: being Irish, being Catholic, and making his money by dubious means, most recently exploiting the end of prohibition, which had come about in 1933. Liquor was not the worst of it; there were well-founded stories that Joseph Kennedy was enthusiastically adulterous and had kept the actress Gloria Swanson as his mistress. His wife, Rose, meanwhile, was reputed to be neglectful of their ever-more-numerous children, though "neglect" is not how most of them would have described what they experienced as a capricious tyranny. But if to cautious, temperate, privileged WASPs the Kennedy name was anathema, to some of their children, especially girls educated at East Coast private schools, it meant a pair of handsome brothers[2] with a history made particularly interesting in the younger one's case by rumors of wildness, ill health, and unexplained changes of college. Despite competition from his roommate Charlie Houghton, Jack Kennedy, currently at Harvard, dated Frances Ann in the intervals of being abroad. She was "a very, very attractive and brilliant girl," Houghton later recalled. "I don't know who found [her] first, whether I did or Jack did. I was in hot pursuit, I'll tell you."[3]

In the winter of 1938–39, the pro-appeasement Joe Kennedy was called back from London to be hauled over the coals by President Roosevelt, who rightly thought him too soft on Nazism and was annoyed, also, by some grandstanding by his ambassador, who had his own eye on the presidency. Jack, meanwhile, had first tried Princeton, been quickly bored by it, traveled in Europe, switched to Harvard, and was beginning to think about his senior-year thesis, the topic of which would eventually be British foreign policy in the 1930s. On various pretexts he had won half a year's leave from college to spend more time in Europe, following Joe Senior to London at the end of February 1939. First, though, he took Frances Ann to the Kennedy villa in Palm Beach for a pre–Valentine's Day weekend. She went on to New Orleans for Mardi Gras, and Jack impulsively pursued her there. Things were clearly getting serious, at least by his not-very-high standards, and according to some reports he proposed marriage. At any rate, Frances Ann's parents were so concerned that her mother carted her off on a world cruise. Himself en voyage for London on the SS *Queen Mary*, Jack was handed a telegram: "CAN ONLY SAY STAY [A]WAY FROM THE HAY GOODBYE DARLING I LOVE YOU = FRANCES ANN."[4]

If what she meant was "Don't make hay while the sun shines," it was a forlorn injunction. Jack was no less promiscuous, and not much less socially ambitious, than his father and made the most of what remained of European high society—quite a lot, actually—on the brink of world war, while soon busying himself on his father's behalf at a quasi-diplomatic fact-finding level. His letters home to friends are full of gossip: about the silk breeches he had to wear at court "which are cut to my crotch tightly and in which I look mighty attractive," about the Kennedy family's ousting of Mussolini's son from the place he expected at the coronation of Pope Pius XII (a personal friend of Joe Kennedy's), and about girls he was dating who'd had affairs with princes. How much of this reached Frances Ann's ears we don't know, but having returned to the States and resumed her semi-independent social life, whether or not directly under her parents' influence, she soon found herself going out with someone much less flippant than Kennedy, and, though poorer, well enough connected. She and Hersey met at a cocktail party of a Yale friend.[5] "You breezed in," he later reminded her, "with an ostrich feather on your head and a telephone number on your lips. I remember it *so* well: Was China interesting?" China apart, they talked about mutual friends, about sculpture, about beagling. They danced the tango.[6] When Jack Kennedy returned to Harvard in fall 1939, invitations to the Cannon parents' New York apartment were waiting for both him and his friend Charlie. They showed up expectantly on Sunday, October 1, and, in a well-staged scene that would have been worth witnessing, were downcast to be introduced to Frances Ann's fiancé, John Hersey.[7]

Life with a journalist, however fast rising, wasn't as zizzy as with the ambassador's scapegrace son. There were wars on in the Far East and Europe, after all, and he had an office to go to. But Frances Ann, who later became a successful theater producer and cofounder of the National Repertory Theater, was as interested in the arts as she was in partying. She and Hersey went to hear Beethoven conducted by Toscanini, to the opening of MoMA's big Picasso show, to *Otello* at the Met.[8] Her mother took them to James Thurber's new comedy *The Male Animal*. Within six months, they were married. Jack Kennedy was at the ceremony in North Carolina on April 27, 1940, having overcome a reluctance he expressed comically to a friend: "I would like to go but don't want to look like the tall slim figure who goes out and shoots himself in the greenhouse halfway through the ceremony."[9]

Their early years together were zestful. "I love you more than the law allows," Frances Ann wrote to her husband while he was away on a working trip.[10] One of her brothers-in-law had told her that John and he had decided that, she wrote, "all Cannon women were so bed conscious that we needed at least three husbands simultaneously to keep us happy. Is that true? I am flattered if it is but a little worried as to how you . . . will last under such strain!" In the marriage's early years at least, he lasted well enough, though in his own letters he never permitted himself anything so explicit. When there was strain, it came at first from what was happening in the rest of the world. Their wedding, by chance, occurred on the day when Himmler ordered the construction of Auschwitz. While that was something known to very few—as a fact, let alone in its implications—everyone who followed the news was aware that in those last days of April 1940 and throughout May the British were crushed by the Nazis in Norway, and Germany overran Belgium, Luxembourg, Holland, and France. The bulk of the British forces that had been sent to support the French were evacuated in disarray from Dunkirk, and a German invasion of Britain was expected any day. At a series of meetings of Churchill's war cabinet toward the end of May, the recently ousted prime minister Neville Chamberlain and Foreign Secretary Lord Halifax, both of whom had been ceaselessly encouraged in their pro-appeasement views by Ambassador Kennedy, argued unsuccessfully that Britain should not continue fighting.

Allies Trapped Here

These events were covered thoroughly by *Time*. Advertising apart, about seventy pages of an average issue were taken up with news:[11] an opening section titled National Affairs followed by half a dozen pages of foreign news treated as a category separate from, and often preceded by, "World War." Then arts, sports, education, and other departments before a sizable section devoted to business. The general effect was designedly miscellaneous—six hundred columns or more were filled with advertising—but the "front of the book" offered seriousness, depth, and pictorial vividness unequaled in other mass-circulation print media. The issue of April 29, 1940, contained maps as well as photographs illustrating the British debacle in Norway, though the detailed accompanying reportage was weakened by some editorializing in response to the Nazi foreign minister Joachim von Ribbentrop's claim that the Germans occupied Norway in order to protect the country from a planned British invasion. If the British had had such a plan, the paper over-loyally asserted, they wouldn't have made such a mess of it. A month later, the invasion of Belgium and France was illustrated by page-width pictures of German armor, plus a four-page color spread of paintings of "France at War" by the artist Bernard Lamotte.

In almost every issue, meanwhile, something was said about ways in which pro-neutrality U.S. public sentiment was shifting in response to events—what *Time* called "the first shocked realization that perhaps soon nothing but a shrunken ocean would lie between Adolf Hitler and

America."[12] How far the magazine was reporting, as distinct from prompting, this realization is a moot point, but there was no ambiguity about the map of France it printed on June 3 highlighting the region between Saint-Omer and Bruges ("1,000,000 Allies trapped here"), or about its sympathies two weeks later, when two full pages were given to an edited version of Churchill's "We shall fight on the beaches" speech.

Early in June 1940 Luce, in Hersey's words, "kicked himself upstairs to the Chairmanship of the Board" and took the opportunity to give a dinner for most of his available top writers.[13] Hersey told his parents that Luce had been in the Netherlands "the days the holocaust began" (the word was then used of any big conflagration, but its later connection with the Nazi Final Solution isn't inappropriate in context). In an after-dinner speech lasting from 8:30 until 11:00 p.m., Luce described his experiences and impressed on his reporters the need for full U.S. support of Britain and defense of Atlantic sea routes, as well as preparation for a possible war on American territory. The effects on *Time*'s already pro-British coverage were quickly visible. With the beginning of the Battle of Britain in July, a cover picture of the U.K.'s ambassador to Washington, Lord Lothian, was captioned "Now there is only one possible ally."[14] Three weeks later, an illustrated account of what the paper described as "history's first aerial siege" was given graphic emphasis in a story printed in a larger-than-usual typeface over two, rather than the usual three, columns per page, accompanied by a double-page map in color.

America was threatened more from the East than from Europe, of course. Hersey continued to be involved in many news items about the region and accompanied Luce to a meeting with the former Chinese finance minister T. V. Soong, who had resigned over what he saw as Chiang Kai-shek's appeasement of Japan. (He later became his foreign minister.) "He is optimistic for Britain," Hersey wrote home, "therefore for the cause of Democracy, therefore for China. He thinks we ought to seek collaboration with Russia against Germany and Japan. He is forceful for a Chinese and clear-minded for *any* nationality. I was very much impressed by him."[15] Understanding what was happening in China also involved listening to what *Time*'s own experts had to say and, from the point of view of relations with Luce, Hersey's recruit Teddy White was proving hard to handle. The issues were difficult and sometimes personal. White was an emotional man, intensely possessive about his copy, which had to go through China's own layers of censorship before reaching New York, where it might anyway not appear for reasons of space. Hersey did his best to reassure him, telling him that there were often occasions when the magazine didn't publish material that everyone agreed was excellent and that White's success ratio was higher than that of most correspondents;[16] but the main problem was the ideological difference between the anti-Communist Whittaker Chambers and White's own expertise and opinions. As the war went on, foreign correspondents other than White also increasingly found their copy altered to suit editorial policy, a battle Hersey was to experience on both sides while also having to field criticisms from powerful people who disagreed with what he and his contributors wrote. The Chinese ambassador to Washington was especially vociferous, writing in longhand and in detail to tell *Time* what its proprietor already believed: "Your statements about Chiang Kai-shek . . . making money and taking bribes; about Chen Li-fu 'privately' [favoring] peace with Japan; about General Tsuing-nan (one of our greatest and most lovable generals) as an appeaser of Japan; about the anti-communist move as an action brought about by these appeasers of Japan;—these are a few examples of strong judgments with no factual basis. They are entirely based on hearsay and prejudicial information."[17]

While the United States was not yet "in" the war, John and Frances Ann's life was dominated by it. At home on Sutton Place on the Upper East Side in July 1940, they had Jack Kennedy to supper to celebrate the publication of his book *Why England Slept*, a version of his Harvard dissertation for which Luce had written a bellicose foreword.[18] Kennedy took the opportunity to tell Hersey what he, increasingly at odds with his father's views, thought about the United States vis-à-vis the European war: in essence, that isolationism was a consequence not of the failings of individual politicians but of democratic constraints. He argued that the British electorate had been, and the American still was, too conscious of what the First World War had cost to allow its politicians to act as decisively as, both morally and pragmatically, they needed to. This was a strong position, albeit one with dangerous implications, and Hersey found his ex-rival "an exceedingly nice person [with] interesting things to say."[19]

American opinion was by no means either as uniformly antiwar as Kennedy believed or as anti-Nazi as Luce hoped (though, like many others, Luce had at first been impressed by Hitler). The following month, John and

Frances Ann went to the cinema in Yorkville, a few blocks north of Sutton Place, to see a German-made film about the invasion of Poland. Yorkville had a large German-born population and was home to the pro-Nazi German American Bund. Whenever the face of Hitler appeared, Hersey recorded, "there was much clapping."[20] By now he was putting together big cover stories for *Time*: about Churchill,[21] about the war in Greece,[22] about the 2,600th anniversary of the Japanese empire.[23] As usual, the words and the information they communicated were not all his own, and in giving shape to material from different correspondents he conformed to *Time* style, which was a matter of structure and balance as well as of idiom. Factual detail had to be fleshed out with "human interest"; current developments given historical context. The results were published anonymously, but it's often possible to identify which stories were his from what he told his parents. With this information, one can also recognize his preoccupations as well as his stylistic brio. The Churchill profile, for example, begins by focusing on the young reporter as man of action: a *Boy's Own*–style story of Churchill's covering the Boer War, fighting "like a professional soldier when a British armored train was captured by the Boers," being taken prisoner and escaping over the ten-foot fence of his jail "with no map or compass, but a little money and some cubes of chocolate in his pockets." What better symbol of Great Britain's "unwillingness to give up when apparently cornered"? The piece is at its best when juxtaposing the strength of Churchill's temperament and utterances with his physical oddities and frailty ("The measured sequences of Pitt, the roars of Samuel Johnson . . . tremble in his sagging, pouting, one-sided mouth"), or contrasting the grandeur of the prime minister's family's—and the country's—history with the humiliating chaos of the Blitz. The vivid last paragraphs, largely composed out of wires from agency reporters in Parliament, drew, too, on Hersey's memories of England as well as his enthusiasm for the sea:

> One day, as a gale whipped white saliva on to the sharp tongues of the Channel rip, and fog set in thick about Dover, Winston Churchill turned the House over to First Lord of the Admiralty A.V. Alexander. As the Prime Minister leaned busily over some notes, the First Lord announced that the destroyers bought from the U.S. would be given names of towns which lie in both Britain and the U.S., that the first flotilla would be given the initial *C*, and that the flotilla leader would be called *Churchill*. The

Prime Minister busily leaned and fumbled, but the bald top of his head blushed.

Cheering and happily laughing, M.P.s shouted "Hold your head up." Like a little boy caught out in pleasant mischief, Winston Churchill raised his pouting face to the Mother of Parliaments.

Hersey's article on Greece is more detached, and also prescient. The ironies in the gap—once again—between the country's past greatness and its modern history were heightened, he pointed out, by the fact that a region so disastrous economically and politically was still of strategic importance. He's very good on Greece's predicaments in the First World War and immediately after, and teasing about its changes of regime: "Between 1923 and 1935, there were 25 Greek administrations plus two dictatorships." The king, described as "this twice-enthroned son of a twice-abdicated father," is called by his nickname, "Gorgeous Giorgios," in a subheading. However pro-Churchill *Time* was, the prime minister's sentimental recklessness in the Aegean didn't have Luce's support.

In March 1941 the Senate had agreed to Lend-Lease, a measure enabling the United States to offer material assistance, though not troops, to "the government of any country whose defense the President deems vital to the defense of the United States." Soon Hersey's topic was the war in the Atlantic ("which seems even more crucial than the Balkans and Africa," he wrote to his parents, "though we hear less about it").[24] Frances Ann was pregnant. And both of them were thinking about what his role would be if and when the United States became totally involved.

Combustibility

When the Japanese attacked the U.S. fleet at Pearl Harbor on the morning of Sunday, December 7, *Time*'s issue dated the eighth was already on its way to the newsstands.[25] So the first number of the magazine to deal with the event and its rapid sequels in Midway, Shanghai, Thailand, Singapore, the Dutch East Indies, and Manila was the one of December 15. By luck, though, the December 8 issue of *Life* carried a cover story by the proprietor's wife, Clare Boothe Luce, about General Douglas MacArthur, recently recalled from retirement to command U.S. forces in the Far East.[26]

On the fifteenth, in a new section, the U.S. at War, *Time*'s opening article told the story of Pearl Harbor, or as much of it as the censors allowed to be told, over eleven pages. The usual mix of range and local color, political grasp and human interest was there, and also an element of what later critics have interpreted as a new and blatant ferocity.[27] "People" in general were alleged to be saying, "Why, the yellow bastards!" and the bellicose words of unnamed individuals were quoted: "We'll stamp their front teeth in"; "I want to beat them Japs with my own bare hands." Apparently Luce himself oversaw and in parts wrote this article, so he must have approved a phrase describing the event as "premeditated murder masked by a toothy smile." It's possible to defend the article's strategy, crude though it was. By beginning with bloodthirsty first responses, it hoped to draw in readers who had those feelings, so as to lead them to a different point: that such reactions aren't best, that "the U.S. knew that its first words were not enough."

The next section, the demoted National Affairs, provided a more reflective account of a confused mood oddly paralleled by unseasonably warm, foggy weather. And in the following week's issue, newly reorganized with additional categories, the magazine resumed its usual ironic factualism: "Some misguided Washington patriot, unable to get at the Japs, emulated the Father of his Country and chopped down four of the lovely Japanese cherry trees along Washington's Tidal Basin." And: "The U.S. made plans to make Eritrea, the sun-cursed, camel-smelling little country . . . on the barren, fever-stricken Red Sea Coast, 1,000 miles from Suez on the Canal, into an assembly plant, an African sub-station of the Democracies' Arsenal."[28] In passing, but to later eyes bleakly, it also mentioned that one of the things the Japanese were concerned about was the high combustibility of their cities.

There was plenty in the current atmosphere that Hersey would react against in his own war reportage. For now, though, he and the paper were at one with most readers in fulsomely supporting the man now chiefly responsible for the country's Pacific defense. From a propagandist point of view, the task was made easier by MacArthur's fame as a hero of the First World War, as a reforming head of the West Point military academy, and as someone whose close association with the Philippines went back to the beginning of the century and had just been endorsed regionally: after his official but, as it proved, premature retirement in 1937, he had been hired by the Philippine government as its military adviser, with responsibility for trying to guarantee security once the islands became independent, which the United States had promised would happen in 1945. Now, though, the war in the region was already going disastrously badly. American focus on Pearl Harbor—that and the Christmas and New Year holidays—provided temporary distraction from the massive loss of U.S. aircraft at Clark Air Base on Luzon, the retreat to safety of much of the mauled U.S. Asiatic fleet, and the withdrawal of Allied troops to the Bataan peninsula, but these facts couldn't be glossed over for long. By March 1942, MacArthur and his staff and family had been evacuated from the Philippines to Australia. Two months later, at Corregidor, the biggest defeat in the history of the United States came to its official end. For the prisoners, much more and much worse was in store: Bataan became synonymous with their death march. At the time, such stories didn't get into the news.

Grand Larceny

The United States needed cheerleaders, and at this stage in his career the young John Hersey was well placed to be one of them. Within hours of the Japanese invasion of the Philippines, an editor at the New York publishing house Alfred A. Knopf had dictated a letter to "Dear Mr. Hershey" saying, "I have been given to understand that you have a great deal of valuable material on Japan and that this material might quickly be shaped into a book . . . There is now a vacuum crying to be filled."[29] In response to events the proposal soon shifted into one for a book about MacArthur, approaching him through what had happened on the Bataan peninsula, or vice versa. Whatever the precise topic, though, there was an underlying problem that both publisher and author had failed not exactly to spot but, as the focus changed, to find an adequate way of dealing with. Little of Hersey's material was his own.

Had he been writing about Japan, of course, he could have drawn on his visit to the country and meetings with some of its leaders. He also had a knowledge of parts of "the Far East" that many Westerners still thought of as all one country. Among the topics *Life* magazine informatively addressed in the war's early weeks were individual Pacific regions, especially its big ports—and, at a more immediate level, how you could tell the difference between Chinese and Japanese people, a matter Chinese Americans had come to care about even more now that Japanese Americans were being rounded up.[30] By February 1942, however, Hersey and his publisher had agreed that he should focus on the Philippines and on the U.S. military, topics of which he had no personal experience though a great deal of material concerning them passed across his desk every day. The bulk of it came from Melville Jacoby and his wife, Annalee, who, like Hersey, were in their mid-twenties and recently married but unlike him had spent recent months in besieged Manila. Time-Life also had another writer-photographer couple on the island, Carl and Shelley Mydans.

Many of these correspondents' cables were now in folders that Hersey used to compile *Men on Bataan*.[31] He was thorough and systematic, and he added to his immediate sources in two main ways. First, through Yale classmates now in the military as well as through *Time* journalists, he contacted people who could give him reliable, vivid information about MacArthur—material that went deeper than Clare Boothe's cover story.[32] Second, from *Life*'s files he compiled a list of "heroes," men whose actions on Bataan had been commended and some of whom had been killed. In a form letter sent to their families, he explained that he was writing a book "on the battle of the Philippines and Douglas MacArthur" and that he hoped, with the recipient's help, to pay tribute to his or her relative. So as to make the book vivid to American readers, he needed information about the man's personality, likes and dislikes; about key aspects of his upbringing: his home, education, hobbies, ambitions, and how and why he joined the army; and also, if possible, one or two stories about him. There was some urgency: he had to send the book to the printer "in a very few days." Replies should be addressed to his home on Sutton Place.

Out of these materials Hersey put together as favorable an account of the disaster as he could. It alternates between two narratives: MacArthur's life—he was born in 1880—and (more or less the same thing) his military career; and what happened in the Philippines between December 1941 and March 1942. The second strand is interspersed with biographical sketches drawn from replies to the letters he had sent. Hersey edited these himself, marking them up like journalists' copy for the printer, indicating where they should be fitted into the text and introducing each with a simple formula: "I think you ought to meet . . ." The effect is respectful, its stiltedness carrying an element of military formality: Hersey stands aside while each man in turn steps forward from the ranks. (Norman Mailer borrowed the method, while making it more elaborate, for the "Time Machines" in his 1946 novel of the Pacific war, *The Naked and the Dead*.) And, such is the power of detail, we end up remembering these soldiers almost as vividly as the general himself: Joe Stanley, a New Mexican sergeant who "got his nose broken playing soldier with his older brother at the age of four"; John Wheeler, a captain from Minnesota who played the piano and loved "slow-moving pieces in the minor key by Sibelius and Grieg"; Bob Silhavy, an engineer with an innate knack for calculating odds, who sprinted a hundred yards under machine-gun fire to blow up a bridge in front of the advancing Japanese, and got back safely.[33]

The story as a whole is intrinsically powerful, and was much more so to readers in 1942 whose knowledge of events was inevitably limited and who had no idea how the war was going to turn out. Hersey doesn't conceal, though he doesn't emphasize, MacArthur's underestimation of Japan's strength, his tactical blunders—the unpreparedness of Manila, the destruction of his air force still sitting on the ground nine hours after the attack on Pearl Harbor—or his ensuing retreats and excuses and falsifications. Nor does he disguise how ominous these events might now prove. There's a frightening hint about the Japanese use of white phosphorus to try to start jungle fires on Bataan, a tactic that worked poorly in humid conditions but that "the guardians of Oregon and Washington and California—if those states are ever defended in their dry seasons—should not forget."[34] This was a war that might go anywhere.

Still, Hersey seems to have been left with a sense that his book wasn't and couldn't have been adequate. After Japan was defeated, and still more after the later fall of MacArthur himself, when his army was humiliated in Korea in 1951, its flaws were increasingly apparent. Explaining that he now found it too favorable to the general, Hersey would not allow it to be reissued. But this wasn't his main reason.

Accustomed to the pooling of information in a newspaper office and to the authorial anonymity of old-style journalism, the novice was surprised and embarrassed by the attention his first book brought to him personally, and the reactions of people close to those whose work he had used. Not that he hadn't acknowledged them. The book's opening pages thank everyone who had contributed, especially the Jacobys, and also the

Mydanses, who by now had been taken captive.[35] A chapter is devoted to the dangers and difficulties of their work, with a pen portrait of Mel Jacoby and a description of his and his wife's eventual perilous escape from Bataan to Australia. Another experienced reporter, Clark Lee, fled with them and went on to report the Allied landings in Italy and France; Jacoby himself, however, died in a flying accident in Australia while the book was in press. There was just time for Hersey to add a commemorative note, but in such a context there's something over-jaunty about the words he addressed earlier on to his battle-weary colleagues: "This book is dedicated to them partly so they won't charge me with grand larceny." The newly widowed Annalee Jacoby didn't find this funny. She and Mel had been married less than six months when he died. Seeing material written by her husband and herself on the pages of a book credited to John Hersey—whole chunks can readily be traced back to *Life* articles[36]—she gave less weight than she might otherwise have done to what Hersey had said, frankly enough, about having drawn on "the magnificent cables to Time Inc. from Melville Jacoby, much of whose material has not previously been published," and about the man whose "fast, observant and eloquent" work on Bataan "beggars description." Decades later, Annalee's daughter, Anne Fadiman, an essayist and a former editor of *The American Scholar*, attacked Hersey, who by then was dead, as a plagiarist.[37]

Ownership disputes are common to all forms of coproduction and, in the case of published books, aren't eased by what one literary historian has described as "the myth of solitary genius":[38] books, unlike films, don't provide comprehensive credit lists, though perhaps they should. Because copyright in an article belonged to the newspaper employing the reporter, the only permission Knopf needed was Time-Life's.[39] Besides, Hersey paid at least some of his sources. There was a fee for Robert Lasseter, who had been helpful about MacArthur's career,[40] and the equivalent of the entire prepublication author's advance of $450 was made over to the Jacobys.[41] And the narrative's shape was Hersey's own; it contained material that was unambiguously his—for example about MacArthur's opposite number, General Homma, whom he had met in Tientsin in 1939[42]—and it was he who had researched MacArthur's life as well as gleaned information about the servicemen to whose families he had written. It's evident from his archive that, rapidly though he completed the book, he put a fair amount of work into it.

His first child, Martin, had been born in October, and in the final stage of pulling the text together, Hersey took Frances Ann and the baby to Palm Beach. They rented a cottage on Seabreeze Avenue, one of the roads that run east to west between the lagoon and the ocean.[43] During the day, Hersey was able to sit out on an enclosed porch, "a wonderfully light and quiet place to work," while Frances Ann cooked and, in the garden, "the little man" slept and got a rhyming "little tan." It was an idyll, particularly in contrast with the experiences soon to be communicated to readers of *Life* by Mel and Annalee Jacoby: their flight from Bataan, described in the issue of March 30, and the scenes they had left behind, the subject of seventeen pages of grim pictures they had taken, which were featured on April 13 and 20. Perhaps the contrast was somewhere in the back of Hersey's mind when he told his parents he had come to Florida "to be away from my sources," somewhere "cut off from the world, where no one could reach me." He was working from eight in the morning until midnight, he said, with just half an hour's swim before lunch and "a little time to play with Martin before supper." He didn't know whether the book was any good and didn't care whether it sold many copies. All that mattered was that it should be thought "fair."

In fact it sold reasonably well—more than seven thousand copies in the first six months—and as a biography of MacArthur has had many admirers, at the time and since. In his three-volume *The Years of MacArthur*, D. Clayton James describes it as one of only two out of "the spate of hasty MacArthur books of 1942" worth reading.[44] Hersey is perceptive about the strangeness of the warrior temperament, the way such a man is separated from others by character as much as power and responsibility. (This would become a lasting theme for him.) He describes the general's most controversial action, clearing Washington of protesting First World War veterans in 1932, in a coolly factual way that leaves the reader to form an opinion. He's quietly amusing about MacArthur's well-known touches of flamboyance, the eccentricities of his domestic arrangements. He is also conspicuously—and for the time daringly—fair-minded about the enemy. There was a story, encouraged if not actually invented by MacArthur himself, that General Homma had committed suicide. This was untrue, as U.S. and Filipino prisoners of the Japanese would discover to their cost; it was Homma who organized the Bataan march. (When he eventually did die, in 1946, it was by firing squad as a war criminal.) Having taken

Homma's measure in China, Hersey was skeptical about the suicide story, emphasizing his vigor and sense of comedy while unobtrusively making what was in 1942 an unorthodox point: that in most wars there's something arbitrary about the sides people find themselves on. Early in his career Homma had spent several years as a military aide in England. In 1917, he went to France with the East Lancashire Regiment and was awarded a Military Cross. Hersey here and elsewhere showed a keen grasp of Japanese military skills and preparedness, by contrast with the view held, at least at first, by MacArthur among others that the country's soldiers and equipment were poor.

Morally speaking, not everything in *Men on Bataan* is so readily defensible. American ownership of the Philippines is taken for granted, as if it had not come about in living memory with the U.S. victory over Spain in 1898. And in another form of appropriation the writing often claims a proximity Hersey simply hadn't earned. This is true of passages of visual description: "From the air . . . you saw" and so on.[45] He didn't use the first-person singular, but the effect is not much different. Two kinds of hazard are involved here, one of them to do with propaganda, hard to avoid at the time; the other an aspect of what was to become known as the New Journalism: How far is it permissible to use essentially fictional techniques in order to make a factual story more vivid?[46]

It's certainly the case that, despite the opening disclaimers, *Men on Bataan* has been taken by even quite sophisticated readers to be a first-hand account. The war veteran William Manchester, for example, in his bestselling 1978 life of MacArthur, *American Caesar*, follows Hersey's book in describing the general, "hatless and with his feet spread far apart," looking up from the Calle Victoria in Manila during the first Japanese air attacks and counting the Mitsubishis flying in formation above him. "'Fifty-five,' he muttered . . . John Hersey heard an aide say, 'Don't you think you'd better take cover, General?'"[47] But Hersey didn't hear this for the simple reason that he wasn't there. Even contemporary reviewers gave him credit for stylistic feats that, when they weren't those of other reporters, were the words of people who had answered his letters. One critic, ironically in *Time* magazine itself, contrasted those elements of the book that tell MacArthur's life story, judged to have been "shrewdly and competently done," with passages where "Hersey" describes "the men of Bataan and their battles," and "feeling and words blend in the unforced flow that is the pulse of music and writing."[48]

His next published book would be more authentic, in the sense of being genuinely the result of firsthand experience.

To Get the Goddam Thing Over

Immediately after delivering *Men on Bataan* to his publisher, Hersey volunteered for the navy. Hotchkiss gave him warm support with a testimonial that described him as representing "all that is best in the young manhood of America." Back at Time-Life, he waited to hear both from the Bureau of Naval Personnel and from Knopf. No one at the publishing house said anything until Alfred Knopf himself telephoned. "I've read your book," he said. A long pause followed. Perhaps Hersey could come "to purchase" some time, the voice resumed. As Hersey told the anecdote almost a quarter of a century later, he wondered whether this was Knopf's way of saying he wanted the author to buy back all the copies of his unsatisfactory work. He didn't realize that Purchase was a place in Westchester County where the Knopfs had a house, and that an invitation there was a sure sign of approval.[49] Cheered by the discovery, he suggested to Luce that Time-Life should send him to the Pacific as a correspondent.

A decisive phase in the war was beginning. In the Pacific in June 1942, the battle of Midway badly weakened the Japanese navy and opened the way to reversing Japan's territorial gains. In North Africa the following month, the German advance was halted; Allied victory in the region would follow before the end of the year. In Russia, German ambitions were to be thwarted by Soviet defiance at Stalingrad in a five-month battle beginning in August 1942, the outcome of which left Hitler for once literally speechless.[50] These events mattered hugely in grand strategy but had no immediate effect on ordinary people still being bombed and shelled in their homes, shot out of the sky, drowned at sea, and taken into slavery. One of the first pieces Hersey put together as an official war correspondent was the story of members of a bomber crew who had crashed into the Pacific, managed to get out of their rusty old B-17, and, before it sank, extricated a leaking, inadequately sized life raft and a handful of moldy rations.

In the desperate week that followed, two of the men died but seven survived to be picked up by a destroyer and then transferred to the aircraft carrier *Hornet*, where Hersey interviewed them.[51] The carrier itself was a survivor, having taken part in the first attack on the Japanese home islands—the Doolittle Raid of April 18, 1942—and the Battle of Midway in June. From August to October, *Hornet* was part of the Solomons campaign, helping guard the sea approaches to the island of Guadalcanal, where the Allies launched their first major offensive against Japan. "Helping" soon became an understatement. Of the four Allied aircraft carriers then operating in the South Pacific, two were put out of action before the end of August, and a third, *Wasp*, was sunk on September 15. When Hersey, under the constraints of censorship, wrote, "During the month of September I was on an aircraft carrier somewhere in the Pacific," he meant he was on the only one. By October 6 he was in Guadalcanal. (Before the end of the month *Hornet*, too, had been sunk.)

In the intervening weeks he had time to observe types of people new to him and in different ways important to his later thinking. The first were black troops, about whom he sent a dispatch, "Negro Gunners," which didn't escape contemporary stereotypes, however friendly, of a kind he would later deplore.[52] A new military phenomenon that at this stage he responded to with more alertness was the aggressive individualist aviator. *Hornet* carried and launched sixteen B-25 bombers in the course of the Doolittle Raid, but numerically its largest complement of aircraft consisted of scout bombers manufactured by Douglas, hence "SBDs": strongly built, powerfully armed, durable small aircraft that could be used aggressively against Japan's flimsier fighters, had the range for long patrols, and were lethal when dive-bombing. An SBD's crew of two marines consisted of a pilot who doubled as bombardier, sitting back-to-back with a rear gunner. The SBD pilot who most interested Hersey on board the *Hornet* was William John Widhelm, known as Gus. As Hersey saw him, Gus was "an exaggerated American, an essence, an extreme. Extremities were his pleasure." How you distinguished this friendly extremism from the versions embodied by the other side—what heroism meant if it was turned against you—was a problem that had bothered many war writers, as it would bother Hersey, too, in his later novel *The War Lover*. For now, though, he simply put in his notebook whatever he noticed about Gus and whatever Gus said or was said about him. He would return to these notes, titled "Sail

Baker Dog" (prewar U.S. naval phonetic words for the letters SBD), the following year, and what he saw next in the Pacific doesn't seem to have affected his attitude to them.

Guadalcanal is the largest of the Solomon Islands. The archipelago, then a British protectorate, had strategic importance because it was close to sea routes between western America and eastern Australia and New Zealand, and between Japan and the oil resources of the Dutch East Indies (now Indonesia). In the first half of 1942 it was occupied by the Japanese, who built a large base on Tulagi and by May were completing an airfield on Guadalcanal. At this point the Americans launched a counterattack—their first major offensive. The Japanese knew about the large force gathering in the region but, assuming it was intended to directly reinforce Australia, were taken by surprise when it invaded the southern Solomons. However, the occupiers quickly regrouped and were themselves reinforced. As far as Guadalcanal itself was concerned, the most prolonged actions, and the most complex reversals and counter-reversals, took place in the jungles and mountains around what the Americans called Henderson Field, particularly over the Matanikau River. After a few weeks of sending background reports from headquarters—"a wonderful American town" with sandy paths, log-frame shelters, cement-floored kitchens, and a Navy Officers' Club equipped with a huge refrigerator[53]— Hersey joined a platoon of Marines in October 1942 on what proved to be an unsuccessful, in some ways disastrous, mission. Moving in single file under at first intermittent fire, the group met fierce resistance as it got closer to its target, and was pinned down by encircling snipers and mortars. What came close to being a rout was just about turned into orderly retreat by the group's "slight and fragile" yet authoritative young commanding officer.

In propaganda terms, what the United States wanted out of Guadalcanal was a positive story that would counter some of the harm caused by Pearl Harbor and MacArthur's humiliation in the Philippines. In Hersey's words, written to his Time-Life editors as background, it was "the first determined, exclusively U.S. initiative in World War II that can truly be termed offensive operations rather than raid." To some extent the propaganda came true, not least because in December the Japanese withdrew. For journalists there were two main questions. One was how the limited amount they saw fitted into the wider picture: a hard matter for a general to be sure of, let alone an embedded reporter, however well informed. More important was what it was like to be there: sights, sounds, smells, feelings. Truthful reporting at that level was wanted at home, including by families and friends of servicemen. But if it helped to know what they were experiencing, there were always deeper, still more personal concerns, for reader as well as writer: What would it be like for me? How would I behave? The Solomons campaign to which Guadalcanal has given its name is more written about than almost any other of the Second World War,[54] but Hersey's account is unusual in the extent to which he directly asks these questions.

Into the Valley is extremely short: about twenty thousand words. There's no "research" in it, in the sense of historical background and secondary sources; Hersey just describes his own experience of being with a platoon in action. The episode itself (he calls it a skirmish) was a failure not because most of the men briefly ran away, though they did, but because they were outfought. It doesn't lack examples of heroism but doesn't come across, either, as if it is trying to deceive the reader. As in Norman Mailer's later *The Naked and the Dead*, which was influenced by Hersey's book, the question of purpose is specifically posed—what were they fighting for?—and receives an uncompelling answer: "to get the goddam thing over and get home."[55] But Mailer wrote after the war was over. This was 1942–43, and Hersey was on official business. It's true that his pessimism is qualified: "Home seems to most marines a pretty good thing to be fighting for. Home is where the good things are—the generosity, the good pay, the comforts, the democracy, the pie." From his own point of view he might have added: the freedom to publish such a book.

Among its most memorable passages is one in which victims of the blast are described, men in retreat, some of them without visible wounds, wordless—traumatized, though that term isn't used—as sad a procession as Bruegel's *Blind Leading the Blind*:

> Our order of march was something like this: First there was a man who kept striking the sides of his head with his fists. The second kept his hands over his ears . . . The middle of the safari was taken up with the worst wounded and their helpers, and then there were two or three more who could walk—men who generally ached and wished to vomit.

In the rear there was a character who shook his head, as if puzzled rather than hurt.

Puzzlement is part of the book's tone. Hersey had gone into the valley expecting to be involved in a brave attack. The title keeps up that expectation with its echo of Psalm 23, about walking in the valley of the shadow of death and fearing no evil, and of Tennyson's "Charge of the Light Brigade," a heroic poem about a military disaster in the Crimean War: "Half a league, half a league, / Half a league onward, / All in the valley of Death / Rode the six hundred." This text, by contrast, includes plenty of fear and less a mass charge than a bunch of individuals creeping furtively from tree to tree. Hersey spent the second half of the foray helping carry wounded men back to base. When he wrote "If I had had any understanding of what Company H might meet, I would never have gone along," he was paying the men a compliment, but he may also have been saying something close to the truth.

Into the Valley appeared in February 1943. In the race to get out a book on Guadalcanal it was beaten, a couple of weeks earlier, by Richard Tregaskis's *Guadalcanal Diary*, a cooler narrative and one that covers a longer period. Tregaskis was in the second wave of the U.S. landings, stayed longer than Hersey, went to more places, and had a greater variety of experiences. He was there for the key battle of Edson's (or Lunga) Ridge and had access to quite up-to-date information about the naval as well as military campaigns. Like Hersey, Tregaskis is uncompromisingly vivid in describing the wounded and the dead, both American and Japanese. The interest of *Valley*, by contrast, comes partly from the intensity of Hersey's story, especially the fact that its focus is on fear, defeat, cowardice. But it may have mattered more that Hersey's name was already known. Tregaskis's book was his first; Hersey's earlier *Men of Bataan* had been reviewed by, among others, Orville Prescott, later the principal book reviewer at *The New York Times*, and had sold well, though it was easily outstripped by *Valley*. Alfred Knopf wrote in person in May 1943 to tell the author that the new book had "just passed twenty-two thousand."[56]

Various things happened in the meantime. After returning from the third battle of Matanikau River, Hersey accompanied Guadalcanal aircrews on rescue operations bringing back pilots who had been shot down, and was twice involved in crashes, the second time during a sea-plane landing that almost drowned him. He thanked his lucky stars, he told his mother in a letter, both that he "had had such a lot of practice at such things as taking clothes off under water" and for the native islanders who "rescued the rescuers."[57] After being hospitalized for a couple of weeks with damage to his rib cage, he made the long trip home for Thanksgiving 1942, the second leg in an overloaded converted B-24 bomber in which, to get the right distribution of weight, some of the passengers had to crawl into the bomb bays for takeoff and landing—"not a comfortable sensation."

In December 1942, he finally received a response to his application for an active commission in the navy but was disappointed to be offered only PR work. "In my time at sea with the Fleet and ashore with the Marines," he replied, "it was constantly pointed out to me that I could accomplish more for the war effort, in a small way, as a journalist than as an Ensign or Lieutenant [in Public Relations]. I believe that this is so . . . *Time* has agreed to send me to a fighting front again in a few months' time."[58] Another Navy office, meanwhile, no less than that of its secretary, Frank Knox, soon sent him an official letter about the courage he had shown on October 7 and 8:

> It has been reported to me that on both of the above dates, during heavy fighting in a ravine, and while severe casualties were being suffered by our forces, you left your own assignment and went to the assistance of the wounded. On each occasion, without regard for your own safety and above and beyond your own obligations, you braved extremely fierce enemy fire in the front lines in order that you might assist in the evacuation of casualties from the ravine to an aid station.
>
> For your heroism and valor on these occasions, I wish to express my highest commendation, and the gratitude of the Navy Department.

Imperative

Early in 1943, Frances Ann had their second son, John Roscoe. Jack Kennedy wrote self-pityingly to his sister and confidante Kathleen, "I see [Hersey's] new book 'Into the Valley' is doing well. He's sitting on top of the hill at this point—a best seller—my girl, two kids—big man on *Time*—while I'm the one that's down in the God damned valley."[59] Hersey was definitely in the news. *Valley* was chosen by the Council on Books in Wartime as one of its "Imperative" works, and a radio adaptation was broadcast. The author was a guest speaker at events held by organizations such as the Civil Defense Volunteer Office of Greater New York and the Red Cross War Fund of New York City. By June he was back on an aircraft carrier but this time in the North Atlantic, heading for the eastern Mediterranean, where he was to join Moroccan Sea Frontier Forces at their headquarters in Algeria.

He used the voyage to pull together his notes for the novella he called "Sail Baker Dog." The "dog" part was appropriate: his portrait of an "extreme" kind of American combatant included an emphasis on macho sexuality. But in the 1940s there was still considerable squeamishness about this topic in the Anglophone world, in part religiously based but also a lot to do with more general codes of reticence that were, as in Hersey's own case, however much he struggled against them, deeply inculcated. There were also taboos specific to wartime, especially against encouraging sexual suspicion or jealousy. Everyone knew that men (and women) away on military service had fears about their distant partners' fidelity and that these were often justified. Some matters were more important than truth, the argument ran, and hypocrisy was generally preferable to causing needless hurt and demoralization to someone already having a hard time. When the end of the war seemed to have loosened these rules, writers who opted for greater honesty were still treated harshly.

In the case of "Sail Baker Dog" Hersey also once again made a fundamental error about ownership. It's not uncommon with writers, especially early in their careers: the words have gone through their minds and hands onto the page and what they read there can seem to be totally their own. The pilot on the USS *Hornet* who had so impressed Hersey was innocently happy with the attention being given to his stories. Hersey made no pretense of believing them all, yet Gus Widhelm may have felt that they were somehow ratified by being written down. At any rate, he made no objection when Hersey, in his own words, "told Gus about these notes." He doesn't say whether Widhelm—by then on a shore base at Quonset, Rhode Island—had an opportunity to read the seventy-page draft of "Sail Baker Dog" that reached Alfred Knopf's wife and business partner, Blanche, in the summer of 1943; it seems not, since the writer refers to having sent him a questionnaire and asked him to return it to Knopf so that they could incorporate the answers in what Hersey assumed would next be an edited text.[60]

The Knopfs were quick to see that Widhelm, who was married and whose wife was now pregnant, might find that she objected to having her husband portrayed (however accurately, and however much he boasted to other men about his successes) as what one in-house reader called "a minor Casanova." Besides, however tolerant his naval comrades were about his antics, it would be something else for them to come to the attention of his superior officers. As Alfred pointed out, "it is the old familiar story of the fellow who gives an interview and is horror-stricken the next morning to see himself quoted in the papers." These fears were tactfully confirmed by a friendly officer in the navy's PR department. Everyone in his office who had looked at the book thought it "beautifully contrived" and "a magnificent job of writing and reporting," he told the Knopfs. But it was their responsibility "to subordinate questions of artifice," whether in matters of security or just to protect serving men and their families, including against themselves. They "could not thank you enough for your quick and sensitive appreciation of these points."[61]

By the time this letter arrived, Hersey was in the Mediterranean, sending vivid cables to his Time-Life editorial colleague David Hulburd about Allied moves in the embryonic liberation of Europe. He wrote about the situation of Cyprus, the island off the coasts of Turkey and Syria, which had stayed loyal to its British rulers throughout the war and had somehow survived as an important naval and air force base. It was in every sense a long way from 501 Madison Avenue, where the Knopfs had their office, and the book and magazine section of the U.S. Navy's PR department, a few blocks northwest at 580 Fifth Avenue. Within days, Hersey was in Licata, southern Sicily.

4. Getting Hurt Getting Through

WHATEVER HE EXPECTED of the European war it wasn't that an old Yale friend would make him cry. Ten months after his frightening experiences in Guadalcanal, Hersey was in a C-47 troop-transport plane over central Sicily. The invasion—the biggest of its kind the world had ever seen—was a few weeks old. With a great show of force General George Patton had captured the unresisting city of Palermo, and by late July his troops had fought their way to Nicosia, a hill town on the route to Messina in the northeast, where the island is closest to the toe of mainland Italy. Hersey, along with the photographer Robert Capa, was among the press contingent in Palermo and subsequently at the tough battle for Nicosia and was now on his way back to the southern port of Licata, where he had a story of a different kind to write. An officer on the flight lent him a five-week-old copy of *The New Yorker*. Riffling through it looking for the authors' names, he came on a Reporter at Large piece by Brendan Gill, who had joined the magazine straight out of Yale. Gill's article was about the civilian captain of a U.S. merchant ship commandeered as part of a large, heavily armed convoy taking supplies from Britain to Malta, fifty miles south of Sicily, where Eisenhower had his headquarters for the Sicily invasion. The convoy came under ferocious attack, and although enough ships got through to help the beleaguered garrison, many others were sunk, including the captain's own. Gill interviewed him on shore leave.[1]

Having described him a little, the article tells the captain's story in his own halting, measured, modest, repressed voice. It's a miniature tour de force of tone, its brinkmanship with sentimentality a matter not of resisting it entirely but of going just over the edge at the right moment. Here, that moment concerns an Airedale puppy given by the daughter of an English skipper to the American, who kept it in his cabin. The dog—"I never got around to giving him a name"—is mentioned early on and quickly forgotten. Two days into the Mediterranean the convoy comes under continual fire from torpedo boats and dive-bombers, Italian and German. An aircraft carrier is sunk with forty planes on board, then a cargo boat goes down in less than a minute. A long day and night later, a torpedo rips open the captain's own ship. He describes counting his surviving crew into the lifeboats:

> "The men were anxious to stand clear of the ship, but, seeing as she was sinking so slowly now, I wanted to go back, if possible, and get certain important papers from my cabin. That was what I told them." Thomson hesitated a moment. "You see, the damn puppy was there."

But the ship has taken on too much water. Thomson turns back and rejoins the lifeboats, which row away in darkness through the warm sea. The next morning the men are picked up and distributed between two destroyers "towing a tanker nearly cut in half by bombs. A German plane lay scattered across the tanker's deck."

The fate of the Airedale was what made the dog-loving Hersey lose his composure. "Goddam war nerves, I guess," he admitted in a letter to Gill:

> And I guess the fact that Frances Ann had written that she had had a very happy meal with you and some wine at the Bistro had something to do

with it. But also what everybody is doing over here, getting hurt getting through, just like your guy, and not being very dramatic about it.[2]

Poor Beaches

Getting hurt was certainly happening a lot, and some men weren't getting through at all. There was controversy about the Allies' strategy at this stage. North Africa had been won and the Germans were in retreat. In Italy, Mussolini and King Victor Emmanuel both wanted to find a way out of their alliance with Germany but were deterred by the fact that Roosevelt, to the alarm of experienced soldiers and diplomats, was insisting on unconditional surrender. Most of the American high command, believing that Italy was now of little military importance and conscious of the difficulty of launching an attack on the Nazi heartland across the Alps, favored a prompt invasion of northwest Europe from Britain, which was also the Soviet preference. Among the main reasons for what in fact took place were that so many Allied troops and so much equipment were now in the southern Mediterranean and that the British, still smarting from the previous summer's loss of Tobruk and the catastrophe of an attempted raid on Dieppe, feared that too early a campaign from their own shores might well fail. Churchill also had demons to contend with in the form of memories of the Gallipoli Campaign in 1915–16—a disastrous attack on the Dardanelles in northwest Turkey that, having been his initiative as minister responsible for the Royal Navy, had led to his resignation from government—and stuck to his idea of Italy's strategic importance. This evaluation was in fact shared by the German command: the Po Valley in northern Italy, was, a German report reminded Hitler, "the key area . . . for the Balkans, for southern France, and for an Allied air offensive against southern Germany."[3]

Once the decision had been taken to invade Italy, with Sicily as the first step, what followed was the war's largest and geographically most dispersed amphibious assault, Normandy not excluded. It was also one of the most accident-prone passages of the war. To assess Hersey's novel set on the island, it's necessary to go into some of the military background that is largely ignored in the book, though relevant to a key part of the story.[4]

Allied command, impressed by German successes with the technique, was determined to use airborne troops to disrupt the defenders from behind. But paratroops needed moonlight, which was the opposite of what suited naval convoys, and few of the available pilots were experienced, or had even received training, in night navigation. As for troops arriving by sea, their information about the southern Sicilian coastline was inadequate—about shifting sandbanks, about areas either too shallow for heavily laden craft or too deep for men to wade in ("poor beaches" the official U.S. military history calls them in a rare moment of blame-shifting). The new amphibious DUKWs ("ducks") were a success, but a great deal of the other sophisticated new equipment brought by the Americans was unfamiliar to those using it. Cooperation between different parts of the vast enterprise—between the air forces and the rest, between the British and the Americans, and, among the latter, between the hotheaded Patton and his fellow generals—was poor. In the longer run, competition between Patton and Montgomery to be the first to reach Messina distracted attention from how best to prevent retreating German troops and equipment from being redeployed in mainland Italy. While the Americans were battling up and down the mountains, the Germans coolly withdrew quantities of matériel and men to the mainland, where they would fight again.

Some of these circumstances were unavoidable consequences of the stage the war was at or of decisions that had already been taken. But at least one was totally beyond human control: a westerly gale on the night of July 9, 1943, that threw aircraft, gliders, and descending parachutists badly off course, slowed down landing craft, and caused seasickness among troops. Once ashore, the British under Montgomery managed at first to make misleadingly rapid progress in the southeast, and the American landings farthest west met relatively light Italian resistance. Not all were so lucky, and a combination of mines and dive-bombers soon reduced the Gela coastline to chaos. A very heavy cost was paid by friendly aircraft overflying Allied troops.

Amid all this, from the immediate point of view of the land battle, the relatively little-damaged port of Licata—the setting for A Bell for Adano—was crucial for supplying an army that had to make its way inland and for bringing in reinforcements. It was a bloody process, full of hazards of all kinds—the cruel terrain giving plenty of scope to the defensively experienced, well-dug-in German army and the more committed among its not-always-so-effective Italian allies. Taking the whole island depended a lot on Licata. Roads in Sicily were far from what even military engineers had hoped for, and the urgency for the Americans of moving traffic through and away from the port was compounded by pileups on the Sicilian beaches, where high waves and soft sand caused vehicles to stall and the congestion of shattered and abandoned equipment presented logistical problems that few soldiers, senior officers least of all, had ever experienced. Patience wasn't much of a virtue in this situation and in any case was one that George Patton had never shown.

Licata intrigued Hersey because in literal historical terms it was where postwar reconstruction began: the first town in Europe to be liberated, occupied, and run by the Allies. It also provided the setting for one of a series of blunders they committed, which he folded into the character of General Marvin, a.k.a. Patton. Military and civilian values, war and peace, collided in a kind of found parable. *A Bell for Adano* was, in the words of the influential New York critic Diana Trilling, "our first fiction of the American government of Italy." The fiction might have been truer and fairer, though, if Hersey had arrived sooner in Sicily, stayed longer, and written less rapidly.

It began as an article for *Life* describing the new work of Amgot—the Allied Military Government for Occupied Territories—as it developed day by day in Licata. He collected historical material in Italian about the town, along with various other documents illustrating the kinds of problems faced by the new administration: mutual denunciations by neighbors; a letter about an alleged misappropriation of olive oil; posters detailing grain prices, the rationing of bread and pasta, exchange rates, curfews, and procedures for handing in weapons.[5] His files also include notes and cuttings about some of the peculiarities of the military situation and its U.S. personnel, who included mafiosi. ("There are men here," he wrote, "who were sentenced to the electrical chair in Brooklyn of New York.") General Patton's behavior was proving problematic: his physical attack on a psychologically disturbed, hospitalized soldier whom the commander suspected of cowardice would soon be notorious. The underlying issue was and remains painfully familiar: What are the problems facing an invading army, benign in its own eyes, trying simultaneously to fight a war against a determined enemy and to bring peace to the civilian inhabitants?

Military vehicles poured through the town toward the interior. Meanwhile, Hersey sat in the office of Major Frank E. Toscani, civil affairs officer in Licata, listening as he dealt with the people of the town. A story shaped itself in his notebook. One thread concerned how the Italian Fascist regime had robbed the community of the church bell it had depended on for timekeeping:

AMGOT-Major Toscani sitting at desk huge room marble floor . . . Talking very fast with exercised Italians . . .
   Last name first.
   Older priest. Bell 700 years old rang time every 15 minutes. Turned into Musso[lini] for arms trying to get another . . . Bell called hours for farmers want to get up listened to bell . . .

Another strand of the article involves a U.S. order preventing local cart traffic from using the town bridge, so as to leave the route free for military vehicles. Working from his notebook, Hersey filled this out a little for his *Life* article.[6] The case was typical of the conflicts of interest and culture faced every hour by Amgot staff, whose much-despised desk role the piece celebrates. In such situations Toscani was both judge and jury and inevitably seemed to local people indistinguishable from representatives of the previous regime. The last case of the day, Hersey wrote, was

both the funniest and saddest. The accused is an old cartman. He stands before the desk with his cloth cap clutched in his hand and as defiant as if his accusers were Fascists, whom he says he hates. The chief of the Carabinieri starts to read the accusation. It appears that the old cartman was driving through the town when a train of American amphibious trucks approached. The old man was drowsing at his reins and blocked their way . . . The Chief of Carabinieri describes how one of his men grasped at the reins of the horse and with towering strength got the cart aside and saved the honor of Licata. The old man stays silent. The Chief now describes how the old man jumped down from his cart and charged the *carabiniere* and tried to fight with him.

Finally, the old man relates his circumstances: the deaths from malaria of his wife and other family members, the earlier theft of a horse by Fascists.

He explains that to see a motorcycle outrider attack his old animal was too much. Toscani dismisses the case, but in the novella Hersey was soon to write, his fictional counterpart, Major Joppolo, recklessly countermands an order given personally by General Marvin.

Adano isn't a war story in any familiar sense, least of all according to the bellicose expectations of Anglophone readers in 1943–44. Joppolo, like Toscani, has to deal with native suspicions heightened by the casual, ignorant behavior of some of his fellow occupiers, including in the highest quarters. In the process he risks "going native." It's a warm, straightforward tale and at the same time a critique of American adventuring, forward-looking when it was written and published, and especially so given the wide audience it was aimed at and soon reached. Today it can seem sentimental and patronizing, and also oddly oblivious to some of the perils surrounding its characters. Reading it, you could imagine (it was what everyone wanted to believe) that the war was as good as won and that the main issue was how best to keep order among the tiny population of a charming fishing port. Yet it makes points that couldn't be more important, now as then, that anticipate the harsher, funnier fictions of the war that stand up best today, by American writers a few years younger than Hersey.

Returning excitedly to New York from Sicily, Hersey left a typewriter case containing his notes and outline for the book in a cab he had been sharing with an army officer he didn't know but whom he managed to track down through the Pentagon. The officer had taken charge of the case, only to leave it behind in turn in a hotel from which eventually Hersey managed to retrieve it. Buoyed by this good luck, he wrote most of the novel in a few weeks during the fall of 1943.[7] In December he filed a promotional article about half a dozen of *Life*'s war artists.[8] He and Frances Ann then went to Mexico for six weeks, where he researched and wrote an over-excitable piece about the right-wing Sinarquistas movement, which the magazine didn't use, though it did print his account, routinely written but painful in content, of a sixteen-year-old's first proper bullfight.[9] It's evident that he felt he was on holiday, with his mind partly on Frances Ann, partly on the imminent publication of *Adano*.

It came out in February 1944, already five months after the Sicilian invasion, and some of the novel's impact may have been related to the slow-developing military situation. Although the Allies had driven the Germans off the island, taken Naples, and begun to move northwest, they were slowed by mountainous territory, winter conditions, and unceasingly fierce German resistance along a line across the whole peninsula roughly one hundred miles south of Rome. January's massive attack farther north at Anzio was literally bogged down. At home it was becoming clear that the war's end was a lot further off than people had hoped. There was some comfort in finding fault in a senior officer. The story invites us to condemn the intemperate General Marvin, who has a local man's mule shot dead to clear the road in front of him: a failure of commonsense diplomacy and a symbol of more general wastefulness of life. True incidents of this kind had initially been glossed over by reporters but had leaked out through returning soldiers. By now, as Hersey's readers knew, Patton had been temporarily moved out of the limelight by Eisenhower. Still, Hersey's satire on the combined high-handedness and crude self-ingratiations of the U.S. Army was braver than it seemed, as was the decision of the U.S. censors to let it be published. Another element, meanwhile, the romance between the married Major Joppolo and Tina, the daughter of a prominent fisherman, though treated with what—at least by contrast with subsequent fictions set in the war—can seem exaggerated tact, touched nerves at home that were becoming more painful as the war grew ever more drawn-out.

It's easy now to devalue the book as concentrating too folksily—too *Life*-magazine-ishly—on the dealings of a small peasant community under its unflaggingly benign new occupying governor, at a time when so many places like it, as well as their would-be liberators, were being bombed and shelled into near oblivion. Hersey voices the problem through Joppolo's hardheaded MP sergeant, Leonard Borth, who finds it absurd that what his officer cares most about is getting a replacement for the town bell. "There's a war going on," Borth says. "Fishermen get blown up in the harbor here. Children get run over in the streets. There's one case of malaria in every six people."[10] He isn't wrong, and in the action of the book it's the war effort that prevails. Although, with help from the U.S. Navy, Joppolo does provide Adano with a new bell, his earlier, more direct humanitarian action—countermanding the commander in chief's ban on local traffic in and around Adano—costs him his post and, we're led to expect, his commission. Joppolo is an attractive hero, somewhat dumb in his idealism and, as an acquaintance of Hersey's pointed out at the time, utterly implausible. "From street-cleaner to Major in two years," he wrote. "Don't you see how you have weakened the main impact of Joppolo's tragedy by this? . . . I think if you had lived with Joppolo [a] little longer, he would have gained density and stature."[11] Onstage, in the actor Fredric March's version, the character went down well with a domestic audience, but on the page it's clearer that Hersey has loaded everything too much in his favor. How much more interesting the book would be if it gave us more of the situation's sheer intractability: the need for aggressiveness in a war like the one for Sicily (there were other Allied generals whom the Germans respected, but Patton was the only one they feared), and also the fact that Patton himself was suffering. More than once he bewildered his entourage by breaking down in sobs.

True, the novella stresses aspects of temporary U.S. rule that were obviously preferable to Fascism and Nazism. Propaganda about the Americans bringing self-determination—Joppolo tells some incredulous Sicilians that "democracy [means] that the men of the government are no longer the masters of the people. They are the servants of the people"—is part of what made the book so popular. Joppolo is a folkloric hero, a Jack Reacher: when he leaves Adano, his "entire possessions consisted of a bedroll, with his clothes rolled into it." (That awkward "bedroll . . . rolled" betrays a larger glibness.) The benevolent outlaw who has restored authority, shown kindness to children, and won the heart of a beautiful woman leaves with no more than he brought and is followed by the sound of celebration: the ringing of the town bell. The extent to which the story gratified domestic assumptions by offering "the Platonic ideal of Americanism, of which the American reality is an active approximation," was objected to by Diana Trilling in her review for *The Nation*.[12] She was also right to concede, though, that "the Joppolo incarnation of American democracy at work isn't a bad star to be shooting at in these practical days." She praised, too, the immediacy of Hersey's concerns, *Adano* being, as she wrote, "occupational history written while it was still little more than a gleam in Amgot's eye." To students of post- or anti-colonialism, the book has a larger claim, what one historian has called its "long-term significance as the pioneer work in a literary tradition of . . . accounts of how Americans behaved in non-Western countries."[13]

Trilling didn't mention that this was the writer's first novel. Most readers at the time loved it, Willa Cather among them,[14] and so did many reviewers. In Britain, the writer and politician Harold Nicolson commented interestingly that "American writers have a gift, which we do not possess, of portraying simple-minded people in a way which renders their absurdities quite dignified. Had Mr. Evelyn Waugh, for example, written *A Bell for Adano* (as well he might) the figure of Major Joppolo would have emerged as . . . ridiculous . . . Mr. Hersey does not render him ridiculous; he renders him symbolic."[15] The book sold fifty thousand copies in its first six months and continued strongly, helped by the award of the Pulitzer Prize for Fiction in 1945.[16] Paul Osborn's stage version opened on Broadway in time for Christmas 1944. Despite some persuasive objections to its comic handling of the Italian characters—present in the original but, Wolcott Gibbs argued in *The New Yorker*, exaggerated on-stage to the point where, in relation to the U.S. conquerors, "it seems to perpetuate the master-race theory"—the production was a hit and ran for eighteen months.[17] A different production, starring Robert Beatty, was staged in London by Hugh Beaumont in 1945, its language bowdlerized at the insistence of a tender censor in the Lord Chamberlain's office who commented, "There are a great number of rather rough words."[18] Negotiations for movie, radio, and TV versions also moved quickly. Directed by Henry King, with Gene Tierney as Tina, the film was released in June 1945. A CBS TV series came later, as did a feature-length TV film in color.[19]

These developments led to some of the side dramas that beset commercially successful fictions, especially ones that are fact-based. Frank Toscani was at first pleased with the book, especially because his new fame helped him win promotion to colonel. Later, he started an action against Hersey for invasion of privacy.[20] Both the writer of the stage version and its star, Fredric March, tried to get in on the film. But these and other distractions lay in the future. For now, Hersey was satisfied that he had made his point. He had written the book "in angry haste," he explained the following year, and with two dominant concerns:[21]

> One of them was the fact, which became evident at about H hour plus
> one minute of the Sicilian invasion, that our longstanding dedication to
> the job of winning the war first and worrying about the problems of peace
> afterwards was not going to work out very well . . . Wars fought without
> politics are wars lost . . .

The other thing . . . was a concern shared by most of the citizens who served in our citizen-Army—namely, that the country should never forget that the military system is repugnant to the democratic system.

The writer was still only thirty years old. The high moral tone of these remarks is heard in the novella, too, though less often in the published version than in his drafts. Early on in the book it's said of Joppolo that "since he happened to be a good man, his works represented the best of possibilities," a sentence that in typescript was followed by another, subsequently deleted: "We should be thinking about the possibilities, and especially the best of the possibilities, in the hope that they may be realized."[22] There's an element of self-censorship in the changes, too. Hersey thought better of saying that Joppolo's feelings for Tina actually enhance those for his wife back in the States, and of describing the Counter-Intelligence Corps as "the nearest America has been able to achieve . . . to the Gestapo." There was nothing empty, either, about his belief in the best in human nature. He gave the royalties from the book to his mother.

Crash Kennedy

Hersey's journalism was also going extremely well, and offers of new jobs were coming in, including from *The Saturday Evening Post*. In November 1943 he and Frances Ann were dined by the *Post*'s editor, Ben Hibbs, and his deputy, Robert Fuoss.[23] Aware of the competition but also thinking about qualities Hersey had shown beyond his writing—qualities (and affinities) by which Luce had always been attracted—Time-Life had already begun to hold out the prospect of a top, perhaps eventually *the* top, managerial-cum-editorial role.[24] *Adano*, though, was being treated as a serious literary work, and Hersey knew that few serious writers spend much time being company bosses. The *New Yorker*'s European columnist Janet Flanner told him, "To have turned reality into fiction, in form, demonstrates your special talent and heart." Confirmation came from a still more persuasive quarter. Damon Runyon was in the hospital with throat cancer. His larynx having been removed, he communicated by writing notes to his visitors, who included the columnist Leonard Lyons. Lyons sent Hersey one of the messages Runyon had scribbled: "Do you know Hersey? He is the best writer that has come out of the war so far."[25]

For now, how and when the war would end was still in doubt, and the Herseys had their children to think of. Aiming exclusively for a literary career was hazardous, but there was one corner of New York journalism where writers were valued above all for their writing. It was by a series of accidents that Hersey found himself being published in *The New Yorker*.

While some of the U.S. military had been completing the occupation of Sicily and preparing for what was to be a bloody and prolonged campaign in Italy, others were still stuck in a tropical version of trench warfare in the jungles and island waters of the South Pacific. As with the Germans, the problem with the Japanese was not so much to get the upper hand, hard enough though that was, as to force them to move and, in the process, to deprive them of the men and equipment they were adroit at evacuating. In part of this effort Frances Ann's old boyfriend Jack Kennedy spent most of 1943 in the Solomon Islands. He came back as a hero, but an embittered one. Hersey made him famous.

A keen sailor and strong swimmer, Kennedy had enlisted in a glamorous but, despite its reputation, not hugely effective branch of the U.S. Navy, the patrol torpedo (PT) boat squadrons. Hersey had written about them in *Life* before going to Sicily.[26] Their immediate appeal to the navy as well as to the general public was obvious: high-speed launches powered by aero engines chasing much larger Japanese destroyers, they were presented as the maritime equivalent of fighter planes. In practice they were quaintly vulnerable (the hulls were still made of wood), their engines unreliable and not all that fast (a destroyer could outrun a PT boat), their torpedoes reluctant to leave their tubes and, when they did so, inaccurate. Still, the legend was strong, and Kennedy at first helped maintain its human side, behaving with his usual reckless aplomb and earning the nickname Crash Kennedy by driving his boat into a jetty. Despite and because of that, and also because he was funny, brave, and skilled, he was very popular in the service. These qualities as well as some of his defects became apparent in the famous episode that Hersey was the first to record in detail.

In total darkness in the Blackett Strait, Solomon Islands, on the night of August 2, 1943, in the course of what everyone now agrees was a badly planned as well as totally unsuccessful attack by fifteen PT boats against the "Tokyo Express" supply convoy, Kennedy's PT-109 collided violently with a Japanese destroyer. Two crew members were lost, and the remainder, after clinging to the slowly capsizing hull overnight, were eventually forced to swim three miles to a deserted island. Kennedy distinguished himself by towing a badly burned sailor the whole way with the help of a leather strap gripped in his teeth. Subsequently he was key in various efforts, some of them equally difficult and dangerous, to find food and water and to raise help. The eleven men's survival and eventual rescue a week later were largely due to his determination. Still, the incident had odd aspects. The PT boat was hunting destroyers: How had they come within ruinous distance of this fast-moving ship without realizing it?[27] What was Kennedy himself doing at the moment of the collision? Japanese propaganda instantly seized on the episode as illustrating the implacable skill of one of its destroyer crews in running down a hostile craft. From the U.S. point of view, given that PT-109 was acting as part of a squadron, it was mysterious that none of the other boats had gone to the crew's rescue and that there was no subsequent search for survivors.

The story has been told many times and from different angles.[28] Kennedy himself resisted talk of heroism. Miserable at having wrecked his boat, having lost two men, having failed to do any harm to the enemy, having experienced moments of sheer physical collapse during the days and nights that followed, and beyond all that at having not only witnessed but been in part the victim of American ineptitude higher up the chain of command, he returned to the States to find that most people knew next to nothing about the war and that their expectations were those of a fairy tale. It would all be over within months, the heroes would come home, and every one of them would have sunk five destroyers or captured a hilltop. By contrast, the story he had to tell was, as Hersey wrote, "a nightmarish thing altogether."

In February 1944, soon after Kennedy left the hospital, Hersey and Frances Ann met up with him and the model-turned-fashion-journalist Flo Pritchett at a Manhattan nightclub called Cafe Society, where they bumped into William Shawn from *The New Yorker*. Everyone in Kennedy's circle and some outside knew the PT-109 story, but hearing it from

Kennedy himself, Hersey saw more in it than action and personality and offered to write it up. At Kennedy's suggestion, he talked first to others involved, members of the crew who were now back in the States at the Quonset Point, Rhode Island, naval air base. After that, he properly interviewed Kennedy himself, by now once more in the hospital, in Boston.[29] A draft was ready by the first week in March, and Kennedy suggested a few changes, mainly to increase the credit given to his fellow officer Leonard Thom and to prevent identification of a member of the crew who had lost his nerve during the ordeal.[30]

Life decided against the piece. On the one hand, Jack's father, Joe Kennedy, Sr., keen for some vicarious glory that might offset his well-earned reputation as a coward and appeaser as well as a crook, was active in spreading the story, and though they were friends, Luce wasn't eager to help him. More of an obstacle in journalistic terms were the facts that *Life* had already carried a piece by Hersey about the PT boats and that by then there were other topics to be dealt with, including that Japan was giving the Americans a hard time in Papua New Guinea and was actively threatening both Australia and India. What was essentially, like *Into the Valley*, an account of glorious failure could have been thought untimely. So Hersey wrote to William Shawn:

Dear Bill Shawn:

Do you remember how, on the night of our most recent meeting at that table in Cafe Society, Jack Kennedy told about his adventure in the Solomons? LIFE was bored with the idea, as I think I told you I expected they might be. But, between other chores, I've seen Kennedy three or four times, and I've talked with some of his crew, and now I'm winding up a story which LIFE says I may sell outside. Since you expressed some interest that night, I wonder if you'd like to look at it before I send it to my agent. I have no idea about your requirements or desires as to length, but I'm just writing it as it writes itself. I'll be done with it over the weekend and could send it to you the first thing next week if you're interested.

My wife and I are planning an evening at Cafe Society some night next March. If nothing comes of this, we'll see you there.

Best,

John Hersey[31]

Shawn and Ross said yes. The article's opening went through a number of changes before being given one of the magazine's signature tunes: a writer in the city waiting for a story to walk in. "Lieutenant John F. Kennedy, the ex-Ambassador's son and lately a PT skipper in the Solomons, came through town the other day and told me . . ."[32]

It was called "Survival." While it relates the events as they concern all eleven survivors, it focuses on a powerful element of Kennedy's own experience—something almost mystical that Hersey later said was what made him want to write it. As soon as everyone had reached relative safety, the skipper, despite having spent more than fifteen hours in the water, decided to swim out again with a lantern to a point where his light might be seen if another group of PTs set out for action. But the loss of PT-109 and presumed death of all its crew had led to a change of route, so no patrol came their way. Exhausted and cut about by coral reefs, Kennedy was seized by a current that took him away from where he had set off. All night he drifted: "His mind seemed to float away from his body. Darkness and time took the place of a mind in his skull. For a long time he slept, or was crazy, or floated in a chill trance." But in a way that both Kennedy and Hersey understood as sailors, the tide in the Solomons

> shoves and sucks through the islands and makes the currents curl in odd patterns . . . [He] moved in a huge circle—west past Gizo, then north and east past Kolombangara, then south into Ferguson Passage. Early in the morning the sky turned from black to gray, and so did Kennedy's mind.

He was back where he had begun, and "for a second time, he started home."

This was what drew Hersey to the story: "The aspect of fate that threw him into a current and brought him back again." It was, he said, a theme that "has always fascinated me."[33] He didn't relate it to how the narrative ends or to the religious belief embodied there, which, according to his own statements, he no longer held. The patrol-boat survivors found they had in common with the Solomon Islanders who rescued them some words well known to almost every Anglophone reader at that time. They were written by a nineteenth-century woman who, as it happens, had lived and died twenty miles north of the Herseys' Briarcliff home, in a house opposite the American Military Academy at West Point.[34] Rescuers and rescued sang them together as the boat took them back to base:

> Jesus loves me, this I know . . .
> Little ones to him belong,
> They are weak but He is strong.
> Yes, Jesus loves me; yes, Jesus loves me . . .

With what in those days was *The New Yorker*'s disregard for journalistic priorities, Hersey's piece about an episode in the Pacific ten months earlier appeared in its pages a fortnight after D-Day. The magazine's timelessness appealed to him, and he also more practically valued the close editorial attention of William Shawn and Harold Ross. In later years he often told a story about a marginal comment made by Ross in a draft of "Survival" at the point where it described Kennedy's having written a message on a coconut. "With what, for God's sake?" Ross asked. "Blood?"[35] If from a news reporter's point of view the article fell short, it had a different and more powerful currency, contributing as it did to the reputation of a man who, with heavy encouragement from his father, would soon be running for office. Joseph Kennedy, Sr., unstoppable in his ambitions for his family but thrown back by the death of his eldest son, Joseph Junior, on a secret flying mission in Europe in August 1944, focused his aspirations on Jack. Riding roughshod over the sensibilities, not to mention the copyright, of the more upmarket *New Yorker*, he persuaded the editor of the mass-circulation *Reader's Digest* to reprint Hersey's article.[36] In this form, much recycled, and reprinted yet again in *U.S. News and World Report*,[37] it played a significant part in JFK's successful political campaigns, first for election to Congress in 1946 and subsequently to the Senate and the presidency itself. If anything, the sheer robustness of the narrative, which inevitably came under hostile scrutiny during the presidential campaign, reinforced Hersey's credentials not just as a writer but, by reputation, as one of the Kennedy team—this despite the fact that, as we'll see, he actively supported the steadier Adlai Stevenson against Kennedy and recoiled from the ruthlessness of the Kennedy machine in action.[38] None of which harmed him as an author who was increasingly a public figure.

Factual Fictions

There were several levels of remove, Hersey knew very well by now, between what happened and what reached readers. Propaganda had its necessities, and he had done his share. Meanwhile, working on larger and smaller scales and in different colors, he had tried the top-to-bottom campaign narrative (*Men on Bataan*), the desperate incident (*Into the Valley*, "Survival"), and the peacemaker's story (*A Bell for Adano*). Some of his reports on the Sicilian campaign would enter the lexicon, being used by writers decades later as they in turn tried to communicate what it was like to be there. "Shelling those hills," he wrote in *Time* of the U.S. advance, "was like shaking lice out of old clothes."[39] He had written thrillingly about the kind of soldier who thrives in action, including in an article about the aggressive new Rangers formation begun in 1943, deeply responsive to the hardheadedness of men who had been brought up rough and were encouraged to develop that side of themselves. "Bomb landed by door—scream—40 men," says one of the notes he made in action, followed by the laconic reaction of one of the Rangers: "Somebody answer that goddam door."[40] Yet he also had plenty to say about personalities of the opposite kind, sympathy toward which had become more open, not least as the result of stories about Patton's bullying. Most soldiers, he had stressed at the end of *Into the Valley*, want nothing more than to stop fighting and go home. In Sicily during the U.S. advance on Nicosia, he witnessed an expressive contrast between a man whose shoulder had been blasted away and a blinded comrade. The first said, "Let's go back there and get those bastards," while the blind man confided, "Eyes are very delicate things."[41] But if he was supreme at the graphic and the human, as an editor he had also dealt with political and strategic stories and had been involved in clashes between what correspondents knew or believed and what editors and proprietors believed they knew. In the case of attitudes to Soviet Communism, such differences were everywhere becoming wider and angrier, but in few places more evidently than at Time-Life. It was in this context that Hersey's role changed. His next posting was to Moscow.

Nothing, of course, was clear-cut, and there were many paradoxes. For example, a reporter was among other things a ventriloquist. The voices of individuals mattered, especially in a magazine as people-focused as *Life*;

yet in *Life*, as distinct from life, their differences of opinion tended to get ironed out. So while Hersey always took pains to interview a range of people on any topic, he sometimes overtly presented the result as a monologue.[42] This could be read as soldierly solidarity, but the process wasn't one he would have wanted applied to his own voice, and the difficulties of genuinely free expression were increasingly apparent to him. He had been able to criticize General Patton in fiction, but the magazines he was employed by had nothing bad to say about him. *Life* published an adulatory profile of the general in November 1942; *Time* did in April 1943 and again immediately after the Sicilian invasion.[43] When the fighting was at its most perilous, the magazines' writers—Hersey among them—had been obliged to celebrate what most strategists at the time and since have regarded as a pointless piece of grandstanding in Palermo.[44] Hersey took pains to let the New York office know some of the other side of the story: the fact, for example, that the U.S. arrival in the more or less open city was prepared for by heavy Allied bombing and produced retaliatory German air raids for which local people understandably blamed the Americans.[45] In the magazine, by contrast, a now familiar photo feature by Robert Capa showed happy Italians lining the streets as U.S. troops drove through the city. One shot varies the cliché of a smiling dark-haired local girl in the arms of a stern invader by foregrounding another soldier, having his shoes polished by a grateful native.[46] This feature appeared directly above Hersey's article about Licata, and although the general isn't mentioned there, nor is the behavior satirized by the writer in *A Bell for Adano*.

MOSCOW

Hersey traveled out from Norfolk, Virginia, at the end of July 1944 on the elderly but recently overhauled USS *Cincinnati*. (In the war's chronology, this was when the United States captured Tinian, one of the Mariana Islands, which was to become the main base for bombing attacks on Japanese cities, including Hiroshima and Nagasaki.) The flagship was escorting a convoy carrying untried, enlisted troops to Western Europe for a war Hitler was patently losing but showed no inclination to give up. There had just been a serious attempt by senior Wehrmacht officers to kill him. The Russians were driving the Nazis back northwest toward the Bal-

tic and Poland, triumphantly reclaiming areas Hitler had accepted, under
the 1940 Nazi-Soviet pact on which he had then reneged, as being in the
Soviet "area of influence." Another historically resonant reverse occurred
the day before the *Cincinnati* sailed: the Soviets reached Brest-Litovsk, site
of the 1918 peace treaty between Germany and the then-new Soviet regime. In northern France, Allied progress was initially slow, but most of
Italy had by now been taken. Everywhere, though, the Nazis continued to
fight hard, and morale on the ship was low. U.S. troops are never told
where they are going, Hersey lamented to Frances Ann,

> much less anything at all about the nature of the people they will come
> up against in the theater where they are going. They go to the cities of
> Europe deaf, dumb and blind, intent only on spending the dough they've
> saved.
>
> We had a movie tonight which insulted the intelligence of morons and
> ten-year-olds. It was called Adventure in Iraq, and it concerned an ori-
> ental potentate, an ex-flying tiger, a drunken but sporting Englishman,
> two priestesses in a trance, etc. etc. . . . It certainly affords our fighting
> men a sad brand of stimulation before going into battle to keep the world
> free—or whatever they go into battle for.
>
> Excuse the homily. It makes me sore.[47]

Still, some of the crew were interesting, among them a few Marines
and a Brooklyn man who had developed a Southern accent so as not to be
identified as being from Brooklyn. "He likes everything and never complains," Hersey wrote; "he likes the ship, he likes the captain, he likes his
gun-boss. He even likes work, and what he likes best is to take his gun
apart and clean it." Meanwhile Hersey was trying to learn Russian but was
distracted by homesickness and often ended up drawing pictures for Martin and Johnny instead.

Pausing in North Africa, he encountered distant versions of his colonial upbringing. Noël Coward was in Cairo being "frightfully imperial,"
and Egypt also communicated something more about the postwar future
than the past: "Lying at the foot of the Great Cheops Pyramid was an
empty packet of Camel cigarettes—with a picture of a camel standing in
front of the very pyramids before which some GI had tossed the pack!"[48]
Even European Moscow was in some ways familiar. Hersey stayed at the

prerevolutionary Hotel Metropol, its art nouveau magnificence still unmistakable though the interior was frayed by the years in which it had served as the Second House of Soviets. Before long, he was interviewing Shostakovich and Eisenstein, visiting Leningrad (Saint Petersburg) to write about the reconstruction of the city, roistering with his outgoing bureau chief Dick Lauterbach and Bill Lawrence of *The New York Times*, and dining à deux with the funny, charming, and shrewd British ambassador Archie Kerr ("my favorite character in town"), whom he had first met in China. He learned to play an early form of electronic instrument invented in Russia before the war, the emiriton.[49]

Just as war journalism was a mode of fiction, so was being a foreign correspondent, and in few places more than in Moscow. Foreign reporters met the people the regime wanted them to meet. In Soviet terms, the regime's own official reporters were perfectly adequate to covering events anywhere near the front, which of itself meant writing what they were told. To keep visitors busy, and at the same time to present Russia in a favorable light, the arts were useful. Today's Western attitudes are still colored by the Cold War, and it can require an effort to recall that since 1941 the Soviet Union had been, with whatever degree of mutual suspicion, a crucial wartime ally—not to say the indispensably sacrificial front line—of the United States and Britain. When the Nazis surrendered at Stalingrad in January 1943, Stalin was *Time*'s Man of the Year. In terms of their human contribution to the Allied victory, it is no disrespect to the United States' 420,000 dead or to the 460,000 from Great Britain and its colonies to point out that the Soviet Union's casualties amounted to 20 million. From a Moscow perspective in August 1944, the Western allies' invasion of Italy had been a costly distraction from what should have been their main effort. Operation Overlord, the attack through northern France, had come very late and even then was moving with what the Russians saw as excessive caution. The real war, in Soviet eyes, was largely being fought and won along its line barging implacably westward from the East Prussian Baltic in the north through Poland and toward the Adriatic in the south.

This is the context in which Hersey wrote both his most sustained articles about the arts and his first contemplations of human atrocity. Like other Westerners, diplomats included, he had little access to ordinary Russians. Communications of any kind were controlled and, when permitted, spied on. Moscow's glitter, such as it was, represented a show of relief that life of any kind had returned to a city that had been vacated late in 1941 in the face of the Nazi invasion, when the bulk of the administration, diplomatic missions, and cultural organizations had been moved to Kuybyshev (Samara), 650 miles to the southeast. But Hersey was both a musician manqué and reasonably knowledgeable about other performing arts, and his new role as a foreign correspondent gave him a chance to show a different side of himself to *Time* readers. Whether or not in the process he gave a full sense of the Soviet Union, its actions and intentions, is a different matter.

What was happening all around him was almost inconceivably confusing. The earliest military action he wrote about from Moscow was the Red Army's entry into Bucharest: the first capital city it had taken in the war (for all its criticism of the Western Allies' alleged dilatoriness in Europe, they had already liberated Rome and Paris). But this was secondhand news. Like other foreign reporters, Hersey had to depend on an *Izvestia* contact for the color he cabled to New York on September 2. Later that month, though, he was taken to the Baltic city of Tallinn, capital of Estonia, where correspondents were treated to excellent food and wine that they were told had been brought from France by the Germans, who had abandoned it when they fled. It wasn't all they had left behind. The party was taken to a former labor camp twenty-five miles west at Klooga, part of the Vaivara concentration camp, which the retreating Germans had tried to obliterate. They saw the cremation pyres prisoners had been ordered to build, with the remains of some of those prisoners strewn over them.[50] Immediately afterward, Hersey was introduced to a man called Benjamin Weintraub, originally from Vilnius. Known since 1943 as no. 339, Weintraub had lost his parents, two brothers, and most of his camp acquaintances. "The camp gave me my first real insight into the German enemy," Hersey wrote to Frances Ann. He now realized that Arthur Koestler's 1943 novel about Nazism, *Arrival and Departure*, was "a true book" and in a coolly powerful article for *Life* he told Weintraub's story and that of "the dark day when the Jews of Wilno were gathered into a ghetto" and of what befell them. He did not mention Stalin's gulag or any other aspect of the continuing Terror.[51]

Meanwhile, other news had to be supplied, "world-shaking things like the menu of the luncheon Stalin gave for Churchill on Tuesday!" or the fact that the British prime minister—in Moscow with the foreign minister, Anthony Eden, for a fateful series of meetings at which, as later became clear, most of the Balkan nations were more or less arbitrarily relinquished to the Soviets in exchange for a British stake in Greece—became annoyed because water had stopped coming into his bath.[52] Political visits of such importance meant entertainments, so Hersey went to the opera, the ballet, and the theater. He met the composer Aram Khachaturian and saw *Eugene Onegin* and *The Cherry Orchard*. For the second time he sat through Boris Asafyev and Rostislav Zakharov's four-hour Pushkin-based ballet, *Fountain of Bakhchisarai*: "And so, sweet Patch, your brave war correspondent has become a ballet critic. Jesus, what a difference from Guadalcanal."[53] At home, plans for the stage version of *A Bell for Adano* were well advanced; it was to be tried out in New Haven and Boston before opening on Broadway at the Cort Theatre before Christmas. The Russians also took up the play, doubtless recognizing the propaganda value of its criticisms of U.S. actions.[54] As if acknowledging this new area of expertise, *Time* unusually gave Hersey a byline for an article on theater in Moscow, then celebrating a quarter century of state control.

He wrote every few days to Frances Ann, who was expecting their third child. Even allowing for the immense difference between current Western approaches to paternity and those of seventy-five years ago, his attitude to what he called her "baby-time" ("maybe you will already have produced by the time you get this") seems casual and, for all the passion and nostalgia in his letters and his exuberance at the news of the birth of his first daughter, Ann, he was evidently enjoying his independence. One of the issues in his letters home, in fact, was his determination to resist new efforts by Henry Luce to persuade him to return to New York as managing editor.

They took some fending off. On November 5, Luce cabled with his much-parodied grandiloquence:

THE TIME HAS COME WHEN WE MUST TAKE DEFINITE DECISIONS REGARDING THE FUTURE OF TIME THE NEWSMAGAZINE ACCORDINGLY IN MY JUDGMENT YOU SHOULD BEGIN WORK AS A SENIOR EDITOR OF TIME NOT LATER THAN JANUARY FIRST STOP FOR THREE REASONS FIRST IN ORDER TO PARTICIPATE IN THE CREATIVE PLANNING OF POSTWAR TIME SECOND TO LEARN THE ART AND TRADE OF BEING AN EDITOR

THIRD BECAUSE WE ARE IN SERIOUS NEED OF A COMPETENT SENIOR
EDITOR[55]

Within a week, David Hulburd weighed in:

LUCE FIRMLY CONVINCED YOUR TIMEINC FUTURE SHOULD BE MANAGE-
RIAL PROLONG PULL DASH NOT THAT HE OR ANYONE ELSE MINIMIZES
YOUR FINE WRITING TALENTS BUT BECAUSE EDITING ETMANAGING ED-
ITING ARE WHERE THE BRAINS ARE NEEDED MOST ETWHERE TIMEINC-
WISE YOU WILL BE MOST SUCCESSFUL ETHAPPIEST STOP . . . FEEL IF YOU'VE
MADE UP YOUR MIND TO HAVE TIMEINC POSTWAR CAREER YOUD BE
WISE TO TAKE TIME EDITORSHIP AS OPPOSED TO CONTINUE AS WAR
CORRESPONDENT ETLIFE WRITER[56]

Hersey's careful correspondence with other, implicitly maligned senior
people at Time-Life confirms that what Luce thought he wanted most was
a "managing" editor—responsible for production, advertising, staffing,
and all other non-editorial, non-journalistic tasks. (Among those who
warned Hersey of the difficulties involved in the role was Luce's own aide
Allen Grover, known in the company as "vice president in charge of Henry
Luce.")[57] Luce said his offer was "OF COURSE MADE IN THE SPIRIT OF OUR
LONG CONVERSATION ON THE SUBJECT OF YOUR CAREER," and it seems
that he held out the prospect of Hersey's becoming editor in chief of *Life*,
though, given the intensity of Luce's own involvement, that role, suppos-
ing he himself ever relinquished it, could never be clear-cut. The urgency
of his solicitations was almost certainly as much to do with well-founded
anxiety about losing his protégé than any willingness to have him take
over. In addition, as we'll see, an in-house rebellion was in progress and
Hersey's decision involved more than simply deciding in favor of his writing. Still, the latter was a crucial part of it, and in his reply he pointed out
that this was something he had mentioned when Luce and he had a similar discussion only a year earlier. At this stage at least he was more interested, he said, in human stories and human feelings than he was in politics
on the one hand or journalistic administration on the other. And once his
stint in Moscow was done, and ideally before the war with Japan ended,
he wanted to go back to China—a trip he had been promised for a couple
of years.[58] Luce gave in with moderate grace and there, for now, the matter

was left—though on Hersey's side with a feeling that nothing much had been resolved.

The distracting Moscow social round continued. One of the foremost American playwrights of her time, the extravagantly pro-Soviet Lillian Hellman was in town. She was the first American to be officially invited by the Russians during the wartime alliance, and a huge fuss was made of her. Though Hersey envied the degree of access she was allowed, and their personalities could not have been more different, over the several months of her stay at the U.S. ambassador's residence—albeit in practice more at the Metropol—they became lifelong friends.[59] On any excuse there were all-night parties at the hotel: for correspondents who had just arrived, or were leaving, or for their birthdays, or for visitors, or for no reason except the wish for a party. The Russians themselves made challenging demands on foreign correspondents' alcoholic endurance, especially around the anniversary parade of November 7, when the expression "Molotov cocktail" stopped being figurative; afterward Hersey went on the wagon for ten days.[60] Frances Ann sent pictures of the children; John replied with stories about poker games, drunken outings to the countryside, the frustration of never—unlike Hellman—being allowed anywhere near the front, while simultaneously not being at the Broadway opening of *Adano*.[61] He was reading a lot in Russian and spent Christmas with one of America's most influential authorities on Russian-ness, George Kennan, who had recently arrived with his wife as deputy to the ambassador, Averell Harriman. The New Year at first brought little change. He wrote an article about a Russian manufacturer. He interviewed the composer Prokofiev and even, "in boredom," dashed off a book about Russian music, which, on the advice of an authority consulted by Alfred Knopf, remained unpublished.[62] And he cobbled together what military news he could, "gleaning the few hunks of wheat from the dreadful chaff the Russian correspondents send in."[63] While the Americans and British were being held up in costly battles with the Germans in the Ardennes, in Alsace, and at Strasbourg, the Red Army plunged toward them.

5. Tu Lu-men, Chu Chi-erh, and Shi-Taling

ERSEY'S ENCOUNTERS in parts of Eastern and Central Europe during the brief intervals between the expulsion of the Nazis and Stalin's tightening of the Soviet hold taught him about extremes of human behavior for which neither Guadalcanal nor Sicily had been adequate preparation. He had already, though, been undergoing a political as well as moral education: one that was being spread on both sides of the Atlantic. In U.S. terms it was essentially Democratic, and the more Hersey identified his own politics with those of Franklin Roosevelt, the more he came into conflict with Henry Luce. The disagreement was intensified by the similarity of their backgrounds and also by a situation directly of Roosevelt's making. In 1943, bothered by Luce's increasing hostility and global maneuverings, the president had imposed travel restrictions on all media chiefs, preventing them (as distinct from their correspondents) from visiting combat areas. So Luce had been grounded in the States while his protégé was seeing action in every corner of the world.

In terms of staving off hostile coverage the ban was badly misjudged, as Luce's biographer Alan Brinkley shows. When Roosevelt stood for

reelection in 1944, Luce—whose wife was by then a Republican senator[1]—
threw all his support behind the Republican candidate, Thomas E. Dewey,
who did better against FDR than any previous contender and beat him in
his hometown. But readers' perception that Luce's magazines had become
Republican vehicles, combined with the mounting exasperation of sea-
soned reporters whose stories were, for political reasons, altered editori-
ally or simply not used, led to an internal crisis, which came to a head soon
after Hersey reached Moscow.

The immediate occasion was Luce's mounting displeasure with Teddy
White's China coverage. In essence, Luce still saw no wrong in Chiang
Kai-shek, whereas White, in common with the regional U.S. military commander Joseph Stilwell, believed that Chiang had lost control of the
country and was now busier with trying to hang on to power and weaken
the Communists than with winning the war. When Chiang persuaded
Roosevelt to recall Stilwell, White was charged with writing *Time*'s cover
story on the matter. His article was rewritten from beginning to end by
Whittaker Chambers, who for some time had liked to boast that he "routinely dropped in the wastebasket" anything White sent in.[2]

The ensuing row involved many of the paper's staff and was a miniature portent of ideological divisions that would spread further and faster
during the Cold War. To oppose Chiang may not rationally have meant
supporting Chinese Communism, but in practice—and certainly in Luce's
opinion—it came to the same thing. Many Westerners closely involved
with China believed that Communism had long been doing more for the
country's people than any other system on offer. As Tony Judt wrote much
later about its European manifestation, "Communism may have been the
wrong solution, but the dilemma to which it was responding was real
enough."[3] Shrewd observers distinguished between Soviet and Chinese
Communism, advocating U.S. support for Mao as a buffer against Soviet
power as well as a pragmatic recognition of the status quo. But in the simplistically anti-Communist mood of mid-1940s America, even this was a
hazardous position to take. Discussing the Teddy White case later in an
article about Luce, Hersey drew a parallel with the postwar fate of two
China experts who took similar lines: John Paton Davies and John S. Service, both of them, like Luce and Hersey, "mishkids," both "hounded out
of the Foreign Service by Senator Joseph McCarthy for the sin of seeing

the China picture, as we now know, far more accurately than Henry Luce was seeing it."[4]

Hersey was never a Communist. His attitude to China was that of "an apprehensive liberal,"[5] and by 1946 he sided with those he himself described as the "mild, gentle, rather frightened-looking, but really quite courageous leaders" of the China Democratic League, begun in 1941 and, while never powerful, still in existence today.[6] Still, to Hersey, not being a Communist was not the same as being dogmatically anti-Communist. On his arrival in Moscow, he brought himself up to date by reading back numbers of *Time* and was shocked by the magazine's partisanship. He wrote to Frances Ann with revealing detachment from the organization:

> I must say I was disgusted with some of their stories. They seem to want to go out of their way to take cracks at Russia. Some of the things they said were certainly partly true; some few of them I have myself felt here—but to work so hard and so deliberately to hit at Russia in every story in which they can, in stories about Belgium and France and Italy and Poland and Finland, in short in damn nearly every story in the magazine, seems to me to do plenty of disservice at the moment.[7]

Meanwhile, the bureau chief he succeeded, Richard Lauterbach, another victim of the Whittaker Chambers pencil, was educating him about the fact—and it was a fact—that Communism "means different things now in italy, spain, france, yugoslavia and russia [sic]."[8] "Luce is so damned biased," Lauterbach wrote, and complaints like this became frequent and open.

The problem was in part a result of the collegially muddled and fluid organizational structure of *Time*, which in the early days had been among its strengths. Now, as the company's official history explains, the relationship between Chambers as the Foreign News editor and his correspondents was ambiguous. The editor of any section, "subject only to the veto of the managing editor, had the last word on what appeared—still anonymously, in those days—in his department. He was expected to be . . . guided by the correspondents' dispatches, but if he believed them to be wrong he was free to disregard them."[9] Chambers, as we've seen, very often thought his journalists were wrong and the difficulty was exacerbated by the fact that while he was responsible for what appeared in his pages, the correspondents themselves were answerable not to him but to the chief of the news service (then Allen Grover, who was the company's vice president). By now these correspondents as often as not had experience in working at senior level in the New York office and for that reason, too, saw themselves as ranking at least equally with Chambers. As the official history says,

> Charles Wertenbaker in Paris and John Osborne [in Europe on a roving brief] had edited Foreign News before him; John Hersey in Moscow, by then an editor of *Life* reporting for all the magazines, had been a senior writer in Foreign News and World Battlefronts; Walter Graebner, in charge of the London office, had served the company in a number of editorial posts before Chambers joined the staff. They openly rebelled when Chambers persisted in ignoring their cables.

In response, Luce ordered a survey of correspondents' opinions. The views that came back were mostly identical with Hersey's own: "Passages used from my dispatches," he complained directly to Luce, were "torn from the context" and made to conform to "*Time*'s editorial bias."[10]

This was the moment Luce chose to try to bring him back to New York—ostensibly to prepare him for "the top job" but, as Hersey interpreted it, to clip his wings. In his reply Hersey reminded Luce of the latter's promise to send him back to China. But he also confronted the political issue, defined as it had been for him by his journalistic encounters during 1944, by the Roosevelt-Dewey contest, and by the in-house dispute: "I will never be a Fascist or a Communist," he told Luce, "but [at the election] I was, and I most certainly am after this experience, confirmed in being politically a democrat, both with and without a capital D. Knowing and admiring the sincerity of your beliefs as a Republican, I am afraid that my stubborn conviction would not help me or TIME if I were to become an editor."[11] In his personal reply Luce dealt gently with Hersey, but he took a characteristically obscure sideswipe at him in a long memo circulated to all his mutinous staff, upholding Chambers's position:

> I have just been told, in a highly confidential manner, that Stalin is, after all, a Communist. I am also somewhat less confidentially informed that the Pope is a Christian. Some will say: what does it matter in either case?

And what does it matter that Hersey advises me that he, John Hersey, is a Democrat? Well, I cannot say for sure what these pieces of information signify, but one must respect the data in each case. A good Foreign News Editor, while guarding against the prejudices arising from his own convictions, will not ignore the circumstances that the Pope is a Christian and Stalin a Communist and Hersey, God bless him, a Democrat.[12]

Hersey and Luce would never be on good terms again, but for now Hersey was still Time-Life's man in Moscow, and he went wherever Moscow permitted him. For example, *Life* published an obliging profile by him of Nikolai Pusirev, director of a heavy-machinery manufacturing plant near Leningrad, "a self-made man who builds machines, owns a yacht and likes to argue about ballet." This was on January 15, 1945, when the Red Army was overrunning Poland, the country that, more than any other, was a sticking point in Stalin's negotiations with the Western Allies over the future shape of Europe. Historically, Poland had always struggled against its German and Russian neighbors. The Treaty of Versailles had given the country one of its brief periods of autonomy—a condition Britain ostensibly entered the Second World War to defend. But in the realpolitik of 1943–45, two things became apparent. One was that Britain and America regarded the regions they themselves liberated as being under their own control: when parts of Italy had been captured they inevitably fell under the immediate victors' rule. By the Soviets, this was gladly taken as a precedent in Eastern and Central Europe. The other, even more basic fact was that few people in the tired West felt like picking a fight with the immense and seemingly inexhaustible Red Army as it rampaged in their direction.

Negotiations of a kind were still going on over Poland, however, and it was in Soviet interests that the world should know what the Nazis had done there. Western journalists, Hersey among them, were shown through the ruins. Hersey's party had as its guide to Warsaw the Communist in charge of "political education" in the Polish army, but perhaps because he was so glad to be let out of Moscow the American doesn't seem to have seen anything compromising in this.[13] As with most wartime journalism, it's difficult to give a fair assessment of the achievement of individual reporters, working as they did under overt censorship—that of their home countries in addition to the places they were filing from—and within agendas set by their media employers, and according to their personal loyalties. The fact remains that very few Western reporters in the Soviet Union told the truth about Stalin. Many broadly egalitarian, democratically minded people wanted to believe that "Uncle Joe" was at bottom a benign, philanthropic kind of man, albeit prone to blunt measures when his social improvements were frustrated. To these well-wishing fantasists, criticizing the means used could seem like opposing the ends.

Besides, the Soviet apparatus was quick to reward those who showed any sign of being on its side. Hersey himself, as someone whose work—especially *A Bell for Adano*—criticized elements of American imperialism, was held up for praise. Being in favor, though, rarely reduced restrictions on movement, which, combined with visitors' own linguistic limitations and the reluctance of ordinary people living under state terrorism to speak out, made most commentators almost totally dependent on official sources.[14] Westerners who knew most often did so because of personal relationships with Russians, their protective feelings toward whom made them easy to control. In the early 1930s an adventurous few had reported on Stalin's savage policies toward the Ukraine. The Moscow "trials" and purges of 1936–38 were more widely criticized, but for many reasons, including the camouflage provided by the civil war in Spain—where Stalin was (and often still is) generally and simplistically thought to have been "on the side of" the Republicans—failed, both then and for many years afterward, to make a deep impact in the West. And by 1942–45, while people in Hersey's position could and should have written about the gulag, wartime imperatives toward an ally kept the story buried. (In 1944, Vice President Henry Wallace managed to tour Siberia without its impinging on his reactions.)[15] Details of the Nazi concentration camps, meanwhile, were clearly news of the greatest importance, and Hersey was among the first to bring them to the United States.

In Warsaw, on the way through buildings flattened by the retreating Germans toward what was presented as their guide's looted suburban home, the group passed a couple of dozen people cutting up a recently killed army horse for food, a scene Hersey vividly described. His strongest writing from the region, though, was prompted by meetings with individual survivors of concentration camps and of the city's ghetto. In one set of notes he transcribed a dislocated conversation held through an interpreter with two ghetto survivors: a Czech woman and a Russian-speaking Polish male doctor, both Jewish. They take turns speaking, a few sentences from one, a few from the next, then back again, and because they are speaking in different languages, there is no communication between them, no connection even of tone in their disconnected speeches—hers heavily ironic, his flatly devastated. The doctor had run a hospital in the ghetto but in the end the Germans took it all away, the patients to Auschwitz, such equipment as there was for their own purposes. Throughout the interview another male survivor, a laborer, perhaps an assistant, stood behind the seated doctor. "When he spoke of the departure of his hospital," Hersey wrote, "the doctor took his glasses off and put his hands over his face. The heavily set laborer let [fall] a stream of tears without seeming to change his expression." For years after, the Shoah occupied Hersey's imagination and was the topic of much of his best work, from "Tattoo Number 107,907,"[16] about a Berlin intellectual who survived the camps by having had the prudence to train as a welder, to *The Wall*.

As in his piece about Kennedy and his co-survivors in the Pacific, one of the matters that most interested him in these stories is the boundary line between chance and personal agency at the extremes of existence—"that mysterious, sometimes almost comical force for life . . . a frightful selfishness that in certain competitive struggles is the margin of survival"—and the problem of distinguishing this morally from man's capacity "to act on the worst in his nature."[17] Even or perhaps especially for someone living among other war correspondents, it wasn't easy to keep such thoughts in balance with day-to-day concerns.

Roscoe Senior died in March 1945.[18] Some of the impact of this bereavement on his widow and children must have been mitigated by his long illness, but that in itself was a grief to John all his life. Forty years later he chose as the epigraph to *The Call* a translation of some lines by the Chinese poet Wei Wen-ti:

> My thoughts are fixed on my sage parent.
> They say the good live long.
> Then why was he not spared?

He and Arthur now took on more of their mother's financial responsibilities. The men's letters to their mother around this time also often concern the middle brother, Rob, an architect in New York who was going through some personal difficulties and whose marriage had become rocky.

Glittering Prizes

Back in the United States, John Hersey was, he had almost forgotten, a celebrated writer. The stage version of *A Bell for Adano* was still running on Broadway, and the movie was on the brink of being released.[19] The novel was that year's Pulitzer Prize winner—Hersey learned about this on a Manhattan tennis court and assumed, at first, that his partner, Richard Lauterbach, was playing a practical joke on him.[20] A congratulatory letter arrived from Secretary of State Edward Stettinius; the Herseys went to a party given by the Knopfs for Jean-Paul Sartre; the portrait photographer and novelist Carl Van Vechten asked them to his sixty-fifth birthday celebration. It was all both exhilarating and worryingly removed from what mattered. In July 1945, to leave himself free for whatever came next, Hersey resigned from his permanent job at Time-Life.[21] He had no difficulty in securing promises of plenty of freelance work, both there and elsewhere.

The war was won, but the question remained when and how it would actually end. American casualties had increased steeply since D-Day. In the Pacific, a new kind of threat came from Japanese suicide pilots. At Los Alamos, meanwhile, a much bigger, more impersonal form of weapon had been developed in the utmost secrecy. During the summer of 1944, when Hersey was on his way to Moscow, U.S. advances in the Pacific included the capture of Tinian, within reach of mainland Japan and already half-prepared as a Japanese air base. By March 1945, with its immense runways and maintenance buildings, it could handle 480 airplanes every hour.[22] While the napalm firebombing of Japanese cities began—itself a savage new technology—crews were already training to deliver nuclear bombs. In June, civilian scientists from the Manhattan Project arrived. They were told to expect a long stay requiring six-month tours of duty. The future Nobel Prize winner in physics Norman Ramsey, in charge of the delivery group, understood from Robert Oppenheimer that around fifty nuclear bombs might be involved.

Hersey, of course, knew nothing about any of this, but bullish reports of the Pacific war reached him from his *New York Times* friend Bill Lawrence, who had been moved from Moscow to Okinawa. "The Jap is putting up a good fight here," Lawrence wrote chirpily to him in May 1945,

> and has been counterattacking for the last two days, including some landings by sea uncomfortably far behind our lines on the Marines' sector. He also is in the middle of what may or may not be his last gasp as an air power, but he's been flinging his bombs, sometimes accompanied by the plane itself, at our fleet, and occasionally venturing over the island to drop a cluster or two on the airstrip. Of course, that interrupts my sleep . . . Anyway, as Uncle Ed used to say, a lot of shooting certainly does annoy soldiers, and war correspondents.[23]

Life put Hersey on to researching and writing a piece about the kamikaze missions, some aspects of which—particularly a summary by the anthropologist Margaret Mead of the findings of a conference called "Japanese Character Structure"—would later prove useful to his writing about Hiroshima. The *Life* article appeared at the end of July.[24] By then Lawrence was in the Marianas and confided to him on Wednesday, July 25, "We've got a new first team in the air out here, and I think it's going to be lots of fun. I expect to have a very interesting piece on the front page Sunday."[25] He was over-anticipating, but not by much. The sporting jauntiness of his tone helps define by contrast what was new in Hersey's approach a year later.

It's not known how he responded at the time to the dropping of the nuclear bombs on August 6 and 9. From a military point of view the weapons were another new means of destruction among the many developed since the war began. As in other cases, efforts were made to conceal the human cost, especially to civilians, and accredited media outlets did their bit, *The New York Times* going so far as to head a September report "No Radioactivity in Hiroshima Ruins."[26] Politically it was to the Americans' advantage to present the bomb as having brought about the Japanese surrender, which thereby became an exclusive achievement of the United States, rather than something aided by the Russians. A separate element contributing to that outcome, the Soviet advance into Manchuria, had been encouraged by Roosevelt and Truman and began at the same time as the nuclear bombings but was now something the Western Allies wanted to stop. There were other massive pressures on Japan resulting from the steady destruction of its naval and air power and cutting off of supplies. The emperor had for a couple of months been seeking ways to surrender that wouldn't produce a rebellion by his army. None of this made headlines. From the point of view of most Americans, the story for the moment was that a devastating U.S. invention had brought the war to an abrupt end and would soon enable the weary troops to come home. As one of the decision makers was to write, "It's all well and good to come along later and say the bomb was a horrible thing. The whole goddamn war was a horrible thing."[27]

Hersey had already been giving some of his attention to the returning troops, their physical and psychological condition, and the problems of readjustment to civilian life, in ways that can be seen as preparing him for what was to become the most important of his themes. Even before going to Moscow, in a long *Life* article about the difficulties experienced by a physically disabled ex-GI, he had paused on an episode in which the veteran and his girlfriend went to the cinema. The film was the propagandist *Bombardier* (1943), the main action of which is set just after Pearl Harbor.[28] "Joe," as Hersey's real-life subject is inevitably called, finds himself unable to watch to the end:

> Everything was fine until a bomb came down on a Japanese; the Japanese was running towards the camera, the bomb went off, the concussion exploded a big oil drum and blew the Japanese to Japanese hell. Joe felt the blows and pains all through his body and his heart began pounding. He said, "Excuse me," to Mary, and he got up abruptly and left . . . Joe felt sick and upset all that night, and from the next day on things seemed to go badly. Joe began to be touchy all the time. People bothered him.[29]

This bellicose recruiting movie was famous for its special effects, and why anyone should have thought it suitable for a romantic excursion with a traumatized ex-soldier is not asked. But it's notable that while the morally convenient climax includes the capture, humiliation, torture, and deaths of the entire U.S. crew of a bomber that has gone ahead of the rest to mark the target, Hersey's damaged hero concentrates on a Japanese casualty.

Another *Life* piece by Hersey, published after the war ended, concerned a form of treatment being tried out on men suffering from post-traumatic stress disorder, then known as combat fatigue: in this case a physical complaint that had no apparent physical cause, "no disturbance in the structure of muscle or nerve or bone such as might have been caused by blast . . . nothing clinically except fatigue and slightly higher-than-normal blood pressure."[30] The patient, whom Hersey calls Erlanger, served in military reconnaissance in Germany and from January 1945 was in continuous frontline action for forty-six days. Dug in one night in a hillside vineyard alongside his friend Ting, Erlanger grumbled about feeling "pooped." Ting offered to do his friend's next point duty—going ahead at the front of the platoon—in exchange for four cigarette butts. The deal was done. Crawling some distance behind Ting through moonlit undergrowth near a farm, Erlanger heard a dog bark, then the noise of gunfire and grenades, then his substitute "hollering and screaming my name." Under fire, Erlanger managed to retrieve what was left of his dying comrade before the platoon was attacked by a mortar. Sheltering under Ting's corpse, he survived but, for reasons doctors hadn't subsequently been able to identify, could no longer use his right leg. He believed he had been recommended for a Bronze Star. Whether or not that was true, he was now in a special unit at Mason General Hospital, Brentwood, Long Island, where researchers were using the hypnotic drug amobarbital combined with psychotherapy in the hope of remedying his condition and others like it. Hersey observed the treatment[31] and, as in "Joe Is Home Now," his approach is to take his human subject on his own terms, describing his behavior and quoting his words without overt editorializing so that as readers we feel we are part, rather than recipients, of a process of assessment and judgment.

From now on, almost everything he wrote about the war concerned damage, irrespective of whom it was done to or by. It isn't difficult to trace a line of development through these and other articles toward *Hiroshima* and beyond, but they have separate qualities, both in themselves and in work he would publish in later years. To Hersey himself, what was most important was that he was now operating as a freelancer, commissioned partly by Time-Life but also by *The New Yorker*.[32] It was in his work for the latter that the advantages were immediately obvious.

In July 1945, while finishing the piece about suicide pilots, he began brushing up his Mandarin in preparation for the hoped-for return to China. Meanwhile, *The New Yorker* commissioned him to review a translation of the Soviet writer Konstantin Simonov's novel about Stalin-grad, *Days and Nights*.[33] Well judged as a piece of criticism, the article is exceptionally informative about the circumstances in which Soviet writers were received at home and disseminated abroad. Simonov's novel had been criticized in Moscow for its relative inattention to enlisted soldiers (Hersey doesn't mention that the author, a devout Communist, came from a once-grand, aristocratic background). Hersey describes an attempt to substitute a Soviet translation for the Western one commissioned by the U.S. publisher, a main difference being that the Soviet version omitted a character in the original who goes over to the Nazis. From the point of view of Hersey's own development, though, the most telling points he makes are about writing in close proximity to historical events and, relatedly, what he calls "the impermanent and local nature of . . . 'truth' in wartime." There's a danger in all wartime writing, he says, of "something editorial, a pamphleteering quality—what the Russians call *agitka*."

The distinction between this and a more neutral-seeming point of view may be ultimately a matter of tone, but after years of wartime stridency, and of Time-Life's homespun optimism, Hersey relished the opportunity to be subtle and complicated. Among the results was a piece of writing that had bigger and more immediate practical consequences than anything he had done before. The most obvious of the changes in his postwar journalism, though, lay in his developing critique of U.S. behavior abroad.

Whats China Doing This Week Questionmark

Toward the end of 1945, Hersey finally persuaded Time-Life jointly with *The New Yorker* to fund a trip to China and Japan. His tour included a journey on the Yangtze River with a *Life* photographer, Dmitri Kessel, which later germinated into his 1956 novella, *A Single Pebble*.[34] The two men also spent time in Beijing (then Peiping), where Hersey filed a vivid piece for *Life* about an entrepreneurial rickshaw puller.[35] The first article he sent back, though, was from Shanghai and appeared in *The New Yorker*. From the outset it focused on the diminution of British imperial power and its replacement by the American equivalent. At a time when the United States presented itself as morally opposed to what the old European empires had been doing, this was an unexpected parallel to draw and cast a cold light on Henry Luce's "American Century" as it was turning out in practice. The first paragraphs give a series of sketches, initially light in tone, of small-scale American cultural intrusion—a hamburger stand on the Bund opposite the Hong Kong and Shanghai Bank; a vendor of the two-string fiddle, the *hu ch'in*, playing a version of "Oh! Susanna"; the replacement of rickshaws with more modern vehicles ranging from a three-wheeled, bicycle-based version to another kind of *ch'e* (cart), the *jeepoo ch'e*, or jeep. But at this point the amiability is undermined by what's described. "It is true," Hersey says disarmingly, "that by American standards, pedestrian discipline in Shanghai's crowded streets leaves very much to be desired." So a number of jeep accidents have occurred— a "shockingly high" number, in fact, and shocking not just in their frequency:

> The worst . . . have happened when American military vehicles have plowed at full speed into the soft, infuriating mass of rickshaws, pedicabs, and humanity at street intersections. Jeep drivers have been able, in this way, to kill three or four persons and wound several at one plunge.[36]

The studied balance here—that "infuriating mass" of Chinese—combined with a sense of achievement on the part of the reckless, often intoxicated American drivers (who "have been able . . . to kill . . . at one plunge") is devastating in a way that, one soon sees, owes something to the contrasting reticence of the Chinese themselves. Visiting a hospital ward full of road-accident casualties, Hersey wants to ask one of them his opinion of Americans. The doctor advises him not to, but a nurse listening to the exchange supplies a caustically deferential response: "Naturally, he feels great discomfort in this connection."

From here, the piece moves on to some of the occupation's larger oddities: the extraordinarily high ratio of senior American officers to lower ranks, their opulent standard of living and their scope for permanent enrichment, whether at the level of cheap personal purchases or of major entrepreneurship. What stick in the mind, too, are some Swiftian images, among them the account of a "rickshaw derby" organized by enlisted men in which coolies, known for the occasion as "horses," give rides to specially chosen pretty girls called "jockeys" in a race for cheap prizes.

Hersey's main informants were Chinese, not Western, and his written sources were Shanghai newspaper stories about U.S. behavior. The next of what became a series of articles by him in *The New Yorker* that implicitly challenged current official opinion was more specifically Chinese in topic. "Letter from Chungking"[37] is focused on a visit to Chiang Kai-shek and his wife and measures the distance between how he found them then and the couple he had written about, not for the first time, in 1939.[38] The article was important to Hersey in further confirming the break between him and Luce, whose formerly energetic, decisive idol immediately struck Hersey as having been personally weakened by a war in which he had been forced into sharing power with his rival, Mao. The difference was still more apparent in Chiang's wife. Both seemed resigned to their eventual loss of power, but there is a personal barb against the West's overindulgence of the couple in Hersey's reference to "a story going the rounds" that Madame Chiang had made much, in a recent speech she gave in Shanghai, of having been among those who "fought the war in Chungking." Hersey comments, "Madame's flights about the world in private planes, her suite at the Waldorf and her floor at the Presbyterian Medical Center . . . are famous here."

He was unduly optimistic about America's chances of success in bringing about a Chinese coalition government of Communists, nationalists, and the Democratic League. There was more realism in his next article, "Letter from Peiping," published in *The New Yorker* on May 4, 1946, in which he showed, among other things, that what had already become civil war in China was further complicated in Shansi Province by the involvement of large numbers of un-repatriated Japanese now lending their support to the Communists. Once again the magazine offered not just space but also enough trust in its readers' intelligence for a richly ironic account of what he called "a war [in Shansi] which, according to official reports, does not exist . . . in which neither side ever attacks but in which both sides lose towns and suffer casualties."[39] He held everyone responsible for the breakdown in negotiations, including the politically unsophisticated and bureaucratically ponderous Americans, but his main charges were against Chiang's Central Executive Committee.

Unsurprisingly, word quickly reached Hersey that Luce was unhappy with the material coming out of their new arrangement. As early as March, Frances Ann, who was "pining for" her husband "something awful" but had been cheered up by hearing from William Shawn how pleased *The New Yorker* was with her husband's work, reported having had an awkward drink with Luce at the opera: "He wanted to know why you had a piece in *The New Yorker* and had done nothing for *Life*. I explained that you had just come back from a trip for *Life* and asked him how he liked the 'Letter from Shanghai.' He said 'I never read the *New Yorker*' in most sneering tones. Lovely guy."[40]

One of Hersey's Time-Life colleagues, Charles Wertenbaker, cabled him parodying Luce's sometimes homespun editorial approach. (Here, because telegrams required punctuation to be spelled out, "CMA" means comma, and "SPRING CHINA WARDS THIS WEEK MAYBE QUESTION-MARK" is a send-up of journalese in general as well as of Luce's appetite for color, meaning "Perhaps spring is arriving in China?")

WHAT WE REALLY NEED IS SOUND CMA SIGHT CMA TASTE CMA LOOK CMA SMELL CMA FEEL OF CHINA THEREFORE NEED BRIEF HISTORY CHINA ALSO EVALUATION CHINA TODAY STOP HOW BIG IS COUNTRY CMA HOW OLD CMA HOW GOOD CMA HOW MANY QUESTIONMARK OUR SOURCES VAGUE SO RELYING ON YOU STOP GIVE PLENTY COLOR LIKE SPRING CHINA WARDS THIS WEEK MAYBE QUESTIONMARK IF SO WHAT ARE FLOWERS CMA BIRDS CMA BEES . . . DOING QUESTIONMARK . . . NEED SOLIDEST DESCRIPTIONS STREET SCENES CMA CHILDRENS LAUGHTER CMA YOUNG LOVE CMA MAIDENS GIGGLES CMA WELL MANNERED BELCHES STOP WHATS CHINA DOING THIS WEEK QUESTIONMARK . . . HOPE YOU CAN KEEP TO 250 WORDS INCLUDING CHART PARA.[41]

Hersey's long "Letter from Peiping," meanwhile, soberly analyzed what the joint commission—including its nationalist representatives—had agreed, in particular about representation on the proposed All-Party National Assembly, and how nationalists not on the commission had subsequently scuppered its decisions by delays, modifications, and procedural manipulation. This wasn't directly, or at all, Chiang's doing, but his poor control of his party was another issue Luce did not want to face. "No matter what the United States does, I am afraid," Hersey accurately warned, "China is in for a long, sharp, bloody struggle."

During May 1946 he had a long piece in every issue of *The New Yorker*. For two of these—essentially a single article run over two weeks[42]—he hitched a ride on a large U.S. tank-landing ship transporting about nine hundred Chinese troops from Shanghai to north China. His aim was to learn more about the Chinese military, but it was about the Americans that he found out the most. The Chinese ranged in age from sixteen upward, and most had seen a good deal of action against the Japanese, especially in Burma. Very badly paid, dressed mostly in castoffs from the U.S., British, and Japanese armies, ill-fed, wholly unused to the sea and prone to nausea, they were humorous, mischievous in response to American discipline, but generally well behaved. The Americans in charge, by contrast, for the most part had experienced little military action, despised the people they called "chinks," ignored the well-intended advice transmitted to them by liaison officers, and treated the sophisticated English-speaking senior Chinese officer "in a manner they would not have dreamed of using to American enlisted men."

Fortunately for his belief in the United States, on his Yangtze voyage Hersey had met an American of whom he could make readers more proud. Walter Morse was a Christian medical missionary working in I-ch'ang (Yichang)[43] whom Hersey clearly saw as a version of his late father. His article is the first of many profiles he was to write for *The New Yorker*, and for various reasons his method—especially the way in which a personal quest of the author's makes itself felt through his scrupulous attention to someone else—is worth watching at close quarters.

Though entirely focused on its human subject and his daily activities, the article is also and avowedly an inquiry into the nature of happiness: a dangerous subject for literature ("happiness writes white," the saying goes—it leaves the page blank) and one that Hersey approached with a degree of trepidation disguised in the published version. The opening section, as it appeared in *The New Yorker* on May 11, 1946, begins and ends like this:

> The first time I saw Father Walter P. Morse, he was walking up the path of his mission compound, reading my calling card, over and over, out loud. I had gone there to talk with him, and his gateman had run out into the streets to find him . . . As he came closer and looked up, I saw a face of benignity, gentleness, humor, and calmness, with round cheeks, a large nose, and tremendous blue eyes; a face flushed a bit by his haste, and, in any case, somewhat reddened by a life spent mostly in the open air. "Hello!

Hello!" he said as if we were friends long parted, though in fact he had never seen me before . . .

. . . As I came to know him better, that evening and later on, I was obliged to decide that although he was a strange man in some respects, he was the happiest adult I had ever known. I thought, too, he realized how lucky he was. Once he said, after a long silence and apropos of nothing that had preceded, almost as if talking to himself, "Oh, yes, I'm a happy, happy man." I have wondered many times since I left Ichang about the basis of Father Walter's happiness; I have gone back over what I know about him, and I'm still not sure what his secret is.

In a draft among Hersey's papers, that last sentence ends differently:

and I wonder now, as I sit writing, whether, by reviewing every detail of the little I know about him, I can get at his secret. I don't know whether I can. I shall try.

The change is explicable as one of process rather than attitude. Hersey began by setting out what he was trying to do and, having tried, altered the wording to reflect his subsequent position. Perhaps there's no more to it than that. The story is, after all, Father Walter's own and can be summarized without reference to the author. Still, what it was about for Hersey clearly involved this "secret." To wonder "many times" about such a question, like wondering whether your parents' lives were worth living, is to ask something about yourself. In its oblique fashion, the profile is about Hersey: his idealism, his sense that if writing is a vocation, it still may not be quite good enough, his search for a hero. To want the secret of happiness may not mean that one is unhappy but must come from something like an absence of happiness, or perhaps in this case of faith. A friend and ally of Hersey's, the Pulitzer Prize–winning *New York Times* columnist Anthony Lewis, was to say, "One sensed underneath, in John, a pain suffered: perhaps personal, or perhaps the pain of knowing so much about man's inhumanity to man."[44]

The article's first part straightforwardly recounts Morse's early life, including a disillusioning period he spent as a Wall Street broker; his taking vows with the Anglican Cowley Fathers; missionary work and language learning in Korea, Japan, and China; and the Sino-Japanese war.

This section culminates in his quixotic determination to learn basic medicine during a period back in Boston; his collecting about a ton of supplies by the simple method of calling in person on the startled presidents of American pharmaceutical companies and telling them what he wanted; and accompanying the cargo via South Africa and India to the middle of China—a wartime journey that, with many frustrations and delays, took him two years. The second part concerns his daily work in I-ch'ang since he got there, supplies miraculously intact, in September 1945. It's a life entirely devoted to the poor except on Sundays, when there are religious observances and solitary recreations: reading, playing the piano, looking out into the garden. Every weekday, Father Walter sets up his open-air stall and is quickly surrounded:

> He wakes up now, literally by cock crow, at about four-thirty in the morning. He has each day a number of devotions to get through, including a reading of Mass. These he does early, and afterward he sterilizes his instruments, breaks out new bandages, and fills his medicine kit with what he thinks he will need that day. At eight o'clock he walks to his home-made clinic—the bombed-out, roofless anteroom of what was once a mission house in the town. He tucks a clean white apron under his beard and sits down on a wooden stall in the open air, walled in by whitewashed ruins, with a couple of piles of bricks as seats for waiting patients to whom standing is painful, and with his medicine kit, a large Gold Flake cigarette tin container holding what he affectionately calls "my various condiments" open beside him on a table made of rubble.
>
> The patients come in by the dozen off the street . . . An old water carrier whom he cured of an ulcer has appointed himself his assistant (at a modest salary) and he crouches beside the Gold Flake box, handing Father Walter bandages and instruments and boiled water or whatever he asks for. The Chinese idea of entertainment is not always ours; the patients crowd around Father Walter and watch with earthy delight as he cleans out a monstrous purple-and-green ulcer on a coolie's leg and covers it with Elastoplast, or probes a deep infection in a small boy's thigh and stuffs it with sulfa powder . . . There is no horror in these sights for them; there is only pleasure in watching Father Walter's gentle work and listening to his quaint remarks. His Chinese is the literary language that he learned in Korea, a tongue quite unlike the vernacular. "It is like talking

on a different plane," Father Walter says, "as if you used nothing but Platonic ideas."

It's irresistible; you want to read it aloud, to copy out the whole thing. Near the end there's a twist. Father Walter once treated a Chinese soldier who took the opportunity to steal his watch. The soldier has never returned the watch but now often comes to see the monk. Walter never mentions the theft directly to the perpetrator but assures him that "however bad a Chinese man may be on the outside, his heart is good." Everything is gathered up here: pragmatism, spirituality, greed, forgiveness, all among the ruins of war.

Still, the reader doesn't quite forget that this is Father Walter's story as told to John Hersey. It looks simple but is actually intricate. The American priest tells the young American writer that the Chinese soldier-thief asked him why he hadn't demanded reparations from the Japanese for his mission's losses during the war: "That's gone and past," Father Walter says he said. "They didn't know what they were doing."

> The soldier suddenly said, "If everyone in the world were like you, Father Walter, there would be no trouble anywhere."
> Father Walter was very gay when he told me this story. He laughed off the soldier's tribute. "I don't know that that's true," he said. All the same, I think he has a sneaking feeling that it is.

These are the last words. In the course of a few sentences we've gone from a sense that we're reading a reliable narrative ("Father Walter said," "The soldier suddenly said") to a sharp reminder of its double subjectivity—Father Walter's account as filtered through, and commented on by, Hersey. And the "I," however quietly the writer reintroduces himself, is momentous. After the opening section, while Hersey has been present as a consciousness, he hasn't mentioned himself at all. Yet we saw that the opening was crucially autobiographical: the account of his meeting the priest and wanting to find his secret, just as the priest is first seen trying to make sense of Hersey, "reading my calling card, over and over, out loud."

Within days of the article's publication, donations from readers for Father Walter's work began arriving at *The New Yorker*. After consultation with him, the money was spent on buying and shipping basic medical

supplies: Elastoplast, multivitamins, rolled bandages in sterile boxes, an-
tibacterial sulfonamides.[45] But the benefits to his project in I-ch'ang
were short-lived; civil war and Communist revolution soon forced him to
move to Tibet and then Taiwan. For many years, he and Hersey corre-
sponded intermittently, catching up with each other in the way of people
whose mutual understanding goes beyond anything to do with news. Social impact apart, the article immediately confirmed Hersey's standing
at *The New Yorker*. William Shawn had cabled the writer at the Wagons
Lits Hotel, Peking: "YOUR MISSIONARY PROFILE ARRIVED [AND] WE ARE
OVERJOYED WITH IT PERIOD A MOVING AND VERY FASCINATING PIECE
PERIOD."[46]

The telegram also outlined thoughts on a major new project. Before
turning to it, Hersey wrote two more articles from China, one for *The New
Yorker*, the other for *Life*. Between them, they add to one's sense of his
greater freedom in his new editorial home while also illustrating the awkward balance involved in his liberal views at this stage in China's history.
Each was about a different village in northern China. Each used "human
interest" as a way toward a wider view of what was happening politically at a national level. The one for *Life* (which didn't appear until August
1946), is safe, conservative, essentially reassuring; Henry Luce could not
have found anything objectionable in it. The *New Yorker* piece is more
challenging—dangerously so in what was becoming the new U.S. political
climate. Both told the truth.

The *Life* article, "Red Pepper Village," depicts a rural world marked by
endurance, communal life, and susceptibility to a combination of luck and
climatic variation—to the laws of "Wind and Water," as capricious seeming and remote as the workings of politics. The village happens to be in
an area garrisoned, at considerable cost to local people, by nationalist
troops. But its people expect no better of the Communists camped on
every side except the north: "All they want is to be left alone to till their
land." Hersey is clear that the community's agricultural methods can't provide for increasingly pressing outside needs as distinct from mere subsis-
tence. One form of modernization strikes him as essential: education. He
describes a teacher's efforts with some care. Still, he is attracted by aspects
of this preindustrial way of life that seemed instructive to the developed
world: "Unlike Americans, Chinese do not make a sharp distinction between work and play." He's vivid about Chinese humor—practical jokes,

nicknames, and small subversions—and ends his story with a scene of children dancing to a "queer, happy song." This is truly a case of "SOLID-EST DESCRIPTIONS STREET SCENES CMA CHILDRENS LAUGHTER": *Life* at its popular-anthropological best.

In *The New Yorker*, his manner is different: brisk, unsentimental, alert to the problems of writing about the Communist-ruled area to which "Crow Village," recently retaken from the Japanese, belongs.[47] He starts out by clarifying the conditions under which he did his research, the freedom he was allowed by Chinese Communist local authorities in contrast with those under whom he had worked in the Soviet Union, his ability not only to ask questions but also to check the answers with other people. The focus then turns to how the local Communist regime is dealing with the situation left by the Japanese, constructing a viable and fair tax system and introducing mildly progressive agricultural methods (Hersey contrasts this in passing with the nationalist-ruled village he had just visited). With hindsight it isn't difficult to see where what's described would prove vulnerable. Still, he doesn't make extravagantly optimistic claims and is persuasive when he turns again to improvements in education, alert to propagandist elements in what's being imparted but also to how new methods, among them the shift away from rote learning and the emphasis on literacy and numeracy, were providing people with the beginnings of ways of interpreting for themselves what they were told. Most valuable of all is the combination of sociology—his account of how the new administration worked, with its complex, self-regulating if often mutually canceling structures of committees—and semi-irrelevant detail of the kind more often associated with fiction. The story ends with an official meeting, immediately followed by an encounter with a local farmer whose opportunism, it's implied, will always be part of what keeps some people on top. As soon as the Japanese left, Mr. Yang went into town and picked up various salable items they had exacted from the locals but left behind—cotton thread, bags of flour. He then sold them back to the Chinese. It was the beginning of a small empire and Hersey found him

> apparently quite pleased, in spite of himself, with the practical benefits of a program which, he was beginning to persuade himself, he had helped to invent. He was pleased, too, with being an official.
>
> After talking for a few more minutes he abruptly announced that he

was going to go and get something to eat, and, taking another cigarette from the pack on the table, he stood up to leave. Then he cleared his throat grandly, spat on the floor, grinned, and walked away.

Over the coming decades, Hersey would write about Chinese politics and education in various ways. For now his thoughts turned to Japan. In May, authorization came through from the U.S. military authorities for him to proceed from Shanghai to Tokyo.[48] He was concerned that fast-changing current events might make what was initially planned as a series of articles on Hiroshima seem unnewsworthy, but William Shawn cabled to reassure him: "THE MORE TIME THAT PASSES THE MORE CON-VINCED WE ARE THAT [THE] PIECE HAS WONDERFUL POSSIBILITIES PE-RIOD NO ONE HAS EVEN TOUCHED IT PERIOD."[49] Besides, although in detail the story had still scarcely been told, its impact had reached every corner of the world. On his travels in rural north China, Hersey met a sophisticated village head who had not heard of "Tu Lu-men (Truman) . . . Chu Chi-erh (Churchill) or Shi-Taling (Stalin)." Nonetheless, he was able to give "the exact circumference, in Chinese miles, of the area destroyed by an American atomic bomb at Hiroshima."[50]

So Far from Home

To most Americans, Japan was, as John Ciardi put it, "so far from home, almost beyond return."[51] The airman-poet, a future translator of Dante and friend of Hersey's, meant among other things that bombing raids took aircrews to the literal limit of their fuel capacity. But he had moral distance in mind, too. In committing murder on the scale achieved by even the "conventional" onslaught on Japanese cities between 1944 and 1945, ordinary Americans found themselves well outside their moral gravity field. Ciardi, a Boston-born child of poor Italian immigrants, had graduated from Tufts, completed an M.A. at Michigan, and done some university teaching before enlisting in the U.S. Air Force and becoming a B-29 gunner. He flew twenty missions over Japan and was one of the war's leading poets. His line half-quotes a Victorian hymn by John Henry Newman, familiar in those days: "The night is dark and I am far from home."[52] Strengthened by this association, Ciardi's poem expresses two things that also lie behind Hersey's account of the bombing of Hiroshima: that the war has taken America beyond some fundamental limit and that—whatever the overall moral balance between the two sides—part of this lies in the physical separation between bomber and bombed.

Much of *Hiroshima*'s power comes from its reduction of that gap. The "Far East" may have been far from home to most Americans, but it wasn't to John Hersey. The by then well-known, well-connected writer keeps himself entirely out of the narrative while recording the experiences of half a dozen Japanese survivors, using words that, as in a novel, are sometimes their own but more often linguistic approximations to how they think. Those individuals, and those experiences, become as "real" to the sympathetic reader as it is possible for anything vicarious to be. No general statements or conclusions are offered, no explicit judgment is reached. In the Hiroshima Peace Museum, looking at a photograph, perhaps of victims opening their parched mouths to drink in the radioactive "black rain" that fell from the famously beautiful cloud caused by the explosion, you remain a spectator: horrified, intimate, but separate. To read *Hiroshima*, by contrast, involves losing consciousness of anything else.

Because the event became so strongly identified with the peace movement as well as with campaigns specifically for nuclear disarmament (or against nuclear proliferation), and because Hersey's writing was so important to them, it's worth acknowledging in advance some of the main arguments against the book. All antiwar literature tells us something we already know: that war is hideous. It does this in part by focusing on individual experience and, where that is factual, it is intrinsically unjust to what other individuals have gone through. The objection—it might be epitomized as "Why Anne Frank (rather than other people who suffered similarly)?"—is important in terms not only of fairness but also of human powers of understanding and representation: all art, all history, fails to encompass the scale of world events, the sheer numbers affected. War seems to require big words, intensifiers, bold type, and while noisy anger can deafen listeners there are those who find quiet irony such as Hersey's insultingly inadequate to the case.[53] Then, too, kinds of measurement beyond the aesthetic force themselves in. What exactly, or even approximately, does the Hiroshima bomb score on the damage gauge? Is it worse than the "conventional" firebombing of Tokyo or Dresden, which caused about 100,000 deaths each? How does it compare with the siege and battle of Stalingrad (approximately two million deaths, taking into account both sides and including civilians)? Or with—at this writing—the latest nonnuclear American weapon, nicknamed MOAB for "the mother of all bombs," dropped on eastern Afghanistan? In any case, numbers seem irrelevant. Perhaps we need an individual suffering-quotient, one that will do justice to the Chinese woman gang-raped by Japanese soldiers, the GI on the Bataan march, the dissident tortured in the gulag, the child looking for her parents in the ruins of Berlin. Then maybe a grade for courage would have to be factored in. If we could arrive at such figures and add up all the scores of all the individuals concerned, would we be any closer to the truth?

Hersey makes no measurements. Many years later, he wrote the text for a book of photographs by Ansel Adams documenting the wartime internment of people of Japanese origin—70 percent of whom were U.S. citizens—in the deserts of the American southwest.[54] Adams's pictures, he said in words that apply even more to his own work, "burn one's eyes."

6. Pyramid, Sun, and Cube

IN THE 1960s Hersey included *Hiroshima* in a selection of his pieces optimistically titled *Here to Stay: Studies in Human Tenacity*. Optimism isn't what most readers have felt as they put the narrative down. True, among his colleagues one or two remained apparently untouched. A perhaps slightly envious Brendan Gill teased him, "Dear Johnnie: All of us are delighted to see . . . that you have more or less put an end to the possibility of war. We can breathe easier now." But most said how moved they were, how proud to be associated with the work. One of *The New Yorker*'s most influential and respected editors, Katharine White, wrote,

> Dear Mr. Hersey:
>
> Among all the letters you will be receiving, one from a New Yorker editor on vacation and an editor whom you've never met, will be just a burden. But I can't help sending you just a word to say how deeply moved I am that we could publish and give over one issue to a piece of writing which will surely prove one of the most influential of our time. It's an amazing piece of reporting which has made me sleepless but thankful.[1]

She added that her husband, the author E. B. White, "feels just as I do about it." The magazine's European correspondent Janet Flanner wrote soberly to her editors about the issue's impact on war-hardened correspondents in Rome: "The impression at the Stampa Estera building here where the foreign press has its offices was like a blow. The installments [individual sections] created complete silence around each man reading, even in the bar."[2]

Practically speaking, perhaps it made no difference. True, there has been no great enthusiasm to use nuclear weapons, but this situation is unstable, and they have scarcely gone out of existence. Arguments continue over the justifiability of deploying the bomb in 1945, both at Hiroshima and in combination with the similarly unwarned-of, bigger weapon at Nagasaki. We know far more now than people did in 1945–46 not only about the cost of last-ditch resistance by Japanese troops to attacks from the sea—at the time, the least unacceptable argument for using the weapons—but also about the hideous destructiveness of nonnuclear bombing raids on other mainland Japanese (as well as European) cities, in the context of which Little Boy and Fat Man were from a military point of view just one more thing after another. And there was the need to discourage the fast-developing Soviet invasion of Manchuria. Afterward, Japanese officials were able to present their people as hapless victims of a war crime, to a degree that helped them shrug off condemnation of atrocities Japan itself had committed in the "long" Second World War, especially in China, where its incursions had involved chemical weapons as well as the torture of captives.

At bottom, the issue was and is less strategic than apocalyptic. Human beings have always imagined some kind of world-ending event, but whatever form it was thought likely to take, until 1945 it was always supposed to be beyond direct human control. Divine anger might destroy everything; so might a cosmic collision. Now, it became clear, a trigger-happy head of state would suffice. And if we began to realize how easily it could be encompassed, we had learned from Hersey what it would be like. All that, presumably, is what silenced the hacks in the Stampa Estera bar. *Hiroshima* still has similar effects. It has never gone out of print.

Box 37

How did Hersey—not Japanese, not an eyewitness, not a scientist—come to be the first person to communicate the experience to a global audience?

Some of the answers are squashed into a fat cardboard box normally kept in a temperature-controlled, secure warehouse in Hamden, Connecticut. This is the depository of much of the vast collection of rare books and manuscripts held by Yale's Beinecke Library, itself on the Yale campus in New Haven and among the architect Gordon Bunshaft's most beautiful buildings, though one that the poet Czesław Miłosz, whose own papers are there, compared to a monumental tomb.[3] Outside the reading room, in a sunken quadrangle, stands a three-piece white marble sculpture by Isamu Noguchi, who—like almost all other Japanese Americans but in his case voluntarily—spent the Second World War in an internment camp.[4] His Zen-influenced "The Garden (Pyramid, Sun, and Cube)" symbolizes what the catalog of Yale's public art calls a balance of cosmic forces and a synthesis of East and West. A similar synthesis, not beautiful to look at but imaginatively still more compelling, is to be found in Box 37 of the Hersey papers.

In it are fourteen individual file folders, miscellaneous in their contents except that all have to do with Hersey's *Hiroshima*: letters from readers, some friends, many strangers; page proofs, contracts, telegrams from overseas publishers; a report that General MacArthur has denied preventing the book's being published in Japanese; details of a braille edition; a list of eighty-plus periodicals that have carried the original article in full. Much comes from later years: letters from children who have read the book at school; details of a grisly U.S. tour arranged in 1955 for the "Hiroshima Maidens," otherwise known as the "Keloid Girls" (keloid is the name of a particularly disfiguring type of scar, and these twenty-five women, all of whom were at school in Hiroshima ten years earlier, were given reconstructive surgery in the States). One folder, though, is more coherent, and revealing about the processes of Hersey's research and writing. It contains

- Hersey's military authorization, dated May 21, 1946, to proceed from Shanghai to Tokyo.
- The Pacific edition of *Time* magazine for February 11, 1946. On

small, flimsy paper, the issue—six months earlier than the famous *New Yorker* number—reprints from a Jesuit journal an article by Father Johannes Siemes, SJ, a German missionary in Hiroshima, describing his experience of the explosion and its aftermath. A carbon copy of Siemes's typescript is also in the folder. (I'll come back to why the piece didn't have the same impact as Hersey's.)

- The calling cards of some Japanese contacts with handwritten English transliterations: "Dr. Sasaki," "Dr. M. Fujii."
- Photographs of disfigured survivors.
- A mimeograph copy of a Japanese technical report written in English headed "Statistics of Damages Caused by Atomic Bombardment Aug. 6, 1945. Foreign Affairs Section, Hiroshima City."
- Lab reports on tests of blood taken from another Jesuit, Wilhelm Kleinsorge, in the months immediately after the bombing.
- An offprint of a 1926 scientific article by Masao Tsuzuki, at that time assistant professor of oral surgery in the medical department of the Imperial University, Tokyo, titled "Experimental Studies on the Biological Action of Hard Roentgen Rays," reprinted from *The American Journal of Roentgenology and Radium Therapy*, vol. xxvi, no. 2, pages 134–150.
- An extract, annotated by Hersey, from *United States News* dated July 5, 1946, titled "Atomic Bomb. First Official Report on Damage to Japan. Full Text of U.S. Strategic Bombing Survey's Findings."
- A note in English to Hersey from the Reverend Kiyoshi Tanimoto, a U.S.-educated Japanese Methodist minister in Hiroshima, apologizing for not having been at home when Hersey called, suggesting a meeting the next day, and enclosing a hastily handwritten account of his experiences of the bombing.
- "A Preliminary Report Prepared by the Research Commission of the Imperial City of Kyoto on the Disaster in Hiroshima City Caused by the Atomic Bomb," again with Hersey's annotations.

Some of what catches the eye among these relics are what the first readers of Hersey's article noticed, too. As we've seen, U.S. media had needed little encouragement from Washington to portray the Japanese as a race of cartoon monsters, bug-eyed, big-toothed, rapacious. Here we find that among these ogres were doctors, secretaries, clergy—people not unlike readers of *The New Yorker*. Over the weeks after his arrival in Japan, Hersey interviewed Kiyoshi Tanimoto and other survivors and found links between some of their narratives, including those of Hatsuyo Nakamura, a woman with three children whose tailor husband had been killed in the Japanese invasion of Singapore, and Toshiko Sasaki, a twenty-year-old woman engaged to a soldier. The article eventually interlaced six people's experiences, a structure that he said later he had taken from Thornton Wilder's *The Bridge of San Luis Rey*, the narrator of which tells the stories of a group of (invented) individuals linked only by their fate: they are all on an Inca rope bridge when it collapses into a Peruvian ravine in 1714. Hersey read the novella during an illness while he was on his way to Japan. But he was being modest. His war reporting had always been about recognizable people, arbitrarily conjoined in their dreadful experiences and seen in all their variety.

This is the first of the things that distinguish his article from Johannes Siemes's, vivid though that is and widely available though it had been, thanks to *Time*. Siemes was writing for his coreligionists, and although his experiences were "authentic," W. G. Sebald was right in his later insistence that this is the least of qualifications; what matters is how well you write.[5] The differences are apparent within a few lines. Siemes says:

> August 6th began in a bright, clear summer morning . . . I am sitting in my room at the Novitiate of the Society of Jesus in Nagatsuka; during the past half year, the philosophical and theological section of our Mission had been evacuated to this place from Tokyo. The Novitiate is situated approximately two kilometers from Hiroshima . . . From my window, I have a wonderful view down the valley to the edge of the city. Suddenly—the time is approximately 8:14—the whole valley is filled with a garish light that resembles the magnesium light used in photography, and I am conscious of a wave of heat. I jump to the window to find the cause of this remarkable phenomenon.

And Hersey:

> At exactly fifteen minutes past eight in the morning, on August 6, 1945, Japanese time, at the moment when the atomic bomb flashed above Hiroshima, Miss Toshiko Sasaki, a clerk in the personnel department of the

South East Asia Tin Works, had just sat down at her place in the plant office and was turning her head to speak to the girl at the next desk. At the same moment, Dr. Masakazu Fujii was settling down cross-legged to read the Osaka *Asahi* on the porch of his private hospital . . . Mrs. Hatsuyo Nakamura, a tailor's widow, stood by the window of her kitchen, watching a neighbor tearing down his house because it lay in the path of an air-raid defense fire lane.

It's quietly done, but Hersey immediately gets more in: information, irony (those futilely self-sacrificial air-raid precautions), immediacy, suspense, and especially—though here there's a caveat—attention to Japanese people.

There were also two surprises. In 1946 readers didn't expect an American to deal so sympathetically with this subject. And whereas *Time* was a newsmagazine, *The New Yorker*, as many reports on the story commented more or less facetiously, was at the time generally associated with light entertainment. (One subscriber complained, "I look forward to my weekly *New Yorker*, not for an informative Treatise, but fun and relaxation. Promise this [the *Hiroshima* number] is the end of such.")[6] Still, Hersey was helped by and quotes from Siemes's piece, which also crucially alerted him to the Catholic mission as a useful source of contacts.[7] The next character he introduces in his article, in fact, is Wilhelm Kleinsorge, "a German priest of the Society of Jesus, reclin[ing] in his underwear on a cot." He's the man whose ominous lab reports are also in this folder: "19/9/45 W[hite] B[lood] C[ount] 3,600. Haemoglobin 50%. Polymorphs 35% . . . Blood Colour Index 0.67%." In a section added forty years later, Hersey described the long, painfully various illnesses these clinical measurements gave the priest warning of.[8] Though less vocal than Tanimoto, Father Kleinsorge is a key figure in the narrative and before that was crucial to Hersey's research, introducing him first to Tanimoto and then, through their joint networks, to all the book's other main characters, as well as writing his own account of his experiences on which Hersey also drew.

The decision to focus solely on people physically affected by the bomb came early on, so Hersey's cast doesn't include Masao Tsuzuki, author of the 1926 paper on radiation, which he nonetheless read and filed. In the 1920s, the point of radiation was to benefit people by looking inside their bodies—the procedure found so worrying in its intimacy by Thomas Mann's Hans Castorp in *The Magic Mountain*—and destroying anything malign that was growing there. Unwelcome side effects of such treatment soon became a concern, and it was these that Tsuzuki had examined in a series of experiments on rabbits: tests of various levels of intensity, some using "the hardest rays such as are employed in the so-called modern deep therapy," with observation of their immediate and subsequent consequences: numbers of deaths, "Average Living Days," and effects on different parts of the rabbits' bodies including their lymphatic system. "After irradiation," he noted, "all animals look as if they were exhausted and gradually become thinner, frequently suffer from diarrhea, and their vital resistance is so much weakened that they die from the slightest injury . . . few of them show power of recuperation." At the time, in rejoinders printed at the end of his article, Tsuzuki's American colleague-critics defensively pointed out that in medical treatment only part of the patient is irradiated, whereas the whole body of the rabbit was exposed in his procedures, but in 1945 his methods proved more relevant than anyone could have anticipated.

By then, Tsuzuki—still based at what is now the University of Tokyo—headed the medical section of the Japanese Research Council. Immediately after the explosion he traveled to Hiroshima and, as best he could, began a research program there, mentioned by Hersey, into the impacts of the event, chiefly of heat, blast, primary radiation, and what the scientist called "radioactive poisonous gas," on people in the hospital. His entire career had been an unconscious preparation for this event, and because of what he was finding out and his eminence, he quickly became an embarrassment to the occupying power. Everything was done to keep him quiet, while U.S. scientists, or so he claimed, were busy pinching his results. All this is another story, told briefly but vividly much later in a 1994 book by a science historian, M. Susan Lindee: *Suffering Made Real: American Science and the Survivors at Hiroshima*. And while *Hiroshima* doesn't involve Tsuzuki, it draws on his and other Japanese research summarized in this folder—particularly the city's official research into the bomb's impact.

The earliest American investigations tended, as Hersey acerbically pointed out,[9] to lay most emphasis on material damage:

> Scientists swarmed into the city. Some of them measured the force that
> had been necessary to shift marble gravestones in the cemetery, to knock

over twenty-two of the forty-seven railroad cars in the yards at Hiroshima station, to lift and move the concrete roadway on one of the bridges, and to perform other noteworthy feats of strength.

Here and elsewhere among his papers, by contrast, are summaries of interviews with his human informants during the six weeks he spent in Hiroshima. Tanimoto and Kleinsorge were especially valuable. The young clergymen's churches were close to each other, and they worked together. Also nearby was one of Hiroshima's most beautiful gardens, Shukkeien Park, formerly land belonging to the town's sixteenth-century castle. When U.S. air raids on Japanese cities began in 1944, the park was designated an official evacuation area for local people—not very sensibly, since the castle itself had long been a military headquarters and was therefore an obvious target. In the event it was close to the A-bomb explosion's epicenter and, for those still alive, on a main route of retreat from the worst of the heat and destruction to a less badly affected area of the city, north of the park but separated from it by the tidal Kyobashi-gawa River. So these Catholic and Methodist missions were at the hub of some of the intensest relief efforts on August 6, 1945. Hersey went to see Kleinsorge as soon as he arrived in the city, and after they had talked, Kleinsorge sent him on to his Methodist colleague. Tanimoto was out when Hersey called, the American left his card, and the minister, worried that he might miss him altogether, wrote him a long handwritten account of his part in the events. A covering note explained the duties that had just taken him away, only nine months since the bomb was dropped: "I am very sorry being out when you visited me yesterday. I have to go to school for teaching this morning as already scheduled."

Hersey returned, and Tanimoto later recorded his impressions of this "tall gentleman with an oval face" who was wearing a uniform but "had about him the refinement of a literary man." Hersey's missionary background and Eastern early upbringing immediately made a connection that kindled the minister's always quick enthusiasm: "I felt as if I had met with an old friend of mine," he wrote, and "now recollecting, it appears I overtalked on it."[10] The two men formed a lasting relationship.

Brought up as a Buddhist, the Reverend Mr. Kiyoshi Tanimoto (Hersey gives all his characters their full names in Anglicized form: a gesture to good manners especially noticeable at a time when the Japanese were still demonized, but also a way of asserting their status in ways immediately graspable in the West) was among the survivors who made indefatigable-seeming efforts on behalf of other people in Hiroshima—in his case, rounding them up, bringing them water, rowing them to what he hoped was safety. He gained particular prominence in Hersey's account because of his distinctive voice, spoken and written, with its touching modesty as well as its confusions and linguistic errors. He was, Hersey tells us in one of his many rapid, precise sketches, "a small man, quick to talk, laugh, and cry. He wore his black hair parted in the middle and rather long; the prominence of the frontal bones just above his eyebrows and the smallness of his mustache, mouth, and chin gave him a strange, old-young look, boyish and yet wise, weak and yet fiery." It's this unlikely hero who plunges into something like hell and saves everyone he can. And the attention to his hair, his bones, his skin on this early page unobtrusively prepares our responses for the kinds of damage we'll soon encounter: people with their hair on fire, melting flesh, broken and putrefying bodies.

To read the finished text against its sources is to see how subtly Hersey preserves the idiosyncrasies of Tanimoto's text while for the most part resisting the easy "color" of just quoting it. But in the silence of the Beinecke Library, with the light shifting across the sculpture outside the window, the minister's own words, written for Hersey that summer night in 1946, carry an emotional charge all their own. "God help and take them out of the fire," Hersey quotes Tanimoto as having prayed as he necessarily ignored the helpless in favor of those for whom he hoped he could do something. But while Hersey gives us the essence of what immediately follows in Tanimoto's hastily scribbled version, he doesn't reproduce it. Here is Tanimoto:

> In the result I made a long round way. As far as I went there were full of wounded people, men and woman, boy and girls, even babies. I was only one who was completely safe. Passing through among them I repeated in my mouth, "Excuse me for having no burden like you do."
>
> When I reached the bank of the river Ota, I jumped myself into the river, knowing no bridge to cross on account of fire. But the river was too wide and deep for me. The stream run as fast that I was about to be drowned, having lost my strength to swim. When I arrived at another bank, I was necked, no shirt and no shoes to wear.

Finally I got back to Sentei, the bank of Ota River, next to my residencial section of the city. As I had told my neighbors, they got together and gathered there. It was my first concern to see my church and parsonage. I thrust into the fire and run about 100 yards, but on behalf of fierceness of the blaze I gave up my desire to see the church.

On having returned to the bank, I found a Jemma-sen, Japanese boat, on the rocks. There were five men who were already dead. With a short prayer I took out these dead bodies and pulled down the boat into the river and rowed across with a bamboo bar instead of oar and let the wounded people cross the river all the day long.[11]

Avenues a Hundred Yards Wide

No other book by Hersey is as famous or as difficult to write about. In the first place, it seems so easily done. Like the best lyric poems, it speaks directly for (but, significantly, not about) itself: the would-be commentator is left feeling redundant. Yet there are things that it's useful for a reader to know about it because they help explain not only how it was written and the context in which it appeared but also how it has grown over the years. It also had unintended, unforeseeable, and occasionally unwelcome side effects.

The immediate research was rapid. In that spring of 1946 Hersey spent six weeks in Hiroshima with his notebook and a translator. Having talked to Kleinsorge and Tanimoto, he interviewed several dozen other survivors. Few of them could become principal characters, but material from many of their stories would be incorporated into the text one way or another. Before he started, Hersey had more or less decided on Wilder's device of focusing on half a dozen people, introducing others through them, and it quickly proved suitable, giving the narrative focus and coherence while also, through human interconnections and sheer coincidences, throwing into relief the smallness of the community afflicted by so vast and mysterious a destructive force. Hiroshima is still a town you can stroll across in half an hour. Because of air raids on other cities, many people had been evacuated by August 1945, leaving a population of about 300,000—or 255,000 if you discount troops stationed there. By the time Hersey arrived in 1946, new roads were being laid, buildings were going up or being restored, and the remaining scorched landscape was covered with the vivid plant life he describes. But the center as a whole, on a plain intersected by rivers and surrounded by hills, remained eerily waste, the ashes of the previously predominant wooden houses throwing into defiant or ironic contrast a sprinkling of more solid structures that had survived. One of these was and is the Red Cross hospital in which Dr. Sasaki did what he could for the tens of thousands who made their halting way there in those first, terrifying hot August days. Another is the staunch granite Hiroshima branch of the Bank of Japan, its uncracked safes the proud work of Herring-Hall-Marvin of Hamilton, Ohio. Among that firm's profitable wartime sidelines had been the manufacture of uranium slugs for atom bombs.[12]

In almost every external way, the Hiroshima Hersey got to know but didn't describe was an American base employing native Japanese staff. The hangarlike curved-roofed labs established on a hill to the southeast of the epicenter—now the Radiation Effects Research Foundation—still stand, but the extent to which Americans were responsible for planning the whole new town is less often remarked. Hersey satirized the grandiosity of these efforts ("avenues a hundred yards wide"), including the notion that a group of commemorative buildings might be erected and named the "Institute of International Amity."[13] (It's true that the eventual Hiroshima Peace Memorial Museum, vividly painful though it and its surroundings are, doesn't escape overoptimism.) Again, we hear about censorship, but mostly as an abstract activity, a concept. There could be a rougher side to the occupation, as a London *Daily Express* writer, Wilfred Burchett, found when he challenged the official denial of radiation sickness at a press conference in autumn 1945. Burchett was quickly subjected by the military to what was said to be a routine medical test, and then hospitalized. There was nothing wrong with him, but while he was shuffled between authorities, his camera and film went missing, and when he tried to go back to work, he learned that his press accreditation had been withdrawn.[14] Stories like this got around among reporters, which may have been why *The New Yorker* encouraged Hersey to keep his stay short and to do his writing back in the United States.[15] The main reason he doesn't talk much about the occupation, though, is that his subject predates all that and from every point of view is more important.

The narrative is in four sections (a fifth was added much later).[16] The first, "A Noiseless Flash," tells what his characters were doing at the moment the bomb was dropped and what immediately happened to them. The second, "The Fire," continues the story over the rest of that day. "III. Details Are Being Investigated" stays with everyone through the agonies of the first night and the following days and weeks, during which many who have seemed unhurt begin to vomit and die; Miss Sasaki, her leg broken, lies helpless beside two hideous near-corpses; those who remain active continue their rescue work in a state of blind exhaustion; and the emperor makes his surrender broadcast. We'll come to the fourth section in a moment, but what's important is the rapidity with which all this was put down, and the very small amount of revision that was involved in shaping it.[17]

Hersey's return trip by boat gave him scope for an uninterrupted review of his notebooks and the printed materials he had collected. He worked like a war poet as much as a journalist. The power of his text is not just a matter of its raw material. There is his startling intimacy with the people he writes about: with poor maddened Mr. Fukai, determined to break free of his rescuers and run back into the flames to die; with Dr. Sasaki, wearing spectacles he has borrowed from a nurse, applying first aid to surviving patients and staff in what's left of the Red Cross hospital, while outside the injured in every quarter of the city begin making their way there; with the clergy's determination to rescue their sacred bits and pieces. Some readers, while understanding Hersey's wish to engage his American readership, are impatient with the unrepresentative predominance of Christians in his narrative, which, while partly a matter of his own background, was more so of his means of access. By poetry, though, I mean something to do with language as much as sympathy. On the one hand, there's his fastidiousness in deploying the idioms of his witnesses. On the other, there's a poet's alertness to what he finds and can use. In this folder in Box 37 we see him searching not just for facts, but for words.

An example is a passage of the Hiroshima City Foreign Affairs Section's report that gripped him when he came to writing the fourth part of his article. The heading is "On the Influence upon Plants of the Atomic Bomb in Hiroshima . . . by 4 Botanists of Kyoto University." Hersey's teenage letters home from Hotchkiss had shown an early responsiveness to his natural surroundings, to seasonal changes in the woods of New England. Now he was reading about enforced change: effects on the vegetation, at different distances from the explosion's center, of temperatures previously unfamiliar to botanical researchers and to which a surprising number of species proved resistant. "It is striking," the botanists eloquently recorded, that

> cassia tora was growing everywhere about the explosion center, as if this plant had been dropped together with the bomb. It stood not only in fragmentary rows among dead remnants of the same plant, but also here and there on riversides on the sites of burned houses. Owing to the[ir] hardness and very remarkable longevity, many seeds of this plant may remain ungerminated in the soil. So it is supposed that such resting seeds were stimulated to germinate by some agencies caused by the bomb.

Farther out, five hundred to two thousand meters from the center of the explosion—an area they called the "second zone"—they noted:

> Fire in this area. Wooden telegraph poles of cryptomeria japonica were charred on radiated side—temperature must have been raised above carbonization point, which, for cryptomeria japonica is ca. 240 C. In this zone many plants were found to survive, such as cercis chinensis,[18] fatsia japonica, buxus microphylla, wisteria floribunda, spiraea prunifolia, trachelospermum asiaticum, parthenocissus tricuspidata, ardisia japonica, celtis sinensis, rhododendron, quercus glauca, bambusa sp[inosa], lespedeza bicolor, aspidistra elatior, colocasia antiquorum, panicum miliaceum . . . If not protected somehow, leaves were burned by fire or radiation. Trees, deprived of branches and leaves, were found to grow new shoots from the stem. Annual plants with well developed stem such as Zea and Ricinus, if not having suffered much from fire, showed rejuvenescence from the survived stock.

Hersey marked some of the Latin names and, in the margins, provided English equivalents: sickle senna for *Cassia tora*; hairy-fruited bean, bluets, purslane. Whether he depended on prior knowledge, a reference book, or informed guesswork, he let his imagination free, a little. *Parthenocissus tricuspidata* is known in the West as both Japanese creeper and Boston ivy. Either way, it's not the same as *Tanacetum parthenium*, or feverfew (a corruption of "febrifuge"). "Feverfew," though, is how Hersey glossed it. As for *Panicum miliaceum*—prosaically, a form of millet—he decided that the more or less literal "panic grass" fitted the situation better, and so it went into what was originally his book's last section, where characters we've come to know for their resilience and resource begin to falter, their hair falling out, little hemorrhages appearing on their skin, gums starting to bleed, wounds reopening, while the vegetable world takes on an eerie exuberance. A little more than a month after the bombing, Miss Sasaki is moved back into the city by car for treatment of her leg, painfully swollen by a compound fracture that has still not been properly set. The passage works together the botanists' report with parts of her own narrative, recounted to Hersey through a translator:

> This was the first chance she had had to look at the ruins of Hiroshima; the last time she had been carried through the city's streets, she had been hovering on the edge of unconsciousness. Even though the wreckage had been described to her, and though she was still in pain, the sight horrified and amazed her, and there was something she noticed about it that particularly gave her the creeps. Over everything—up through the wreckage of the city, in gutters, along the riverbanks, tangled among tiles and tin roofing, climbing on charred tree trunks—was a blanket of fresh, vivid, lush, optimistic green; the verdancy rose even from the foundations of ruined houses. Weeds already hid the ashes, and wild flowers were in bloom among the city's bones. The bomb had not only left the underground organs of the plants intact; it had stimulated them. Everywhere were bluets and Spanish bayonets, goosefoot, morning glories and day lilies, the hairy-fruited bean, purslane and clotbur and sesame and panic grass and feverfew. Especially in a circle at the center, sickle senna grew in extraordinary regeneration.[19]

"Panic Grass and Feverfew" became the title of the fourth section, and the words have in turn engendered a small jungle of unreliable explanatory notes on internet sites devoted to the book. It's one of many moments when this work of observation inevitably reads like science fiction. People often speak of it as a novel, a description that exasperated the writer.

Titles for the individual parts became less of a question once William Shawn and Harold Ross had made an unprecedented decision: not only to print the long article in one issue of the magazine rather than spread it out over several weeks, but to give over the entire number to it. Accounts of its impact have understandably tended to focus on this aspect, but more important to most readers was not so much what they expected in *The New Yorker* as what they had been thinking about in the previous weeks. Early in July 1946 the U.S. Navy carried out the first of a monthlong series of tests of its latest nuclear weapons at Bikini Atoll in the Marshall Islands. The islands are in an empty-seeming spread of the Pacific, but it's empty only in the sense in which Africa seemed empty to Conrad's young Marlow,[20] and in recent history the region echoed with the 1942 Battle of Midway, a turning point in the war and symbolic also in that during the conflict's early days the islands had lain at the outer edge of Japanese power, just beyond U.S. control. Put at its simplest: in the immediate lead-up to the first anniversary of victory, the Americans returned to this spot to enact a brutal reminder of their power.

No secret was made of the fact that Micronesians living on the atoll were forcibly evacuated to what was thought to be safety; that scores of ships converged on the area to provide experimental stations, workshops, and living quarters for troops and researchers; that surplus craft were put into the explosion zone to see how they stood up to the experience, along with a mass of military equipment—and animals—loaded onto them. In case the symbolism of all this should have escaped anyone, the fairground targets included a former Japanese cruiser, the *Sakawa*, which duly sank. All this and more was elaborately publicized: between late March and early October 1946, *Life* magazine alone carried five long, illustrated articles about the tests.[21] *Hiroshima* can be seen as, among many other things, answering the triumphalism.

No serious effort had previously been made to dispel the effects of wartime anti-Japanese propaganda. Although the last of the camps in which Japanese had been interned was closed in March of that year, widespread hostility against the innocent former inmates often prevented them from returning to where they had previously lived. This was an America, after all, in which it was possible for a writer to refer in print to "the sweet pungent odor of baked Japanese."[22] The effects of radiation were being systematically lied about. Advances in U.S. military technology—the development of radio-guided missiles and of an aircraft (the B-36) capable of carrying a nuclear bomb for six thousand miles, air bases on Alaskan ice floes—were continuing apace, as were ever-increasingly outrageous actions by the Soviet Union in Eastern Europe.

Damn Smart of You People

All this helps explain much of the impact of what from one point of view was just a magazine article. Its reputation spread in part simply by word of mouth, followed by reprintings in other newspapers, radio broadcasts, translations, book publication, and more translations. Before all that, though, how it was handled by *The New Yorker* helped create the initial excitement and in turn became an aspect of the legend. It was Shawn who persuaded Ross that it would have more impact as a single item than as a serial—a decision that didn't necessarily entail giving over the whole magazine to it but that, once this, too, had been decided, was powerfully reinforced. The magazine's identity has always included its strong sense of itself, and part of that has been consistency—of tone and outlook, but more recognizably what would now be thought of as visual and sequential branding: cover style, typography, the order in which items appeared, the already idiosyncratic names of the individual sections or departments, the very fact that those departments were regularly there. Surprise, then— journalistic impact—was something the magazine generally achieved surreptitiously, if at all. But by the same token, in a professional world of gossip, of scoops, and of spoilers, a surprise really had to be one. To decide something a few weeks before a given issue appeared was almost always for it to be known about, at least in midtown Manhattan; by definition, publishing is a world in which secrets tend to get out. So up to the last minute only two small groups of people were in the know: Ross, Shawn, and Hersey, plus, a few days before the issue went to press, a couple of handpicked senior writers at *Time* (because it had partly funded Hersey's trip) and, for the sake of fairness, *Newsweek*—founded in 1933 and the key rival of Henry Luce's magazines. Not even Hersey's mother was in the know.[23] Meanwhile, in *The New Yorker*'s own offices, writers turning in regular items were kept wondering why the usual urgency about them was missing and where their proofs were.[24]

The previous issue, August 24, contained no hint of what was in store. Henry Luce had to put up with a little needling in it about *Life*'s current obsession with Barbara Laage, a young French actress, which seemed to contrast with his high claims for his papers' moral, political, and generally American purpose. (The Talk of the Town slyly called it Laage's being "tapped by the Skull-n-Bonesmen.")[25] It was summer, after all, and *The New Yorker* led with a light story by A. J. Liebling set in newly liberated Paris. Many of the cartoons had a holiday theme—three middle-age ladies in a hotel lobby complaining to the manager that "a strange woman" (seen in a rocking chair facing out to sea) "is sitting in our corner of the porch." In a tiny gesture to the Bikini Atoll tests, a drawing by Alan Dunn showed "Laboratory X" with a horseshoe pinned for luck above a pair of closed doors marked "Nuclear Physics." Andy Logan wrote about a transatlantic crossing on the newly demilitarized *Queen Mary*. A Reporter at Large was about cattle-breeding in Connecticut. There were the usual reviews of films (Hitchcock's *Notorious*) and new books (Edmund Wilson on John Dos Passos's *Tour of Duty*—"probably the best thing he has written since he finished *U.S.A.*"): in general, a light editorial diet between ads for Parker 51 fountain pens and Park & Tilford's Private Stock American whiskey.

Still in the cause of secrecy, the cover of the August 31 issue gave no more away: Charles E. Martin's sketch is of a holiday resort seen from above, people swimming, sunbathing, sailing, horse-riding. And the contents started out familiarly enough: full-page ads for Nolde nylons and women's clothes from Bergdorf Goodman and Lord & Taylor. At the last moment, though, the issue was wrapped in a white band with heavy black type. Between pages 15 and 27 it contained nothing other than the first part of Hersey's piece. There was no special typeface, no change in layout, just the usual *New Yorker* logo, "A Reporter at Large," and a heading in small capitals: "HIROSHIMA." No cartoons whatsoever before page 27, Hersey's byline at the bottom of page 68 (but, filling the back cover, a final injunction to "Always Buy Chesterfield [Cigarettes]"). Only a single short paragraph, at the foot of the middle column of the article's first page, offered any overt editorial comment:

TO OUR READERS
The New Yorker this week devotes its entire editorial space to an article on the almost complete obliteration of a city by one atomic bomb, and what happened to the people of that city. It does so in the conviction that

few of us have yet comprehended the all but incredible destructive power of this weapon, and that everyone might well take time to consider the terrible implications of its use.

—THE EDITORS

On newsstands the issue was a sellout. A vendor at one of the entrances to Grand Central Terminal told a *New Yorker* staffer that instead of having a few copies remaining on Friday evening as usual, he had sold all his stock by 2:00 p.m. on Thursday. Purchasers "rush in and rush out, people that I've never seen buy the magazine."[26] One in a group of Japanese American soldiers noticed the cover strap, bought a copy, "showed the others, and they all came over and bought copies . . . and took seats and began reading silently." Several people had bought multiple copies. "Damn smart of you people," the vendor added.

Inevitably, some of the reaction in the months that followed was hyped. Yes, Albert Einstein ordered a thousand copies, but this was for a mailing to members of his organization the Emergency Committee of Atomic Scientists.[27] No, Penguin U.K., which published the book version throughout Britain and what was still (just) its empire, didn't print a million paperbacks. They anticipated doing so, and the initial print run was 250,000, but sales were somewhat dampened by extensive international newspaper serializations, which Hersey insisted had to reproduce the text in full, so when the British edition appeared, every potential buyer had already had a chance to read the whole thing and tens of thousands of copies remained in the warehouse. Myths notwithstanding, the fact remains that *Hiroshima* has been read all over the world. Many other books on the subject followed, taking many different approaches, but, now as then, whichever of them anybody was talking about, one question would be asked: Have you read John Hersey?

Luce, of course, was irritated, and his papers tried to minimize what he felt as a humiliation, claiming that *The New Yorker* "had practically stumbled into" its scoop. *Time* claimed that Harold Ross, "a man given to juvenile and profane tantrums," had only agreed to the idea of publishing the article as the entire content of a single issue because he needed to disguise how short the magazine was of good material at the time.[28] The *Time* piece praised Hersey as a journalist. His career had been established, after all, on the staff of Time-Life. Yet even though the costs of this particular trip had been shared by the company, it had ended up with the less interesting of his articles from China.[29] Besides, had they not themselves published an eyewitness account of the bombing, six months earlier? For *The New Yorker*, by contrast, the article represented a step up in reputation and sales, as well as confirmation of the value of a writer who would go on publishing most of the best of his work there for the rest of his long career.

Financially Hersey now found himself able to help others while also becoming significantly richer himself. He made over his income on serialization (secondary newspaper publication and broadcasting of the article) and book-club sales to charities, principally the American Red Cross, but retained substantial earnings from primary book sales, a source of income that continued throughout his life. The Red Cross arrangement was messy at first, thanks to the attitude of that least charitable of institutions, the IRS, which despite the cause—and the fact that the situation of a correspondent in Russia, China, and Japan in 1944–46 hadn't been ideal in terms of medium-term tax-planning—didn't like the fact that Hersey had not made the commitment in advance.[30] Once settled, though, the deal guaranteed a substantial overall donation, and Hersey was later able to add support for other charitable activities. Out of revenue from the Book of the Month Club, for example, he asked Knopf—which published the book in the States in hardback—to send the first $4,000 to Einstein's Emergency Committee of Atomic Scientists before the balance went to the Red Cross, and the ECAS also benefited when Alfred Knopf decided that some of the firm's own profits on the book should go to charity.[31] With Kiyoti Tanimoto's help, royalties from the book's eventual Japanese publisher were distributed to relevant individuals and causes. (Already in 1948 Hersey had 9,000 yen in a Japanese bank ready to be handed out as soon as the Americans unblocked the account. This was just his advance on publication in Japan and, while not a large sum, represented more than six months' earnings to someone on an average wage there.)[32] Hersey also supported Tanimoto in his fund-raising visits during the early postwar period, which included his addressing a youth rally at Camp Mahackeno on the Saugatuck River, sponsored by the writer's local Westport Community Council of Churches.[33]

Now a freelancer with a family to support, Hersey arranged his American contract for the book so that in the short term it guaranteed a regular salary: $500 a month for two years from January 1, 1947—about $144,000 or more per annum in terms of pay today.[34] This was over and above the sums that were coming in from stage and film versions of *Adano* and also from magazine writing in a range of well-paying outlets, including *Cosmopolitan* and the *Herald Tribune*[35] but mainly, now, *The New Yorker*. In 1947 the latter published a story by him, "A Short Wait," about a survivor of the Warsaw ghetto arriving unexpectedly at the apartment of relatives on Park Avenue.[36] Meanwhile, it commissioned him to write a three-part series on the financier and influential political adviser Bernard Baruch, recently appointed as U.S. representative on the new United Nations Atomic Energy Commission.[37]

Not everyone admired *Hiroshima*. The novelist and critic Mary McCarthy, in particular, writing soon after it appeared as an article, saw it as normalizing rather than attacking America's use of the bomb, and regarded the very facts that it had been written by a Time-Life author and had appeared first in *The New Yorker* as compounding this effect:

> What it did was to minimize the atom bomb by treating it as though it belonged to the familiar order of catastrophes . . . which we have always had with us and which offer to the journalist, from Pliny down to Mr. Hersey, an unparalleled wealth of human interest stories . . . The interview with the survivors is the classic technique for reporting such events—it serves well enough to give some sense, slightly absurd but nonetheless correct, of the continuity of life. But with Hiroshima, where the continuity of life was, for the first time, put into question . . . the existence of survivors is an irrelevancy, and the interview with the survivors is an insipid falsification of the truth of atomic warfare.[38]

McCarthy reinforced her point by satirizing the advertisements published in that issue of the magazine (though not, of course, in the book version) and by saying—reasonably enough, but with a rider whose illogicality didn't help—that "to have done the atom bomb justice, Mr. Hersey would have had to interview the dead. But of this Mr. Hersey is, both literally and temperamentally, incapable." (Did she think anyone else, literally or temperamentally, would have been less so?)[39]

The fact that the dead can't speak to us is, of course, a given of all war literature ("The only heroes are dead" is both a cliché and untrue), and by minimizing the value of surviving witnesses' accounts McCarthy implicitly scorned the work of a host of survivor-writers, not to speak of great writers about war who hadn't had direct experience of their topic, Tolstoy and Stephen Crane among them.[40] At the same time it was unfeeling of her, to put it no more strongly, to insult the courage of those whose efforts to help victims worse affected than themselves Hersey describes, but whom she patronizingly and inaccurately lumped together as "busy little Methodists." An implication of her words ("The existence of survivors is an irrelevancy, and the interview with the survivors is an insipid falsification of the truth of atomic warfare") is that these brave men and women somehow ought not to have survived, if for no other reason than that their having done so defeated her own drama in which the atom bomb canceled that possibility.

Tone was to become a particular battleground in literature of the Shoah, when writers—including some, like Primo Levi, who had been in concentration camps—would be criticized for seeming insufficiently angry and/or for not explicitly laying blame. Something similar is involved here with nuclear warfare. Careful readers of *Hiroshima* must judge for themselves whether it is possible to reach the end of the book—or, indeed, to reach its second or third page—without feeling angry oneself and without grasping what the moral issues are and that these feelings and thoughts have arisen directly because of what Hersey writes and how he writes it. Still, McCarthy wasn't the only person to experience the work differently.[41] Others, by contrast, interpreted it as indulging a remorse the Americans had no need to feel, or at least not to advertise. One of these was the novelist Thomas Mann, whom Knopf had been considering as a possible translator of the book into German. To Mann, the article was a daring piece of reporting and of "American self criticism," but, he wrote, "I have not the slightest interest to have the Germans read it. It is . . . their only pleasure to enjoy the mistakes and sins committed anywhere else in the world."[42] But most readers simply thought it a masterpiece and one that should be read everywhere. Hersey was showered with honors—the Journalist of the Year Award, invitations to lecture, honorary degrees.[43]

For now, he remained almost entirely unknown in one country: Japan. As early as October 10, 1945, former U.S. war correspondents had been freed from the requirement to submit their work for censorship,[44] but in Japan itself the misnamed Civil Information and Education section of

Allied Command continued to exert muddled but intimidating control over what might appear. When it objected to a proposal for publication of Yoko Matsuoka's translation of *Hiroshima*,[45] attention in the media at home forced General MacArthur in person—who owed a debt to Hersey for *Men on Bataan*—to deny that this had happened, and he seemed eager to praise the book to visitors.[46] There's ample evidence, however, that the translation was obstructed at every turn. Necessary licenses were refused, cuts in the text were demanded, and personal pressure was put on the translator. Bureaucratic delays were introduced by supposed legal problems to do with yen earnings, or a rumor that Penguin had an arrangement with a different translator, or the inability of the Japanese publisher-in-waiting, Hosei University Press, to produce a formal letter from Hersey saying it had his authorization. Yoko Matsuoka told Hersey that a "Mr. Brown" at Supreme Command had claimed that a couple of Japanese acquaintances said they feared the book would "remind the Japanese of the war again." It evidently hadn't occurred to him, she wrote, "that his own existence reminds us more vividly of war than anything else . . . SCAP [Supreme Commander for the Allied Powers—an abbreviation for the occupation bureaucracy] seems hopeless. Their sense of value, their understanding of the Japanese and their problems seem completely out of focus."[47]

Various individuals did their best to help move matters along. Because mail was censored, acquaintances passing through, such as Irita Van Doren, the literary editor of the *Herald Tribune*, carried letters between Matsuoka and Hersey.[48] An unidentified colleague called Berry, based in Tokyo, pursued the tenderhearted Mr. Brown while admitting that to negotiate with him, "you just sit on a merry-go-round that's gone out of whack and watch the world turn into a kaleidoscope in which nothing is definite but everything is kinda pretty or kinda ugly, according to the colors used."[49] Negotiations that were going on simultaneously for a Japanese translation of *A Bell for Adano* gave scope for further delaying tactics, while Berry vividly described SCAP's attempts to pretend that there had been no ban on either book:

> Yesterday I talked with Brown and with a new fellow in CI&E, Romney Wheeler, who handles the issuance of licenses (in a vague and unauthoritative way) . . . Wheeler wishes nervously not to be quoted at all about

anything and assures me of nothing. He says that the whole thing was a terrible mix-up, and that there was considerable misunderstanding and that he "thinks" that now, if you will write to Lt. Col. D.R. Nugent [in charge of "Information and Education" at the San Francisco headquarters of Supreme Command] asking for a license to publish the books under SCAP circular 12, 9 May, 1948, and that you are willing to accept blocked yen pending future regulations on exchange, you will get your license . . . What Wheeler wants you . . . to do is to write Nugent and re-apply for licenses . . . just as if nothing had happened in order that "this ghost" of censorship can be exhorcised [*sic*]. As we all know there never was any censorship here at all. It was all a very great and regrettable accident.

Forty months after the bombing, the Japanese version of *Hiroshima* finally appeared. Paper was still rationed, so the first printing was limited to forty thousand copies. It sold out in a week.[50] Seventy years on, it is still in print.

For Hersey's subsequent writing, *Hiroshima* was both an opportunity and a challenge. In some ways it was also a liability. He could be fairly confident now that whatever he wrote would be published and publicized. And he would never lack the financial freedom to write whatever he chose, on any subject, in any way. This meant, among other things, that there was no obstacle to his ambition to be a novelist. As for the hazards of success, he was too self-controlled to fall prey to the most obvious of them. There would be no long silences, no months in the drunk tank, no all-consuming litigation. Still, *Hiroshima* told an unmatchable story. Hersey had researched it with a lot of help from ideal participants and had written it quickly. It was only sixty thousand words long. Could he ever again write anything quite like it? The puritan in Hersey told him not only that he couldn't but also that he shouldn't, or not with the same ease. He had always been thorough, but henceforth any research he did would be yet more painstaking. He would take immense trouble to find a narrative approach, the right style. He would tax his imagination. And in the first instance, all this would be in the cause of the only subject in human history that seemed even bigger than Hiroshima: the Nazi Final Solution.

7. Listening to the Dead

OWARD THE END OF 1947, Knopf issued a press release summarizing *Hiroshima*'s success: reprints in eighty newspapers and magazines; translations into eleven languages to date; a braille edition and an edition for schools; total U.S. book sales (including through the Book of the Month Club) of 613,500.[1]

The more successful a writer is, the more past work can be an obstacle to whatever should come next. Hersey had already experienced the demands a popular book brings in its wake: public appearances and interviews, decisions about reprints and translations and adaptations, and written contributions on related topics. Who would check that a new foreign-language edition was faithful and complete and that extraneous illustrations or typographical conventions had not been introduced, or that the casting of a stage version was appropriate? He was a perfectionist— the more so as the size of his readership increased. Meanwhile, like other authors of nonfiction, he found himself treated as an expert, liable to be called on to speak at conferences and to join ever more advisory bodies and pressure groups. *Hiroshima* continued, would always continue, to bring in correspondence, both in its own right—problems with payments from foreign publishers in the aftermath of war, contests between British publishers over who had the closest personal relationship with the author,[2] issues of censorship, compliments and requests, many of them fatuous, from readers—and as a source of attention to himself.

Celebrity wasn't easy to avoid. He was voted Journalist of the Year in 1946–47 and, along with General Eisenhower, Laurence Olivier, Bing Crosby, Ingrid Bergman, and others, one of Ten Outstanding Celebrities of 1946.[3] He headed off most requests for public appearances and interviews but accepted a few positions on public committees and agreed to a request from Yale to give the university library the manuscript of the work (though this caused a mild ownership flurry at *The New Yorker*).[4] He had to struggle to remind himself, let alone others, that he was more than the author of a single book. Both out of his own intellectual interests and in order not to become typecast, he agreed in the short term to write reviews and articles on a range of topics. All this consumed time and, less easily measured but more important, imaginative space. And—as became the norm with him—the subject he was now thinking about differed so substantially from that of previous works that his life had to be lived on ever more separate imaginative and intellectual levels, in addition to simply being lived.

In the last respect, he was busy enough. In 1948 he, Frances Ann, and their three small children, Martin, John Junior, and Ann, had moved out of Manhattan to Greens Farms, Connecticut.[5] Roughly halfway between the city and New Haven, and about forty miles from Briarcliff Manor, it's the oldest part of Westport, on Long Island Sound, then still semi-rural but already a commuter town. In those days, even fathers who worked at home weren't involved in every hour of their children's upbringing, and parents didn't communicate as much to other people about parenthood. Among the few sightings Hersey left of himself as a father in his published work is a brief description of an outing with Martin and John Junior, then seven and five years old, to "look at" President Truman on an election tour of Connecticut in the 1948 campaign.[6] (Another, more oblique, is a 1954 article complaining about the sorry state of children's primers and suggesting that jollier authors such as Dr. Seuss should be persuaded to write such books. *The Cat in the Hat* is said to have been prompted by Hersey's idea.)[7] His and Frances Ann's letters to Grace, on the other hand, are full of stories about the children's development, birthday parties, school achievements, holiday arrangements, pets, and favorite books.[8] In 1949, Frances Ann gave birth to their fourth child, Baird. Early in the 1950s her husband urged his mother, "Come and visit us and our dog, canary, tropical fish, chickens (four given us for Christmas!), live shrimp, pet turtle, and assorted crickets who've been attracted by the chicken feed. We are numerous and active."[9]

After the end of the war, Frances Ann increasingly wanted professional as well as domestic projects. She had managed alone through John's long absences in Moscow and then in China, dealing not only with her young family but also with older relatives, particularly her wayward father.[10] Now the couple were jointly enlisted by the sinologist Pearl Buck to help a journalist acquaintance, Jerome Ellison, start a magazine co-owned by John Steinbeck, John Dos Passos, and others. It was given the unambitious but, as it proved, disappointingly accurate title '47 (subsequently '48): *The Magazine of the Year*.[11] Hersey did his bit by contacting big names like Rebecca West and Thornton Wilder and contributing material of his own, including a short story[12] and a not especially well-informed review-essay on a book of pictures by his colleague Robert Capa.[13] He also secured U.S. rights to the first chapter of Ralph Ellison's *Invisible Man*, which he had read in the British literary magazine *Horizon*—it was the beginning of an important friendship.[14] But the enterprise didn't flourish. In any case, whatever the gaps in Frances Ann's life, her husband was consumed by work of his own that increasingly involved big, overtly political topics. He was preparing an essay in support of the new United Nations[15] and a profile for *Collier's* on Secretary of State George Marshall, soon to be the architect of the European Recovery Plan,[16] as well as the *New Yorker* series on Bernard Baruch.

All these pieces concerned civic responsibility, but what absorbed Hersey at least as much was his ambition as a fiction writer, and here he was encountering discouragement—or perhaps not encountering it: it's hard to tell whether he noticed the warning signs, which were inevitably muted. At *The New Yorker*, which, like most fiction writers of the time, he regarded as the gold standard, internal memos show that stories he submitted were causing some awkwardness. The trusted fiction editor Gus Lobrano told Harold Ross he was unconvinced by them. Hersey was too valuable to treat lightly, and when Ross discussed the problem with William Shawn, they decided that the fiction department should make a point of dealing with him not directly but through Elizabeth Otis, of the agency McIntosh & Otis, who, though Hersey continued to handle most of his own business affairs, acted as a gatekeeper over some matters.[17]

In the short term, Ross was relieved to hear from Lobrano that one of the Hersey pieces he had looked at "could be fixed." (This was "A Short Wait.")[18] Ross himself quietly plugged away at suggesting nonfiction topics to his author[19]—in one respect unnecessarily: Hersey was researching his next novel with greater factual thoroughness than for anything he had previously written. Having spent some time thinking about Auschwitz with the notion of setting a book there, he turned instead to the Warsaw ghetto, which he had visited in 1944. In February 1948 he told his mother that although he still wasn't sure whether he would "go through with it," he was finding the investigations "most interesting."[20] He pondered histories of the Jews of Central Europe, books by Jewish political philosophers and theologians, works on the Bund and on Zionism, histories of Poland, maps of the ghetto, details of wages and rations in Warsaw in 1940–41, and a typescript translation of the Stroop Report—a book-length account of the Warsaw Ghetto Uprising and its context written for Himmler in May 1943 by the senior SS general who had been sent to crush it.[21] Acquaintances were pressed into service, among them the artist and educator Jacob Landau, who came to dinner and was quizzed about Jewish rituals.[22] Then there were the most painful of sources: people who had written accounts of their own experiences of the ghetto, some of whom had survived, most not. These writings were in Polish and Yiddish, and Hersey had the idea of paying translators to speak their more or less unprepared versions directly into a wire recorder (a forerunner of the tape recorder—used, as it happens, for some of the first interviews with Holocaust survivors).[23] The effect, Hersey said, was of "a tremendous interview": he was "listening to . . . people talk for hours on end," while at the same time avoiding anyone still available for a real interview, fearing, he said, that they might give him too limited a perspective while coming to dominate his story. By February 1949 he hoped "to have my first draft finished in about two weeks!"[24]

Circles Around Numerals

An account that Hersey gave of these labors and scruples at a sales conference for Knopf representatives in December 1949[25] made a big impression on its hearers, but to anyone less involved reveals some of what, for readers today, makes the first half of this tremendous book a bit too literal, too fact-laden: so burdened with its sheer responsibleness that it has difficulty taking off imaginatively. This was long before readers had become familiar with Shoah narratives and long, too, before the deterrents introduced by those who have argued, at one emotional extreme, that only those who suffered the Holocaust should write about it.[26] Hersey recognized that the subject was one that an outsider must at least find a special way of handling: this was why he chose not to base his novel in one of the camps. And both then and later he talked in—for him—unusual detail about the tortuous process of deciding what kind of a book could come out of his hundreds of pages of notes and his scores of hours of recordings. He often changed his mind about what exactly his subject was, even whether he could write about it at all. He compiled indexes of his materials "so that I would remember where to look." He made a chronology, a list of themes (nineteen of them), a list of characters (at first fifty, at a later point seventy-one), then a tabular arrangement linking people to themes and vice versa, and both to specific episodes: "Circles around the Roman numerals indicated that characters dominated the episode." Drafts accumulated, both in number and in length.[27] To aid concentration, Hersey had his phone disconnected. His editor at Knopf, Harold Strauss, wrote to him respectfully but apprehensively, at the end of 1948,

> Your entire progress report was happy news, but the best part was the implication that you yourself are pleased with what you are doing. You have always had extraordinary clarity of mind about your own work (making my job as your editor something of a sinecure). In the case of almost anyone else, I would have to make grim noises at the prospect of a novel 200,000 words in length; but if you really feel that the novel must be that long, I'm sure that you have the soundest reasons.[28]

Until now, point of view had been one of Hersey's main problems: Who did this narrative belong to? How (he didn't put it this way, but some of the eventual reviewers did)[29] could a privileged, healthy young WASP in New England pretend to even a fictional grasp of the ordeals of Central European Jews under Nazism? Eventually, as Hersey explained, he "handed" the story (the verb is still revealingly proprietorial) to his narrator, Levinson.[30] The decision necessitated another round of adjustment, then entire new drafts. Characters were built up only to be later "absorbed" or "cut out." Repeatedly and explicitly—four times in as many minutes—Hersey spoke about his confusion in all this and about feelings of pain, depression, fear, and discouragement.

By unburdening himself about these agonies to an audience of what he increasingly thought of as the Knopf family, Hersey was reinforcing a personal, psychological claim to which the company had already responded. Alfred Knopf's son Pat wrote, "I don't think any of us have ever worked on a book which means so much to everyone. I certainly never expected to find within the five short years I've been here as much pleasure in my job as THE WALL is giving me."[31] In the background was the fact that Alfred and Blanche Knopf had been the first Jews to make a major impact in the largely gentile male world of pre–Second World War New York publishing. They brought an international range of authors to attention, with a new degree of commercial flamboyance. The Knopf list was not overtly Jewish, and as well as being the first American novel of the Shoah, *The Wall* was among the Knopfs' first publications on a centrally Jewish theme (theirs was one of many Anglophone publishing houses that turned down Anne Frank's *Diary*).[32] Pat Knopf himself had spent the Second World War in the 446th Bomb Group, Eighth Air Force, winning a Distinguished Flying Cross flying missions over Germany from Bungay in Suffolk.[33]

Complicated allegiances and taboos were at work in all this. In 1950, discussions of how the Shoah could be written about were less common than late modernist challenges to fictional authority in general. Hersey kept abreast of the arguments while knowing too much about literary history to think that they were entirely new, and among mainstream writers was unusual at this stage in the extent to which his work, in depending on a narrative put together by a collector of stories with the help of a later "editor" from what was told or given to him by people, most of whom, like himself, are now dead, allows for uncertainty about those stories' credibility.

Certain aspects of *The Wall*, of course, were well beyond doubt. As with Hersey's journalistic work, the facts came first—but here without journalism's pressures of time, of the requirement to move on with a changing situation, and, especially, of a busy, skeptical first reader in the office, blue pencil hovering over the page. In some ways this situation was advantageous—one assumed by every writer (at least every writer who hasn't accumulated evidence to the contrary) to be ideal. But it deprived Hersey of a stimulus to which he had always responded exceptionally well: the physical presence of other human beings in all their difference and strangeness, telling him their stories with their own accents and gestures. Using taped spoken translations of written texts was pragmatic but also eerie, and dark in its implications. It was as if, after Guadalcanal, after Sicily, after Moscow and northern China, after Hiroshima, he felt he needed to put a both literal and metaphorical wall between him and all those suffering faces—a wall and also a physical landscape and seascape, a continent—but not, he hoped, any imaginative barrier. Yet he had no need to. The voices themselves, the faces, the bodies—most of them no longer existed. He was listening to the dead.

A New Bible

Another of the many ironies *The Wall* presents is that in being the first American novel, or, seen another way, the first piece of New Journalism, to re-create imaginatively one of the more hideous situations of the then-recent past, it was bound to be overtaken by genuine historical narratives—and also by other novels (such as Leon Uris's *Mila 18*, about Nazi Poland, published in 1961). The facts, very briefly, and as reliably told by Hersey, are these. In German-occupied Warsaw and other cities in Poland, where there was considerable support for Nazism, restrictions on Jews began to be imposed as early as November 1939. Over the following twelve months, existing Jewish quarters were, by fits and starts, turned into places of imprisonment and starvation. Warsaw's ghetto was the biggest. Non-Jewish inhabitants having been moved out, Jews in vastly greater numbers were moved in from all over the region. Soon it was a staging post for what the Germans pretended were far-distant labor centers but in fact consisted of the Treblinka death camp, fifty miles away. As in other places ostensibly under their own administrative rule, Jews were categorized according to the soon all-too-familiar rudimentary categories: age; state of health; trade, "useful" or otherwise. Following these criteria the Judenrat (Jewish Council) was obliged to identify those who would be transported. In May 1943, a proportion of those remaining took part in an armed, brave, but doomed rebellion: the biggest act of Jewish resistance in the war and one that in its early stages caused the first retreat ever of German troops under fire from Jews. A handful of the latter escaped and survived. What remained of the ghetto was razed in the course of the battle, and its ruins were blasted again as the Russians invaded. At this point in the tragedy of Europe's Jews, the family of Anne Frank had so far been in hiding for less than a year, and Primo Levi had not yet been arrested.

When Hersey visited Warsaw early in 1944, hardly anyone knew that buried beneath the rubble were thirteen hidden containers of documents written by inhabitants of the ghetto. With a handful of exceptions, those involved in creating this archive were dead.[34] They had been led by a powerful, charismatic historian and political activist, Emanuel Ringelblum, who was himself among the victims. Ringelblum's archive was part of a project begun as early as the 1920s devoted to recording Jewish life from "below"—itself part of a wider historiographical movement involving "ordinary" people as distinct from rulers, aristocrats, and powerful or starry figures of other kinds. The existence of the Warsaw archive had been quietly communicated among trusted members of the wartime Jewish resistance, and in September 1946 excavations began under the guidance of one of Ringelblum's former companions, Hersh Wasser. Not everything was found at the time, nor has it been since. More documents turned up in 1950 in a couple of milk churns. Others may remain somewhere in the ground under today's busy city. The world above them has changed. The Chinese embassy stands on what was for some time believed to be the site of one container. (An excavation there proved fruitless.) The town where Ringelblum grew up—Buchach, or Buczacz, in Galicia, once part of the Austro-Hungarian Empire—is now in Ukraine.

Some of those who wrote their stories for Ringelblum in the early 1940s did so hoping that "they were fulfilling a national mission of the highest importance." But to everyone, what mattered most was "to remind future generations that they were individuals."[35] There were dissenters. One of the documents in the archive bitterly dismissed the whole enterprise. "History does not teach a thing," the anonymous skeptic wrote. "Jews have no history, all of it is only myth. We are worried about gathering material for history? Forget it. Fight hunger." Still, history went on being compiled. In 1943 the American Federation for Polish Jews published *The Black Book of Polish Jewry*, a selection of refugees' firsthand reports and other documentary materials put together by a team led by Jacob Apenszlak.[36] (It was followed in 1944 by Ilya Ehrenburg and Vasily Grossman's *Black Book of Soviet Jewry*, written in Yiddish, suppressed in the Soviet Union, and not published in Russian until 1980.) A small number of articles on the subject, including about the Ringelblum archive, appeared in the years immediately afterward. Among them, in 1947 and '48, were a personal piece by the writer Rachel Auerbach, a key figure in the enterprise who had survived; an account of the archive by a Polish-Jewish historian, Nachman Blumenthal; and a pamphlet biography of Ringelblum by one of his friends.[37] But it wasn't until the belated awakening of public consciousness about the Shoah in the 1980s that translations of the documents began to appear on any scale.[38] Meanwhile, even among stories of the Warsaw ghetto more generally, *The Wall* was by a long way the first book-length narrative.

In terms of later para-controversies about the Shoah—controversies not about the phenomenon itself but about how it has been described and discussed—Hersey's book couldn't be more troublesome. As with *Hiroshima*, he was writing for all sorts of people, including those not unlike himself: members of what was then still the WASP American ascendancy, people who, in common with Anglo-Saxons in other parts of the world, might have had friends who were Jews but were not especially philosemitic and showed no overwhelming curiosity about, let alone sense of vicarious responsibility for, what had been happening in Central Europe. For readers like these *The Wall* was one of a handful of works in the postwar years that opened minds, changed attitudes, and introduced a dimension of human knowledge that would take decades to become more fully understood. At the time, it had comparable effects on Jewish readers, too.

What Has Made Our Life Worth Living?

This awkward, intense, and—as a recent historian of the Ringelblum archive, Samuel D. Kassow, has said[39]—underrated novel is conceived on the scale of other American war "epics" of the late 1940s and early '50s such as Norman Mailer's *The Naked and the Dead* (1948) and James Jones's *From Here to Eternity* (1951). But unlike them, it includes no American characters and is only toward the end about military combat in anything approaching the traditional sense. Again distinctively, its most important fighters are women: Rutka, who while pregnant is spirited out of the ghetto to procure arms for the resistance, and Rachel, who leads one of the resistance groups. The pace starts out slow, and to many readers at the time the stealthy accrual of fateful events came, as it did to the victims, as a shocking surprise: the apparently random construction of walls connecting buildings at points around the ghetto; the departure of non-Jewish residents and arrival of more and more Jews; the establishment of increasingly arbitrary rules; the selections required of the Judenrat; Slonim's mission that establishes where all the railway trucks destined for "the east" actually go and why they return so soon. All this has its own painful inevitability for later readers, too, though for many it is the details that are most powerful, at least up until the tense action of the last third of the novel, relating the final preparations for and carrying out of the rebellion. In what happens here, some of the book's most fully developed moral-philosophical passages occur, representing an aspect of the Russian influences both on the book and in Hersey's imaginative development more broadly.

From the perspective of writing about the Shoah, *The Wall* is distinctive, too, in its sense of the continuities of life in the ghetto, seen as extensions of the deprivations and migrations forced on Jews at various points in their history and also as examples of the courage of some but also the weakness and cupidity of others. Even within the ghetto, society is sharply stratified in relation to power, opportunity, and accommodation. Rachel's jeweler father is so wealthy that he is able to escape into the city, though it does him no good. At the other end of the scale are humans living like wild animals. Material distinctions are matched by ones of intellect and imagination: music and poetry still matter here, but so does religion, whether seen as socially ameliorative (with all the ironies that entails in such a context) or as purely spiritual. Charitable activities continue almost until the end—the inmates run a hospital and schools. Custom and ritual are preserved, from Rabbi Mazur's fixing a menorah on the door of his new accommodation at the novel's beginning to Rachel's singing "Raisins and Almonds" to Rutka's baby in the closing scenes. Gradations of opinion are intensely argued and make a difference, whether the ideological scruples of socialists who still hope to find common cause with their Polish allies outside the wall, or the quarrelsome hopes fixed on the Soviet Union or on Palestine. Among the few who get away before the uprising is Rachel's young brother David, though whether he'll make it to the Holy Land we know no more than she. A definite fate befalls Halinka's baby Israel, and of a horribly unanticipated kind.

The book contains patterns and dreams and moments of some beauty, but the occasions when it seems most inclined to indulge them are not allowed to last. We are never to forget how desperate the situation is, yet the evidence, as the book's historian, Noach Levinson, is forced to recognize, is always open to interpretation. A rabbi is turned into a clown by the Germans, but then we learn (as they don't) that he wasn't a rabbi at all but an ordinary Jew who has been perfecting this act as a kind of resistance. So far so cheering; but Rachel wants to know why the watching Jews laughed. Later, she and another of the book's most vivid, developing characters, Bergson, become sexually involved and take a forty-eight-hour holiday from the main action, a kind of honeymoon that has either been carefully planned or is an accident—the versions Levinson himself provides at first differ and may in any case be distorted by his own feelings for Rachel, confided to his diary but not to anyone around him. Yet ten days later Bergson gives Levinson another account. Asked by Levinson why the previous one had obvious flaws, Bergson answers "I'm not a practiced liar," to which the diarist adds a note: "And that, at least, I feel sure, is the truth."[40] In the book's final movement, too, a fighter whom everyone has presumed dead returns from a three-day concealment, wounded and in despair over his personal failures. He tries Levinson's patience with his need "to evacuate his poisonous and embarrassing sadness . . . I could think of answers to Rapaport's self-abasements . . . But it is hard to argue with a man who declares and repeats and insists that he is worthless."[41] Yet the next day, at a May 1 meeting of the ghetto's socialist Bund Group,

Rapaport makes a rousing speech. Levinson subsequently reflects that "the greatest mistake we can make is to try to judge a whole man from the few things we hear him say and see him do."[42] Moral judgments may err, but it is Levinson who makes Hersey's own habitual point, "We are all talking about one question: What has made our life worth living?"

Amid all this some of the resistance fighters, close to beginning their action, gather to hear Levinson lecture on the work of the Warsaw Yiddish writer I. L. Peretz. They meet in a bunker in the dark, and Levinson begins by talking about Jewishness. His diary records that in his opening words he aimed to evoke

> a definition of Jewishness that was at once exact and yet broad enough to cover all ages, all loci, and all conditions of Jewry . . . to move our small group of desperate men and women out into the great universe of Jewishness, so that we might take a short vacation from our self-pity and (perhaps) . . . feel sorry for all who are more comfortable and noticeable than we. Not as superiors, not in condescension; as fellow human beings . . . I thought this feeling might do us good.[43]

For those trapped in the ghetto to feel sorry for those outside! It's an audacious moment in a bold book, and typical of the depth that immediately brought it many admirers.

Hollywood

Dealings over jacket copy took what was becoming their usual form: minutely detailed exchanges over how the book was to be described and strong resistance by the author to the inclusion of any personal information. In this he was overruled: a biographical note on the book's back flap naturally mentioned his visits to Poland and Estonia. A description of the novel at the front, by contrast, drew away from particulars in favor of a wider claim for its "universality" as an account of "the full stature of man in the face of catastrophe."[44]

Outside Knopf, early reactions were a matter of the pre-publication grapevine and came mainly from filmmakers and from British publishers who still controlled Anglophone book-publishing markets outside the

United States. Among movie producers, the most committed, as we'll see, was David O. Selznick, whose attempts to get the novel into cinemas continued for the next fourteen years. Among British publishers, the entrepreneurial socialist Victor Gollancz, who after some delay had published *A Bell for Adano* in the U.K., offered an advance of £1,000 for *The Wall* simply on the strength of what he'd heard about it, arguing that despite Penguin's publication of *Hiroshima* he and Hersey had an "unspoken gentlemen's agreement" and stressing the relevance of his Jewishness.[45] Solicitations also came in from W. H. Allen, Hamish Hamilton, Macmillan, and Secker and Warburg. Both matters, film and overseas publication, seemed important enough to warrant a trip to Europe, so at the beginning of 1950 Hersey set off on the *Queen Elizabeth* for what he described to his mother as a "two-month tour,"[46] one of the effects of which was to keep him out of reach during the buildup to the book's U.S. appearance in February. In the course of it, he met and liked Hamish "Jamie" Hamilton, who, with the help of a warm recommendation from James Thurber, became his regular U.K. publisher.[47] He was also approached by at least one European film producer.[48]

With an important exception, the reviews were overwhelmingly favorable. The general tone and stance are represented by two very different long articles. The first to appear was a front-page item in the *Herald Tribune* books section written by the author of *Berlin Diary*, William Shirer.[49] The headline, "John Hersey's Superb Novel of the Agony of Warsaw," followed the publicity in emphasizing that the book was an "Epic" not just of "the Jews Who Lived and Died there," but of "All Men Facing Death." The implication that the story itself may not be enough[50] is continued in Shirer's opening sentence, which assumes that few gentile readers were ready for this topic:

> As everyone knows—but who remembers now, or cares to remember?—many millions of decent, innocent, non-combatant human beings were barbarously done to death by the Germans during the recent war though they had no direct part in it and certainly no responsibility for it and were not even guilty of provoking the *Herrenvolk*.

That the victims were "half-forgotten," their culture so "strange and baffling" that Hersey had to communicate it "in terms that we of the predominantly Christian world of the West can comprehend and feel"—all this, along with the notion that the novel is "much more interesting and significant on a higher level as an epic tale of man on this planet," continues through the article. As for Hersey himself, Shirer wrote that it was as if the journalist of *Hiroshima* had "leapt, overnight . . . to the forefront of our creative writers," among his many gifts ("scope and depth and power") being a formal grasp and polish for which he could think of no precedents since Flaubert.

More critical but at the same time more inward and still more enthusiastic was *The New Yorker*'s own review, by Alfred Kazin.[51] If it was a little weakened in impact by Hersey's closeness to the magazine, this was outweighed by its authorship. The son of uneducated, Yiddish-speaking Russian immigrants, Kazin was Hersey's contemporary and one of the rising generation of Columbia-educated Jewish intellectuals in New York. He had reservations about *The Wall*. He thought it politically inadequate, an opinion debatable in both relevance and truth and further weakened by the fact that while Kazin instances Koestler as the kind of writer who would have gotten this right, he later concedes that Koestler could never have achieved the book's strengths. He is more telling about some of the story's narrative limitations: how slow it is to get going, its occasional artificiality and implausibility, how middle-class and "nice" Hersey's main characters are,

> so one misses the verve and tang of those masses of poor laborers and small traders who were the greater part of Polish Jewry, the implacable fervor and mystical intensity among the orthodox, and the mockingly ragged and marginal life of the *Luftmenschen*—Jews so poor, even for Polish Jews, that it was proverbially said they "lived on air."

Despite all this, to Kazin the book succeeds because of two all-answering triumphs: the character of Noach Levinson and the ways in which the novel—indeed Hersey himself—supplies a partial yet optimistic answer to the evils recounted:

> the quick and affectionate understanding, the superlative human sympathy, the wealth of love itself, with which Mr. Hersey has interested himself in a tradition so different from his own . . . He has made of [the Jews'] unspeakable last years in the Nazi ghettos . . . one of the most encouraging

examples we have that there can be an understanding between peoples, and that the possibility of it lies in just such an imaginative act of human solidarity as this book represents.[52]

We'll come back to a different take on these views. For now it's relevant that when *The Wall* appeared, Hersey's mailbag was as full of praise from Jewish readers as from others, and that people working for David Selznick who investigated its appeal came up with similar findings. In March, Selznick received two cables reporting on inquiries among booksellers in Los Angeles. "ALL CLASSES ARE BUYING THE BOOK. AND NOT ONE COMPLAINT REGARDING THE RACIAL ANGLE [*sic*]," the first reassured him. A couple of weeks later, another researcher summarized his own findings: "BOOK IS SELLING FAST . . . HERSEY POPULAR TOO. BUYERS KNOW WHAT THEY ARE GETTING. NOT A BOOK FOR LIGHT READING. EXPECTED TO BE ONE OF BEST SELLERS OF YEAR IF NOT BIGGEST. ABSOLUTELY NO DIFFERENCE JEWISH AND GENTILE REACTION."[53]

Selznick moved toward consolidating a deal with Hersey. Then in his late forties, the producer was and is most famous for *Gone With the Wind* but early in his career had developed a strong literary reputation with George Cukor's *David Copperfield* and the Greta Garbo *Anna Karenina*. After Hersey's return from Europe they met, the amphetamine-loaded, impulsive Selznick shaking with enthusiasm. Hersey had plenty of respect for the producer's skills as well as for his reputation. He could see the possibilities in a movie of *The Wall* and understood that there were aspects of the book that, however indispensable to his writing of it, wouldn't translate well to the screen. At the same time, its reception had confirmed what he knew all too well: the story could not be darker, its milieu was deeply foreign to many Americans, and he was going to have to fight to ensure that its uncompromisingness survived in any adaptation. There had certainly been nothing like it from Hollywood. Selznick promised him this was what he found so exciting. He was determined to avoid stereotypes. What about the character of Rachel? Hersey asked. The point about her as a heroine is that her beauty is not physical. Indeed what Hersey, like his narrator, bluntly called her ugliness is compounded by the conditions into which she and the others have been forced. She is emaciated as well as fierce and troubled (the adjectives are Hersey's).[54] Could Selznick contemplate such a leading character?

Privately, the producer was worried that someone else—"[Darryl] Zanuck and others"—would be after the rights before he could nail them down.[55] Selznick gave Hersey the assurances he wanted, but the writer remained doubtful. A very long contract was drawn up in which his conditions included approval of the screenwriter, director, and leading actors, the last all specified by role. Within Selznick's company everyone was also urging caution but for different reasons. He was in financial trouble. His factotum Dan O'Shea cabled him at the Paris Ritz begging him to drop the project along with another that he was pursuing.[56] In Hollywood as a whole, earnings were "terrible," O'Shea reminded him; there was so much uncertainty; *The Wall* would be expensive; he simply didn't have the money and would therefore need to find a coproducer . . . But Selznick had a pressing reason to do the film: his new wife, Jennifer Jones, had won an Oscar in *The Song of Bernadette* (1943), produced by his competitor Darryl Zanuck. Much of Selznick's work after the end of the war was focused on providing vehicles for her. They married in 1949: What better wedding present than the role of Rachel? And if she played the part, surely revenues of the kind he was accustomed to would pour in once again.

One of Selznick's ways of thinking about a matter was to dictate enormously long memos to expensive advisers, setting out questions to which the answers were all too obvious. (Another was to ask the same advisers—often over and over again—what the questions involved were. This included requesting lists "of all the stories that we own," or details of contracts that had already been summarized for him many times.)[57] His vast archive at the Ransom Center in Austin, Texas, which makes the Hersey papers look like a few notes on a paper napkin, contains folders full of unproductive to-ings and fro-ings about *The Wall*. O'Shea was right; his boss knew that he simply couldn't afford to take on another project at this stage, though Selznick himself put the matter more elaborately:

> The enormous number of problems with which I am faced as a result of financial disappointments of a drastic nature . . . mean, not so much that I cannot finance the picture with myself as producer, but that I shall simply not have the time to personally produce it, because I shall have to devote myself to a wide variety of other problems to cope with reverses.[58]

He wasn't yet committed. The contract with Hersey hadn't been signed. And already there were significant setbacks. Two artistically respected directors Selznick had approached as possible partners declined: Elia Kazan, according to Selznick, because "he didn't want to do it," and Vittorio De Sica, because he was "too busy." Still, the vision of a gigantic win that would solve all his problems hovered before the gambler's eyes, and what seemed to him bound to make *The Wall* a near-certain hit was to cast Jennifer Jones as Rachel. But would Hersey consent? Eventually, the question was put directly to him.

Most though not all of Hersey's tactful, carefully thought-through reply is about the Jennifer Jones question.[59] Though she was a glamorous star, she was not an actor of great ability, but he couldn't say this, so he focused on the impossibility of making her ugly. Whatever the makeup department might achieve, he said, "*all* your audiences would see, in their mind's eyes . . . the image of a lovely, healthy-faced American woman" who had never ("thank her stars") encountered what the characters in *The Wall* have to live through. He reminded Selznick of his assurance that he wanted to break with Hollywood stereotypes. If the project went ahead, Hersey would not, he promised, be inflexible. The whole point of the "approval device" in the contract was "to create a situation in which, beyond the approvals, I could rely 100% on your judgment." But in the casting, "I believe that the criteria of truthfulness, fidelity to the story, and fittingness are the only ones which it is fair to ask me to apply."

This was an oblique way of saying that he wouldn't entertain casting an actor simply on the ground of box-office appeal. But he didn't know about Selznick's financial troubles and was surprised to learn that he was looking for a coproducer. He had imagined a more direct relationship between the film and the man who had approached him so zestfully and thought it best to begin his letter with this point. He said that although he hadn't anticipated a coproducer, he was sure that one could be found. For example, before meeting Selznick he had been approached about film possibilities by Lazar Wechsler, producer of the pioneering 1948 film *The Search*, about a young survivor of the camps looking for his mother across the ruins of Europe.

Whether or not Hersey knew this would be the effect, mention of a potential rival galvanized Selznick still further. Having failed to secure Hersey's agreement to the one condition he believed would guarantee the project's success, instead of abandoning the contract Selznick signed it. For Hersey, even if the film was never begun, this meant $100,000 paid over ten years: an income now roughly equivalent to $250,000 or $300,000 per annum. If it was not a fortune, in addition to his substantial other literary earnings it contributed security to what was already a good standard of living.

Between 1950 and 1964 Selznick made many attempts to induce other people to work with him on *The Wall*, or to buy the project from him, or to find a way of getting out of the continuing payments, or to persuade Hersey to relent over his degree of control, or any of these in combination. It had become a personal struggle, and in dealing with others about a different adaptation later on, Hersey was to prove much more flexible. In October 1960, a stage version opened at the Billy Rose Theatre on Broadway. Adapted by Millard Lampell, among whose major credits was the fact that he had refused to testify to the House Un-American Activities Committee (HUAC), it dispensed entirely with the narrator and incorporated fifteen Yiddish musical numbers.[60] The English actress Yvonne Mitchell, who played Rachel Apt, was Jewish, as it happened, and there was anyway enough distance between her performance and that of Jennifer Jones a couple of years earlier in Selznick's version of *A Farewell to Arms* for Hersey to have had no regrets about his earlier decision on that front.[61] George C. Scott—at the time a classical stage actor—was Dolek Berson. "The theatre flames with fury," wrote Howard Taubman in *The New York Times* at the outset of one of those reviews that make one sorry not to have been there.[62] Morton Da Costa's production ran for almost two hundred performances.

Lampell much later also wrote the screenplay for a three-hour TV movie version,[63] but by then Selznick was dead. Among all the sad craziness of the Hollywood producer's correspondence on the topic, nothing speaks more clearly than a two-page, single-spaced letter he sent to Hersey's agent in May 1964 about a recent expression of interest in *The Wall* by Paul Newman and Martin Ritt. The obstacle, once again, was casting approval, but surely Paul Newman "would be ideal for the male lead." Selznick talked of all the money he had spent on the project, including on his "overhead costs and on the costs of attorneys who have been engaged on these negotiations," not to speak of the expense of borrowing in order to pay Hersey the annual sums due under an arrangement that, Selznick said, he hadn't anticipated becoming onerous "since [he] assumed the picture would be made," but that in the end had become part of "a very large loss." It can be an effort to remember that what all this was about was a narrative of the fate of the Jews of Central Europe, twenty years earlier.

Confused Commentary

Over the same period, members of a new generation of Jewish literary intellectuals found themselves in contention over what was, in effect, another version of the old assimilate-or-not debate. *The Wall* was caught up in this when the highbrow journal *Commentary*, published by the American Jewish Committee, had to deal with an internal disagreement about the book.[64] *Commentary*'s eventual reviewer, the respected scholar-critic David Daiches, praised the novel lavishly as a "miracle of compassion" in the issue of April 1950.[65] But a younger, more idiosyncratic contributor had a different opinion. Leslie Fiedler published fiction and poetry in the magazine as well as some tough, original criticism, including an article arguing that William Faulkner belonged to Orwell's category of the "good bad" writer.[66] It was Fiedler whom Irving Kristol originally commissioned to review Hersey's book. He sent in his piece promptly. *The Wall* is badly written, Fiedler judged, its characters have no convincing inner life, and its account of events and of the people destroyed by them is sentimental and patronizing. The article was suppressed. Fiedler protested, to no avail. His original review finally appeared, decades later, in a collection of his essays,[67] but a different, more imaginative attempt lay undiscovered in *Commentary*'s archives, along with a mild cover letter to Kristol and some scraps of paper recording the divergent opinions of others on the magazine's staff.[68] This version is a dialogue, in its opening stages a kind of revue sketch but by the end a Shavian intellectual and moral contest, in which a Critic, who in the course of the dialogue voices all the criticisms made in Fiedler's original article, argues with a Kibbitzer—Yiddish for a talkative bystander—who has read the piece and who represents what Fiedler viewed as conventional Jewish opinion (as it were, Kristol's),[69] and with the Kibbitzer's father (standing perhaps for *Commentary*'s founder-editor, Elliot Cohen) about whether it should appear.

The sketch has much of the "verve and tang" Alfred Kazin found missing in Hersey's novel. The Kibbitzer and his father are concerned about the culture and circumstances in which the book will be read, the Critic about what he sees as transcendent literary value:

> KIBBITZER: You don't seem to realize, this is not just any book to be classified as middle-brow and laughed off. Rabbis will preach sermons about it, their congregations run out to buy it. It's not only my father who cried [when he read it]. Why, I was talking just last night to an eminent Jew, I won't mention his name, a member of the . . .
>
> FATHER: Go ahead, mention the name. Maybe it'll have some influence.
>
> KIBBITZER: The only point is, he wept, too.
>
> CRITIC: A stock response. Some people weep over Mother's Day cards . . .
>
> FATHER: Leaders of the Jewish community, refugees from Poland will cry their hearts out over this book, and you, you should excuse my expression, a young snot, *you* say it's no good!

The Critic persists. By condemning the book, he says, he's insulting neither the Jewish community in general nor readers of *Commentary*. On the contrary, he is treating both with respect, whereas the book preaches a kind of Jewish disappearance into Western civilization via "the Higher Assimilation." The Father protests: What about this scene or that scene, "the concertina playing the *Hatikvah*"? But everything by which he has been moved confirms the Critic's exasperation. A point raised by the Kibbitzer, that the novel was thoroughly researched, has no relevance to its value as a work of art, the Critic says, because art belongs in a region "where truth can't be apprehended by statistics." From here he moves briefly into a wider, indeed prophetic attack on the "documentary novel" before returning to *The Wall* and what he argues are its failures of characterization—especially with Rachel, "the ugly girl with the usual heart of gold, and a sex of gold, too."

As the years have passed, readers have de facto taken Fiedler's side in this argument. *The Wall* has been reprinted and translated but is best known today for cultural-historical reasons, as the first example of what has become a crowded genre. Fiedler agrees with Kazin that Hersey tidies up his characters too much: these Polish Jews do sometimes talk and behave as if they have been privately educated in Connecticut. The young Critic puts this with characteristic robustness in his original review: "like someone with good intentions retelling a Yiddish story, but avoiding the extreme intonation that makes the point, to keep from giving offense." The Critic has the last word, but there's a moment just before the end when the Kibbitzer expresses a more persuasive, more lamentably resigned view. The Critic has worked himself up into a statement that rages, as the Kibbitzer recognizes, not just against the book but against the seeming incommunicability of its subject:

> CRITIC: The mountain of torture and struggle has labored and brings forth—what? "The Jewish ethical tradition . . . the basis of all Western monotheism . . . human understanding in politics . . ." [T]he glibbest Friday night sermon or Sunday morning editorial will tell us the same thing. Is this the best one can imagine from the survivors of such terror?
>
> KIBBITZER: As a matter of fact, I've heard one or two survivors speak, and this seems to me, for better or worse, very much the sort of thing they do say . . . You miss the real point. Isn't there a kind of nobility, even grandeur, in hanging on to these very platitudes?

It's a pity that this lively response wasn't published. The decision seems to have been close and to have involved the editor's overruling several of his colleagues. The typescript is marked up for the press, and the folder it's in also contains a scrap of paper with internal readers' comments. While Robert Clurman thought the dialogue form added nothing, Clement Greenberg said it was "perfect for *us*" and Robert Warshow agreed. Irving Kristol couldn't see how they could not publish it. The resigned last words are on a separate note: "File this somewheres. IK."[70]

Elsewhere the book fared much better. It sold half a million copies within a year in the United States.[71] Celebrated writers wrote enthusiastically to Hersey, among them the war journalist Martha Gellhorn, herself an aspiring novelist though a much better reporter, who thought it "a masterpiece; the scholarship and the craft are dazzling, and the imagination which made it possible to recreate a world only known in the imagination, is breath-taking." With this novel, she said, Hersey had established himself as "the best that is writing in English."[72] Norman Mailer told his Japanese translator he thought it one of the "ten or fifteen best" recent American novels.[73] In May 1950, Philip Goodman wrote to Hersey to tell him that the Jewish Book Council of America had awarded him its prize for "the best fiction work of Jewish interest." Yet more celebrity swept him along in his new roles as a historian, a friend of American Jews and of the newly founded State of Israel, and someone with special insights into interracial relations. He was invited to attend a symposium of the United Survivors of Jewish Persecution.[74] Solicitations came from Israel, including one from the Israeli delegation to the UN proposing that he spend a year in the country and "produce the first real novel about the struggle for independence." He was awarded honorary degrees at Jewish universities, became a Fellow of the Society of American Historians,[75] won the Anisfield-Wolf prize for a book on race relations,[76] and was invited by Arthur Koestler to be a patron of the Fund for Intellectual Freedom.[77]

And his previous books continued their busy afterlives. *Hiroshima* had finally been published in Japan.[78] TV adaptation rights to his Guadalcanal narrative *Into the Valley* were bought by CBS,[79] *A Bell for Adano* was still popular, and he returned to nonfictional work while thinking about a new novel. Most immediately, he had a profile of President Truman to write.

8. Mr. Straight Arrow

SINCE THE END of the Second World War, Hersey had been one of many who had watched with increasing dismay what he saw as a fundamental cultural change in the United States. He described how the signs appeared

> in various kinds of loyalty oath . . . instanced by the way the Columbia Broadcasting Company, in devising an oath that was intended to separate the sheep from the goats in a particularly sensitive industry, abandoned the time-honored affirmative formula, "I swear allegiance," and instead required every employee to swear that he had never been a member of any of the organizations cited on the Attorney General's consolidated list of subversive groups.

True loyalty, he insisted, was a positive impulse, not a matter of promising not to be disloyal.

He didn't specify the shift's source, but everyone knew what he was talking about. The bluntly named House Un-American Activities Committee went back as far as 1938 and in 1945 had become a standing (i.e., permanent) committee of Congress. It investigated the Communist Alger Hiss with the help of Hersey's erstwhile *Time* colleague Whittaker Chambers. In 1947 it began an intimidating series of inquiries into the political affiliations of people working in Hollywood. Meanwhile, the hard-drinking, volatile Senator Joseph McCarthy, encouraged by a number of more publicity-shy informants on the right, had been going about seeking reds to devour and finding them, at least to his own satisfaction, everywhere he looked, including in the White House. How perfectly his worldview would have been confirmed had he known about Hersey's remarks, which were made in a talk at Yale's Skull and Bones Society in June 1951.

The event was held in secret—even the existence of the club is supposed to be a secret, though its fame depends partly on this pretense. The typewritten text of the talk, not very furtively headed "SB" in Hersey's hand, is among his papers.[1] At the outset he spoke about allegory, which was beginning to interest him for his own writing. But after deferring to the club's quasi-Masonic origins through various coded references, he turned to his main topic, which, while treating it in broad human, clubbable terms to do with friendship, he also tied to the dangers of what he didn't need to name as McCarthyism. It was a subversive speech, all the more so for being made to ambitious young men in one of the nurseries of the American establishment. The political climate changed as the 1950s went on, but at this stage many liberals were reluctant to condemn McCarthy's redbaiting, and the elder Kennedy brothers, Jack and Robert, actively supported him.[2] That the author of *Hiroshima* had spoken in this way was quite a secret for members of his audience to keep. What neither they nor McCarthy could know was that only recently, in another but much more powerful private gathering, Hersey had heard the president of the United States himself speak against McCarthy and had witnessed his dignified dismissal of a suggestion that in order to deal with the senator's destructive methods, a McCarthy-like procedure might be used.

This meeting, held at the end of February 1951, was the culmination of a series of otherwise more openly planned encounters between Hersey and President Truman for a *New Yorker* series whose level of access Truman's biographer David McCullough has described as unprecedented.[3] It was crucial to all Hersey's best writing that he was both an outsider and at some level not. In cases like those of *Hiroshima* and his article about Walter Morse, he gave practical assistance to a cause after the writing, but there was generally a prior degree of involvement in terms of imaginative sympathy and, even before that, of trust: he was someone whose decency was recognized by other decent people, so they let him in. The process was complicated and differed from case to case. For the most part, as with loyalty, Hersey's kind of truth didn't often consist of a negative—of stripping away falsehood, exposing wickedness. There were times when these were necessary, but his first impulse was to establish positively, painstakingly, and sympathetically what the facts of a case were. It required, of course, that facts should be there in the first place. The things that had made *The Wall* a success were not primarily to do with fiction, and any assessment of his career must acknowledge that, despite his own ambitions and beliefs, his first though not sole talent was for journalism. If Hersey misjudged his own gifts, other people continued to push him into doing what he generally did best.

The Truman articles are a case in point, as also, before them (and elements in what led to his being given the access to write them), was a series he had done in 1947 for *Collier's* on George Marshall, who had just become Truman's secretary of state, and one for *The New Yorker* on the philanthropist, recently appointed as head of the Atomic Energy Commission, Bernard Baruch. As a journalist Hersey was no pushover, yet at the same time he didn't assume that powerful people were necessarily villains in need of being taken down. Baruch, though, for all his merits—his persistence, keen instincts, generosity, sagacity, and willingness to pass off as good luck what were in fact the results of his own hard work and of taking other people's good advice—was a monster. Hersey's skill is a matter of letting him convey his monstrosity out of his own garrulous mouth, while including himself, the observer-writer, as no more than a respectful, tolerant near-absence, entering the story only when, as if to correct a less favorable impression Baruch himself might be in danger of making, good things need to be said about him.

The reader wants more. Baruch advised statesmen. He had a new responsibility for atomic energy. What his political and philanthropic activities added up to, as distinct from the balance sheet of his businesses (summarized here with remarkable clarity), isn't assessed, and Hersey's avoidance of probing is a limitation. What he communicates, though, is his subject's blend of charm, shrewdness, sentimentality, probity, patriotism, extraordinary head for facts and details, and simultaneously hungry and controlled zest for pleasure: horse racing, showgirls, food. The profile— it consists of three articles—is varied in texture and focus, but the opening gives a good sense of how Hersey's visual scene-setting can be accompanied by a similarly filmic approach to "presence" as an aspect of character. Part of what happens here is that through the hierarchy of a racing stable we are led up to two powerful personages, only to find that someone still more important has yet to arrive. Another part is to do with a muted, unresolved, but, in the piece as a whole, never-quite-absent hint of risk.

> Dew was heavy on the grass beside the long row of stables. A thin, blue plume of smoke stood up from the chimney of the mess shack across from the stables, and the early sunlight glistened on the tents of the swipes and exercise boys ranged along the outer edge of the field beyond the mess shack. Few sounds broke the stillness of the morning—stamping in the stalls, muffled human and equine coughs now and again, occasional ejaculations and sharp bursts of laughter from the boys, and a distant jubilee of peepers in some flats not far from the track. Many of the stalls were empty; this was the last week of the Saratoga season, and quite a number of horses had already been shipped to other tracks. It was about eight o'clock. Robert J. Kleberg, Jr., owner of the King ranch, in Texas, of Assault, and of all the other horses in these stables, sat alone in a garden chair under a brilliantly colored and incongruous beach umbrella, up towards one end of the row of stalls. Max Hirsch, Kleberg's trainer, stood under a tree talking with some of the exercise boys. Hirsch, a sharp-faced man with glasses, was wearing a gabardine shooting jacket, with a shoulder-patch to couch the butt of a gun; he kept his hands in his pants pockets and his shoulders hunched, and talked in a husky voice. A black mongrel dog lay by the trainer's feet.
>
> A Cadillac limousine drove up the road that led into the Kleberg stable area. It stopped on the grass not far from the mess shack. "Here's the boss," Hirsch said.[4]

Bernard Baruch is not much remembered today, but no one who reads this profile will forget him. The sheer intelligence behind the writing must have been among the reasons why Hersey's weighty human subjects in this period allowed him to get close to them and revealed so much of themselves to him. Everything he put into the portrait adds to it. There's a beguiling, deceptively digressive-seeming passage in this same first scene when the trainer shows off his dog, throwing coins for it to find in a field of long grass while Baruch looks on admiringly as it "darted back and forth in the tall growth." "I always enjoy watching a good dog," the financier says. He is "entertained," Hersey writes, "by the dog's earnest money-grubbing."

Whatever Baruch's importance, Harry S. Truman was clearly as big a step up as any magazine profile writer could aim for. His staff took some persuading—more, it seems, than the president himself. The first approach was made by Harold Ross at *The New Yorker*, who was a friend of Truman's press secretary, Charles G. Ross. The reply seemed negative. There had been so many similar requests that to favor one magazine over another would be invidious. Hersey might, though, be given background access to people who knew the president, and could take it from there. He thought about the idea on his European trip and decided to try. In June 1950 he had a long talk with the press secretary, who was one of the oldest friends and closest presidential confidants in a famously intimate entourage. He then spent several weeks in Washington with current and former colleagues of the president and talked to his music-student daughter, Margaret. He went next to the home territory of this close-knit, deep-rooted family: Kansas City and Independence, Missouri. Contrary to Truman's then-current reputation as, in Hersey's summary, "the hack politician who succeeded the great F.D.R. . . . . shelterer of second-rate cronies; spunky, crass, impulsive, and slightly rattled," the writer began to find more. He called it a "moral texture . . . as strong and durable as brake lining." Where this came from, he later wrote, in a passage that is revealing, too, about what Hersey valued in his own background, was

a frontier probity, sorely toughened in pain and conflict; his ancestors were pioneers, westward-removed Kentuckians, and every family in his Scotch-Irish-German-Dutch Independence circle had had some relative who had been killed by redlegs or bushwhackers. There had been much Bible—Old and New Testament—in his youth, and humility had been drummed into him, without, however, depriving him of the capacity for feeling pleased with himself a lot of the time . . . This man wouldn't pose for pictures in Indian headdress when campaigning, and wouldn't kiss babies . . . Politically, as far as I could dig to find, he was as clean as a whistle.[5]

At last, a short face-to-face interview was arranged. But rather than using the time to ask the kinds of questions that might have helped fill out a routine though solidly researched profile, Hersey talked to the president about his passion for history. Roosevelt, he pointed out, had surrounded himself with historians; Truman not. Didn't he have some kind of obligation to let himself "be glimpsed . . . for history"? It was a specious argument. Plenty of people who came close to Truman, whether day by day or at special events, kept diaries and wrote letters. Historians wouldn't be short of information. But it won Truman over and, during a period of three world-historically important months, allowed Hersey an extraordinary amount of proximity.

Thinking of the Truly Great

Just five years earlier, ninety-five days into his unwanted inherited presidency, after spending the afternoon inspecting the U.S. Second Armored Division outside Berlin and then the ruins of the city itself, Truman had written in his diary about his fear "that machines are ahead of morals by some centuries and when morals catch up there'll be no reason for any of it."[6] He didn't specifically mention the A-bomb, though that very morning the world's first nuclear explosion had been brought about in New Mexico. Truman hadn't yet learned of the test's success, but he knew plenty about the weapon and its likely consequences. Six weeks earlier, the advisory committee in charge of the project had given him its unanimous recommendation that the bomb should be used against Japan as soon as possible, and without warning. Other groups and other individuals advised differently, and the new president was well aware of every conceivable objection to, as well as argument for, the weapon's use. From a moral point of view, even Secretary of War Henry Stimson, an ardent supporter of the bomb's use against Japan, called it "the most terrible weapon ever known in human history." It was ultimately capable, Stimson told Truman within a couple of weeks of the latter's taking office, of bringing about the complete destruction of modern civilization.[7] As for immediate practicalities, other ways of ending the Pacific war had been debated and presented to Truman, including at a White House meeting in June 1945,[8] as had the risk of a nuclear arms race, sooner rather than later, with the Soviet Union. At Potsdam the following month, having told Churchill about what the latter called "the Great New Fact"—the result of the Trinity Test at Alamogordo—and discussed the details with his military advisers, he discreetly but unnecessarily dropped a hint about the weapon in the ear of Stalin, who already knew. This was July 24, 1945, and Truman had made up his mind.

No one in the world had communicated the results of that decision more powerfully than John Hersey. Later, some critics, among them the moral philosopher Elizabeth Anscombe, would call Truman a mass murderer.[9] But Hersey had in common with Truman a pragmatic understanding that the world is not managed by moral philosophers. If machines can run ahead of morality, so can the human beings who make them, and over the past few years Hersey had spent most of his time contemplating another of the best documented cases of that happening. Neither the Warsaw ghetto nor the camp to which it was a gatehouse required anything advanced in the way of military technology. As for the nuclear bombing of Japan, Hersey wrote in 1951 that "no more needs to be said than is well known: Truman's decision was essentially a tactical one—namely, that bringing up that gun at that time would save footsoldiers' lives."[10] The synecdoche was apt. In September 1918, Truman had distinguished himself as an artillery commander in the Meuse-Argonne offensive, then the largest action in American military history and one that helped bring about the end of the First World War. Knowing how and when to use a big gun was part of his formation.

Only a year after being returned to the presidency in the election of 1948, Truman was once again intensely beleaguered. Hersey's purpose wasn't to hold him to account—almost everyone was doing that—but to show what he was "like." The familiar expression is odd, not least because it implies that nothing is unique: What was Hiroshima like? What was it like to be in the Warsaw ghetto? Description, the phrase suggests, is a way of finding resemblances where perhaps none exist, so that we can begin to understand what may be incomprehensible. In the case of biographical profiles, William Shawn preferred an older phrase used, as "likeness" also once was, in visual portraiture: to "get down." The pre-photographic idea was that by writing or drawing you could fix a person or place for memory. Hersey, Shawn thought, "could get Truman down," and he suggested that there was something necessary in this: "possibly Truman has some sort of obligation to let himself be got down."[11]

Classically self-educated, Truman was not averse to the notion. A translation of Plutarch's *Lives* of important figures in ancient Greece and Rome was always on his shelves, as was a book he had been given by his mother for his twelfth birthday: C. F. Horne's 1894 *Great Men and Famous Women*. The boy read about the emperor Constantine and the Babylonian king and lawmaker Hammurabi and never forgot what he had learned. He might well have said what a poet of his own time wrote: "I think continually of those who were truly great."[12] For Truman, this wasn't a matter of fantasy or escapism. He believed, as was generally believed in almost every age before our own, that life stories could benefit readers both morally and practically. The career of a powerful military figure or politician was likely to involve situations that, one way or another, would be repeated, and whether the challenges were met well or badly, useful lessons could be learned from the process. In the first weeks and months of the provincial countryman's inheriting the presidency from Roosevelt, everyone who met him found him more impressive than they had expected—usually much more so: better prepared, more knowledgeable, more decisive to a fault, and also more human and funny. Amid the political and economic struggles of the war's immediate aftermath, this changed: even for a politician, the swings in Truman's reputation were startling. Really getting him down, conveying what he was like, was a complicated as well as an important thing to do, and Hersey was the first person to achieve it.

As so often, he gets a purchase on his subject through his way of talking and also what would now be called his body language. The articles appeared in two different sequences, one in *The New Yorker* between April 7 and May 5, 1951, the other as Hersey later organized it for book publication.[13] In the latter, which represented Hersey's own preference, the downbeat opening episode concerns the president's daily ten o'clock meeting with his staff: the deceptive routineness of it and the mix of efficiency and mutual informal good humor involved. The date was November 28, 1950, and the profile's first readers the following spring didn't need to be told that for some months previously the United States had been at war with the Communist bloc in Korea.[14] Yet Hersey's narrative takes its leisurely tone from Truman's own refusal of drama. Being head of state, we are to understand, is something that continues every day of every week and is not best done on nerves or through histrionics. The advisory group considers a list of legislative recommendations for Congress, a draft proposal for naming a committee, an ongoing issue concerning steel prices (explosive then as now, and it was to become more so), an appropriation for assistance to Yugoslavia, some decisions about government appointments.

All this takes up about six thousand words—three-quarters of the installment. But there's tension. The normally "exuberant, defiant mien" of Truman's morning greeting, its "mock impatience"—as usual, he has been up since 5:30 a.m.—is missing; his laughter at his colleagues' jokes lacks heart. When everyone's main business has been dealt with and a certain amount of gossip has been indulged, Truman, writes Hersey, "centered himself at his desk."

> For a few moments, he shifted papers back and forth and straightened a pair of scissors and two paper cutters lying on the leather margin of his desk pad. He had suddenly drooped a little; it appeared that something he would have liked to forget was back in his mind, close behind his hugely magnified eyes.
>
> "We've got a terrific situation on our hands," Truman said in a very quiet, solemn voice. "General Bradley called me at six-fifteen this morning. He told me that a terrible message had come from General MacArthur. MacArthur said there were two hundred and sixty thousand Chinese troops against him there. He says he's stymied. He says he has to go over to the defensive . . . The Chinese have come in with both feet."[15]

With what we'll learn was, for good and ill, his usual firm clarity, the president goes on to describe how he intends to proceed. He'll meet the cabinet, along with General Bradley. Other senior figures will hold meetings with the Treasury and the congressional committees. A national emergency may have to be declared; he'll wait and see about that. Anyway, there will be a radio message to the people: "a simple, four-network hookup from right here, about ten days from now, I would say." Certain current plans will have to be remade. Amid all this, the product of the hours between Bradley's phone call and the meeting, the president pauses: "Suddenly all his driven-down emotions seemed to pour into his face. His mouth drew tight, his cheeks flushed. For a moment, it almost seemed as if he would sob." But he gathers himself quickly, resumes his instructions, and brings the meeting to an end with a joke.

A lot has been communicated, the narrative has accelerated, and if we were reading a novel we might expect it to turn now to the battlefield. Instead, the next episode is entirely devoted to Harry Truman's daily morning walk, or march.[16] Once a hardworking small farmer, then a highly effective soldier, the president still regularly strode a couple of brisk miles at the beginning of every day before doing some gym exercises and having a swim. Security men were in the background, but no advisers were at hand, and Truman soliloquized in Hersey's presence, prompted from time to time by a quiet, knowledgeable question but essentially telling his own story, volunteering his version of events. Inevitably some of this was propaganda, as when Hersey mentions the bad news from Korea and is told that "a general can't be a winner every day of the week," but even here Truman reveals something of himself, including his passion for history: "I advise you to study the lives of Alexander the Great, Tamerlane, Gustavus Adolphus, Hunyadi—and Robert E. Lee and Stonewall Jackson. You'll find they all won most of the time, but they all had their troubles, too." At other times, what comes out can be unpredictable, intriguing, vivid in the way that irrelevancy can be what makes a novel most truthful-seeming. "I like being on the road," Truman says at one point. "Fact is, I like roads." He reminisces about the responsibility he and his father took on for maintaining the roads around their farm before the First World War and how the job's importance stayed with him in the early stages of his subsequent political career. As "got down" by Hersey, it's a wonderful piece of talk, personal, digressive, detailed; and in its sly allusion to Westchester County, where Hersey had grown up in Briarcliff Manor, it shows that if Truman was in a way on his own, he also knew perfectly well who he was talking to:

We took the work, my father and I did, and we had the best roads in Missouri, in and around Grandview. We didn't get any richer, but we had good roads . . . In '28, I went out to build the county some new roads. I had two engineers, Colonel Edward M. Stayton—he's a retired general now—and N. T. Veach—he was and is a Republican. I could then, and I still can, get along with a decent Republican, though Mother never let one, decent or otherwise, land on the front porch if she could help it. Anyway, I took these two engineers, and we drove over every inch of the three hundred and fifty miles of surfaced roads in Jackson County—only you couldn't call them surfaced roads, really: they were just roads with piecrust on them, water-bound macadam that would scale off in no time. The people voted me ten million dollars to build roads—the first bond issue was six and a half million, then in '31 they voted me three and a half more—and I gave them two hundred and eighteen miles of roads that they're still driving on . . . as fine as the system in Westchester County, New York State.

These roads lead Truman's talk in many directions: to other people he worked with on them, to his own habits as a (fast and sometimes negligent) driver, to his oversight of public spending as chairman of the Truman Committee, to corruption and from that to the relative evils of theft and lying. Occasionally Hersey steers him somewhere different: to his reading, to the passage of Tennyson he carries in his wallet; and occasionally Truman himself introduces a wholly new topic: meteorology, for example, or botany. In all this we see him, as the poet Dryden said about the heroes of those character sketches by Plutarch that Truman admired, "in his undress, and are made familiar with his most private actions and conversations. You may behold a Scipio and a Lelius gathering cockleshells on the shore, Augustus playing at bounding-stones with boys."[17] Part of the informality comes from his exchanges with those around him in these precious off-duty moments: his driver, the security detail, his trainer. There are moments of staginess, but Truman's friendliness, his grasp of other people's personal lives, of their existence *as* people, are unmistakable and were often commented on by contrast with the breezy but distinctly removed relationships of the aristocratic Franklin Roosevelt with most of those who worked for him. Meanwhile the marching president indulges a countryman's quiet teasing of the citified writer he has in tow: Can he keep up? He'll probably need a nap.

That ease—the relaxed but perilous self-confidence often remarked on in Truman once he had emerged from Roosevelt's long shadow—is evident again in his handling of the press corps, which is the topic of the next episode. This concerns the occasion when the president made his notorious slip (if that's what it was) of conceding under questioning that the use of nuclear weapons was not excluded from consideration in the Korean War, that such consideration was "for the military people," and that any decision would not be a matter for the United Nations, which had overall responsibility for the action against China, but for the "military commander in the field." This admission, or threat, or gaffe, caused near-panic among America's allies, and in describing it Hersey quietly deploys all his authority as an experienced reporter. Just how the president gets boxed into his corner, how the media then build the story, and what its international repercussions are is an absorbing narrative in itself. It's also adroitly used to lead into the fourth section, "A Weighing of Words," which concerns the minutiae of drafting the president's radio speech about the war.

The five-part series ran in *The New Yorker* until May 5, 1951. In 1980 it was reprinted in Hersey's *Aspects of the Presidency*, where it was joined by the results of a similar project on President Gerald Ford undertaken in 1975.[18] At the time of its first publication Hersey's work on Truman was important in telling readers about the underlying strengths of a man about whom public opinion continued to swing violently, and also in putting his weaknesses into perspective. John Updike, then a student at Harvard, wrote home avidly that "it is an extraordinarily skillful and uneditorial coverage on one of the most important men in the world, a man who only recently has given the world evidence of his great personal courage."[19] For later historians and biographers, however rich their other sources, it has provided a fund of factual material and also an interpretation both of the role of the media in politics at that stage and, relatedly, of the extent to which the president saw himself simultaneously but separately as the holder of his job and as himself: a division long familiar in the history of monarchy but one that, or so the series implies and some political scientists have come to agree, has become impossible for any individual to bridge adequately in a global world. If this is true, the Second World War and its aftermath were the historical moment when the impossibility became clear. As the political scientist Robert A. Dahl—by then a colleague of Hersey's at Yale—wrote in 1980 in some mild words that seem ever more relevant today, the book "reveals aspects of the Presidency the Framers [of the Constitution] never foresaw—and would have found worrisome if they had."[20]

Among these is foreign policy. One seeming aid, of course, was the United Nations, of which both Truman and, with such means as were available to him, Hersey were advocates. If the main existential problem the UN was established to face was the sheer disunity of nations, this was nowhere more apparent than in the Cold War. It wasn't until 1980 that Hersey revealed that his meetings with Truman had included a session in which the president asked the opinion of a group of trusted advisers about how to deal with "the poison of Senator Joseph McCarthy." McCarthyism had brought about a weakening of public trust in some of the country's most valuable leaders, among them Secretary of State Dean Acheson and Secretary of Defense George Marshall as well as the president himself, and in general had caused bitter divisions that made attempts to calm a series of international crises ever more difficult. Truman's and his colleagues' struggles in Korea, a country whose partition had been among the more casual-seeming outcomes of the Second World War, heralded yet more damaging conflicts in the region, most of all in Vietnam and Cambodia. One proposed solution in the late 1940s, that of General MacArthur and others on the more or less extreme right, involved exploiting the United States' current superiority in nuclear weaponry to wage all-out war against both the Soviet Union and Mao's China. The apocalyptic atmosphere was encouraged, to Hersey's dismay but not surprise, by Henry Luce's magazines and gained support from a series of spy scandals, among them those involving Alger Hiss and Klaus Fuchs. It was also exacerbated by Truman's handling of the press conference described by Hersey.

Hersey was only one among very many writers and artists, as well as public figures of other kinds, who were appalled by the new atmosphere. Threats to artistic and intellectual freedom were part of it, but the corruption of public debate, the credence given to lies, the exploitation of any opportunity for political advantage—none of it in essence new, yet all of it always necessary to resist—these plainly required something more of him. But what? He was already a prominent member of PEN, the international organization devoted to protecting freedom of expression (in 1949 he had been offered its presidency).[21] Where he could, he used his writing in support of the causes he believed in, the UN among them. He and the playwright Arthur Miller were part of a group that met informally in a mutual friend's New York apartment to discuss opportunities to place and orchestrate articles and other forms of public argument opposed to

McCarthyism.[22] The Skull and Bones talk was part of this campaign to maximize influence, consolidate support, and encourage waverers. It wasn't nothing, but could he do more? Late in February 1951 he was invited to what he had been led to believe would be a private dinner with the president; his wife, Bess; their daughter, Margaret; and perhaps a close friend or two of theirs.

The White House was undergoing a major program of restoration and reconstruction, so the Trumans were living at Blair House on Pennsylvania Avenue. Hersey arrived promptly at 8:00 p.m. and was shown into a room at the rear, where, to his surprise, a bunch of men, among them the president's counsel, Charles Murphy, stood around a large table covered in green cloth. Murphy explained that there was to be an off-the-record discussion and that Hersey should not take notes. More people drifted in; the group eventually included the attorney general and half a dozen senators and congressmen. The president entered, sat next to Hersey, and without preamble said he wanted everyone's advice about how to counter McCarthy.[23] After some discussion, one of those present ("not from the Justice Department," Hersey wrote much later) announced that a dossier existed that revealed what hotel rooms McCarthy had stayed in, with whom and when, over a period of years. Publication of its contents would destroy the senator.

It was one of the occasions when Hersey noticed that Truman distinguished between his private person and his office: "His third-person self spoke in outrage: the President wanted no more such talk." The writer later reconstructed the sense of his words from memory:

You must not ask the President of the United States to get down in the gutter with a guttersnipe.

Nobody, not even the President of the United States, can approach too close to a skunk, in skunk territory, and expect to get anything out of it except a bad smell.

If you think somebody is telling a big lie about you, the only way to answer is with the whole truth.

The rest of the evening was, he said, an anticlimax. It was the last occasion when he met Truman in office, and he had to write his articles without mentioning it. Whether or not anyone was thinking about Hersey himself as a potential politician—a notion that surfaced a few years later when he was working for Adlai Stevenson[24]—his reputation for trustworthiness was consolidated. As for his own ambitions, he continued to focus on social responsibility—civic virtue—as communicated by the written and spoken word, how to pursue it, and how to defend its freedoms. Public education and the environment would soon be among his concerns. How politics were conducted, though, and how human beings found ways of getting along together, preoccupied him at a utopian as much as a practical level; or rather he found himself, in both journalism and fiction, considering the ways in which utopias fail.

Versions of Family

The plainest and most moving example came from a trip to Israel. *The Wall* had produced many invitations to visit the country, and Hersey opted for one that gave him the opportunity to see what had become of the egalitarian rural kibbutz movement, founded early in the twentieth century around the time of the Russian Revolution but inevitably affected by the changes that had taken place subsequently in Palestine: the arrival, first, of idealistic volunteers from different cultural backgrounds, then of very large numbers of refugees from and survivors of Nazism; the establishment of Israel as a state; and developments in agriculture and industry that had had impacts everywhere in the world. Hersey's article is clear, detailed, and respectful but bleakly unromantic. The social organization of the early kibbutzim, with their absolute equality of labor and reward, their undifferentiation of gender, their segregation of parents and children, was dependent for its success, he implies, on a mix of self-selection (the original kibbutzniks were more often volunteer immigrants than refugees) and opposition: an element of excitement in confronting the British Mandate was removed with the foundation of a self-governing Israel. It was also a youthful movement: the early kibbutz was not designed to accommodate how people's ambitions grow and their capacities alter. Men and women newly arrived from Central Europe, many from the concentration camps, were disinclined to eat in communal barracks. Many had skills, trades, and professions that didn't easily fit into the by now well-established kibbutz rule of nonspecialization, and further tensions were caused by the fact that those who had grown up in and with the system formed a de facto ruling class—one that was challenged now by another aristocracy, that of resisters to Nazism. Agricultural communes came under pressure because the new national government, needing to feed its large population, had to keep food prices down at a time when costs to those dependent on selling their produce were going up. Some of the kibbutzim visited by Hersey were perpetually in debt. Meanwhile, new technology required expertise that required specialists. The entire economic and social basis of the old Zionist movement, it seemed, was being undermined by, among other things, the fulfillment of Zionism.

Hersey reveals the predicament sensitively but without sentimentality, and without touching on its perilous geo-strategic context.[25] By the end, the promise he quotes from the Old Testament prophet Amos—"They shall also make gardens, and eat the fruit of them. And I will plant them upon their land, and they shall no more be pulled out of their land which I have given them"[26]—comes as an irony, all the more so for his passing reference earlier to a kibbutz of Polish Jews, some of them survivors of the Warsaw ghetto, whose output is prosaically specialized in manufacturing metal beds.

He had seen Stalin's Russia. His sympathies in Israel were for the individualistic, the enterprising, and the colorful. In a strange novel written at this time called *The Marmot Drive*, also concerned with utopianism, he imagines a New England community that has kept the customs and values of its origins into the present day. An educated city girl comes to spend the weekend there with her boyfriend and is caught up in a somewhat desolate rural sport: a hunt for woodchucks. During this event the attentions of different men make her feel sometimes like a hunted creature herself, though in one case she's the pursuer. A recriminatory, puritanical village trial seems to echo Arthur Miller's *The Crucible*, first performed the previous year, including in its hints of the proceedings of HUAC. Hersey's book has had chasteningly few admirers but is a reminder that the more oppressive forms of government can be local and familial as much as national. The fable's depiction of a father uncompromisingly severe with his son, while not autobiographical—Hersey was a warm, affectionate parent—suggests something he resisted in himself, as well as the tensions familiar to anyone responsible for a boy moving into his teens.

On the surface the Herseys—John, Frances Ann, Martin, John Junior,

Ann ("Boo"), and the toddler Baird—were living very comfortably. The film deal with Selznick for *The Wall* guaranteed a solid income throughout the 1950s, and plenty more was coming in. In 1952 CBS TV bought adaptation rights to Hersey's Guadalcanal book, *Into the Valley*. Writing proposals arrived from all sides—for a film about Hungarian former refugees and articles on McCarthyism and on Eisenhower. He also kept a shrewd eye on his backlist, drawing Knopf's attention around this time to rights sold in India and the Middle East, where earnings were currently very low. Guessing that they might increase "in a distant and generally more literate future," he insisted on contracts that ensured that rights would revert to him within a fixed period.[27] This affected, for example, sales of *A Bell for Adano* in Arabic and Hebrew translations. Although he had passed on to the American Red Cross *Hiroshima*'s revenues from serialization and the Book of the Month Club, royalties continued to come in from the book itself and from translations. Over the latter, he successfully argued with Knopf that when foreign book clubs bought his works, his share should be calculated not in the same way as that from sales to U.S. book clubs, on which Knopf took 50 percent, but as for foreign publications, on which the firm was entitled to only 20 percent and he himself to 80 percent.[28]

All this enabled him to buy and build on twenty-six acres overlooking Long Island Sound. He and Frances Ann engaged an architect named Eliot Noyes, "a young modern who used to be architectural consultant for the Museum of Modern Art, a friend who knows our ways and lives near here."[29] As a member of the Pequot Yacht Club in Southport and a regular, keenly competitive participant in the Larchmont Regatta and other contests, Hersey spent much of every summer on the water, sometimes chartering sizable boats for family excursions out of Long Island Sound to Naushon Island and Martha's Vineyard. He later articulated more fully his always intense relationship with boats—and their relationship with the water, and the relationships between people on and with boats in and with the water—in various literary forms. From today's perspective, among the most striking, though somewhat artificially presented, are the ecological discussions in the later *Blues*, his 1987 book about sea fishing.[30] A more traditionally eventful symbolic novel published in 1967, *Under the Eye of the Storm*, presents, in a way that may have drawn on unwelcome new tensions in his private life in the mid-1950s, the painful, ambiguous crosscurrents between two couples on a boat hit by a tornado. These works were still to come, but meanwhile he thought back to his trip on the Yangtze at the beginning of 1945, out of which came one of his best novels, *A Single Pebble* (1956).[31]

Sailing was not his only recreation. He was good at poker, and, almost as tense, there were family word contests. He and Brendan Gill took their sons to football games, at one of which Gill teased his friend about *The Marmot Drive*: "Your *next* novel begins 'Bang! Was that a gun I heard? Speaking of guns—.'" He added, "The next 69,990 words will cost you $1 a word."[32] But for all the laughter, especially around the dinner table, something of Hersey's former newsroom ease had left him. Unlike most male and several female American writers of the time, he wasn't a big drinker. Gill himself was one of the habit's prose poets.[33] Many people in Hersey's wider circle were alcoholics, at least by today's standards, and his moderation as well as his seriousness about life and everyday decisions increasingly separated him from some of them. (Robert Brustein later recalled Hersey's switch from Heineken to Beck's beer as having seemed "almost as momentous to me as the end of the Vietnam War or the breakup of the Soviet Union.")[34] It meant that he had more time for his work, and also— but it's also "but"—that almost everything he did, wrote, and said was more careful, more circumscribed than was the case with writer friends like Lillian Hellman and William Styron. Some described his calm as almost Confucian. His life had friendship, variety, prosperity, and—what for a while seemed to distinguish him from so many others—stability. The house was built, trees were cleared, and the garden was coming along. "Our acres of honeysuckle have begun to be flecked with white," he wrote to Grace in June 1953,

> and the whole hill smells good. Frances Ann has put in a rock and cut-flower garden on the slope coming up towards the house, to the right of the driveway. Like everything else around the house, it will take a couple of years to come into its own, but it is already very pretty. I've begun to experiment with propagating stripes of periwinkle and ivy, as we are much in need of ground cover in various places.[35]

The following summer, they were persuaded to open their house and garden for an event organized by the Fairfield Historical Society. A glossy magazine came to take pictures.[36]

Making a new home can sometimes be a way of trying to repair what has begun, invisibly to outsiders, to go wrong. Problems had been growing. John's brother Rob was unhappy and sometimes unwell, and in the mid-1950s his marriage broke up. John had his own share of family difficulties, including with some of the children, their health, and their education. And while he and Frances Ann kept up a good front, in private they had begun to get along less well. New political activities were taking him away a great deal; Frances Ann wanted more of a life and career of her own; some relationships collided and caused friction. But the causes of marital breakdown are often no more clearly identifiable by the afflicted couple themselves than by anyone else. Why, a reader of *In the Eye of the Storm* might ask, why do hurricanes happen?

By 1957 the couple had decided to part. It was the second such situation Grace Hersey had had to face as a mother-in-law, and now she drafted a letter to Frances Ann with truthfulness and dignity:

> It is no use saying my heart is as light as a feather . . . because it isn't—it is heavy as lead with sadness. This contemplated break can only bring . . . disillusionment, and a sense of loss of highest values. But—you two parents love the children you have brought into the world . . . You are old enough to know your own minds and hearts. How can I say "God bless you—go ahead"? I only say "Be *sure* you are right—then—then only—go ahead."[37]

They were divorced in 1958. The children were between the ages of nine and sixteen. Hersey had written reassuringly to his mother, "I have a feeling that everything is going to turn out all right in our family. Thank you for your love and understanding."[38] Something of his sadder feelings may be guessed from his description, around this time, of a man who leaves his household and his sense of loss not so much over the place as "over the words said and the things done in these rooms over twelve years of the prime of his life."[39]

Hersey always separated work from domestic life, and not just in the discipline he applied to removing himself into his writing. In these difficult years he had found, or fallen into, various new involvements. One was directly political: in the first (1952) presidential campaign of Adlai Stevenson, who was among the architects of the United Nations and Truman's chosen successor, Hersey chaired the Connecticut branch of Volunteers for Stevenson.[40] The intelligent, lucid, moderate, and modest Stevenson had considerable appeal for artists and intellectuals among many others, and although these gifts didn't translate into enough popular appeal for him to defeat General Eisenhower, Arthur M. Schlesinger later saw him as having been JFK's forerunner.[41] Hersey was busy, too, with journalistic assignments and pro bono activities in literature and education, and campaigns against nuclear proliferation. He worked hard for the Authors Guild, helping to secure better contractual arrangements for his peers. He judged prizes: the American Academy of Arts and Letters' 1952 Prix de Rome, for example, was decided by a panel on which he sat with W. H. Auden and Van Wyck Brooks. It went to William Styron. In 1953, when Hersey was still in his thirties, he became the youngest writer ever elected to the academy, an honor he found specially cheering, as he confided to Alfred Knopf, given that "published news about Hersey writings has not all been happy lately" (he meant the poor reception of *The Marmot Drive*). At the academy's beaux-arts building on West 155th Street he was proud to find himself in a chair behind one bearing the name of an earlier author of Alfred Knopf's, Willa Cather.[42] In 1955, with help from Robert Penn Warren, he secured the Rome Prize for Ralph Ellison.

Some of Hersey's admirers wondered whether cultural diplomacy abroad would appeal to him. In September 1954 the U.S. Information Agency offered the possibility of his becoming a cultural representative to India.[43] But domestic politics also had its attractions. He was busy in the antinuclear movement, arranging a visit by Kiyoshi Tanimoto to a Christian youth rally in 1949 and, on the tenth anniversary of the bombing in 1955, writing a big article about the latest Geneva Summit. He was also doing a lot of work on public education. The topic had come to interest him particularly during his postwar travels in China but was a strong part of his family background and had been on his mind ever since he left Yale. On the boat to Cambridge, the young idealist had met James Bryant Conant, a reforming president of Harvard. During what Hersey at the time called "one of the most interesting half hours I have had," they talked about "education methods, the blessings and curses of work in education in general and, in particular, that of a University president."[44] Now, almost two decades on, he sat on an educational committee of inquiry set up by the state of Connecticut and was a trustee of several schools, and spent the early part of 1955 on a series of visits to schools and individual educators that took him to Chicago, Berkeley, Stanford, Portland (Oregon), Los Angeles—where he managed to fit in some vacation with Frances Ann, Johnny, and friends—and Albuquerque. Researching in Kansas, he took the opportunity to visit the retired President Truman.[45] At the specialist Hartt College of Music in Hartford, Connecticut, he was daunted and thrilled by being loaned, albeit briefly, a Stradivarius.[46] A novel was emerging from this research,[47] so when, soon afterward, Henry Kissinger contacted him on behalf of the Rockefeller Brothers Fund about a major project concerning gifted students in public schools, Hersey declined.[48] Still, the 1956 election again saw him out on the campaign trail on Adlai Stevenson's behalf, this time as an adviser and a speechwriter specializing on education policy and nuclear proliferation.[49] There are signs that he was torn between the claims of his writing and this new degree of political engagement. In July, Stevenson wrote to him about the problem, apparently hoping to persuade him into a closer involvement. While the candidate showed sympathetic concern about "a very improper balancing of values," Hersey had evidently expressed to Willard Wirtz, a future labor secretary who was part of the campaign's inner circle, "a willingness to help" that seemed to go beyond his current efforts, and Stevenson asked directly whether he could "give us a few weeks of your fuller time in September or October."[50] These were the weeks immediately before the election on November 6. In the event, Stevenson was once again swept away by Eisenhower, but it sounds as if he may have been holding out to Hersey the possibility of a future job if things had gone differently:

> No one could appreciate more fully than I do your expressed feeling that it is very hard to function under the extraordinary and inordinate pressures of a campaign editorial bullpen operation. I do have the feeling, however, that if there is any prospect of your having time available we could work out some arrangement which would permit our calling upon you in a somewhat different manner.[51]

That summer Hersey joined Ralph Ellison, Pearl Buck, John Steinbeck, and Arthur Miller on the U.S. delegation to PEN's annual meeting, held in London.[52] The following year took him and other PEN delegates to Japan. It was inevitable at the time that some of his activities and the personal connections they involved would sooner or later lead to accusations that he was a Communist, though no one seems to have taken the charges seriously.[53]

American Troubles Abroad

Korea had made it obvious that in some regions the Second World War still hadn't ended, a fact brought closer to home in Europe when Hungary was invaded by the Soviet Union in October 1956. Hersey interviewed one of the refugees who had reached the United States and wrote up his story in *The New Yorker*. The article is justly hard on the Soviet Union; somewhat soft on Austria;[54] vivid about Vilmos Fekete, the former anti-Communist politician who provides the main human focus; and interesting about the combination of idealism, energy, and organizational inefficiency among various religious aid groups working with refugees. Later the piece was among a number collected under the title *Here to Stay: Stories of Human Endurance*, but there are many signs in Hersey's writing that the places to which his imagination was now taking him were too dark to be readily articulated.

While the ostensible focus in *The Marmot Drive* is on Hester, the most brutal emotional encounters are between her boyfriend, Eben Avered, and his father, Matthew, whether over the relative merits of rum and whiskey or what's really to be found in the Bible. After the Ten Commandments in Exodus 20, the next chapter, Matthew points out to his son, "tells us believers how to organize polygamy and slavery, and that's where it says, 'Eye for eye, tooth for tooth, hand for hand, foot for foot, burning for burning, wound for wound, stripe for stripe.'"[55] Hester tries to figure out what lies behind the bitterness of Matthew's attacks on sanitized religion and on his cultural surroundings in general, but her efforts distract from the conflict between her boyfriend and his father—a conflict she has played a part in through the sexual attraction between her and Matthew. In letting these ideas loose, Hersey doesn't quite either control them as a novelist or let them control the novel: we see things through Hester's limited understanding, which gives us very little purchase on Eben; and the physical potential of what's going on—the possibility of a real (rather than desired and, by the townspeople, suspected) sexual act between her and Matthew—is repeatedly deflected by events in the wood-chuck hunt. But there's unmissable psychic energy in all this, of a kind that is more clearly if also less recklessly expressed in *A Single Pebble*.

The 1956 novella returns to some aspects of the China of Hersey's boyhood via his Yangtze trip in 1945. The narrator looks back on a time "in the century's and my early twenties" when, as a young engineer, he was sent upriver to identify possible sites for a dam. From I-ch'ang, he travels through the gorges and rapids to Wan Hsien by junk, under sail on the rare occasions when the wind is favorable but for the most part propelled by a dozen oarsmen and hauled by scores of "trackers" harnessed together on the hazardous towpaths. Early on, the young man suffers a malarial fever, which intensifies his encounters with what he sees at first as the cruel, superstitious slave economy of the river. To make a separation between what he "concludes" and the experiences themselves is to suggest a narrative more prosaic than the one Hersey offers, but this representative of technological progress comes to recognize that the ancient, apparently wasteful, and inefficient methods of navigating dangerous waters give thousands of people not only employment but a sense of individual meaning. What that meaning consists of is obscure to the engineer, and he is as bewildered by the contradictions between the Chinese, and within individual Chinese, over their attitudes to ritual as Matthew Avered is by the customs and beliefs of his fellow villagers in *The Marmot Drive*. It's perfectly clear that the river is capable of being subdued by a series of dams that would be of immense value for energy and irrigation while allowing for transportation through locks and lifts. But by the end of his voyage the engineer knows, too, that everything he has experienced and valued in it would be nullified by such an intervention. The traditional ways now seem better, for all their precariousness, poverty, danger, and hardship. There are many moments that could illustrate that point, as well as the simple poetry of the language used. One occurs when he comes on the sailor called Old Pebble preparing for the journey's hazardous next leg. He is

mending a parrel, a small collar of bamboo rope which held the crude iron snatch-ring for the towing hawser against the mast . . . What struck me now was the affectionate care with which he worked. He had a shell of callus on his palms, so that it was almost a wonder that he could make a fist at all: his fingers were as thick as my thumbs—yet he drew out and replaced crushed strands of bamboo from the braid and fed in fresh lengths with the care and precision of a surgeon, and if the new strand did not lie absolutely flush with the rest, he would take it out and shave off a few delicate fibers with a tiny knife and thread the filament in again. Workmanship! All my life since then I have watched for such love of perfection in men who work with their hands.[56]

The novella has been taken as elegizing the China that some on the American right believed they had "lost,"[57] but for all his evocation of the past, what the engineer comes to understand is that America never had a China to lose. The country he experiences is too big, too old, its people too separate and too superior in their separateness to be appropriated by another culture. The tough wisdom of Old Pebble, the legends related by the junk owner's wife, Su-ling, the sacrifices and rituals enacted by various members of the crew at different times—all these exist of themselves, untouched by the engineer's presence. The special tone of the story comes from the double regret of the narrator as he looks back over a failed career that "began and ended" with that journey and recalls a world that history has taken away. The distance between narrator and his past self allows him to moralize in a fashion that Hersey always felt he needed but that elsewhere he doesn't always manage so well. David Sanders is right that *A Single Pebble* is Hersey's "most nearly perfect fiction."[58]

He was still thinking a good deal about the natural environment. For Alfred Knopf's sixtieth birthday in 1952, he had written an affectionate piece focusing on a little-known aspect of the publisher's life: his enthusiasm for national parks. Born in New York City, Knopf was well into his fifties before he saw anything of the United States except its cities. Having decided to find out what existed in between them, he approached the project with his usual energy and thoroughness. With advice from the similarly assiduous Hersey,[59] and accompanied by small armies of expert guides and minders, he and Blanche made trips to Yellowstone and after that to many of America's other curated wildernesses. Among the results was Knopf's commissioning of the environmentalist Freeman Tilden to write *The National Parks: What They Mean to You and Me* (1951). The power of nature was Hersey's topic in an exciting narrative-cum-portrait of an elderly woman caught in a hurricane and flood when Connecticut's well-named Mad River burst its banks in the summer of 1955.⁶⁰

Meanwhile, for the UN he scripted a documentary film about Hungary. And during his return to Japan in July 1957 for PEN he followed up a strange, grim, all-too-resonant story about a U.S. military exercise held earlier in the year in Gunma Prefecture, northwest of Tokyo.⁶¹

The occupation of Japan had officially ended in 1952, but U.S. troops continued to be based there. During the war, Gunma people had become impoverished when they were required to set aside their traditional work of silk production in favor of farming for food. After 1945, their new main source of income was scrap metal gathered on the local U.S. military range. As soon as the fateful exercise began, troops of the Eighth Regiment, First Cavalry Division were overrun by scavengers, and in the confusion the event proper was abandoned. Bored, two soldiers played a game in which they scattered shell cases to tempt the opportunists, then fired spent cartridges on them from a grenade launcher. (It later emerged that this was a common sport on the range.) A Japanese woman was hit in the back at close range, the metal traveling four and a half inches into her chest cavity and hitting her aorta. She died instantly. The soldiers' clumsy attempt at a cover-up was reinforced by U.S. military censorship, and the story only gradually leaked out. It was, as Hersey wrote in *The New Yorker*, "so loaded with symbols, emotions, complexities, lessons and ironies that the case became a classic representation-in-small—an image with the authenticity of an antique limner's crude miniature—of American troubles abroad."

In attempts at recompense soldiers made a collection of money, and private individuals—some of them American—gave generous presents. No one, though, seems to have tried to find out what practices were customary locally in situations of bereavement and of grave offense. Japanese fury was heightened by recent memories of one of the U.S. atomic tests at Bikini, the first "Castle Bravo" test in 1954, which had been three times more powerful than anticipated and exposed native fishermen working far outside the exclusion zone to radiation from which at least one died. Meanwhile, issues of international legal jurisdiction arose, and also military ones of what did and didn't fall within a soldier's "official duty" on an exercise. These escalated into a dispute over sovereignty, with Washington under pressure from American veterans and other "patriots," and the Japanese government similarly embattled from within. And then there was the matter of the killer, William Girard, a not-very-bright, hard-drinking twenty-one-year-old specialist third class from the Midwest, who had a Japanese girlfriend.

The initially penitent Girard was content to be tried by the Japanese and found a local lawyer. His elder brother, though, was contacted in Ottawa, Illinois, by a New York publicist who told him that William was a hero and held out the possibility that a group of lawyers might be persuaded to take a case against the U.S. government, which, after some to-ing and fro-ing, had conceded that Japan had the right to deal with the matter. Hersey sharply describes the personalities involved and the predicament of Girard's girlfriend, whom he had promised to marry, seemingly in the belief that this might stand in his favor with the courts, and who despite being noisily abused on both sides patiently continued offering acts of propitiation to the bereaved family. Meanwhile Girard enjoyed "soaring self-esteem" when his situation was mentioned publicly by the president, and the Supreme Court deferred its vacation to deliberate over it.

Girard's case was heard in August. Hersey's alertness to Japanese ritual and tradition gives this story—which, like his articles critical of U.S. behavior in postwar China,[62] has never been reprinted—extraordinary depth of texture:

> As a courtesy to the defendant, every Japanese word in court was trans-
> lated into English, but there was no way of translating, at least in terms
> that could be quickly grasped by the Americans, the essence of the Japa-
> nese meaning of any trial—and especially of this one. To the Japanese, a
> trial is a kind of public penance; feelings are weighed along with facts.
> This trial was supposed to be Girard's chance for a humble apology to
> Japan for what everyone could see had been a stupid, brutal, gross, inhu-
> man act.

Instead, in a stifling room where some members of the public had fallen asleep, Girard "fidgeted, crossed his legs, slouched, heaved, turned this way and that." Meanwhile, not so much in the background as part of the situation's essence stood every insult and humiliation suffered by the Japanese at American hands since Hiroshima—abuses, not all of them conscious, which Hersey lists in an excoriating paragraph. A short time before the trial, in the region where the killing had happened, a group of "huge, drunken" GIs laid into white-uniformed Japanese police in a pinball parlor. As President Clinton was to say much later, in a moment of concern about the impact on the Russian leadership of Western successes in former Soviet territory in Europe and their possible repercussions, "We keep telling [them] . . . here's some more shit for your face."[63]

Strength of Character

In June 1958, Hersey was remarried in a Congregational church in Fairfield, Connecticut.[64] Barbara Kaufman, formerly Addams, born Day, was doubly on the rebound. Her first marriage, to the cartoonist Charles Addams, had foundered on his infidelities and his resistance to her wish to have a baby. A compromise seemed to have been worked out in the form of adopting an older child, but Addams balked at the last minute. Vivacious, determined, resourceful, beautiful, and, as her daughter stresses, utterly down-to-earth, the thirty-one-year-old simply walked away on June 15, 1951, leaving behind all her personal possessions but happy to be turning her back, also, on Morticia, the cartoon character who had preceded her arrival in Addams's life but whom, being slender and dark-haired, she was said to embody. A new relationship, with a wealthy war veteran named Joe Kaufman, was less long-lived—indeed, in her own later summary, was "unmentionable."[65] Barbara had known John Hersey since the 1940s: the Addamses were neighbors of the Herseys in Sutton Place, and once the writer became, like Charles Addams, a *New Yorker* fixture, their social worlds overlapped. The intense, saturnine Hersey was very different, though, from the gregarious, hard-drinking, apolitical Addams, with his black jokes, his racing cars, his collection of Gothic oddments. One *New Yorker* staffer, contrasting Barbara's husbands, gave Hersey the nickname "Mr. Straight Arrow."[66] This wasn't meant kindly, but by her mid-thirties Barbara had begun to tire of the vagaries of a life she had come to feel excluded her. The straight and narrow had its appeal and in Hersey was combined with social-political commitment and a strong sense of family life, the latter more than confirmed when he took her home to Briarcliff.[67]

Afterward, he wrote to Grace, "I think that with [Barbara] I have known for the first time in my life the meaning of a deep, calm, truthful, and wholly reciprocal love." Late in 1959, in her fortieth year, Barbara gave birth to a daughter, Brook. Arthur Schlesinger was among those who wrote to congratulate the couple. "I think John's capacity to face a crisis like this at his age," he joked, "exhibits great strength of character."[68]

9. Those Breakthroughs I Yearn For

FOUR OF HERSEY'S BOOKS so far had given voice to one or other op-
pressed, ignored, terrorized, or patronized group: Sicilians under
American occupation, Japanese under American bombing, Jews
under Nazism, and Chinese peasants on the brink of industrialization. He
had also made readers share his concern with children marginalized and
adults mesmerized by ineffective kinds of education and assessment. Now
the civil rights movement, too, claimed his attention, though he couldn't
anticipate just how intensely he would become involved.[1] Meanwhile,
America's blunderings in Indochina led him, as it did other writers, to look
for fictional analogies in the Second World War. He hadn't lost interest in
John "Gus" Widhelm, the dive-bomber pilot he had met on the aircraft
carrier *Hornet*,[2] and was also fascinated by conversations he'd had with
Pat Knopf, who'd spent the latter part of the war as a B-22 bomber pilot
based in England. Although Hersey was famous for having revealed just
how bad war could be, for him and many others it had an undeniable fas-
cination, even appeal, and he had seen enough to know that if you accept
the possibility of a just war, you have to accept, too, that for it to succeed,

people are needed who enjoy and are good at being warriors. There were limits and qualifications: *A Bell for Adano* was in part about a general— Patton—who liked war too much; and in Hersey's earlier *Men on Bataan* he had, he now believed, been too kind to the similarly trigger-happy MacArthur. But the issues—endurance, self-sacrifice, heroism, and the links between these and insecurities of various kinds—hadn't gone away, and they had cropped up again in his thinking about Harry Truman. Out of all this came a flawed but at its best enthralling novel, which was almost immediately turned into a film, *The War Lover*.

Structurally among the most ingenious of Hersey's books, the novel is made of four main threads. Two concern the life of a U.S. Air Force base in Britain and the crew of a particular bomber: the novel alternates between sections on the one hand telling the tense story of a single mission lasting fifteen hours and, on the other, covering the six months in 1943 between the men's arrival in Cambridgeshire and the beginning of this last raid. The retrospective narrator is a copilot, Charles Boman, whose close relationship with his pilot and their contrasting attitudes to the tasks at hand—to danger, fear, the physical actualities of aerial warfare—form another strand. Their enforced mutual dependency is complicated by the copilot's love affair with an English woman, Daphne, and her separate relationship with the pilot, Buzz Marrow. The psychology of all this is intense, and intensely subjective on Boman's part, which almost but not quite justifies what can seem overdetermined elements in the characterization of Buzz, with his obsessive sexuality and linkages between flying and sex, fighting and sex. (He names his plane *The Body*.) Daphne, on the other hand, is portrayed with real subtlety, and her pragmatic, autonomous approach to her fragile affairs—fragile because the men are under such stress as well as because they are liable to disappear from her life at any moment— is communicated with respect and vivid circumstantiality. The novel is unusual among books by men about war in the assurance with which it handles a woman confident in her intelligence as well as in her sexuality, someone who has learned to survive in a world where the common knowledge that men can't be relied on is true at the most existential level (her father was killed in the London Blitz; a former airman lover didn't come back from his last mission). Her feminist premise that war is a disease of masculinity, or at least of a very common form of it, is a large aspect of what the book is about, though the theme is less interesting when Buzz is being diagnosed rather than simply "got down." The boisterous, egotistical, opportunistic, exhibitionist pilot is a convincing character, and the nature of his appeal to other men as well as to women doesn't need explanation. More compelling is Daphne's question to Charles: "Why do you men have this conspiracy of silence about this part of war, the pleasure of it?"[3]

While she's one of the book's main strengths, another lies in its sheer narrative tension and descriptive verve. The latter reaches a new poetic level early on, when Boman first sees the crew's American plane in its English fenland setting: "Surrounded . . . by vague, lumpish trees and shrubs, our ship huddled in the mist like a great dark sea lion among some waveworn rocks."[4] Hersey hadn't forgotten what Cambridge felt like to a young American. He has the rare skill, too, of depicting work: the practical professional tasks of each member of the crew, how painstaking the preparations for a mission are, how long everything takes, and then the slow build as one plane after another takes off, the squadron forms in the air, then the group. All this is matched and intensified by Boman's turbulent, confused, traumatized sexual behavior as well as his fluctuating feelings about his professional tasks. In these respects the book is unequaled in war fiction of its date (*Catch-22* had still to appear and shows signs of having been influenced by *The War Lover*)[5] and holds the reader not least through how fear is communicated by a narrator who, precisely because he is the narrator, we know will survive.

And if much of the book's tension and sadness derives from the high risks of the bombing campaign, few readers even in 1959–60 were previously aware how unsuccessful bombing missions over Europe had been in terms of impact on military-industrial targets. Just what the campaign was actually achieving is made fun of in a riotous scene in the mess when the men sing, "What shall we do with a drunken pilot?" with its exultant, bitter refrains: "He will bomb the blind and pregnant . . . he will bomb their homes and churches . . . he will bomb their turnip patches . . ."[6] A mix of futility and guilt presses on Boman, and the accumulation of his experiences—of different missions, of his dealings with other airmen, and of his gauche, perilous relationship with Daphne—in turn influences his behavior: his irresolution and the Daphne-like way in which he compromises with circumstances. Both characters are too idealistic not to regret their ultimate pragmatism, and too pragmatic for idealism to be anything but a source of pain.

This psycho-moral muddle owes something to Ford Madox Ford, whose 1915 novel of bewildered honor, *The Good Soldier*, is mentioned. Boman's cultivated friend Lynch—a precursor of Heller's Snowden in *Catch-22*[7]—has read it. Boman himself is "flummoxed" by it—"I couldn't have told you who was who"—and gets more out of Antoine de Saint-Exupéry's fraught poetic novella *Night Flight* (1930). It's a plausible choice. Saint-Exupéry was a hero to wartime aviators; having escaped from France in 1940, he became a reconnaissance pilot for the United States. (He and his plane went missing in July 1944.) His account of the tensions between ground controller and pilot, between notions of duty and those of love and life itself, between the beauty of the night sky and the terrors of a hurricane—all this spoke readily to anyone involved in air war.

If Hersey was helped by his literary reading, he also characteristically did a lot of basic factual research. USAF Information Services in Washington facilitated a visit to the Air University at Montgomery, Alabama, on a military flight: "I shall cut some invitational orders," his Washington contact told him, "and you can hitch-hike down there and back."[8] The research division of the U.S. Air Force Museum in Dayton, Ohio, lent him various books and manuals, including a copy of the flight operating instructions issued to pilots of the B-17F.[9] Preparations of such thoroughness can go wrong in Hersey's novels, but in this one they supply anchor points for events that become increasingly vertiginous, as when Boman forces himself to do what he can for a bombardier he doesn't like, whose leg has been blown off in a plane that, one way or another, is clearly going to crash.

The physicality is frightening and gruesome—Boman kneeling on a sheet of ice incorporating the bombardier Max's blood—but more horrible still is his revulsion at the look of imploring affection Max directs at him "from a bundle of bloody trouser material," a look containing "a marked degree of love":

> I believe this tender begging look increased my sense of terror by many fold, because I hated Max, I really did hate his deep aggressive drives, the love of dropping bombs that made him jump on his seat, after bombs-away, like a baby on a kiddy-car. I think he was one of them, one of the men with the taint Marrow had, a war lover . . . And his eyes were saying,

"My dear Bo, my dear fellow man, my brother, sharer with me of life, do you understand what I am trying to say with my eyes?"

The idea of a war lover takes on a different meaning here, and in acknowledging the way warriors' mutual dependence becomes mutual loyalty and sometimes more, Hersey brings his story close to its complex end. By then, both Max and Buzz, among many others, are dead. Daphne has already made clear that, for her, the relationship with Charles, too, is over— in part because he has been unable to make any long-term commitment to it, and in part (and relatedly) because his tour of duty is complete. He survives, of course, to tell his story; yet that story is nothing more than what's in it. His voice is maturely retrospective, he has had time to reach this degree of understanding, but there's no indication how long an interval has passed between these events and their narration, or what has occurred during that time.

Educating Janet

The book was well received, including by former airmen who had served in the campaign, whose letters Hersey, as always, kept.[10] Other popular war writers admired it, too: Irwin Shaw, author of *The Young Lions* (1948), told him, "The whole business of flying in wartime has never been presented, as far as I'm concerned, with more skill and precision . . . The idea of war as a pleasure, as an amusement, as a gratification and necessity, to certain men, is one that I find convincing and real."[11] Hersey's reputation among Cold Warriors as a crypto-Communist was reinforced, meanwhile, by an enthusiastic article in the Soviet *Literaturnaya Gazeta*, knowledgeable about his work and making mention of discussions about *Adano* between him and Soviet critics in Moscow near the end of the war. The reviewer described *The War Lover* as an indictment of what he implausibly claimed was a specifically American kind of militarism.[12]

Negotiations for a movie were quickly concluded. While David Selznick, near the end of his expensive ten-year lease on *The Wall*, was still trying to get that project into production (and now to renew the contract with Hersey on different terms),[13] Columbia agreed to pay $75,000 over six years for *The War Lover*—in today's terms, roughly $600,000. This meant that Hersey's annual income at the end of the 1950s included (after he had paid his agent's percentage) $19,000 from movies, in addition to what his accounts for a typical year show was around $1,150 from stage rights,[14] $1,350 for stories, $780 from royalties on *Hiroshima*, and a further $55 miscellaneous earnings.[15] All told, then, his writing was bringing in the current equivalent of about a million dollars a year. This could decrease sharply, he was aware, with the end of the extended Selznick contract in 1962 and of the Columbia payments in 1966. For now, though, he remained very comfortably off, and the film of *The War Lover* was a success. Shot on location in England and released in 1962, it consolidated the reputation of the young Steve McQueen, who plays Buzz Marrow (called Rickson in the film). The role of Boman (now Ed Bolland) gave scope to Robert Wagner, already familiar as a shell-shocked soldier in *With a Song in My Heart*. Howard Koch's otherwise reasonably faithful script doesn't allow Shirley Anne Field the full scope of Hersey's Daphne, but she communicates some of the character's ambivalence, and the dramatic situation carries her and the rest of the film.

This was Hersey's last major literary engagement with the Second World War.[16] Other historical and international themes would come into his writing, but his main interests were now with U.S. domestic politics: public education, still, and, as an inevitable corollary, though one of which he so far had little direct experience,[17] the condition of those who were still called Negroes. In the first instance, though, his subjects were poor whites. He had already described what military service at its best could achieve in dealing with illiteracy.[18] Now he wrote about the predicament of a girl in southern Illinois, a voracious reader (and writer) whose intelligence had been occluded by the muddle of her home background, failings of both expectation and individual assessment in the local school system, and the fact—which Hersey prophetically treats as important, though he doesn't develop the point—that she is obese.

In its attention to an "ordinary" yet extraordinary individual who is put before the reader with all Hersey's attentive sympathy and subtlety, the piece continues the strong biographical vein of his writing. The omnivorous reading of the girl he calls Janet Train inevitably lacks direction, what with her parents' distractions and her teacher's amiable passivity. The issue is not race, but that is something the article keeps the reader guessing about, in a Faulknerian way.

There are twenty-six children in the teacher's class, we are told, nine boys and seventeen girls. Wilson School was recently integrated with a nearby all-black school, and Mrs. Hottelet has four Negro pupils. She recognizes that Janet has talent but not that, as a teacher, she can develop the gift. Racial stereotyping would identify the untidy tenement home in the first paragraphs as a black one, but nothing is explicitly said about this except that the area is racially mixed. Once the narrative turns to Janet's mother, the background becomes identifiable as poor rural white. And the predominant concern is to resist national-utilitarian pressures on education, pressures that in turn derived in a strange way from international politics. (This would be the scenario of Hersey's next novel, *The Child Buyer*.) The new context is defined in an introduction by Hersey's Yale friend August Heckscher II, then president of the Woodrow Wilson Foundation, who commissioned the essay for a collection under the title *Education in the Nation's Service*.[19]

Heckscher was soon to become John F. Kennedy's special consultant on the arts. His current concern was how the arms race was affecting ideas about schooling. With the successful launch of Earth's first satellite in 1957, he wrote, "Man had embarked, however crudely and tentatively, upon a journey of hitherto impossible dimensions. He had not shown himself particularly capable of dealing with the complexities of his earthly environment, yet now he was about to cast himself forth into other realms. A renewed interest in education would have seemed a proper, and a fittingly humble, response to the challenge of space." Such a response was complicated for Americans, though, by the fact that the satellite was Russian, and that it was seen as a new element in the Cold War. Russia, Heckscher recalled ("with a certain effort of the will"), had been looked upon as "intellectually backward." So a renewed focus on U.S. education had been contaminated by deriving from an impulse to "beat the Russians." The foundation wanted to consider what, if not something like this, Woodrow Wilson had meant when he had spoken of education "in the nation's service."[20]

The contributors were mostly academics and/or professional educators, though the poet Archibald MacLeish had served as assistant director of the Office of War Information under FDR, and McGeorge Bundy, the youngest-ever dean of his faculty at Harvard, would later become Kennedy's national security adviser. Robert F. Goheen, son of medical missionaries in India, had recently become president of Princeton. Among the others were Logan Wilson, president of the University of Texas, a state-university alumnus and an educational sociologist; Harry D. Gideonse, president of Brooklyn College; and Jacques Barzun, provost of Columbia. (At least three—MacLeish, Bundy, and Hersey—were, like Heckscher himself, members of Skull and Bones.) Eminent company, then, and an early hint of another direction Hersey's career might take.

Whether or not a move into academia had occurred to him yet, he would soon agree to give a lecture series at Yale and to sit on a university committee looking at student admissions and financial support.[21] His article, meanwhile, shifts from the idiosyncrasies of its opening subject into a convincingly argued attack on the group-based (and therefore cost-saving) IQ testing regime that he argues has failed Janet. He also has interesting things to say against the prevailing "democratic" educational culture of middling-ness and "social adjustment." Professional resistance to over-early reading, for example, was partly driven by a dislike of the "special," of the undemocratic "privilege" of honoring intelligence, an attitude influenced by theorists such as William C. Bagley. From here Hersey moves on to a persuasive discussion of the ancient debate between "nature" and "nurture," emphasizing what he calls "the unlocking of human gifts." Democracy can work well only if underpinned by education, he argues, because "each child in each classroom in our schools" is not only a unique human being but someone who—in a peroration that today sounds sadly overoptimistic—"one day must make choices and give consents that will help to perfect us all." The late 1950s, one remembers, were about to turn into the 1960s.[22] This is the fervor that had come down to him from his missionary parents and that he increasingly wanted to find a way of putting into action. But fiction was still his obsession, and his next novel was a satirical fable about education.

The topic is the one identified by August Heckscher: attempts to appropriate education to national interest by commercial means. From a presentational point of view, *The Child Buyer* is superficially modeled on Swift's *Modest Proposal for Preventing the Children of Poor People from Being a Burthen to Their Parents or Country, and for Making Them Beneficial to the Publick*. In homage to Swift's satire, the cover and title page are set out like those of an eighteenth-century volume, with a period profusion of capitals and italics: "A Novel *in the Form of* Hearings *before the Standing* Committee *on Education, Welfare, & Public Morality of a certain* State Senate, *Investigating the conspiracy of* Mr. Wissey Jones, *with others, to* Purchase *a* Male Child." But the plot is more Orwell/Huxley than Swift: Clever children are bought from their parents by a company called United Lymphomilloid, which, working under government contract, subjects them to a program of confinement, sensory deprivation, and indoctrination leading to maximization of highly specific forms of intelligence. The style, meanwhile, is fashionably absurdist, as if Eugène Ionesco had combined with Max Frisch to send up American small-town democracy in action. Indeed, the targets of much of its robust humor are the procedural intricacies and personal vanities of officialdom: a venting of steam, perhaps, that had built up in Hersey during many long meetings. There's also a fair amount of conservative exasperation at the linguistic mix of modishness and euphemism common to most social programs.

Though short-listed for the 1961 National Book Award for Fiction and regularly reprinted until the late 1980s, *The Child Buyer* hasn't worn well. Yet if its targets were soft, they deserved to be hit, and among educators as well as literary critics the reception was warm on both sides of the Atlantic. In a symposium on the book published by *The New Republic*, the novelist Margaret Halsey regretted that Hersey wasn't running for president.[23] Teachers used parts of the book as a basis for classroom discussion. A stage version by Paul Shyre ran at the Garrick Theatre in Greenwich Village, as well as at the celebrated Hull House community theater in Chicago.[24] And it was profitable: film rights for a TV series yielded $25,000; the BBC paid $1,000 for a radio dramatization.

Hersey had practical as well as moral support in his work from Barbara—*The War Lover* is dedicated to her—and whatever challenges they faced, the marriage was deeply happy. Affectionate correspondence between Barbara and his mother in February 1960 tells of her checking the typescript of the novel between the baby Brook's feedings while waiting for John to return from a Monday-night bowling session.[25] She was friendly, and attentive to her friends, in a way that enriched the couple's social life.[26] The previous weekend, these letters tell, Teddy and Nancy White came out from New York to spend the night. At dinner, other guests included the *New Yorker* writer and novelist Peter De Vries and his wife, Katinka Loeser, along with Pat Knopf and his wife, Alice; the composer

Richard Rodgers, his wife, Dorothy, and their composer daughter, Mary, with her producer husband, Hank Guettel. "Baird was wonderful," Barbara wrote of Grace's now eleven-year-old grandson. "He loves guests and always has better manners than anyone many times his age."[27] Thank-you letters the couple kept are full of small tributes to the warmth and attentiveness of their hospitality. The English writer Laurie Lee, whose bestselling bucolic memoir *Cider with Rosie* first appeared in the States at the same time as *The War Lover*, was introduced to the Herseys by the British publisher they had in common, Hamish Hamilton, and came for lunch. It was only after he left that he realized his visit had coincided with the publication of Hersey's *Child Buyer*, which his hosts had evidently been too polite to mention. Meanwhile, an apologetic Lee wrote, "I was . . . particularly touched by Barbara's compassion in warming-up my beer."[28]

Not that being a Hersey, like being in any extended family, didn't sometimes feel like taking part in a continually self-renewing problem-solving exercise. Though Baird won places at both Pomfret School and Hotchkiss, it was eventually decided that the liberal, experimental Buxton School in Williamstown, Massachusetts, would better suit his already unmistakable musical and artistic gifts. (He later became a professional composer and performer of experimental rock music, from which he moved into a more meditative, yogic, Indian-inspired sound world.) For health reasons, Martin's schooling was often interrupted. Grace was eighty in 1962, and her circumstances were complicated by the fact that Rob was still living with her and, in his brothers' mildly expressed view, not doing much to help about the house. Early in 1963, John and Barbara took her to Florida. She was beginning to have difficulties with memory and communication. Soon, there was correspondence about finding a housekeeper.[29]

If Hersey was ever tempted to relax a little there was no sign of it, even after he broke an arm sailing.[30] Sailing had become a literal way of getting himself and his family offshore. For two weeks at a time in June and August that year he chartered a yacht called *Land's End* from a well-established business run by Ted Okie. The first trip took them from Rowayton Marina between Stamford and Westport, down the coast to the picturesque Southport, in North Carolina; the second from Padanaram, Massachusetts, across to Naushon and Martha's Vineyard, which was becoming a favorite place.[31]

To be sure, part of what took up his time was saying no: regretful answers to requests from this national committee and that national institute; to the Rockefeller Foundation declining to write its history;[32] to various archives, the Library of Congress among them, that had asked for manuscripts he had promised elsewhere.[33] On the other hand, while he declined many, though far from all, invitations to speak at more exalted gatherings, when a Japanese journalist from Hiroshima came to talk at a local junior high school he immediately agreed to take part in a discussion with him.[34] He continued to sit on local school boards and on the governor of Connecticut's Committee on Libraries. He was active in campaigns defending copyright, one organized by the American Academy, another by the Authors' League, and on behalf of the latter wrote in 1962 to a couple of people he knew who were high up in the administration: Arthur Schlesinger, by then special assistant to the president, and Nicholas Katzenbach, deputy attorney general.[35] As a private individual as well as a committee member, he took up cases of publishing freedom, for example on behalf of booksellers threatened with imprisonment for offering Henry Miller's long-banned *Tropic of Cancer*, a saga that ended up in the Supreme Court.[36] He joined the board of the important educationalist journal *The American Scholar* and the University Council at Yale.

In June 1963, after the death in office of Yale's president Whitney Griswold, Hersey was among those asked to give their views about a successor. He responded not with names but with a job description:

> He should be a teacher, a scholar of the widest scope, an intellectual, a shaper and guardian of standards of mental discipline; he should not be . . . chosen for his . . . knack for military command . . .
>
> Institutions like Yale stand in danger of becoming instruments of public polity. Yale should never be a servant of the society, or of national needs; it should be society's conscience . . . [Its president should be someone who] cannot be influenced or bought or pushed around by the transient requirements of the state.[37]

Was there a hint in this that he himself was interested? If so, it was indirectly picked up, as we'll see,[38] but the job went to Kingman Brewster.

With his writing, too, Hersey was no less busy than usual, though he was beginning to suffer, as he confessed later, from a feeling that while topics pressed in on him, his imaginative means for dealing with them had grown stale. In 1962 Knopf published a selection of his articles under the title *Here to Stay: Studies in Human Tenacity*. Eight stories, filling 336 pages: survivors of concentration camps, of Hiroshima, of the flooding brought to Winsted, Connecticut, by Hurricane Diane; a traumatized war veteran recovering at home; a family escaping the Budapest of 1956. "The great themes are love and death," Hersey wrote in his introduction; "their synthesis is the will to live, and that is what this book is about." More demandingly, he was working on *White Lotus*, an allegorical novel about race influenced by Ralph Ellison. It could easily have stood as his main, very distinctive contribution to current debates on the topic and perhaps would have done so, but in November 1963—before it was complete— President Kennedy was shot dead.

Practically speaking, there were immediate consequences for Hersey. His much-discussed *New Yorker* article about Kennedy's wartime heroism, which had played a part in the election campaign, had recently been put together with four other "True Stories of World War II by a Famous Combat Correspondent" to make a book titled *Of Men and War*.[39] Though not in the Kennedys' innermost circle, Hersey had come to know JFK reasonably well. And while never subscribing to the Camelot myth, he was a friend of one of the people who invented it, the journalist Theodore H. White,[40] as well as being close to the regime's adviser, propagandist, and historian, Arthur M. Schlesinger. Within weeks of the assassination, JFK's brother Robert Kennedy invited him by telegram to be a trustee of the late president's library.[41] As a member of a kind of memorial circle invited to dinner by Jacqueline Kennedy and to the anniversary mass in St. Matthew's Cathedral, Washington, but above all as a conscientious citizen, Hersey was anxious to help preserve and extend Kennedy's belated moves in favor of civil rights. Politically the issue became prominent in the election year of 1964, when the Republican candidate Barry Goldwater stood against the policies of Kennedy, of his successor Lyndon Johnson, and of Robert Kennedy in the latter's role as attorney general to both administrations. Goldwater took the classic white conservative position that the practicalities of racial equality were best left to state and local law, and individual action.

As so often, Hersey's first openings for involvement came through journalism of various kinds. *The American Scholar* is a broadly educational, not just academic, journal run by Phi Beta Kappa, the oldest of American liberal-intellectual campus societies and at the time something between a philanthropic foundation and a huge network of elite college fraternities and sororities. It had taken its name from an inspiring lecture given to the Phi Beta Kappa Society at Harvard in 1837 by Ralph Waldo Emerson, and it now included on its board, along with Hersey,[42] Hannah Arendt, Alfred Kazin, and the historian Richard Hofstadter. Titled "Our Romance with Poverty," Hersey's article overtly challenged not only Goldwater's views but also, more interestingly, the educational claims of the "War on Poverty" campaign launched earlier that year by LBJ. Hailed by its supporters as a continuation of Roosevelt's New Deal and seen by its critics as, among other things, an attempt to camouflage America's increasing expenditure on the war in Vietnam, the poverty program was arguably both those things but mainly an idealistic and, in the eyes of most liberal-left reformers ever since, modestly successful effort to improve the conditions of America's worst-off. Still, the problems Hersey identified in it were real: the strength of resistance among Southern whites to any such scheme, and the fact that it wasn't generous enough.

He told the stories of two experiments. First was that of a privately funded free school in Prince Edward County, Virginia, set up to fill the gap left when in 1959 the county's board of supervisors had withdrawn all funding from public schools, leaving 1,700 black children without formal education and also without the social welfare provision that schools help provide for the poorest. (This decision was later ruled unlawful by the Supreme Court.) Second, he discusses New Haven's Community Progress Incorporated (CPI), which at the time had spent $8 million on helping 220 children in pre-primary nurseries and 114 young people in work crews. From these examples his argument moves out into a range of propositions, starting with *"No single approach will suffice"* and *"A truly massive attack is needed."* He pointed out that at a time when, nationwide, about 35 million people—19 percent of the population—were reckoned to be living in poverty, the amount Johnson had promised for his whole effort was $350 million: $10 per head. It was, Hersey wrote, "pitifully, even absurdly, inadequate."[43] The potential beneficiaries of any such project should be involved in planning and executing it, he said, and, still more important given the tendency of philanthropy to stay close to home, he warned that the places where it would be hardest to set programs up would be precisely those where they were most needed. It was one thing to raise money and volunteers in New Haven, quite another in Jackson, Mississippi.

"Romance" in the title could have been read as pointing to a lack of realism, but there were other senses in which the word applied to what was happening in the 1960s. The involvement of privileged white Americans in race-related projects that were often described as domestic versions of the Peace Corps (and in Hersey's personal terms reprised some of what his father had tried to do in China) was truly romantic in its aims and, although often unsuccessful in specific ways, formed part of something that did bring broad improvements. And if Hersey was challenging LBJ, he was also quoting a New Haven activist: "We're having a romance with the poor."[44] This largely meant with deprived African Americans, with the kinds of people who had been abandoned in "a glacier of human needs":

> Their families' average annual income was less than $1,800, and after four abandoned years the children were half-starved, their clothes were ragged, their teeth were rotting, their souls were set away from the world; many of them were apathetic, silent, cowed, sullen, uncommunicative.[45]

As happens in romances, the more Hersey's heroes achieved, the more new challenges appeared before them. While education helped lift some bright, ambitious young black kids out of poverty, it also exposed the plight of those who, for whatever reasons, weren't bright or weren't ambitious, or were bright and ambitious but in ways that teachers and other humanitarians couldn't, for all their hard work, get any purchase on. Hersey was aware of the difficulty but at this stage prone to brushing it aside. "Our Romance" explicitly answers critics of programs that favored those most likely to benefit quickly from them: the hope had to be, he said, that the example of successes with the more tractable "might make the hard core more amenable to treatment."[46] The somewhat lofty briskness of tone here would be modified by his experiences in the coming years. Among the first was his participation in the "Freedom Summer" of 1964, when he stayed on a Mississippi cotton and soybean farm owned and worked by a couple called Norman and Rosebud Clark, who lived there with their eight children. Among Hersey's objectives was to act as a prominent witness to Norman Clark's attempts to register as a voter along with some of his neighbors.

Locally, he soon found, such power as he had was not much respected. Everywhere he went with Clark, they were followed by a pickup driven by whites with "a shotgun prominently displayed."[47]

Mississippi Yearning

The Freedom Summer and other projects of its kind have been criticized from the obvious point of view that while middle-class reformers, mainly students and mainly white, dedicated themselves to the cause of people whose basic rights had been denied, these gestures, however honorable, were only temporary. The visitors could leave, and before long most of them did so—those, that is, who weren't killed, as were Henry Dee, Charles Moore, and others and, on the night of June 21, James Chaney, Andrew Goodman, and Michael Schwerner. The deaths of the last three, a Mississippi-educated young black man and two Jewish whites from New York, their fate later grimly dramatized in the 1988 film *Mississippi Burning*, help highlight what was really important and, in retrospect, uniquely promising about the movement. It was precisely the voluntariness of the action and the social status of some of those who participated, along with the fact that they worked side by side with brave local people, that guaranteed attention to the cause for which they gave up time, comfort, and safety.

Hersey himself was a case in point. In 1964 his tax return showed that he was earning more than ten times the median wage of all men then at work in the United States, twenty times that of "non-white" men, and almost forty times that of entire non-white families living on farms: people like those among whom he stayed in the summer of 1964.[48] In the following year's return, $6,000 of Hersey's income came, indeed, from the article he wrote about them for *The Saturday Evening Post*. The magazine was ailing but still had a circulation of millions, and it was to its mildly prosperous, mildly conservative readers that Hersey wanted to bring what until recently had been news to him as much as it would be to them. He was, after all, someone they could recognize as being like themselves. A couple of weeks before his voter-registration article appeared near the end of September, they might have read him in *Life*, celebrating the America's Cup yacht race.[49]

For people such as the Clarks, as Hersey wrote in his minor classic of civil rights literature "To Whom a Vote Is Worth a Life,"[50] the franchise was "the real issue":

> School integration, job opportunities, cotton allotments, social mixing, mongrelization—all other problems, all slogans, all shibboleths give way to [this] issue, which is the means to power. In a few counties . . . the vote is in truth a life-and-death matter.

He begins with the emblematic scene of narratives of the time: a group of country Negroes shuffling nervously toward the county seat, in front of which stands a threatening sheriff. Anyone reading the story today is likely to do so through Ava DuVernay's film *Selma* and its episode outside the courthouse when Martin Luther King, Jr., leads a mass attempt at voter registration. But as so often and so important with Hersey, his was among the first treatments of the topic to be aimed by a well-known writer at a mass readership. It was illustrated by Tracy Sugarman, who had been a U.S. Navy war artist in World War II and himself spent that summer in the Delta making ink wash drawings of what he saw. The article tells that in the county where Hersey stayed, blacks outnumbered whites by 19,100 to 8,200. Yet, or rather so, in all the years between the State Constitution of 1890 and the spring of 1964, "only twenty-six Negroes have had their names entered in the book of qualified voters," and the whites "mean to keep it that way."

Quick to see the historical ironies of the situation, he concentrated on them as much as on its more immediate injustices and risks, powerfully though he presented those, too. A statue of a soldier stood in the courthouse yard where would-be voters were kept waiting on the ground under the watchful gaze of police sitting on chairs. The effigy commemorated the War Between the States. At its unveiling, Hersey recorded,

> Miss Annabell Tull, of the C. R. Rankin Chapter of the United Daughters of the Confederacy, spoke these words in dedication: "From his hands came down to you a wealth of priceless heirlooms: patriotism from his forefathers . . . heroism that did not fade in all the many changes from wealth to poverty, nobility that rose above defeat, faith in the right, generosity, courage, every trait of a people that make a nation great."

Now, Hersey comments, "the latter-day vessel of those valued heir-looms, Sheriff Haralson R. Lee, came out, put his hands on his hips, and in what seemed . . . a very loud voice said, 'All right, now, who wants to go first?'"[51] Intimidation and obstruction apart, he explains how all those who that day began trying to register failed the test. (They weren't told why, but one element may have been that a section of the U.S. Constitution chosen for them to read out and then explain contained the expression "viva voce.")[52] He relates the life story of his host Norman Clark under his protective pseudonym Varsell Pleas: a tale of deprivation, misfortune, punishingly hard work, ambition, luck, wise choices, and brave decisions—and increasingly of serious help from prosaic-sounding central initiatives and institutions such as FDR's New Deal, with its Farm Tenant Act of 1937, and the Farmers Home Administration, which helped people like him buy land. Then came the Council of Federated [Civil Rights] Organizations (COFO), offering citizenship classes and advice. Now that the volunteers were here in force, two stayed with the Bankses: "a doctor's son from Roslyn, Long Island, a Yale student, quick-witted and intense; and Bud Samson, a light-skinned Negro, a lawyer's son from Michigan who had been through the civil-rights wars as campus chairman of CORE [the Congress of Racial Equality] at a Midwestern university—he had a hundred-day jail sentence on appeal at home."[53] They shared a room, one bed each: a unique comfort in this household. Hersey himself stayed there, too, but the narrative doesn't tell us this. He is invisible in it, as he was in *Hiroshima*.

Omniscient invisible narrators were becoming unfashionable in journalism, as they were in fiction—or rather, extremely visible ones were becoming more fashionable. It wasn't for modish reasons, though, that later in the 1960s Hersey would emerge from behind his protective narrative curtain. Among all that crossed his horizon in the decade's first half, the civil rights workers' murders and their aftermath made the deepest, longest impact on him, in part because of the extreme difficulties experienced by JFK's brother Robert in securing successful prosecutions. The fact that in order to serve on a jury you had to be registered to vote was one among many viciously circular elements involved. Righteous anger at legal and procedural obstructionism, the realization that it was hidden and depersonalized by institutions like the police and the judiciary, all worked away in John Hersey for years before he felt forced to come out against them, in person as well as in his writing, by the events of 1968. Meanwhile, his work continued in its busy, orderly way.

American Coolies

In fiction, Hersey's negotiations between China and the United States continued without any overt acknowledgment of his personal investment in the process, and now in his part-allegorical way. It wasn't fanciful to suppose that sooner or later the relative power of the two countries might be reversed. What if white people became the coolies of the Chinese? If it could happen in the future, it could also be imagined as having done so in the past. He began work on a novel along these lines around 1960 and delivered the result to Knopf early in 1964. *White Lotus* is a fantasy blending themes from Ralph Ellison and from American history into a scenario in which the United States has been conquered by China and many of its people have been shipped east into slavery.

The novel begins and ends with a public confrontation between the central character, an emancipated white female slave taken originally from rural Arizona, and the Chinese emperor. Her story fills the six-hundred-odd pages between: her capture at the age of fifteen; passage to China; successive periods of slavery in roles whose social deterioration is largely the result of sexual involvements with mutinous male slaves; escape with one of these men to a technically emancipated but nonetheless racist and profoundly unequal Shanghai; participation there in a protest, violent at first but, with her and her partner's help, eventually peaceful. All this roughly mirrors the history of American blacks between slavery and the summer of 1964, and has the clear aim of startling the reader into a few questions: about the political and economic origins of cultural difference; about the flimsiness of conventional moral absolutes; about the arbitrariness of East-West divisions in addition to black-white ones; and, in the central character's own development, about what freedom consists of. White Lotus is another of Hersey's strong female protagonists.[54]

He didn't make his ambitious project any easier to pull off by presenting it entirely through her. Lack of variety apart, the problem, again, is one of voice and, with that, of individual perception. You can open the book at any page and think: Whatever an American woman transported to China might sound like, it's not this. In his 1991 *John Hersey Revisited*, David Sanders mounts a sophisticated defense of what he sees as an "invented language" purged of cultural references by the circumstances of White Lotus's slavery: "With white family, white homeland, and white god all utterly gone, her situation may seem about the same as that of the characters in *Hiroshima* and *The Wall*, but . . . Hersey has further imagined a loss of language—consequently of memory."[55] This was evidently his intention, but does it work? To take an example almost at random, someone who has no memory of American idioms and who we've just been told had never previously seen the ocean would surely be incapable of the confidently nautical—in other words, Hersey-like—idiom with which the crossing is described: "We sailed day after day on a measured following swell . . . One evening the wind increased . . . The shallow-draft fisherman [i.e., their boat] was no match for an ocean gale."[56] Passages like this aren't just occasional slips. The narrative is too ready to forget about being this individual woman's story, in favor of providing something between a sophisticated report by a diplomat and a political lecture. Here, for example, is how the undereducated White Lotus, sixteen years old and en route by donkey cart between one Chinese slave owner and another, is supposed (albeit by her older self looking back) to have understood the situation that has developed nationally with the arrival of a new emperor:

> The great dynast Yung-t'ai had a long rule, during which he subdued the Manchu warlords, so the northern part of the land massif has been more or less unified. In the coalescing North, in the so-called "core provinces," into one of which we have been transported, the repressive measures of Yung-t'ai had prepared the ground for a rank growth of liberal ideas. His successor, Emperor Ch'ang-lo, a scholar and philosopher, has accordingly promulgated a set of principles by which his prefects and magistrates are to conduct civil life; it is called the Nine Flowers of Virtue. Despite this decree, real life has not changed—everywhere are bloodshed and turnover, greed and graft and injustice, disgusting cruelties in the name of progress; but the words of the Imperial edict are powerful, and hope has leapt up in the hearts of the have-nots.[57]

At the level of action, *White Lotus* is often compelling. "Yellow"-occupied America is convincingly portrayed as a fearful, impoverished, supersti-

tious region where foreign power is exerted through exploitative collabo-
rators. Once arrived in China, the white slaves develop hybrid local
cultures, their exaggerated loyalties to feebly recalled American beliefs
mingling with the customs of their new owners, while in a day-to-day existence that gives little scope for pleasure, initiative, or responsibility it
seems to White Lotus normal, or at any rate unavoidable, that she should
be sexually abused, that the men she's attracted to should be self-destructive
and unreliable, and that any wish for a larger good should give way to
the needs of sheer survival. Her pragmatic promiscuity is among the
more convincing things about her, especially once she's living among
the well-imagined chaotic half-freedoms of post-emancipation Shanghai.
And the existential question of what freedom is, especially once you've
achieved what you thought it would be, provides the novel with much of
its eventual resonance and surprisingness. "I was free!" White Lotus says,
but immediately pulls back from romantic cliché:

> Somewhere in these confused moments I had come to realize that freedom
> could be felt at best only for moments; that even for the powerful, even for
> yellows, it was inconstant, elusive, fickle, and quickly flown. It turned out to
> be an experience rather than a status. Ayah, much needed to be changed
> in our lives to give us, not freedom, but mere humanity. Freedom was
> not to be bestowed but grasped—and only for a moment at a time.[58]

This is of a piece with the unexpectedness of how the tense framing episode ends, which also relates to a neat turn involving rival memories and
interpretations of events earlier on.[59]

Hersey's heavy cargo of research had once again made his fiction
clumsy to steer. In preparation he studied nineteenth-century China, including the Second Opium War of 1860, in which Britain and France, fighting with American support under the flags of free trade and of "opening
up" the Far East, defeated the imperial army, put Emperor Xianfeng to
flight, and destroyed Beijing's Old Summer Palace. The files in his archive
contain dozens of pages of notes on all this, but they are nothing beside
his hundreds of pages on the history of emancipation, particularly John
Hope Franklin's 1947 *From Slavery to Freedom*,[60] and the works of African American writers such as W.E.B. Du Bois and Langston Hughes. It
would be some years before the effects of this reading on Hersey's moral

imagination would become apparent in a quite different book. *White Lotus*, meanwhile, though an extended parable rather than a piece of fictional realism, is at the same time too firmly anchored in the everyday to take off imaginatively. Knopf published it in the States at the end of 1964, Hamish Hamilton in the U.K. the following year, but foreign-language publishers were reluctant to take it on, as were paperback imprints outside the United States.[61] While a few academic specialists in Hersey's work have written about it admiringly, or at least defensively,[62] general critical opinion was represented by the Irish writer Anthony Cronin, literary editor of *Time and Tide*. Writing anonymously in *The Times Literary Supplement*, Cronin acknowledged that "John Hersey's virtues are too well known to need re-emphasizing. He is an energetic, adventurous, skilful writer who sets himself a new subject for each book and works out the implications of it with intelligence and honesty."[63] In his opinion, though, *White Lotus* was a tract and quickly became predictable.

I Feel Very Successful. It Is Strange. I Do.

Hersey was thin-skinned about such reactions, these days. Colleagues did their best to flatter and cajole, Alfred Knopf telling him he was reminded of what happened to some of his other authors in midcareer such as Willa Cather and Thomas Mann.[64] The older novelist John O'Hara, whose *Appointment in Samarra* had given him an early fame comparable to Hersey's, consolingly joked that each of his own books since *Samarra* had been unfavorably contrasted with the one that immediately preceded it, while subsequently being praised to the disadvantage of the next: "When I published *Butterfield 8* in 1935, they expressed their indignation as if the author of *Appointment in Samarra* had betrayed them. Then, as I kept writing away, *Butterfield 8* receded into my personal literary history and was lumped with *Samarra*, to the discredit of *A Rage to Live*."[65] Months later, Hersey was all the same still licking his wounds. He grumbled to Knopf about young critics with little experience writing "carelessly and foolishly."[66] *Time* magazine's review had been particularly cruel, saying that some of the novel "is so dull it couldn't even be used in the Hollywood epic [it] seems destined to become." As for the language, "whenever Hersey needs an idea and can't find one—it happens all the time—he uses a big word instead: cangue, coffle, fulvous, hame, jingal, liripipe, métayer, panyar, purlin, psora, shroff, sycee." The novelist guilelessly reported the excuse made to him by the literary editor involved, who claimed that the item "slipped into the magazine at a time when he had just fallen and broken both ankles." Even Henry Luce apologized, Hersey told Knopf, when the men bumped into each other at a birthday party for Teddy White (another burying of hatchets).[67]

Literary judgments can seem so unpredictable a combination of the culturally determined and the subjective that most serious writers end up depending either on the opinion of one or two trusted readers or solely on their own instinct. The trusted reader may be imaginary—typically some past mentor or object of admiration whose standards the writer tries to reconstruct and apply. Or she may be a partner, amatory or professional. Agents and editors often fill the role, but not always. Late in life Hersey spoke appreciatively of the close editorial attention for which *The New Yorker* has always been famous and regretted that, in his experience, there had been no equivalent at Knopf. Certainly the approach of Alfred A. Knopf, Sr., was mainly a matter of backing his instincts with encouragement and trust, while making occasional suggestions for future topics. Hersey's editor at Knopf, Harold Strauss, was more cautious but deferred to Alfred, and had an unhelpful habit of saving some of his criticisms until after a book had appeared and the reviews were in.[68] For his own part these days, Hersey, while nurturing his relationships with Alfred and Blanche, could be imperious with others in the firm. Though courteous in his correspondence, he also always stressed his artistic independence. "One isn't a good judge of his own things," he had written to Strauss about *The Marmot Drive*, for example, "but I think the book not so awful as most of the reviewers did, and that it will find its day." Reading through the letter, he made an insertion so that this part read, "I stubbornly, and possibly wrongly, think." But he was, he made clear, already well advanced with his next piece of fiction: "proceeding in my own blithesome way as well as I can see it, regardless of the disciplining the critics would give me."[69] That new book was *A Single Pebble*, and his judgment then was right. In any case, whatever Strauss thought, he had to bear in mind Alfred's general position, which was that "John must be kept quite *happy*."[70]

And happy he seemed to be, including in this overt confidence in his own powers. He kept to himself the pangs he was beginning to feel about what he later described as a loss of mental fluidity and ease. Having seen critics overpraise and overdisparage other writers' work, he had no reason, he told Strauss, to trust their opinions of his own. It helped that he regarded himself as, by birth, an outsider. His early life in China meant, he explained to a graduate student in 1972, that there was "something subtly alien in my work" that perhaps helped account for its being "against the grain, both of literary fashion and of establishment values."[71] And, he wrote with a mix of self-deprecation and artistic pride to another correspondent, he wasn't even popular: "I make a living, but my books don't sell particularly well, though some of the early ones have had a wide circulation." And yet, "alone in my limbo, I feel very successful. It is strange. I do."[72]

As for imagined readers, Hersey went on to confide what kind of person he had in mind and what a fluctuating, chimerical kind of recipient that person was:

> I visualize a reader as I write; I see in my mine [sic] a person to whom I am writing. This person is like a figure in a dream: the face of the person may give way at any moment and dissolve into another face, and that one in turn may give way to another, so that the person to whom I am writing shifts identities while I am in the act of writing. Whatever the identity, I feel very close to this person. I want to share with this person—this must be my purpose in writing—my vision of life, my bewilderment, my wonder. All that sounds very grand, but it isn't. I am just writing a letter, a kind of letter, to someone I love and trust.

You don't have to be Freud to see that uncharacteristically uncorrected typo—"mine" for "mind"—as compounding the introversion of this account.

These confidings came from someone who still disliked discussing his work, or claimed to. "I've just turned down propositions to be interviewed . . . by *The New York Times*," he wrote, "and on television by Robert Cromie ('Book Beat')." Cromie was a celebrated interviewer, formerly a war correspondent, and it's intriguing not just that Hersey turned him down but that he's keen to tell his young correspondent that he has done so. Still, such exchanges, first with his editor, then with people hoping to write about his work, illustrate what was his steady picture of himself as an author over a twenty-year period. It was in the middle of that time that he wrote *Too Far to Walk*, which appeared in 1966.

Faust

The novel is another parable but the opposite of *White Lotus* in that whereas the earlier novel's allegorical situation is generally more interesting and persuasive than the fictional actuality it's being applied to, here the story of a clever, wayward boy negotiating and failing to negotiate student life is better done than the framework, which is a Faust story.[73] John Fist, to whom the lecture theater seems too far away to walk to, is a plausible enough character, and there are some vivid and funny moments throughout the book. His arguments with his distraught parents and well-intentioned tutors are painfully believable, as are the clever-competitive-serious-scandalous conversations of students over refectory dinner. The account of a political demonstration watched by John lacks the autobiographical brio Mailer brought to such topics a couple of years later in *The Armies of the Night* (1968) but nonetheless has plenty of sharp detail, as does the boy's spell in a psychiatric hospital. There's also a good scene between John and a prostitute ("Look, honey, *please*, none of those social-studies questions," she begs him) who enjoyably satirizes her older academic clients, forever turning up with the excuse that they're celebrating because they have either just been given tenure or prevented someone else from getting it. But you only have to think of the name Salinger to see this narrator's removedness from what's being described. "On the jukebox the Rolling Stones sounded as if they were trying to roll bricks," he tells us; and "There was, as usual, quite a cluster of guys around Laetitia, a runaway girl from Boston whose only talent in life was swimming topless." Nudges such as the fact that John's dissolute experiences always cause a smell of burning increase the pedagogical distance.

Did Hersey think the novel might be read by young people—his older children, say—and to their advantage? Could they have been his imagined readers? At the end, a reformed John tells the tempter Breed,

I've come to see that there can't be any shortcut to those breakthroughs I yearn for. You can't imbibe them, or smoke them, or take them intravenously, or get them by crossing your legs and breathing deeply for twenty minutes. Guess you just have to work like hell for them, grub for them with the other grubs, and maybe you won't have them even then. But they aren't worth having any other way. Not your way.[74]

He is planning a visit to his parents and considers linking up with the Nice Girl. In the immediate, he attends a lecture on Catullus. I was a student when the book came out but am not surprised that I never heard of it. If it gained no traction in the central character's age group, though, it pleased some of Hersey's older readers, not least by helping them feel less pessimistic. And it was as both a patient listener to and, especially, an apologist for the young that Hersey was to make some of his most valuable contributions in the second half of the 1960s. He was needed in this role and, by the time *Too Far to Walk* appeared, had found a new way of fulfilling it.

10. The Master

Y ALE'S NEW PRESIDENT, Kingman Brewster, was a wealthy Massachusetts liberal Republican, handsome, charming, and a descen-
dant of not one but two of the Pilgrim Fathers. A star at Yale just
after Hersey left for Cambridge, he was too independent-minded—or
perhaps too grand—to join Skull and Bones. As editor of the *Yale Daily News*,
he argued against American involvement in the Second World War. Having gone on to a dazzling academic career at Harvard Law School, he
became provost of Yale in 1960 and the university's president in 1963.
Among the first of his many controversial actions in that role was to ask
a student political group to "postpone" an invitation to the segregationist
governor of Alabama, George Wallace. Soon afterward, Brewster arranged
an honorary doctorate for Martin Luther King, Jr. He wanted more black
students and staff at Yale and also wanted women to be educated there.
Chiefly, his aim—treasonous to his own class, or so it seemed to many
members of it—was to turn Yale into a "meritocracy," doing away with a
system in which being the son of a Yalie and/or having attended one of
a handful of elite schools more or less guaranteed a place. This was less

revolutionary than it seemed. Harvard had already moved decisively in the same direction and for similar reasons: awareness, heightened by the Second World War, that vast numbers of capable Americans were being denied opportunities to realize their talents; and, more pragmatically, increased competition from state universities with their more welcoming admissions policies and their emphasis on the sciences and professional subjects.[1]

The extent to which America had changed has often been epitomized by the simple fact that for the first time the country had more students than farmworkers. And this newly large pool of energetic young Americans engaged in critical thinking coincided with there being plenty of topics to think critically about. Civil rights apart, it was a period of rapid escalation in the U.S. military's entanglement in Indochina, formerly confined to special forces such as the Green Berets, who were described as "military advisers," but by 1965 greatly expanded, with open participation by regular U.S. combat troops combined with a serious bombing campaign. The influential body Students for a Democratic Society, begun in 1960, which had acquired a ringing manifesto by its president, Tom Hayden, and was already nationally active against racism and nuclear proliferation, reacted quickly to these events with a series of teach-ins and marches. Hersey was among the public intellectuals who took part.

His dissidence may look unremarkable amid that of his more flamboyant contemporaries—the pugnacious iconoclast Norman Mailer, for example, or William Sloane Coffin, Jr., who had worked for the CIA in the Korean War before becoming chaplain of Yale in 1958 and acquired a separate fame for his participation in the Freedom Rides of the early 1960s. Hersey never went to jail. It is the deceptive cautiousness of his temperament that makes his behavior in the 1960s so remarkable.

In June 1965, the White House held a celebration of the arts. The event attracted media attention in itself but also because the poet Robert Lowell announced that, as a protest against the war in Vietnam, he had declined an invitation to take part. Hersey said he would use the occasion to make a point in his own way. At ten in the morning the visitors were greeted in the Blue Room by the president's wife, Lady Bird Johnson. A bestselling biographer and historian, Catherine Drinker Bowen, was there, and the novelist Saul Bellow, and Phyllis McGinley, a popular writer of children's books and vers de société. So, too, among many others, were

Hersey's distinguished old Moscow acquaintances the Kennans: George was to give a lecture titled "The Arts Today" after everyone had had a chance to look at some of the White House's paintings. Lunch was to be at the National Gallery, and then Leonard Bernstein, Ira Gershwin, and Ned Rorem would provide musical entertainment in the East Room.[2] Helen Hayes, Arthur Miller, and Tennessee Williams were among representatives of the theater who would read and perform after the music. There was to be a film narrated by Charlton Heston and more opportunities to look at pictures, followed by drinks in the Rose Garden, after which Gene Kelly would act as master of ceremonies during a buffet dinner with music from Duke Ellington and, tactlessly in the circumstances, the Air Force Band. (The previous day, the USAF had managed to bomb a leprosy hospital in North Vietnam.)

The writers began at 10:30 a.m.: ten minutes each, Bowen first, then Hersey, then Bellow and McGinley. Hersey was on familiar ground in the White House. During the Second World War he had more than once been a guest of Eleanor Roosevelt. President Truman had shown him every exposed corner of the building while it was being restored and expanded. Since then, Hersey had often been there to see one or another of the Kennedys. But if the arts were to be celebrated here, the reason, as far as he was concerned, was that they offered something more important than light entertainment combined with a chance for those in favor to be taken behind the scenes. He had decided to deliver an extract from *Hiroshima* and to add some comments on its immediate relevance. "I read these passages," he began in his dry, dignified, intense way,

> on behalf of the great number of citizens who have become alarmed by the drift of our foreign policy toward belligerence and an increasing use of force. Let these words be a reminder. The step from one degree of violence to the next is imperceptibly taken, and cannot easily be taken back. We cannot for a moment forget the truly terminal dangers in these times of miscalculation, of arrogance, of accident, of reliance not on moral strength but on mere military power. I address this reading to the conscience of the man who lives in this beautiful house.

The course of events wasn't shifted, of course, not in the East Room let alone in Indochina. LBJ wasn't even there to hear Hersey read, though

Lady Bird was in the front row. There were mutterings among some of the participants. Saul Bellow was reported as saying somewhat stuffily that while he, too, disagreed with the president's policies, he attended out of "respect for his intentions and to honor his high office." Hersey's stand, by contrast, was more direct, more provocative than any he had taken in public before. A few months later, he gave a full explanation.[3]

Immediately after the White House celebration, *The Saturday Evening Post* offered to send Hersey to Vietnam as a reporter.[4] But he had already accepted a very different assignment, as master of one of Yale's residential colleges.[5] While Kingman Brewster was busy loosening the establishment's hold on Yale, he continued to operate in a distinctly establishment way. Fellow sailors, he and Hersey had become good friends—John and Barbara rented a house on Hatch Road on Martha's Vineyard, next door to the Brewsters, close to the Vineyard Haven Yacht Club—and the job idea came up after a conversation about where they might find a home in New Haven. However cozily done, it was a clever hire. One of the main strategic elements in Brewster's plans for Yale was to overhaul appointment policies. He saw this primarily as a matter of seeking out the best-qualified people in the world, rather than those who were thought most likely to fit in. Brewster was enough of a Yalie, however, not to ignore the value of other Yalies in working from the inside. Among the most powerful campus dissidents was the chaplain, William Sloane Coffin, scion of a wealthy family, nephew of a member of the Yale Corporation, himself a Bones man. Another member of Skull and Bones, R. Inslee Clark, was put in charge of student admissions. Hersey himself was appointed over the heads of a number of insiders[6] but was as loyal as anyone to what he and Brewster both saw as the university at its best. This didn't protect either man from criticism, especially from alumni. A Yale graduate from the 1940s, by this time in the defense industry, was among those who used Hersey's White House protest as an opportunity to attack Brewster's policies:

> It seems that the experiment of appointing a non-academician to a senior post in which his personal voice can be confused in the public mind with that of the University, has already been proved to be a stupid undertaking by the Corporation. I advert specifically to the incredible performance by the recently appointed Master, Mr. John Hersey, at the Arts Festival in Washington the other day. Criticizing one's host is distinctly

not in keeping with any element of good manners, ancient or modern. This breach of elementary proprieties patently disqualifies him from taking part in the education or guidance of young men. Academic freedom is indeed to be cherished since practically all human progress results from the views of well informed dissenters. Whether or not Mr. Hersey's views are correct, or based on any form of valid information, is therefore, immaterial. What is material is that his egregious boorsmanship reflects great discredit on him and on the University which appointed him. As a practical matter, I suggest that you institute a cram course in basic etiquette, with our in-house novelist as the first student.[7]

Hersey's installation ceremony as master of Pierson College took place on November 15, 1965. Twelve days after the formalities, he took part in a big antiwar rally in Washington, D.C., an action for which his Yale inauguration speech carefully prepared the ground.[8] After some gentle jokes about institutional life and the "inertia of a great University," the tall, robed eminence turned to the responsibilities that writers and academics have in common. "It is too late now," he said, "for politics in the traditional sense." The self-exclusion symbolized by Yale's fortresslike Gothic frontage had to be replaced by active traffic with "the world of Mississippi and Alabama, of Hiroshima and Vietnam." He ended with another symbol, and a rallying call to his students. His old rooms in Trumbull College had become a lounge for fellows. Now paneled in maple, the place seemed to defend what he had earlier criticized as a seclusion that made "society seem the unreal, and education the only real, world." For him, Trumbull was still redolent of "rebelliousness, alienation, bewilderment, unrest." He added, "Yet also—yes, I will claim this kinship with you now these many years later—echoes of irrepressible hope, of yearnings beyond expression, of a ravenous hunger for life."

Hersey was quick to act on these passionate hopes in his new job but in doing so experienced some of the exclusiveness he criticized. Given Brewster's aim to recruit teachers who would attract and act as role models for black students, Hersey suggested offering a post to Ralph Ellison. It didn't seem like a far-fetched idea and would have had the support of other friends of Ellison's at Yale such as Robert Penn Warren and R.W.B. Lewis. With *Invisible Man* (1953) he had quickly become one of the most celebrated serious writers in America, and he had recently published a book of autobiographical essays that focused on aspects of his experience as a black American author, especially of some establishment stereotypes.[9] He had already taught at Yale on a special fellowship, as well as at Bard and Rutgers. Yet resistance to Hersey's proposal took forms so plausible, so innocuous-seeming, but so adamant that he was exasperated into taking a sheet of paper, dating it, and simply writing them down. The chair of the English department, he recorded, "said that there would be serious objections to having Ralph Ellison teach an Early Concentration seminar in English, because the senior members of the . . . department would feel that teaching should be done by members of the department; they would object to having a person 'from outside,' over whom 'the department would not have jurisdiction.'"[10] Another scholar-bureaucrat, meanwhile, raised obscure technical difficulties based in the constitution of Yale College.

In their polite way, it seemed to Hersey, these professors were using the rules not unlike small-town white officials in the South faced with Negroes who wanted to register to vote. They were treating Ellison in the way he himself had satirized in *Invisible Man*. Hersey was new to the intricacies of academic politics, of course, and it may be that other factors were involved. Ellison's earlier temporary post had been vaguely defined, and according to some accounts he hadn't taken his duties overseriously. Whatever the background, Hersey felt snubbed, but within his own college he had room for maneuver—room, too, for what he called "the ventilation of my mind," as well as the minds of his students. He arranged a series of visits by celebrities, sometimes interviewing them, as he did Ellison,[11] more often asking them to give talks (or sing or play). Kurt Vonnegut, Arthur Miller, and Lillian Hellman came, as did Washington insiders like Averell Harriman and Arthur Schlesinger. The jazz musician Dave Brubeck performed with his fourteen-year-old son. Classical musicians from the university put on a program of English theater music from Shakespeare to Dryden. During his first year in the college Hersey ran seminars on Vietnam, on civil rights vis-à-vis New Haven—a city with a huge underemployed black population—and on the duties incurred by privilege.

His determination to develop his students' moral imagination is clear from a talk he gave to the freshmen at the beginning of his second year.[12] It began conventionally enough, with the atmosphere of the college, its activities, the achievements of individual recent students, and the need for everyone to ignore any preconceptions they might have had about Yale. From here, though, he turned to his Ruskinian insistence that all education, including undergraduate life at a university, should be part of adult existence and not merely a preparation for it:

> You are living now; you are daily moving into your futures. There is not a now and then another time later when you will be "going out into life." If you manage not to make this separation, you may also manage to see through the false and life-postponing modes of playing it cool, playing at finding yourself, and going mechanically along in the cynically careerist line. None of these are enough in a time of Vietnam and Vista [Volunteers in Service to America, a social program initiated by JFK], and the anti-poverty program and Stokely Carmichael and Red Guards and John Birch and General De Gaulle standing in a rubber suit on the deck of a cruiser watching a blinding flash over a Pacific atoll for the glory of France. To be alive in such a time one must have the courage to gamble one's own person. One must give oneself—to ideas, to ideals.

It's hard to know how many of the specific allusions his audience of eighteen-year-olds would have understood: references to a leader of the civil rights campaign as it, and he, segued into Black Power and the Black Panthers; to student activists in Mao's Cultural Revolution; to the U.S. extreme right; to the beginnings of France's nuclear armory. Some students may have found the master's tone overzealous, or undercomprehending of the nuances—and the importance (to them)—of "cool," or just of slowly and obliquely finding oneself. Hersey's appetite for preaching was a common source of complaint among critics of his fiction, and just as he may have been asking too much of late teenagers en masse, he was also disparaging efforts at self-individuation that, to many, really mattered. Besides, if there really was no division between college life and life of other kinds, why *were* colleges sequestered behind such gates and walls? For some, though, his challenges were exactly what they wanted. Students themselves increasingly took responsibility for what became known as the Pierson seminars, which were soon, along with series modeled on them in other colleges, authorized for credit toward degrees. The "Pierson Tutorial" followed: a one-on-one project of private study devised between student and tutor. Senior Yale scholars who believed they had long ago lost interest in undergraduate teaching were lured back in to give talks on such topics as "The Brain," "American Leaders and the Cold War," "Medicine and the Social System," and "Experience and Ideology." Reading groups tackled texts on topics ranging between black nationalism, ancient lyric poetry, and keyboard music from Bach to Brahms. Pierson was, as Hersey said in his pep talk, a kind of "mini-multiversity." And among the main beneficiaries was the master himself. In his own reading, as well as in classes for students, he pondered work by James Baldwin, Eldridge Cleaver, LeRoi Jones, and Richard Wright, and the recently published *Autobiography of Malcolm X*.

The job of master, as a former Yale student has written, "entailed playing counselor, mentor, and surrogate father to 350 students and 75 fellows living in one of Yale's 12 residential communities."[13] There were tiresome aspects to this. Although other staff dealt with most of the domestic concerns, it was to the master that college members went if their grievances were unresolved, and the vigor of Hersey's involvement in all aspects of the community's life had the effect of exposing him to everyone's foibles: one fellow had been away for some years and wanted his old suite of rooms back; another had asked a student to water his plants during a short absence, only to discover afterward that the student had used the opportunity to sleep with a girlfriend in his fellowly bed. On the latter occasion someone called in the campus police, who found pot in the suite: But did it belong to the students or to the resident fellow himself? Hersey dealt with such matters efficiently and fairly but was rarely ingratiating. Grayhaired now, his dark eyes so deeply set that they were shaded by his brow, he was found remote by some. He fought tenaciously for his college and was a tireless defender of its students. But day by day his writing still came first: literally so. Every day, he got up at about 7:00 a.m., went to his study at 8:00 a.m., and wrote until 12:30.[14]

Too Far to Walk appeared in 1966. He had been careful to make clear that he finished the book before returning to Yale: however relevant to university concerns, it was not, he said, a roman à clef.[15] The claim seemed at odds with his earlier involvement in the committee on student discontents, but those who knew him thought it most likely that the novel's subject was closer to home. Hersey's own children were growing up— John Junior was in his senior year at Yale when his father was appointed to Pierson—and already in *The Marmot Drive* the writer had dramatized intergenerational family tensions. Aspects of his past experience are also detectable in a novel he completed while at Pierson: a marriage under strain; a man's struggles with on the one hand his sense of the past, particularly of his father, and on the other the fast-changing present.

The Sheer Downhillness of Everything

Published in 1967, *Under the Eye of the Storm* is one of Hersey's most exciting stories. It combines Conrad's *Typhoon* with Edward Albee's relatively recent *Who's Afraid of Virginia Woolf?*, using the sheer drama of a small yacht out in a hurricane to force open the tensions between four friends—two married couples. In the process, various of Hersey's themes are put under new pressure. The book is philosophical; it doesn't hesitate to pay tribute to Camus. It's also psychological, though at its weakest in the sexual rivalry between Tom, the reflective central character, and an alpha male who seems wholly unconscious of his competitor's feelings. All this is doubtless what Hersey wanted his reader to be most aware of. But what in fact come through most strongly—as much so as in *The War Lover*—are danger, fear, and struggle, all heightened here by the fact that unlike in the earlier novel, the reader can't be sure the protagonist will survive.[16] In one remorselessly headlong sentence Hersey communicates the existential drama of his main character, a liver surgeon named Tom Medlar, at his yacht's helm:

> The spray from those breakers astern, when she was half way down a wave, seemed to be leaping over the spreaders more than half way up the main-mast, and when *Harmony* fell into the out-of-control squirming of her consternation at the foot of one of those troughs and Tom looked up and around, he found her in a bowl of raging water, an amphitheater with steepest galleries, the topmost of which seemed to tower over the wind-vane at the head of the mast, which he knew to be thirty-eight feet high, and again when, a few seconds later, she trembled at a crest in the froth of a breaker reaching up her flanks with its willful steel fingers deceit-fully camouflaged by millions of soft white bubbles, she seemed to be on a pinnacle, an Alp of water capped with snow white, commanding a peak's panorama if one could overcome his vertigo and look, and yet again, when

she started the headlong descent of that mountain and Tom looked ahead and downward, he half expected the sea to part down there at the bottom, to open up all the way down to sand and rocks bearded with glistening kelp and barnacled shells and fishes flapping and gasping on dry land and green lobsters scrambling in terror across the open place seeking the cover of the salt sea.[17]

In less vertiginous conditions Tom's recreational sailing enables him to escape from what he fears is his inner bankruptcy, as well as from the high-tech artificiality of the contemporary world. But in the storm he finds himself reconsidering his youthful break with his father's values. Probity, decency, these "big and good words" had seemed inadequate to "the bomb tests and the Calcutta famines and the white response to the Montgomery bus boycott and the exposure of Stalinism . . . the sheer downhillness of *everything* since the Korean war,"[18] but in the hurricane what gets these poor humans through in their flawed craft is ultimately a combination of the boat's traditional strengths with Tom's hard-practiced navigational skills and the efforts of his crew. There's plenty of the familiar moralizing here, but it's complicated by ways in which at various points Tom's own judgment and behavior go awry.

Among the reasons Hersey had wanted to move back to New Haven was that, besides being the home of his alma mater, the city was among those that seemed at the time to be successfully tackling the worst consequences of industrial change. In the nineteenth and early twentieth centuries, the arms-manufacturing port had attracted large numbers of job-hungry immigrants from Europe and then, between the world wars, African Americans and Puerto Ricans. An exodus of middle-class workers and declining opportunities for the unskilled and semiskilled were among the main issues facing the town's long-serving mayor, Richard C. Lee, who since 1954 had built up a reputation as an urban renewer. Under him, New Haven became what Hersey overoptimistically described at the time as "one of the most exciting cities in the United States."[19] He was referring to the many schemes Lee had brought in with support from the federal government and foundations: by the time of Hersey's arrival the city was spending fifteen times more per capita than New York on major social projects.[20] But Hersey also sensed danger. Urban race riots, usually in the summer and sparked by overheated white police action against provocative young blacks, had already flared in 1964 in Rochester (NY), Harlem, and Philadelphia, and in 1965 in Watts. Over the next years they multiplied and intensified: North Omaha, Newark, Detroit, Minneapolis, Chicago, Washington, D.C., Baltimore, Cleveland.

Hersey's work in the public school system put him in close touch with these concerns, and his period in Mississippi, as well as his research for *White Lotus*, helped focus his thinking about their origins. While he had already shown that he could be stirred into active involvement, it's as if his having formally become a member of the establishment—almost the very fact of his being head of a college—freed him into what he might earlier have thought of as irresponsibility. Comparable adjustments were happening all around him. Clergymen, university presidents, and suited heirs of Republican conventionality were discovering that the supposedly empty symbolism of their positions in fact gave them considerable power to oppose a status quo of which they had seemed (and from a more radical point of view still were) hereditary components.

Meanwhile Bantam bought paperback rights to all his works for an advance of $100,000.[21] Paramount paid $150,000 for a movie option on *Too Far to Walk*.[22] For tax reasons these sums were spread over five to ten years, supporting a degree of luxury well beyond what Hersey's Yale salary and free house would have provided. For Christmas 1965 he took the family to the Virgin Islands. The following summer they again went to Martha's Vineyard. It had become a favorite destination, among other reasons because Lillian Hellman was there—sometimes with her friend the novelist Peter Feibleman, of whom John and Barbara both became fond.[23] Since their Moscow days the stormy, hilarious, self-dramatizingly radical, hard-living Hellman had always been Hersey's doppelgänger, challenging his opposite personality while extravagantly voicing many of his sociopolitical beliefs. Their seeing more of each other coincided with and encouraged a new incautiousness in his writing. For now, though, he was a busy, successful man on vacation. Between bouts of Pierson College work and reading Melville, he skimmed around on a sunfish—"one of those little surfboards . . . with lateen sails." There was, he said, "nothing in the world so relaxing for me."[24] In his study overlooking the bay he watched fishing boats negotiating the tide rips and worked on *Under the Eye of the Storm*. Later he chartered *Land's End* once again. The older children joined them "on and off,"[25] the weather was perfect, and they made daily trips, described in letters to his mother:[26] to Woods Hole on the mainland south-west of Falmouth, to Tarpaulin Cove on Naushon Island, or around the coast to Oak Bluffs and the sprawling bay of Cape Poge. Friends who joined them included the *New Yorker* writer Daniel Lang, a former war correspondent and a specialist on the nuclear arms race. ("In all his life," Hersey was to write with revealing solemnity, "Dan never touched . . . a trivial subject.") Lang and his wife, Margaret, had been among the people responsible for luring the Herseys to the Vineyard. There was no television in the house they were renting, Hersey told his mother that summer, and ("you'll be glad to hear") Brook was making frequent visits to the public library. He sent news of the family's pets: their dogs, Abigail and Quincy, but also "the cat, whose name is Mouse, and the gold-fish, four in number," who "have fortunately not met each other."

Arthur Schlesinger was coming to Pierson to talk; Benjamin Spock, too, with whom Hersey was in contact about the National Committee for a Sane Nuclear Policy (SANE). Given what was happening in other universities, Schlesinger, who had been educated at Phillips Exeter and Harvard, was surprised by what he called "the squareness of the faculty and the blandness—or was it timidity?—or boredom or contempt—of the under-graduates."[27] This impression was soon to be belied, and amid Hersey's pastoral dealings with young men who had discovered LSD, not to mention stashes of phenobarbitone left hitherto untouched in bomb shelters built into Yale college cellars in the 1950s,[28] he had a grief to overcome: in October, Grace died. A memorial service was held under the bright Tiffany windows of Briarcliff Congregational Church, where he had been christened and had worshipped as a teenager. She had had a heart attack at home at 44 Valentine Road, where the unhappy Rob continued to live amid Grace's possessions and the relics of his childhood.

While Hersey kept urging his students to move beyond the shelter of Yale, everything in the outside world seemed to become madder and sadder. The following summer Yale was hit by one of the first local squalls of what was elsewhere becoming a social hurricane. A community-educational program sponsored by Hersey called Upward Bound, an effort to fill gaps in the teaching of "hard-core" disadvantaged local teenagers in the hope of helping some of them get into university, ended with the students' trashing rooms in the residential colleges where they had been taught. Hersey did his best to see the event as providing a lesson for the teachers, giving, he said, "some of us in the university a glancing education in the desperation which vented itself, alas, in recent days."[29] His own already considerable education in this area was about to be radically deepened.

Seven hundred miles west of New Haven, on a hot Sunday late in July 1967, a police raid on an after-hours drinking club in Detroit—a city where, as in New Haven, vast efforts had been made to ameliorate some of the worst social problems—was followed by what became a riot. Today the story has gained new currency through Kathryn Bigelow's powerful 2017 film *Detroit*. Amid widespread looting a false rumor spread that organized, politically motivated blacks were operating as snipers. Pressures on local police, already at odds with the administration over their low wages, were intensified rather than relieved by arrests on an unmanageable scale and by poor tactical integration with reinforcements from the National Guard. Men on duty for days and nights with little sleep and no proper meals, frustrated by a policy decision not to stop unarmed looters, frightened by the violence of the rioters and by the rumors of organized killing, were further destabilized when one policeman was killed by the shotgun of another in the course of a confused arrest.

At home in Pierson, the master watched television, appalled by the sight of "American tanks rolling through the streets of an American city on the hunt for American citizens, and of military helicopters hovering over Detroit rooftops."[30] During what he called an "insane night," a four-year-old black girl was killed in her family's apartment by a burst of .50-caliber machine-gun fire from a tank "when someone in the room with her lit a cigarette and the flaring match was taken for the flash . . . of a sniper's weapon." (A .50-caliber bullet is as thick as a thumb.) In the course of those days, forty-two individuals were killed, at least six by the National Guard, eighteen by Detroit police, and five more by bullets fired by members of either body. Three of the deaths occurred in a motel where two white girls and half a dozen young black men, one of whom had just ended his military service in Vietnam, were hideously beaten, insulted, physically and psychologically tortured, and in at least two cases shot dead by a group of men composed, at different times and in varying combinations, of police, National Guardsmen, and a private security guard. One of the forms of torture used was to instruct an already beaten man to pick up a knife from the floor. He knew that if he did he could legally be shot. But when he didn't, he was again beaten with a rifle butt. The girls were stripped, battered, and sexually molested. Two of the dead men were later found to have had their sexual organs shot off. During the ensuing outrage and attempts to bring the culprits to justice, survivors of the "incident" and their families were continually harassed and intimidated by police. One way or another, every individual charged with involvement in the atrocity, however unambiguous the evidence and even if he had confessed, was eventually acquitted.

In the immediate aftermath of the Detroit riots and those in Newark two weeks earlier, President Johnson established the National Advisory Commission on Civil Disorders. His private aim, according to his aide Joseph Califano, was to head off a congressional investigation in the lead-up to next year's election.[31] Hersey may have suspected some such motive but had anyway been less than reassured when Johnson sent Cyrus Vance to Detroit as his representative. Until very recently Vance had been deputy secretary of defense and the conjunction of the riots with what was happening in Vietnam was in everyone's mind. Two needless wars were now going on, it was widely said, one in Indochina, one at home. So when the commission's executive director, David Ginsburg, invited Hersey to take part in the official inquiry, he declined, saying that he "did not want to attach my work to a document over which, as a whole, I would have no control at all."

The Kerner Report (named after the commission's chairman) was published in March 1968. It turned out to be a surprisingly outspoken attack on what it described as the racism of a country that was "moving toward two societies—one black, one white, separate and unequal." Far from praising President Johnson's efforts, it argued that "white society is deeply implicated in the ghetto . . . White institutions created it, white institutions maintain it and white society condones it." No more welcome to Johnson was the fact that the report sold more than two million copies. Hersey shared its views but by now was deep in a project that approached the issue in his own way.

One of Them Vietnams

As usual, "his own way" also became what was for him a new way. In the early stages there was a notion that what he wrote might take the form of an article for the *Detroit Free Press*, one of whose reporters gave him paid-for assistance.[32] Even this arrangement, though, seemed to Hersey too limiting. *The Algiers Motel Incident* is unique in his work because he himself is openly, outspokenly, intensely—and vulnerably—not only present in but also the investigator, prosecutor, and judge of all he relates. He had learned from Ralph Ellison, he said, that invisibility could be a disguise for nonaccountability.[33] Beyond that, he knew that in telling this story he could not be objective.[34]

At the outset, however, he approached it as he approached every piece of journalism. He read everything he could find about the recent riots, their context, and their aftermath. He went to Detroit and interviewed officials, commentators, black leaders, and militants. Gradually, he met the key participants and won their confidence: the survivors of the motel outrage, the bereaved families and friends, even those specific policemen who, as he but not the courts would decide, were the abusers and the torturers, the executioners—all talked to him in words that, through his telling, we hear and interpret for ourselves.

In the *Financial Times* a respected British critic, Philip French, called *The Algiers Motel Incident* "a masterly piece of reporting, fit to stand alongside . . . *Hiroshima*."[35] This is right. The book is also unsurpassed among Hersey's works in what it has to say to readers today. As Thomas Sugrue, a historian of twentieth-century America has written, the book communicates a "tragedy of power, inequality, and injustice . . . whose consequences continue to poison race relations in America today."[36] Comparisons with Truman Capote's "nonfiction novel" *In Cold Blood* have been inevitable, but race was not a component in the murder of the Clutter family, and Capote wrote half a dozen years after the event, Hersey while his story was still going on. Because in his own eyes no one else would do it, he believed he had a duty to bring the culprits to account. In an agonizing tirade that fills seven pages, Mrs. Pollard, the mother of one of the victims, tells him, "It hurts more for all of us to know that they call this justice. Write the book! Write it!"[37]

The Algiers Motel Incident begins where the immediate atrocities themselves ended. For the surviving black boys, that is—there was a little more in store for the white girls, though what exactly that involved they were subsequently still too frightened to reveal. It's about three in the morning. Warning the men that if they look back they'll be killed, the police send them out the motel's back door. Semi-naked, badly cut and bruised, they make their escape. One of them manages to call the mother of one of the dead men. Another is picked up by some railway police and taken to the hospital to have his head stitched. As they make it to their complicated households, Hersey's narrative turns to the parents and step-parents and siblings and part-siblings for their recollections: not all at once—the story moves around, bewildered and appalled, from place to place, person to person. We hear a little about the motel, a little about how and when the police department first learned what had been going on. Some of this is pieced together in Hersey's calm voice, some of it in the agitated or melancholy voices of those he talked to. In the mix, there's a steady, limited, Faulknerian poetry of family—a poetry derived in part from how these idiomatic falterings look, set out in the conventions of the printed page— as when the father of Auburey Pollard tells of hearing that a son is in trouble, and then which son it is and that he's dead, and leaves his workplace to go to the morgue:

> On the way I said to myself, "How in the world could all this be?"—you
> know. I said, "Maybe it's a mistake." That's the way I wanted to feel. So,
> my maw was there. My maw said, "Well, Baby, I tell you. We'll go see."
> I said, "Maw what's this? A mistake?" I said, "It couldn't be Auburey, I
> know Auburey's got more sense than that." Maw said, "Well," she said,
> "Baby," she said, "you never know. So let's go see." So we goes down to
> the morgue.

What they see there is too much for this slow, hardworking, gentle man. In time it drives him away from his family and then tears the rest of the family apart. One of Auburey's brothers, Chaney Pollard, is allowed home from Vietnam on compassionate leave and goes with his mother to the undertaker's to see the body. "Momma," he says,

> They don't kill them in Vietnam like that! They don't torture them then
> shoot them or blow them up when they got through with them. Momma,
> they don't stand them up and beat their face off before they kill them . . .
> Momma, they did worse than if they caught one of them Vietnams
> out there.

Chaney at first wants to get the rest of his "crew" over from Vietnam to avenge what has been done to Auburey. Like his father, he goes "out of his head." He ends up in a military psychiatric hospital.

Through scattered-seeming, confused, sometimes mutually inconsistent part-narratives like these we try to grasp more of what has happened: how it began, what the sequence of events was, who did what to whom and why, what the consequences have been and may yet be. Some facts become clear; many don't.[38] There are multiple investigators: public administrators, family members, journalists, police, Hersey himself. All are differently motivated, in different ways unreliable, and some are under threat—among the troubles the bereaved have to deal with are racist phone calls and messages. The coolest voices here are paradoxically those of the culprits, and part of Hersey's skill is in holding back what he knows about the degree of participation in each case. Somehow he persuaded them to talk, not so much about the incident itself as about their lives as policemen, the parts of the job they like and that interest them, the puzzles it involves. Because they are policemen, they approach some of these questions with an awkwardly formal attempt at factualism that makes strange harmonies with the different but similarly revealing inarticulacies of the black speakers: "I believe that if we had acted before they started looting," says David Senak, never finishing the sentence, "and before these people saw the instigators go and actually in front of us burn places down, arson, which they all know is an offense punishable by imprisonment, you know, a felony, they saw this, they saw these people carrying gasoline cans into stores and actually burning them in our presence and nothing done."[39] Much of Senak's normal work, we learn, and what he's really good at, involves entrapping prostitutes. He and his colleagues also spend a fair amount of their energy catching convicted petty criminals in new petty crimes for which, given the cumulative approach to punishment, they will serve long sentences. While a white policeman who has confessed—confessed—to having taken part in the motel atrocities is sitting at home on bail, a brother of one of the victims is serving a three-year jail sentence for stealing seven dollars off a paper boy.

Hersey is very fair to the police. Unlike Bigelow's film, his book has space to allow a generous sense of their home backgrounds, their concerns, their limitations but also their better qualities. It has less patience with the buck-passing National Guardsmen involved, erratic in all their actions except ensuring that responsibility doesn't fall on themselves. And it has no time at all for the white lawyers whose job is to prosecute the accused white police and who adroitly avoid calling key witnesses or otherwise rocking the law-enforcement boat.[40] Here the question of the legality of Hersey's book is important but also easily dealt with. Much was said at the time about the risk of prejudicing the trials, and the lawyers made play with this, but there has never been any sustained argument that publication could or should have been prevented, or that Hersey or Knopf committed any offense. Postponing a hearing in Michigan in the summer of 1968 because of the amount of attention the newly published book was receiving, Judge Robert Colombo blustered about taking the matter to the American Bar Association and other professional bodies, but lawyers acting for Knopf had already prevailed. The leading New York firm Weil, Gotshal & Manges asserted that *The Algiers Motel Incident* was a report on matters of "overwhelming public importance" that had received widespread press coverage, and was therefore protected by the First Amendment as interpreted by the Supreme Court in several recent named cases.[41]

As for the right to a fair trial, the court was in a position to take adequate protective measures (such as the temporary adjournment which Judge Colombo put in place), and again the Supreme Court had shown its support for the principle of freedom of comment. Hersey's own position was impeccable. He took no money from the book, paying some of the income as fees and expenses to those who helped him and putting the rest into a new charitable foundation.[42] As for justice, it was clear to him, he said, that nothing would bring about convictions of the murderers and their accomplices. Dismissing a review in the journal *Commonweal* that argued that Hersey had undermined the judicial process, a friendly lawyer wrote, "One might ask what judicial process, or better yet, whose?"[43] The best that could be achieved was, as Mrs. Pollard had urged him, to write, and to do so with all the involvement, passion, and technical skill at his disposal.

To date there has been only one reprint edition, by a university press.[44] To some extent the book's appearance early in July 1968 was overshadowed by the murder of Robert Kennedy a few weeks earlier, and by the electoral turmoil into which that event, together with LBJ's earlier decision not to stand for reelection, had thrown the country. Yet it was widely reviewed and sold well. It was both helped and hindered by appearing so soon after the Kerner Report and the assassination of Martin Luther King, Jr., which both the report and the book did much to illuminate. Hersey's work could be read as a case study vividly illustrating Kerner's conclusions.

Living History

At Yale, Hersey was encouraged by the friendly reaction of a senior figure in the English department, Eugene M. Waith. "I was reminded of the 'good' Dos Passos of the USA [trilogy] period," Waith aptly wrote. "I suppose it was your combination of vignettes, news stories, straight narration, and incidents that illuminate a milieu."[45] This contrasted with the grumbles of some lazy critics that the book was confusing to read, as if confusion of all kinds were not its topic, and as if such a series of events could usefully be simplified. It's true that for a lawyer's purposes a more orderly—say, strictly chronological—telling might have seemed necessary. This was the point of view of a Harvard Law School graduate, Stephen Schlesinger—son of Hersey's friend Arthur—writing at length in *The Atlantic Monthly*.[46] But when he complains, "One is swamped in detail and description, lost in an amalgam of impressions, some boring, some irrelevant, others perceptive," the obvious response is that this is what the experience of trying to understand that situation, those people, these events, was like. Nothing Hersey records is irrelevant, though the reader must ponder—and it's part of what makes the experience so gripping— what the relevance of any given detail may be.

There's an example when Officer Senak tells Hersey a contorted story about recently finding himself, while suspended from duty, and against all regulations and common sense, pursuing some men whom he suspected of having stolen their car. He got lost, he says, in a hazardous quarter of the city where two prostitutes, one black, one white, got into his own car against his will and one of them pulled a knife. When he fought with the women, they reported him for assault but dropped the charge once they realized who they were dealing with. In legal terms the story has nothing whatsoever to do with the Algiers Motel case. The account is rambling, circumstantial, part plausible, for the most part wildly unconvincing. Psychologically, though, in terms of our understanding of Senak as a protagonist, it's fascinating both in the obsessions that characterize it and that it dwells on—a desire to chase down possibly harmless suspects; the motif of entrapping and/or being entrapped; prostitutes and cross-racial sexual entanglement—and also in Senak's muddled, self-pitying, self-justifying thought processes. "The reason I got into trouble all over again," he laments, "was because I was overzealous. It was my instinct of a police officer."[47]

Using the book as a peg for a retrospective essay on all Hersey's work, Herbert Mitgang in *The Saturday Review of Literature* said that though in his fiction "the thread of compassion" that runs through all his writing often becomes sentimentality, it results in a "rare fairness" in his reportage. *The Wall*, Mitgang pointed out in passing, "took the form of a 'nonfiction novel' long before that form was claimed by Truman Capote," and what made Hersey always worth reading was that "he is still going where the action is in living history."[48] Living history was exactly the point, and there was much more of similar kinds to be lived in the next couple of years, including in New Haven.

Among the consequences of the skewing of the justice system against blacks was a retaliatory, despairing drift toward armed resistance, formalized in the Black Panthers' movement founded in the wake of Malcolm X's death. Events of the kind Hersey had described contributed to the group's momentum, and support for it grew, too, as it became clear that it was being actively infiltrated and undermined by the FBI under the bureau's increasingly uncontrollable founder-director J. Edgar Hoover. By the end of 1968, Hoover had been running the FBI and the organization out of which it grew for almost forty-five years. Whatever and whoever had led to the belief that black snipers were killing police in Detroit, the lie would have been welcome to him.[49] The Panthers set up offices in black communities, including, for almost accidental reasons, one in Orchard Street, New Haven, just six blocks west of the main Yale campus.[50] As with Columbia on the edge of Harlem, the proximity of the university to deprived residential neighborhoods was crucial in what happened there.

Hersey dedicated *The Algiers Motel Incident* to his students at Pierson. Many of them, whether or not in direct response to his exhortations, were involved in local community projects of various kinds. The number of black students in the college had increased, and some held influential positions in student organizations, one as president of the National Black American Law Students Association and two as leaders of Yale's branch of the Black Student Alliance. John and Barbara engaged with radical students directly, in a pragmatic, friendly spirit.[51] Unlike some contemporary academics, Hersey did not tailor his views toward attracting favorable attention, any more than he was among writers who used their personal behavior to attract attention to their work. He was never as radical as the chaplain of Yale, William Sloane Coffin, or as politically adroit as Kingman Brewster. But his views both on Vietnam and on institutionalized racism brought him into open conflict with the system, and in various ways he sailed close to the wind.

In the summer of 1967, Hersey and three Martha's Vineyard neighbors—the novelist William Styron, the cartoonist Jules Feiffer, and Robert Brustein, dean of the Yale Drama School—placed an ad in the *Vineyard Gazette* denouncing another holiday resident, Nicholas Katzenbach, who had recently become undersecretary of state and who, they reminded readers, while deputy attorney general, had defended the Gulf of Tonkin Resolution, which enabled the escalation of the Vietnam War. To have used a local newspaper for such a matter may seem unambitious. On the contrary: To its many prominent regular visitors, the Vineyard was a kind of club and, like other clubs, was treated as a sanctuary. Kingman Brewster, who was a friend of people on both sides of the argument, told the advertisers their gesture was "bad manners at best," calling it "an offensive infringement of the long standing ethic [*sic*] of the Vineyard as a place where even a public man's life can be lived quietly."[52] This was tantamount to saying what the similarly well-born Katzenbach himself said privately: that the advertisers "were not gentlemen."

The incident is rich in implication. Brewster and Katzenbach had in common that they were liberal centrists from powerful backgrounds who, while conscious of the injustices of the system and in various ways working to change it, at the same time enjoyed and beneficially exploited their inherited opportunities. To "ordinary people," it's true, they would have been hard to distinguish from their local opponents, all in their own ways prominent and well-off. Their being at home on the Vineyard was part of that. But the four protesters had either been scholarship boys (Hersey and Styron) or were publicly educated (Feiffer and Brustein), and it would be easy to identify other elements that set them apart and that allowed

Brewster and Katzenbach to see themselves as occupying a more elevated plane. In 1967, this was the point. Where were the boundaries between private and public, between inherited seclusion and voluntary exposure, between governors and governed? In his White House protest and his Pierson speeches, and metaphorically in *Under the Eye of the Storm*, Hersey had shown that there could be no such boundaries, no safe havens. Individuals, even students, even presidents, were responsible for their actions and had to be held to account even in places—physical or otherwise—that might previously have given them shelter. There was a strong puritan element in this, and something naive, even adolescent, too. For a senior statesman to be denounced on Martha's Vineyard by his artist neighbors was a bit like being insulted at home by your student kids (an experience known to several of those on both sides, Hersey among them). But Hersey valued naïveté. One of the things he wanted, and got, from Pierson was a strong shot of youth and idealism. To him, the question wasn't whether the polite, amiable Katzenbach should enjoy a kind of socio-moral immunity on the Vineyard. It was whether being on the Vineyard should let Hersey and others ignore what was happening elsewhere: tens of thousands of American troops going to a war whose military aims their rulers were unable to articulate; nuclear tests by the United States and the Soviet Union on the same day, August 4, 1967.

The Algiers Motel Incident's dedication, "To the students of Pierson College," paid tribute to how, in steering them toward social and political involvements outside the campus, Hersey had been stimulated by their energy and was educated alongside them. In a big departure for him, the second chapter of the book is about his own involvement and procedures in the investigation. He is vehement that "every white American with any pretensions to racial understanding" should read "that surpassingly remarkable document of our time *The Autobiography of Malcolm X*." Like Ralph Ellison's *Invisible Man*, Malcolm X's book—now known to have been ghostwritten by Alex Haley—exposes the built-in racism of American life, not only in the South and not only after slavery. If there is an original sin more recent than that of Adam and Eve, it is, according to this view, the genocide of Native Americans. Like many of his students, Hersey accepted these arguments. And in writing about Detroit, he decided that for the first time he had to be present in his book, in the way that writers associated with the New Journalism made a point of being.[53] He had also discovered how little he knew, despite all his reading and all his seemingly relevant experience:

> My own education in the course of the researches . . . was a staggering one. At the outset I learned . . . that experiences I might have considered as credentials for this task had not given me sufficient insights for all that I was to confront. I had been born in China, had felt as a child the puzzling guilt of being pulled through the streets in a rickshaw by a yellow man; I had witnessed death and pain in war; I had tried to learn something about racism while writing several novels with racial themes; I had lived for part of the anxious summer of 1964 in the home of a black farmer (*I* was anxious; it was truly dangerous for him) in Holmes County, Mississippi, and for the past two years I had lived in intimacy with college students, the most open, most threatened, most serious, most generous people I had ever known. But these were not enough.[54]

That Hersey should have seen students as a threatened category tells a lot, and it seemed to some at Yale that the master of Pierson occasionally went too far in that direction, had gone native, or just regressed—as many academics of the time did—in the sense of thinking himself at one with the kids.[55] And kids is what they were: intelligent by definition, in some cases mature and responsible, but for the most part sheltered offspring of a period of exceptional prosperity, members of the "Spock Generation" brought up without scolding in a climate of non-authoritarianism. Hersey's past experiences may not have been adequate to Detroit but were a great deal more than most of his students had had, and now they were faced with being told that, one way or another, they were implicated in two shocking cruelties: what their country was doing in Indochina and what it had inflicted on black people at home.

Nationally, the guilty rage of students who were still saved from military service by the fact of being students; the anger of black people, some of them students but most not, who had become increasingly conscious of the historical origins of their predicament and who also now believed that getting something substantial done about it had to involve making white Americans scared *not* to do something—all this produced a perilous situation. One aspect, as is clear from the rumor about black snipers in Detroit, was people's ability to buy firearms and ammunition. When activists threatened violence there was every reason to be afraid, and the behavior of police and local administrations, though in some places impressively restrained, all too often exacerbated what it was supposed to control. And just as an urban crisis was simultaneously a campus crisis (not least because some of the most privileged campuses were in poor urban districts), so the campuses became identified by conservative parents and politicians as hothouses of dangerous ideas and forms of behavior. This wasn't wholly mistaken. Student life did encourage extremes of many kinds, not least of self-identification with everything a student for the moment thought he or she wanted to be. As Hersey was to write vividly, out of his years of sympathetic observation and participation:

> The drive is to purge the self, through new and ever new experience, of the whole station-wagon load of junky white middle class values and of the guilt the wagon carries on its chrome luggage rack. The greatest need, hidden from the mind though it may be, is to be purified by having the experiences one cannot have—being poor, being black, for some even being a member of the opposite sex—and the experiences one does not want—above all, if male, most unwanted yet most deeply wanted without knowing it, being a soldier in an evil war.[56]

The last adjective seems perverse. Did even the most rebellious of male students really want, however unconsciously, to fight in an evil war—in this context, Vietnam—more than (say) a "good" war such as the one against Nazism? Or at all? It's tempting to take "evil" as the imagined student's description of any war: an expression of the view that war is intrinsically bad. But as we've seen, Hersey had always been fascinated by bellicosity, by the strange pact between heroism and violence. And his students are not wholly imaginary: he's talking about people he knew well, to some of whom he had become a kind of confessor; talking, too, about a part of himself. Hersey had learned in Guadalcanal, Warsaw, and Hiroshima that there are virtues that only war at its most vicious makes possible. What's at stake in this part of his diagnosis is nothing so rudimentary as a test of masculinity (though it may involve that among other things). It is a profound metaphysical paradox.[57] A soldier in an evil war: It was one of the ways Hersey saw himself.

On the Green

While he deeply understood what the young were going through, and encouraged their more radical instincts, his aims were always moderate and constructive: community social programs, not armed struggle. He preached that the world could be made fairer through positive changes of heart, of thinking, of social organization, yet without violence. Like Brewster and many others, though, he also sometimes despaired of this view. When Brewster brought down the wrath of politicians, alumni, and parents by confessing that he was "skeptical of the ability of black revolutionaries to achieve a fair trial anywhere in the United States," Hersey admitted that he himself "would have gone further."[58]

The times could not have seemed worse. Thanks in part to Brewster's initiatives on race as well as to his excellent personal relations with students, faculty, and New Haven community leaders, Yale had not seen protests directed against the university itself on anything like the scale experienced in the second half of the 1960s at Berkeley, Cornell, Harvard, and Columbia. The mishandling of demonstrations at Harvard also taught Yale some lessons, while the fact that they had occurred on the campus of the university's traditional competitor and not-so-distant neighbor was a warning in itself. But Yale now had a unique problem to face. A member of the Black Panthers was murdered in New Haven in 1969 on suspicion of being an informer. The movement's leader, Bobby Seale, had been in the city at the time and was implicated. A trial was to be held at the New Haven courthouse, diagonally across the Green from the main gate of Yale College itself.

New Haven Green is the city's historic center and symbolizes more about the United States than some care to recall. Most of the area around it was purchased cheaply and more or less forcibly from Native Americans. The Quinnipiac people, commemorated in the name of a traditional club close to the courthouse and much frequented by its officials, have the distinction of being the first groups of Native Americans to have been enclosed in a "reservation"—by white settlers at East Haven, on the opposite side of the harbor. That was in 1638. New Haven's first Christian church was established on the Green the following year. A couple of generations later, the university arrived. Today, the Green has three old churches at its center, the courthouse on one corner and the university's Old Campus along its western side.

It's also a focal point for homeless people. The contrasts between its soup kitchens and the prosperity of everything around, between vulnerable human indigence and the fortresses of law, church, and academia, are unmissable. And of course the Green is an obvious space for open-air meetings. Now additional pressures converged. Brewster's many successes inflamed radicals suspicious of what they saw as "repressive tolerance," the deceptive and coercive power of liberal gradualism. Then in November 1969, Yale members of the powerful national group Students for a Democratic Society took up the cause of a black employee in one of the residential college halls who had been dismissed as a result of a dispute with a student manager. A building was taken over—the first such occupation in Yale's history. Soon, jury selections began for the Black Panthers trial and rumors circulated that May 1 would see huge demonstrations. In mid-April, the presiding judge became incensed by a disruptive conversation between two Black Panthers in the visitors' section of the courtroom and sentenced both to six months in prison. The extravagant penalty was soon lifted, but the damage had been done.

Through a remarkable conjunction of political strategy, civic diplomacy, cunning, goodwill, and luck, Yale was saved from what could easily have been an explosion. Brewster's statement that he doubted that black revolutionaries could get a fair trial was an element in this triumph, not least because black activists who knew him knew, too, that he meant it. The university's nonconfrontational handling of the situation included a decision not to suspend classes but to allow faculty and students personal discretion in what classes to hold or attend. Students themselves contributed through an imaginative, thorough set of preparations for an invasion of a size that didn't in the end occur: designated places where marchers could rest or take refuge, receive first aid, and get food and nonalcoholic drinks. Pierson students were prominent in all this, and Hersey encouraged and later proudly defended what they had done.

The irony, as he observed, was that journalists, politicians, and alumni reacted as though Yale had burned down—indeed, as if it had burned both itself and the courthouse down in an orgy of revolutionary self-hatred. Vice President Agnew pressed for Brewster's resignation; letters came in calling him a Communist, an appeaser, a traitor. Conservative alumni already displeased by the shift against easy admission for people with Yale connections, and by the introduction of coeducation in 1969, withdrew financial support.

Hersey's period as master of Pierson was due to end that same summer. Tired, disillusioned, and deeply apprehensive about his country's future, he sat down to write the last of his annual letters to the college's alumni. It is an unsettled, unsettling document.

His previous official communications—end-of-year reports, eulogies, exhortations—had always combined seriousness with a decorative border of learned wit, mild in-jokes: the mannered geniality of the WASP academic establishment, elegant and correct. The previous June, when coeducation had been among his main themes, he joked about the failure of attempts to achieve this at Yale by persuading Vassar, a women's college, to move to New Haven; he called it "Vassar's jilting of Yale after a long flirtation." True, he pulled no punches when it came to explaining student "unrest." The malaise stemmed, he argued, from "revulsion at the prospect of being asked to give or take lives in a war that seems to them immoral and mad; at the way we continue, often for the sake of profit, to poison the skies and rivers and seas; at the horrible multiple sclerosis of our great cities; at the undertow of racism that tugs at all of them, black and white alike."[59] But however pressing the issue, these writings were basically measured and calm. He made clear that while he wanted to maximize useful student involvement in decision-making, he agreed with Brewster that universities weren't democratic governmental organisms. Nor, though, despite the view of some alumni, were they businesses, and he said it would be disastrous to regard students as a product. The main concern in student governance, he believed, was one of communications, particularly between the leaders of student organizations and those affected by them.

His 1970 letter takes a different tone from the outset. "All is not bullshit that is now called by the name," it announces. And although the early part of the ensuing discussion concerns students' use and misuse of language, particularly the language of revolution, a different impetus soon becomes clear. Hersey wants the alumni to understand a phenomenon many know about only from the media. This is going to be the case for the defense. "I charge you not to become blindly enraged by what you hear in student throats as pure b.s.," the outgoing master writes; "you must search out the reality. The reality is that changes are coming. They must come. They are beginning to come now. You must share in bringing them. Or else."

He was directly responding to what had been said by alumni in letters to the university, as well as to Pierson College. And this was to be a public document, one that, after it had been circulated to former members of the college, appeared in the *Yale Alumni Magazine*[60] and quickly after that as a book: *Letter to the Alumni* (1970). The basis of the argument is that readers should look beyond appearances—unkempt youth with long hair shouting revolutionary slogans—and identify the often admirable reality behind them, a reality to which Hersey presents himself as a trustworthy guide. He was confident that he had earned that trust during his five years at Pierson and throughout his career as a writer, and it's evident that he both understands and shares the motives of his students at their best. There's a risk, though, one that he doesn't quite avoid, of taking their side to the extent of patronizing his readers, "those of you who lead steady, unruffled, protected lives."[61]

Some passages are clumsy, especially when the aim is an undisguised plea for the restoration of lost financial support. The more apocalyptic passages about what will happen if the elders fail to act in the way Hersey advocates are exaggerated in tone, and anyway weren't borne out, though events almost half a century later have given a new currency to his fears. For all this, his inside knowledge of student motivations and of the enterprise, commitment, and practical good sense that many—faculty as well as students—brought to the preparations for and handling of May Day are revelatory, if as much about Hersey's sympathies as about the situation itself. He mentions an attempt by one student group to set up a free breakfast program for New Haven children that wasn't connected to the Black Panthers. He describes the organization of ad hoc lectures and seminars covering every angle on the current unrest. He tells of the successful efforts of a football "jock" to set up a community child-care center, and the same man's impassioned short speech to the faculty, imploring it to provide moral leadership.

To some students in the thick of all this, as well as to several reviewers of the book, the master's enthusiasm was naive.[62] The future Yale professor David Bromwich, a member of Pierson, participated early on in canvassing New Haven middle-class homes, trying to assure residents that there was nothing to worry about, but was perturbed by how much of this effort was directed by student propagandists for the Panthers. Having visited about three dozen houses with a friend, he reported back that people were genuinely afraid: "The violent talk of the Panther leaders turns them off." To his disillusionment, an organizer on the student steering committee told the editor of the strike newsletter, "You can't print that."[63] Still, Hersey relates undeniable examples of courage and pragmatism, both from students and faculty members. Among the latter is a psychologist who, on the day, helps organize a first-aid center and, when the National Guard's teargassing of the crowd seems to be getting out of hand, steps into the street wearing a white coat and stethoscope and accosts an officer with a highly effective improvisation: "This is a medical area. I have a hundred and fifty severe cases of conjunctivitis."

There is a much wider agenda. A few days after May Day 1970, four students protesting at Kent State University were shot dead by members of the National Guard. Written in the aftermath of that event among others, *Letter to the Alumni* is not only about Yale or even about students' idealism in general but about the potential for what Hersey calls "American repression." Here the author's feelings break through in a way he had only recently learned to permit himself:

> Do you think I exaggerate? My Lai. Our official acquiescence in the Vietnamese prison of Con Son, with its unspeakable "tiger cages." We are capable of this future.
>
> In fact, this is the easy future to reach. All we have to do is keep on going the way we are now.
>
> I think this is an intolerable future for my five beloved sons and daughters and for my dear young friends that I have made in the last five years. The thought of it tears me apart.[64]

This was a step too far for many of his readers, some of whom, especially Pierson alums and Yale faculty, wrote to him at considerable length. A staff member at the Yale Dean's Office commented specifically on his dark vision of the future: "I agree fully alas that [it] is one of the possibilities. But I am not sure that there is not yet another option—which is not the status quo, but a less dislocating type of evolution."[65] Others ranged from a supportive conscientious objector now living and working in a California commune dedicated to a free-schooling project to a highly articulate military officer on active service in Quang Nam Province who confessed to having "suffered a number of internal contusions, caused by colliding loyalties to two of my favorite institutions," Yale and the Marines, and argued cogently against what he saw as Yale's new anti-militarist ethos.[66] Kingman Brewster himself was more in tune with his friend's pessimism, as well as grateful to him:

> My feelings are so involved, my ego so enlarged by your generous treat-ment of me in your pages, that I have refused to comment publicly. But to you I can only say how very much I appreciate what you have done— for Yale, for Country, and for whatever is that mystery which others call God. I guess I am most appreciative for country. Yale is doing alright— for the moment, as you so rightly and so often say. God I suppose is too. But not so for Country.[67]

Among the most encouraging responses was one sent to Brewster him-self, who passed it on. Charles E. Odegaard, president of the University of Washington, Seattle—which, under his care, had become one of the lead-ing public universities in the United States—said he regretted the book's focus on private institutions but was glad of how thoroughly it dispelled false versions of what had happened at Yale, and of Brewster's actions in particular. At a recent dinner, Odegaard had heard two wealthy Yale alumni-benefactors "lashing into" Brewster. He was sending them copies of Hersey's book.[68]

11. Sweet Land of Liberty

F REED FROM THE RESPONSIBILITIES of college leadership, Hersey also took a break from the Nixon regime. A one-year fellowship at the American Academy in Rome gave him time to reflect historically on the relations of intellectuals to political power.

His focus was Nero's Rome. In the wake of *The Algiers Motel Incident* and *Letter to the Alumni*, he was wondering what it would be like to live under a government that prevented him from writing those books. Published in 1972, *The Conspiracy* is a thoroughly researched, inventive epistolary novel reimagining a famous plot led by an orator and literary patron in ancient Rome, Gaius Calpurnius Piso, against the emperor. The project brought various problems, particularly how to invent voices for people in the ancient past: characterization through style was not among Hersey's strengths, and the letters his ancient Romans write to one another, though very different in content, sound samey, whether the authors are secret police, poets, or philosophers. The main issues, though—Do intellectuals have any real power? What are their obligations under a repugnant regime?—are as pressing as always, and Seneca's words to his nephew Lucan are true and melancholy: "A writer cannot change the world; his duty is to describe it."[1] Yet even description, as the novel tells us, is subjective. "Where you see horrors," Seneca tells Lucan, "Petronius sees picnics."

No one saw picnics in the American situation in the early 1970s, and after a decade of intense activism Hersey could be forgiven for drawing back a little, for coming close, even, to despair. What was it to be a writer? Where would his work take him next? Were there obstacles in its way? And could he help others to develop the skills he had learned? One of the things Italy reminded him of was how much he loved Yale and still had to contribute there. Having moved out of the master's lodgings at Pierson, he and Barbara bought a modern house on Humphrey Street,[2] a pleasant, tree-lined residential neighborhood within walking distance of the main campus. For cash-flow reasons, the father of five persuaded Knopf to help with the financial arrangements for the purchase.[3]

While Yale's English department was keen to have him teach a course, it was unforthcoming with money. There were serious intellectual doubts, some of which Hersey shared, about "creative writing" as an academic subject. On the other hand, competition with developments in other institutions continued to drive the university forward, and it was evident that students wanted opportunities to work with writers and that other places were managing much better to meet the demand. As early as 1960, a Yale contemporary of Hersey's called George de Mare, then working at Price Waterhouse and the author of a novel about corporate life, unsuccessfully tried to enlist support from him, Brendan Gill, and others in an effort to set up a Yale creative writing workshop.[4] After arriving at Pierson College in 1965, Hersey had managed to secure one-term appointments for Lillian Hellman,[5] Arthur Miller, and William Styron, but there was nothing in New Haven with the éclat of Harvard's long-established Charles Eliot Norton lectures and Boylston professorship for a poet, or the Ferris and McGraw professorships begun at Princeton in 1964. These were the comparisons Hersey himself drew on, knowing what his Yale colleagues regarded as serious competitors. He was well aware, though, that Iowa had been teaching creative writing since the 1920s, that the subject had been taken up at Stanford in 1946, and that the writing program in Columbia's not much younger School of the Arts was flourishing. At Yale, Hersey himself apart, the sole established writer in residence was the illustrious Southern poet, novelist, critic, and editor Robert Penn

Warren. Brought into the Drama School in 1951 to teach playwriting—one of the few genres of which he wasn't an acknowledged master[6]—he was made a professor of English in 1961.

Warren was not only a very good and prolific author but also an originator: a key figure, with John Crowe Ransom and Allen Tate, in the poetry of the Fugitive movement, cofounder of *The Southern Review* with Cleanth Brooks, and, again with Brooks, coauthor of a number of highly influential works on what for half a century was the dominant approach to literary criticism in schools and universities, "close reading." He had done graduate work at Oxford at the same time as Brooks, who from 1947 was Gray Professor of Rhetoric in Yale's English department. Warren himself was coming up for retirement.

Professing Writing

Back from Rome, Hersey taught for the college seminar program he had begun at Pierson, working as an untenured lecturer in the English department at the rate of $3,000 per course.[7] It wasn't nothing, and the freedom from bureaucratic responsibility suited him. Still, for someone of his international standing and with his track record at the university, the situation was a shade exploitative. He didn't know the then chair of the department, Dwight Culler, at all well, but late in 1972 he phoned him. One conversation led to a second, over lunch. Having broached the topic of how practicing writers should be represented on the faculty, he mentioned Warren's imminent retirement, apparently in such a way as to have been understood as hinting that he might be considered as his successor—though if this was his implication he quickly pulled back.[8] In the eyes of Culler, a scholar of nineteenth-century literature, Hersey, for all his honorary degrees and teaching experience, might have seemed disqualified by his lack of either literary-historical or critical credentials, not to speak of the still essential-seeming Ph.D.[9] Behind Culler, Cleanth Brooks was making his weight felt, as also was the eighteenth-century scholar Maynard Mack. At the same time, setting aside the needs of traditional scholarship, there were other claims on the department's resources, among them its innovative program in the newly expanding field of African American literature, which for good reasons had Brewster's support.[10] Whatever the ins and outs of the processes involved—and negative views of Hersey's recent fiction may have played their own part—several new heavyweights joined the department on full professorships in the 1970s, and Hersey wasn't among them.[11]

Students competed to get into his classes: either "The Craft of the Writer," on fiction—which made use of readings from an anthology he had published—or "Form and Style in Non-Fiction Writing." With rare exceptions they were not allowed to take both.[12] One said later that being accepted was like getting into Yale all over again.[13] As a tutor Hersey was formal but good at letting discussion occur between students in a group and meticulously attentive to the work submitted to him. Each of his ten students would write a two-thousand-to-three-thousand-word draft one week, revise it the following week in the light of discussion, then repeat the process. In addition to meeting with them as a group, he saw everyone individually once a week. To them all, he communicated the importance of writing as a vocation, as a way of improving the world, and "the difference between striving for fame and striving for excellence."[14] Several made careers as journalists, among them the brave war correspondent Marie Colvin, later killed in Syria, and the influential *New York Times* critic Michiko Kakutani. A few became novelists.[15] But Hersey was careful not to treat either of his courses as a series of "how to" exercises, seeing them instead as "a serious inquiry into what it means to be a writer, what it means to live by and for writing." In any case he didn't believe it was possible "to 'teach' or 'learn' how to write masterpieces."[16] Implicit in his approach was that writing existed in order to be read and that reading was essential to it. Like the old teachers of rhetoric, he treated classic texts as models for imitation, asking students to use Virginia Woolf's *Mrs. Dalloway*, for example, as the basis for an account of a day in the life of a fellow student. In the nonfiction class he stressed that "nonfiction" meant what it said, getting students to discuss the relation between the verifiable and the invented in passages from Hemingway, Truman Capote, or Tom Wolfe.

As far as his own writing was concerned, he kept it for the longer, non-teaching part of the year. As his sailing novel *Under the Eye of the Storm* had shown, he was instinctively and increasingly hostile to most new things. A Yale researcher temporarily beguiled him, though, into acting as an experimental subject for a project on whether using a computer might be helpful to people working imaginatively. This was in 1972, so the equipment occupied much of a building. Hersey's first approach was to work as he would previously have done with a typewriter: keying in a draft of his next novel, which he had first written in longhand, and then revising on-screen. But he wasn't slow to cotton on to the new practical possibilities offered by the technology—word-searching, multiple replacement, instantaneously "clean" revised pages—and after a month of trial and error became a convert. Of a kind. Subsequently, he never felt much need to keep up with IT developments. Having acquired a Lanier "No Problem" word processor of his own, he remained faithful to it almost until he died.[17]

Yale apart, this was a time of professional uncertainty for him. There were questions about the future of the agency that dealt with his film deals, McIntosh & Otis, where one of the staff was retiring and another was unwell. Elizabeth Otis herself, who had founded the business in 1928, was finding Hollywood less susceptible to authors who, like her and like some of her best-known clients, were getting on in age.[18] Hersey's lifelong publisher Alfred A. Knopf, Sr., was eighty now, and while the list continued under his name, it had been an imprint of Random House since 1960; in 1968 the dynamic, opinionated Robert Gottlieb became editor in chief. A year before the merger Knopf's son Pat had left to start his own publishing company, and Blanche Knopf had died in 1966.

Hersey continued for now to work with his original editor, Harold Strauss, but he, too, was feeling the years[19] and in any case had never been the kind of editor who saw his job as helping to transform a text. For closer attention Hersey had depended on *The New Yorker*, yet the magazine never published much of his fiction. In August 1972 the latest of William Shawn's gentle rejections arrived via Otis.[20] Hersey knew that Shawn had declined to take an extract from *The Conspiracy* but not that in 1968 he had protected him by killing a negative review of *The Algiers Motel Incident*.[21] Of Hersey's other recent books, *Under the Eye of the Storm* was the only one to have been noticed in the magazine, and then in a brief anonymous note describing it as a "heavy-treading allegory." His name is so intimately associated with *The New Yorker* and was so often mentioned in its columns, in reviews of stage and film adaptations of his books, or of biographies of people who were or had been his friends, or articles about the magazine's own history, that it comes as a shock to realize that fifteen years had passed since he had written for it.[22]

These circumstances weren't all new to him and of course were of kinds shared by most writers. But as he approached his sixtieth birthday he was inevitably beginning to think not just about how he was doing in the present but about his future reputation. In 1966 he had had a mild spat with the reference books series *Contemporary Authors*, which, following its normal practice, had sent him a draft article about his work to check. The essay was essentially factual and drew heavily on reviews, but to Hersey's way of thinking too many of those used were negative. He sent the editor concerned a list of more favorable items, and the article was changed accordingly.[23] In the early 1970s, though, he was increasingly hearing from graduate students interested in writing about his work, whose letters to him tended to mention how little it was discussed these days. If uningratiating, this was true, and had the effect of making him think more than he had in the past about the possible reasons. In one letter, responding to an approach from a future academic, Sam Girgus, he tackled them at length.[24]

It took him five months to reply. After apologizing for the delay and after the usual provisos about his dislike of anything that smacked of either autobiography or literary self-interpretation, he suggested possible reasons why he had become neglected. (Unlike with *Contemporary Authors*, he didn't argue that the opposite was true.) Setting aside "quality, or lack of it" to consider later, he described himself as writing "against the grain, both of literary fashion and of establishment values." Even *A Bell for Adano*, he pointed out, though in many ways "a sentimental novel about a 'good guy,'" had been an attack on a senior American officer as "a dangerous shit"—one written, he added, "several years before Mailer wrote about Croft and Cummings in *The Naked and the Dead*, by which time this was precisely the thing to do."[25] Second, there was perhaps something "subtly alien" in his work as a result of his Chinese childhood. Third, he didn't repeat himself in form or "apparent content," and this upset critics' preconceptions.

Then came a digression on the world's crowdedness—it was to be the subject of his next novel, but the implication here is that there are just too many writers—before he turned to a separate question Girgus had raised, about journalism versus fiction. Hersey defended the idea that fiction was a report on life. He also made a claim for the imaginative engagement required by the best journalism. But it was possible, he hinted a little belligerently, that suspicion of journalism as an inferior form was a further reason that his novels were undervalued: "If the fact that I still write journalism puts off serious critics of fiction, then that will have to be their problem." As for the postponed matter of quality, he returned to it only briefly and gave little away. It was possible, he said, that his work was poor and therefore not worth writing about. "My own view is that some of it is (poor) and some isn't. That which isn't will have its day. So I won't worry about it."

It's scarcely surprising that in a letter to an unknown student Hersey didn't reveal which of his work he felt most and which least confident about, or that he didn't engage with specific criticisms that had been made by reviewers. What he does betray is deep defensiveness. However controversial its subject, *Adano* had not been neglected but on the contrary widely hailed, awarded a Pulitzer Prize, and turned into a successful play and a film. And the idea that critics were deterred by the variety of his work ignored the fact that versatility had become one of the things they expected from him and generally praised. (As the critic Clifton Fadiman put it, Hersey "remains one of our few distinguished novelists incapable of repeating themselves.")[26] It's worth observing, too, that while Hersey makes so strong a claim for journalism at its best at the same time as hinting that a prejudice against the genre may have caused some critics to fail to take him seriously, he had not discouraged the academic David Sanders from writing about his work in a way that, though exhaustive in its coverage of the fiction, does less than justice to his factual work.

If he was thin-skinned, he was also tough, and in terms of his earnings from his work he went on the offensive. He had suspicions about the accounting system at Random House and asked the Authors Guild to audit the figures for *The Conspiracy*, his novel about ancient Rome, on his behalf.[27] The investigation proved him right, but such satisfactions can be short-lived when, as in any author's dealings with publishers, one is negotiating with human beings about intrinsically sensitive matters. His publishers should have been more careful, but in various ways the company had been accommodating to Hersey, bringing out whatever he wrote even though the most recent books were not doing well either critically or commercially. Sales of individual new titles continued, on the back of his fame, to be respectable enough immediately following publication but after that dropped off dramatically, and it was becoming increasingly difficult to find foreign publishers for them. The problem was scarcely unique to Hersey. As his friend Peter De Vries wryly joked about the simultaneous publication of his comic novel *Mrs. Wallop* and Hersey's *Letter to the Alumni*, which De Vries admired, "All in all these works between them should sell several hundred copies."[28] But although it was unrealistic to compare *Hiroshima* with Hersey's later books of very different kinds and on less obviously compelling topics, anyone looking at the balance sheets would have noticed that while in the 1960s the 1946 book was still selling in the United States at a rate of more than 100,000 copies a year, *A Single Pebble* had dropped to the low four figures within twelve months of its first appearance.[29] And whereas *Hiroshima* was translated into fourteen foreign languages and *The Wall* eleven, *The Marmot Drive* had made it into only two (German and Danish).[30]

Meanwhile, like many authors at the time and since, Hersey was exasperated by a false but widespread perception that copyediting—essentially ensuring that the published text is free of errors—had replaced a fuller, more sympathetic involvement in what the text itself was. We've seen that Harold Strauss was never an interventionist editor, but it would be easy to show that such people still existed, among them Knopf's own Robert Gottlieb. Hersey's feeling, though, that he wasn't as much valued by his publishers as he had been in the heyday of Alfred and Blanche—indeed, that new people at the top didn't have much of a clue about him—can only have been reinforced when, shortly after Harold Strauss retired, one of Knopf's (in Hersey's eyes) relatively new senior editors, Ashbel Green, asked him whether he would be interested in writing a biography of Sam Goldwyn.[31]

Whatever his concerns, they didn't affect his output. A flurry of writing followed *The Conspiracy*. *I Married You for the Fun of It*, his translation of a play by the Italian writer Natalia Ginzburg, with whom the Herseys had spent time when they were in Rome, opened at the Yale Repertory Theatre in February 1972.[32] He collected a volume of critical essays on Ralph Ellison and a coherently organized anthology with his running commentary titled *The Writer's Craft*. He wrote a new novel and another big article about Israel for *The New Yorker*.

The novel, *My Petition for More Space* (1974), is an Orwellian fantasy about a dense line of people queuing for accommodation. One of those shuffling forward is the narrator, who believes that the fact that he is an aspiring writer entitles him to slightly more room than others. Yet being pressed against a pretty girl in the crowd complicates his sense of what personal space means: a disturbance not unlike the one Hester caused to some of the older men in *The Marmot Drive*, twenty years earlier. The underlying fear is easily recognizable—Hersey had recently been appalled to see a picture of a hundred thousand people on a Chinese beach where, when he was a child, there were rarely more than two dozen.[33] But it's too much so because for no necessary reason the fiction is set in New Haven: an "anachronistically suburban" setting for this Malthusian dystopia, as one reviewer pointed out.[34] Unusually for Hersey, the plot depends on a mathematical nonsense: for two generations, we're told, couples have been prevented from having more than one child—a situation that would surely by now have freed up ample living room for everyone crushed against the wall around the Green. Among the lukewarm reviews,[35] T. A. Shippey's comment in *The Times Literary Supplement* was on target: the book is "less chilling or disturbing than teasing," he wrote. "At times there are even coy hints that it is a novel about writing novels."

This was true, too, of Hersey's very different satirico-realist next fiction, *The Walnut Door* (1977), again set in New Haven and also concerning living space but in this case an apartment in Wooster Square into which Elaine Quinlan has moved on the rebound from a bad relationship. The novel plays with geographical and generic boundary lines, with physical-cum-social-cum-psychological spaces—human accommodation versus bureaucratic and authoritarian structures, outdoors and indoors. But to say this is to apply one academic exercise to another. Several of Hersey's friends had warned him that university teaching might not be good for his work. Despite the evidence of his own early triumphs, he maintained on the contrary, "It really doesn't matter what a writer does; the argument that you should go out and meet raw life, work on the crew of a freighter . . . doesn't seem to me valid."[36] There's an unmistakable sense that the explorations in the New Haven books come out of and feed into pedagogy. Few readers other than Hersey's students can have responded so alertly to their setting; and again in a more self-congratulatory-seeming than imaginatively productive way, these fictions, along with another from Hersey's late years, make extensive allusions to classical music.[37] There's no reason at all why the scarily predatory locksmith employed by Elaine in *The Walnut Door* should not be an opera enthusiast, and perhaps the novel aims to dignify and complicate him by this. But here once more Hersey does too much, leaves too little room for the reader. Anyone who prefers a lighter touch will find the book overexplicit. Locks and keys are themselves a metaphor best used sparingly, if at all. And a novelist writing about inarticulate young people needs either a good ear or an inventive vocabulary (an allusion to *A Clockwork Orange* draws attention to what *The Walnut Door* doesn't achieve).[38] It's hard to say which works less well, an exchange between two carpenters who, deafened by the volume at which "The Temptations are giving the lucky world 'With These Hands,'" confuse the words *plywood* and *walnut* ("Walnut? Come on, Cube I ain't had my coffee yet")[39] or a narrative full of arch sentences like "He . . . takes an admiring gander at his not quite detumescent selflet." In the end, as one of *The New York Times*' reviewers of the book complained, the protagonists are shallow, what draws them together isn't evident, and "why, in the final analysis, we should care about them for over 200 pages remains unclear."[40]

An aspect of the New Haven novels is exactly what he always said he didn't want: they are so unresolved and seem to come from such awkwardly sexual parts of his imagination that the reader is in danger of feeling required to attempt an amateur psychoanalysis. Yet the part-concealments, part-divulgations are explicit in the sense not that they're overtly interpretable but that it's obvious they are going on. He wrote often in these years about how the writer delves into the unconscious, about the role of dreams and fantasies. Later, despite his supposed refusal of all forms of self-revelation, he talked about it to interviewers. Part of the introduction to *The Writer's Craft* about "the altered state of consciousness that any act of writing seems to require" gives an idea of the straightforwardly Freudian ideas involved:

> During most of our waking lives the conscious mind, the intellect—alias the censor—is in more or less full command. In the throes of writing, when it is going really well, the writer seems to surrender himself to a state something like that of daydreaming, or even something like that of real dreaming, but apparently not exactly either one. He gives himself over, it seems, to some kind of struggle between the supplier and the censor. The supplier is aroused, almost dangerously active; the censor, who has serious formal work to do, is hard put to it to keep the supplier in hand.[41]

He was still busy with other genres and public roles. Although he had pulled back a little from the intensity of his 1960s engagements, he remained a civic activist: one whose most important activities took the form of writing but who continued to work hard on behalf of many causes. His long championship of public education had been acknowledged when a new school in an expanding suburb of Chicago was named after him in 1968. He spoke with pride and delight at the opening, paid several later visits, maintained a keen interest in its activities, and in 1993 endowed a scholarship there.[42] While his recent thinking had inevitably been more focused on university-level concerns, those weren't always separable from how students were taught earlier on, as contributions by him on the harm done by exaggerated divisions between sciences and humanities showed.[43]

Yale's having used him as an IT guinea pig was to come in useful when he joined Congress's National Commission on New Technological Uses of Copyrighted Works, an innovative turn in another of his long-standing engagements.[44] His battles with the judicial system also continued and developed, especially in relation to the plight of impoverished defendants. He wrote a provocative document commissioned by the Forum for Contemporary History in 1972 arguing that among the system's failings was the widespread misuse of plea bargaining, which had the effect of eroding the defense of the innocent.[45] By this time, procedural corruption was an issue at the pinnacle as well as the base of American society. The first Watergate arrests took place in June 1972, but there had always been concern about the Nixon regime's onslaught on liberal values and institutions. The Committee for Public Justice had been founded by Lillian Hellman in 1970 with Hersey on its executive board, and he helped organize a 1973 meeting on the implications of Watergate, out of which was formed a group specially concerned with government secrecy.[46]

Hersey's distrust of and opposition to the Nixon regime had been prompted early on by the president's refusal to rein in the crude outbursts of his deputy, Spiro Agnew, against students. After some hesitation he turned down an invitation to become involved in a new national volunteer scheme on the ground that it was compromised by emanating from a White House that had hitherto shown nothing but contempt for young people.[47] During the Watergate scandal he was vocal in arguing against all Nixon's prevarications and proposed loopholes. When the president stepped down and was succeeded by Gerald Ford, whom Hersey had known as a Yale football coach in the mid-1930s, Hersey wrote a long, cautionary article for *The New York Times Magazine* about Ford and about the seemingly untrammeled power of Henry Kissinger in his administration. The underlying issues here were still the war in Indochina—which, as we now know, Nixon and Kissinger had for domestic political reasons jointly caused to be protracted in time and then massively extended in reach[48]—and more broadly the arms race, to which Hersey would return ten years later.

His involvement in writers' organizations, meanwhile, continued to take him abroad. In 1974 he accepted an invitation from the popular mayor of Jerusalem, Teddy Kollek, to return to Israel, this time with Barbara and Brook, who was now fourteen.[49] They stayed in the oldest of the Jewish settlements built outside the walls of the Old City in 1860, Mishkenot Sha'ananim, and recently turned into a VIP guesthouse for visiting artists. Among the outcomes was an article on the children of Holocaust survivors, published by *The New Yorker*.[50]

Generations

It was a year after the Yom Kippur War and thirty years after the Soviet Union had driven the Nazis out of Poland. Several of Hersey's Israeli contacts were survivors of the Warsaw ghetto, people he had first met in connection with *The Wall*. In writing about the Israeli second generation he was influenced by his own children and consciously sought out familial situations. The voices in his article are argumentative and reactive, and cross-generational disagreements as well as mutual affection and pride come through noisily.

The participants were almost all from Israeli versions of the Herseys' own world: educated, articulate, comfortably off. An element in the story is that those who fought against Nazism and for the State of Israel have become a kind of aristocracy and that just as this has consequences in their relations with immigrants of other kinds, it also affects the children's feelings. The survivors' version of class is one of experience, not birth, and can't be passed on. Palpable resentments result, and in the artificial surroundings of these interviews they emerge with a force that is sometimes heightened, too, by individuals' suspicions of the American interviewer.

All this happens without preamble. The article begins arrestingly:

> Shimon and Yael.
>   Now we are in the family room. One whole wall is covered with books—angular Hebrew characters on their spines. The hero sits with his back to the books.[51]

Eight meetings, or short sets of meetings, are recounted, each titled after the children who appear in them, and in each, as here, the figure of a hero and ideas about what heroism means are important. In the first, both parents are former leaders of the Warsaw ghetto resistance. As the weekend-morning conversation gets going, they are joined by their unwilling-seeming son, Shimon, a military reservist, and more dutiful daughter, Yael, a psychology student, both in their twenties. In a pattern that will be repeated, the father speaks first and most, but the focus is on how the children react and on the separate current preoccupations they increasingly reveal. If there are hesitations, we see that they are a matter partly of deference to the parents but also of caution about what the WASP interviewer's prejudices may be. Always, though, what comes out un-prompted sooner or later is to do with "the Arabs": sometimes belliger-ent, sometimes anxious, sometimes liberal-pacific. The young men are for the most part the more aggressive, though on one vivid occasion a pregnant wife, translating for her soldier husband (who it later turns out has perfect English), takes over his story of the Yom Kippur War and his attitudes toward it and fiercely amplifies them:

> Look, there have never been better pilots than ours. Not English, not American, not German, not Russian, not Japanese, not Chinese— none! . . . You know what stopped us? The major powers stopped us. It was political. We could easily have taken Damascus, but the politicians listened to the two big powers, and it was the politicians who said no, and we actually had to retreat. If the major powers hadn't stopped us, we would have had total victory—for all time.[52]

On another, Hersey helps us notice a boy's compulsive self-contradictions and the way they heighten one statement he leaves unqualified: "Personally, I don't believe there will be peace. I think the aim of the Arabs is very clear—not peace but the opposite. It is very naïve to think there won't be another war."[53]

Among the recurrent elements, again related to how members of the children's generation establish identities separate from those of their celebrated parents, is their impatience with the Holocaust as a topic. "Yes, yes, we know," one says; "we know, we know." There's no consistency here, either, and the tones adopted differ as much as the attitudes. This density of texture, to which is added the richness of the physical context—family homes, furniture, books, ornaments, habits (everyone smokes a huge amount; someone has a cigarette lighter disguised as a grenade), food, and drink—is deeply communicative, as also are the rare moments when Hersey directly reacts to what he describes. Early on, there's a passage about a Holocaust museum set up by one of the fathers in the kibbutz. A grimly iterative catalog briefly rises through simple repetition and a moment of pathetic fallacy into poetry:

> Brassards with the Star of David, insignia of the S.S., tools of torture . . .
> a cake of Jew soap—and rooms full of photographs, scenes from the
> ghetto, glimpses of the process, many of the pictures slightly blurred, as
> if to look at the faces and faces and faces of those who were lost caused
> the camera itself to quake and tear its lens away before the shutter was
> even closed.[54]

It's Hersey at his best: subtle, attentive, but unintrusive, himself a camera.

All the Appalling Trivia

He was never an investigative reporter and, while vocal against Nixon, played no part in the Watergate revelations, but he produced a quiet confirmatory scoop in the sequel. Using as a precedent Hersey's celebrated articles on Harry S. Truman—another "successor President"—*The New York Times* persuaded the White House to allow the writer similar access to Nixon's successor, Gerald Ford. As Jack Rosenthal of the *Times* pointed out to the White House press secretary, Jerald terHorst, the new president was relatively little known to the public. And in what was presented as his new-broom approach, Ford had promised "an open . . . a candid administration."[55] Rosenthal made his approach the day after Ford's swearing-in. A delay was asked for, time for the new administration to settle in, and during that period hopes were quickly put to the test when, without formal consultation or public preparation, Ford pardoned his predecessor. After terHorst resigned, further delays ensued, but on February 7, 1975, Hersey and Ford had a preliminary conversation.

The writer had had much less time to prepare for this than for the Truman series, and his article, though published as a single item, was almost as long. Whereas he had been a supporter of Roosevelt and came to admire his successor, he loathed Nixon, had no high expectations of Ford, and on closer acquaintance found little that impressed him. Writing about him again some years later, he couldn't have anticipated the resonance his words would have, seven presidents on:

> He seemed to revel . . . in all the appalling trivia—Barbra Streisand, Bob Hope, Bella Abzug's hat; and Miss America and the Cotton Maid, who seemed to be given almost equal time, if not equal value, with Cambodia and Vietnam . . . The limited historic data bank in President Ford's memory made him think of each day's dealings with The Hill as almost the whole of "how it works."[56]

Ford was, Hersey acknowledged, an essentially decent man: the profile is a study of limitedness rather than overreaching or criminality, and among the things it reveals is how easily a limited president can be outflanked. Not for nothing are the article's first two words "Donald Rumsfeld," and if Rumsfeld ("bright, jealous, crafty, and fiercely combative")[57] is a key presence, still more so is an absentee: Kissinger. At the outset, albeit as an afterthought, Ford had told Hersey that the only events he couldn't attend would be the president's "daily meetings with Henry."

As it transpired, the week Hersey spent in the White House in 1975 began on Monday, March 10, when the Khmer Rouge were closing in on Phnom Penh, the last Vietnam offensive was beginning, and Kissinger was shuttling around the Middle East in preparation for what was to prove a disastrous meeting with Yitzhak Rabin.[58] The White House had for some years been under pressure because of its secretive and in many people's eyes illegal conduct of the war in Southeast Asia, so it wasn't surprising, and didn't surprise Hersey, that he was kept out of all discussions involving foreign policy. What did take him aback was what he learned, almost by accident, from the press secretary: that with the exception of Kissinger's deputy, Brent Scowcroft, and occasionally Secretary of Defense James Schlesinger, "nobody, but nobody . . . went in with Henry to discuss foreign policy with the President." Scowcroft later confirmed this to Hersey, and the article's most important insight—though even this arguably overestimated Ford's own involvement—was that "United States foreign policy [was] transacted man-to-man between Henry Kissinger and Gerald Ford."

> I had seen endless meetings of six, eight, ten advisers sitting with the President to hammer out policy on the economy and energy and Congressional tactics and everything else under the sun; there the President had heard numerous advisory voices. But foreign policy was apparently of a different order. Of course, Dr. Kissinger had the whole weight of the State Department behind him, and I was told that he did occasionally appear at senior staff meetings to brief the President's advisers; but in the formulation of settled policy, this President, who had had a minimal exposure to foreign affairs before he came to office, heard, I was told, only one voice, and a mercurial voice it was, Henry Kissinger's. Yes, this was the most alarming thought I had had all week.[59]

Given the apparent absence of Hersey from (or, more accurately, the reticence of his presence in) most of his journalism, it's noticeable that at this moment of being actually excluded he makes his voice heard—not, he stresses, on his own behalf, but in quiet protest at the powers gathered by Kissinger to himself and the president's acquiescence. It's toward this that much of the portrait has been directed: the attention to Ford's guileless hand movements, his imperturbability, his absorption in the details of his own clothes. He just doesn't care enough, or not about anything that matters: doesn't care about a bill to help the unemployed, doesn't care "how a decision would look five—or fifty—years hence."[60]

In 1976 Ford for the first time stood for election as president. He was narrowly defeated by Jimmy Carter, an outcome that gave Hersey, now in his seventies, an opportunity to publish a kind of manifesto. It takes the form of a utopian inaugural address, the speech Hersey wished Carter might give, and combines historical insight with a sharp, controversial sense of what's happening in the present. It also speaks to our concerns forty years on. Yet it has never been reprinted.

The targets of the article are many but are summed up as "the military-industrial complex"—the phrase coined in a "near horror of self-recoil," Hersey reminds his readers, by President Eisenhower in his startling fare-well address to the nation in 1961. We must "guard against the acquisition of unwarranted influence" by this cohort, Eisenhower had said, and must never let its "weight . . . endanger our liberties or democratic processes." The more he thought about this warning, "so uncharacteristic of that dull, fair-minded President," said Hersey speaking as Carter, "the louder it has sounded in my ears. It was like a wild cry of pain, for he was a lifetime soldier, a golf and bridge crony of powerful businessmen, a Republican not famous for startling and unorthodox insights. The danger must have stared him in the eye so starkly that he was forced to blurt out the alarm." It hadn't, of course, been heeded, and much of what follows is a catalog of the damage the United States had inflicted on itself and other countries as a result. Here are the key passages:

> I need only mention the interests of multinationals in such resources as the gold, chrome and asbestos of Rhodesia; the manganese, copper, chrome, antimony, nickel, tin and uranium of South Africa; the nitrates and copper of Chile; the oil of Iran, Saudi Arabia, Nigeria and Venezuela. These business interests have directly affected our policies on apartheid, the Palestinians, Israel, Latin American dictatorships . . .
>
> At home, meanwhile, business influence has managed to keep the government from taking effective action for the safety and well-being of the citizenry: Kepone in the James River, PCB in the Hudson; slowdown of controls of automotive pollutants; inadequate safety precautions in nuclear plants; fantastically hazardous negligence in the transport and disposal of nuclear wastes; headlong sale to private companies of leases for oil-drilling on the Atlantic shelf; a bill to limit strip-mining vetoed . . . ; sale of arms to Saudi Arabia, among many other countries; handguns a glut on the open market; computer networks building up data banks of

private information on individuals; the recent drift of health insurance back towards the private sector while hospital costs skyrocket.

The list continues with an accounting of military-industrial collaboration at its most obvious: "Three times as many tons of aerial munitions were dropped during the Vietnam War as . . . in all of World War II. This kept many factories humming." At bottom, Hersey wanted Carter to say, all this was caused by greed and had led to decadence, corruption, and the neutralization of whatever moral authority the U.S. might have had in the world. It had also produced "growing alienation of the populace from 'Washington.'"

While this wasn't what President Carter eventually said outside the White House on January 20, 1977, in most ways it could have been. And the fictional speech attracted a great deal of attention, in part because of an attempt to silence it. The article had been commissioned by Norman Cousins, the veteran editor at *The Saturday Review*.[61] When it came in, Cousins got cold feet and commissioned a second article to "balance" what Hersey had written.[62] (The writer approached was James Kilpatrick, author of a widely syndicated regular column called A Conservative View.) Learning of this, Hersey called Cousins to object and raised contractual issues as well as ones of editorial and authorial integrity. Whatever nerve Cousins had left now resulted in his spiking Hersey's article at the last minute and writing a tame one himself to replace it.

The story quickly got out through discontented staff of the *Review*, and Herbert Mitgang wrote about it in *The New York Times*,[63] plausibly claiming that Hersey's criticisms of General Motors, Exxon, IBM, ITT, and General Electric had bothered Cousins because "*The Saturday Review* frequently carries advertisements from some of these companies." The article had meanwhile been picked up by *The New Republic*, appeared there on December 11, 1976, and was widely syndicated. Other writers, among them the novelist Shirley Hazzard, reported having had similar experiences with the *Review*.[64] Cousins now falsely claimed that what he had asked for from Hersey was something that would "rally the people to large challenges in a spirit of post-electoral reconciliation and goodwill" and that Hersey's reaction to what had occurred between them was "unfair and unwarranted." In a withering private letter to Cousins, Hersey said, "An editor who thinks his writers have a responsibility to him, and not vice versa, had better look to his own vineyard."

The Potential of Being Tremendously Absorbing

Hersey now began work on another major literary venture. Like his earlier long novels *The Wall* and *White Lotus*, the new project, though fictional, is built out of extensive archival work and other historical reading.[65] But it was also helped by a more immediate and intimate journey of self-discovery in the form of his return to Tianjin to write his vividly personal articles for *The New Yorker*, "The House on New China Road."[66] That series appeared some years before the book he was preparing, *The Call*, and was a reminder, if any were needed, of Hersey's paramount skills as a reporter, which remained intermittently on show almost despite himself. During the "Second Cold War"—the period of the Soviet war in Afghanistan and the election of Ronald Reagan as president on promises of increased military spending and implacable hostility to the Soviet Union—he researched and wrote a sequel, "Aftermath," to *Hiroshima*, almost as long as the original, bringing the stories of his survivors up to date with an interlaced accompanying chronology of nuclear proliferation. He also produced a moving historical essay on the 1940s internment of Japanese Americans, to accompany a series of photographs taken in 1943 by Ansel Adams at the Manzanar Relocation Camp in California.[67] These two works continued and crowned Hersey's oeuvre at its strongest and most natural. As always, though, he was intensely busy with other, to him more satisfying creative projects, and since the first and longest of these also began to occupy his time in the 1970s, it makes sense to take them together. They concerned his family history, his wish that his father's career had not been truncated, his private passions—sailing, fishing, music—all at an extreme of informativeness.

The Call (1985) is a study of vocation: of what can be involved, for the individual but also for contiguous people—family, colleagues, friends—in giving one's life to the service of others. It was what Hersey most admired and wished he had achieved more fully, and he understood the difficulties. To live a life, Boris Pasternak had written in 1957, is not as easy as to cross a field, and it was clear to Hersey that he himself had made compromises. Early in his career, he had been attracted by relatively simple forms of sainthood like that of Father Morse—"simple" because Morse had no dependents, no love life in the ordinary sense, and was not, as far as we can tell, concerned to extend his activities beyond helping those immediately around him. Hersey's father had had similar but more ambitious ideals and was also a family man. By education, talent, and opportunity, the writer was almost bound to have followed a different course, but in *The Call* he maps his moral origins and, implicitly, what he felt were his failures. In common with most of his liberal contemporaries, he found his political and social times intensely challenging, exciting, and painful, and the 1970s had brought no relief. But to him these years were a time for reflection and reassessment. Some of the results appeared at the time—*The Conspiracy*, *My Petition for More Space*, the Gerald Ford article (itself reissued in 1980, along with the earlier profile of Harry Truman, as *Aspects of the Presidency*). Others were much longer in gestation, and of these the biggest and to him most satisfying was *The Call*.

It's a hybrid of fiction, family history, and the history of the YMCA in China and more generally of China itself in the late nineteenth and twentieth centuries. A third of a million words in length, it recounts from the eighteenth century on the family background of David Treadup, in some but not all respects a fictional version of Roscoe Hersey, Sr., and then Treadup's personal story from his birth in 1878 to his death in 1950. The resemblances between him and Roscoe Hersey are complicated by differences—most obviously, Treadup stays on in China long after Hersey Senior's early retirement and is interned by the Japanese—and even more by the fact that the "real" Roscoe appears at various points in the narrative, playing himself. Besides, Treadup is also John Hersey: in his furious curiosity, his insatiably wide interests, his passion for reform and for education, and other, more personal battles. "What is moving in his story," the unusually engaged narrator tells us at the outset, "what may in the end be thought to redeem the obvious failure of his mission . . . is his lifelong struggle to subdue the greater but sicker saint in himself and give himself to a more modest state of being: one of balance, sanity, serenity, and realized human love in the face of a shifting and violent and mostly hateful world."[68]

All this is done with an encyclopedic wealth of detail—about Chinese

languages, literature, and customs; about Chinese politics (the Boxer Rebellion, the rise of President Yuan, relations with Japan, the New Confu-
cianism) and social history (the harvesting of ice for ice boxes, how a
late-nineteenth-century rowing crew trained); about the organization,
staffing, and finances of the YMCA. The temptations of get-it-all-in-ism
are not disguised. David Treadup tends to be close to wherever the historical action occurs and whoever is behind it: he meets Li Yuanhong, soon
to become vice president of the Republic of China, and through him President Sun Yat-sen; his admirers include the warlord Feng Yuxiang; nationalist troops attack Nanking while he's there on one of those impulses
that tend rather obviously to serve the novel's purposes; and we are privy
to Bertrand Russell's visit to China with Dora Black. There's a lot to hold
a Western reader's attention and sympathy: immense amounts of historical action and the immensity of China itself, geographically and demo-
graphically; all in contrast with the brave, puny efforts of the missionaries,
whose frustration and despair mount as the years pass and they themselves
grow old. One woman develops dementia and goes around naked, de-
claiming bits of *Lysistrata*; a doctor whose hospital has been repeatedly
robbed shoots a Chinese intruder dead.

In so big a book it's inevitable, perhaps, that at close quarters the writing lacks edge. There's also too little variety of tone and voice or tension
in the development of characters and their interrelationships. As with
White Lotus in the earlier China novel, everything is focused on Treadup,
whose feelings and thought processes always strictly follow whatever track
they're currently on, never admitting irrelevancy. If he's dealing with the
Japanese, he's not thinking about his wife, Emily, and vice versa. *War and
Peace*, which similarly blends fiction and history and is similarly rooted
in the author's family background, offers lessons that, for all his admiration of Tolstoy, Hersey hadn't absorbed.[69] During the five or six years
over which the book was researched and written, he was warned about
some of these problems. Despite what he often claimed was a lack of creative editorial involvement by Knopf, his new editor, Judith Jones, read the
work in progress with considerable care as early as 1981. Before commu-
nicating her response to Hersey, she discussed the material with her boss,
Robert Bernstein, then president of Random House, whose instincts, she
said, were "always so good," though Jones herself was the more formida-
ble reader. It was she who, as a young editor at Doubleday, had rescued

Anne Frank's diary from the rejection pile. She worked with several of the most important American writers of the generations coming up behind Hersey, among them John Updike and Anne Tyler. Anyway, on Hersey's new project, she said she and Bernstein saw "very much eye to eye."[70] The raw material was "wonderful," and she praised how Hersey managed to synthesize his various sources. She more than hinted that these were so vivid of themselves that they might be made to tell the story unaided: in other words, though she wasn't explicit about this, a nonfictional version might work better. Certainly it had "the potential of being a tremendously absorbing narrative." The problem at present was that the story was overexplained.

This was what critics had been saying about his novels ever since *The Wall*, and the problem is familiar to every writer and reader: in D. H. Lawrence's way of putting it, too little of the tale, too much of the teller. One effect, counter to Hersey's intentions, was that the all-analyzing narrator separated Treadup from the reader. Jones went into the problems in detail, writing comments on the typescript as well as in her letter. She found the tone wrong: not only was the narrator overbusy "explaining, analyzing, paraphrasing, justifying in contemporary terms the motivations behind the actions and scenes," but he did so in a contrived, ornate language "almost to the edge of satire." The objections couldn't have been put more plainly. She followed them with a more emollient paragraph about parts of the typescript she liked and an acknowledgment that her author might well have reasons for sticking to his approach.

Stick to it he did. While later acknowledging the "wonderful editing" she provided on *The Call*,[71] he paid no attention to her most substantial suggestions. He felt he still hadn't successfully imparted the message he had spent most of his career trying to get across to readers about the difficulties of imposing one set of cultural ideals on another. Christianity is his overriding example, but democracy is part of the argument, too. Treadup explains to his brother that the early-twentieth-century founders of the Chinese Republic, influenced as they were by their admiration for America, and inexperienced in most practical matters of government and administration, "had overlooked the fact that the American Constitution was the product of a long, slow evolution of European ideas that suited the Occidental mind. The Chinese mind, so long habituated to authority, was far from ready for 'democracy,' registered with the U.S. patent office."[72]

So Hersey persisted; his book appeared and was very respectfully, though not enthusiastically, received. The sinologist John K. Fairbank gave it qualified praise in *The New York Review of Books*, finding it "fascinating to read," in part because of its organization—how Treadup's day-by-day narrative is measured against the long memoir he writes while interned by the Japanese—and "authentic" in the sense that it gives of "the sights, sounds, and smells, the amenities and disasters, of the old China."[73] To Fairbank, who, though he didn't say this, had been involved in Hersey's project from its outset,[74] the book's main value was as an essentially positive account of U.S. involvement in China, one with useful lessons for the present day. But he saw it, too, as in many ways autobiographical, not least in Treadup's "disillusionment with the letter of Christianity," which "seems to tell us more about Hersey than about Treadup."

Ever-Spreading Lava of Knowledge

Judith Jones's most striking influence on Hersey's work may have lain in a decision he made in his next book, which is about sea fishing: that it should include recipes. Jones had a specialist sideline—it had become what she was best known for—in cookbooks. In 1961, a few years after joining Knopf, she had published Julia Child's *Mastering the Art of French Cooking*. Marcella Hazan and Claudia Roden were also among her authors. Each of the twelve days' fishing recounted by Hersey in *Blues*, days spread over four months from mid-June to late October, ends with a different way of preparing his catch for the table.

He hadn't always fished. In the 1970s he gradually reduced the scale of his boats to a Soling called *Rumor*, an Olympic-class open keelboat that he raced at the Vineyard Haven Yacht Club. Later he added a succession of lobster-style craft from which he taught himself to fish, and on which he took family and friends for picnic lunches or suppers; Barbara's picnics were famous.[75] Eventually he didn't sail at all but transferred some of the energy it had involved into an almost scientific study of when the bluefish would bite. He charted weather conditions and tides and reached a point where he could plan a dinner party, go out that day, and be sure of catching enough fish. The recipes themselves were an important part of the ritual, developed with his usual intensity and precision and executed by himself for every dinner party. His daughter Brook later recalled hearing the screen door slam and seeing "Dad, trailed by his lab Kettle, making his way down to the beach to row out to his boat. He knew how to squeeze the essence out of a summer day."[76]

Blues (1987) is about this happy recreation. But there's something deeply awkward in the end-of-day moments when Hersey and the fictional inquisitive Stranger with whom he has been out in the boat arrive at his house and meet Barbara, who, though she is named, is given no words. It's as if, having kept readers out of his personal life all these years, the writer abruptly lets us in but is then too embarrassed to do anything except lecture us about food. And if the domestic passages are stilted and artificial (in addition to including a recipe, each is followed by a poem about fish), the main body of the chapters is still more so. They take the form of Platonic "dialogues" in which the Stranger occasionally asks a short question or interrupts, while Hersey discourses at length and often fascinatingly on boat construction, lighthouses, piscine taxonomy, the underwater food chain, fish in religion, fish in literature, types of seabirds and of seaweed, and pollution and overfishing. Environmental deterioration is one of the book's main themes. Whether or not in all this the Stranger has anything to teach Hersey, we don't get to hear it, and such words as he's given ("That was a spunky little perpetrator") are peculiarly arch. The reader may think that at this price for a fish dinner, the Stranger would have found a table at a harborside restaurant more relaxing.

As in *The Call*, much of what seems to be going on is the author's compulsively recording for posterity large parts of the immense body of knowledge, reflection, and opinion he had accumulated. (It seems relevant that *Blues* is dedicated to his grandchildren.) Getting it all into the right containers is more important than considering whether anyone will ever dig out what's in them. It's among the familiar frustrations of age: the impossibility of imparting to the young all that, after a search so painful and so long, one has learned. These encyclopedia entries make an odd contrast with a repeated motif in *Blues*: that fishermen should be highly selective, never taking more than they need for supper. Hersey disliked didacticism in others. As his narrator waspishly says of the polymath Dr. Wyman in a 1987 story, "God's Typhoon," "We could imagine no subject on which he could not bury an adversary under the ever-spreading lava of his knowledge."[77]

This same exhaustiveness, not necessarily showing off (though it can read like it) so much as using up everything he's got, is more overtly combined in Hersey's last novel, *Antonietta* (1991), with the notion of what happens to an artist's work after his death. Here the subject is a fictional Stradivarius violin: its personal importance to the maker, whose workshop is vividly brought to life, and its continuing career long after Stradivari's lifetime. As with the poems in *Blues* but more centrally, the form allows Hersey to play some of his favorite tunes—the book is full of musical notation, staves of quotation with footnotes identifying the works they're from. He himself was a musician manqué, we remember, and had even once played a Stradivarius. The opportunity he was given in 1955 on a visit to the Hartt College of Music, he said, "rewarded me for all the years of practice I'd done, that one experience, it was just wonderful." He and a Stradivarius-owning acquaintance played the slow movement of Bach's Double Violin Concerto together. "It was ten times the sound that I'd ever been able to make before."[78]

In the novel, he tells stories around and through music about musicians' lives, some of them true, some not—about Mozart and his father, about the violinist Pierre Baillot and his collaborations with Berlioz, about Hersey's own teacher, Pavel Federovsky, imagined here in a complex relationship with Stravinsky in Lausanne. Between periods of high musical activity the instrument suffers many vicissitudes, including as the latest acquisition of a crooked financier on Martha's Vineyard—a believable enough fate, though the two women suborned by the owner, a violinist and a pianist, are depicted with oddly lascivious shallowness. As in the New Haven novels, it's clear what Hersey is "doing": much of the novel is about fiction—people's fictions about themselves and about others, the intergenerational game of Chinese whispers about Antonietta's own history. And there's much to learn from it if one is patient. But the historical insights don't rise to any dance of the imagination. Invented or factual, straight or parodic (the Vineyard chapter seems to be sending up Ian Fleming), too many of the episodes sink under their learning.

"And" and "But"

More successfully, his work continued, during the last decade of his life, to have the strong nonfictional dimension he still undervalued. This included biographical writing, though now mostly in the form of orations celebrating prizewinners and honorary graduands, and memorial tributes. *The New Republic* commissioned a piece from him about Henry Luce,[79] and *The New York Times Book Review* one on Sinclair Lewis.[80] When Erskine Caldwell, author of some of the more coruscating stories of life in the South, died in 1987, the Academy of Arts and Letters asked Hersey to speak about him.[81]

He also wrote a vivid anecdotal preface to a new edition of James Agee's *Let Us Now Praise Famous Men*, published in 1989. The article appeared first in *The New Yorker*.[82] Among those who read it was a biographer of Agee's, Laurence Bergreen, whom Hersey had helped but who complained that not all Hersey's anecdotes were his own. Plagiarism always makes a good news item, and *The New York Times* ran the story.[83] But is it plagiarism to re-relate facts that have been put in the public domain? It's true that many of the facts in Hersey's article, though not the language he used, were drawn from Bergreen's book, but, as Hersey argued, Bergreen didn't own them. Like any biographer, Bergreen was dependent on his sources—who had included Hersey himself—and although we expect a scholarly book to acknowledge prior materials, this tends to be done in footnotes and other apparatus not used by magazine articles. Hersey had the better of the argument, but some of the mud stuck. The Agee piece, this time with full acknowledgment to Bergreen and another biographer, was collected, together with other biographical articles by Hersey done since his earliest years—including those on Walter Morse, Jack Kennedy, and Lillian Hellman—in a book titled *Life Sketches*, published in 1989.

Tributes apart, he still found time to attempt more practical favors for people he liked, though not all of them succeeded. He wasn't able to persuade Isaac Bashevis Singer to write a prologue for a Chinese translation of Singer's novel of pre–World War II Warsaw, *Shosha*, done by an old acquaintance.[84] Nor did he manage to get Yale to take Norman Mailer's son Stephen as a student, though having met and talked to the boy he joked to Mailer, "My basic position (which I didn't put in the letter to the Dean of Admissions) is that anyone who has learned to ride a unicycle deserves a Yale education."[85] The Lillian Hellman oration in *Life Sketches*, which had been delivered when she was awarded a literary prize in 1976, had trodden lightly, even humorously, around the question of her veracity.[86] Though known as a moral force, she was more "a *life* force," Hersey began. He went on to give some examples of her "powers of invention" at their most comical and harmless; there's some mellowing of his usual sternness about truth here. Hellman herself asked, as Hersey would not have done, "What true story is there ever in this life?"[87] But she taxed even the most relaxed standards, and it's strange to find him angrily defending her a few years later, when Mary McCarthy famously said on *The Dick Cavett Show* that she lied with every word she wrote in her memoirs, "including 'and' and 'but.'"[88] Those memoirs, Hellman's most successful work after she stopped writing plays,[89] did contain many inventions, and her allies were apprehensive when she embarked on a defamation action against McCarthy—a battle averted by Hellman's death in 1984. The least pompous response to the squabble was Norman Mailer's: he took out an ad in *The New York Times Magazine* imploring both women to back off. Hersey, by contrast, wrote sternly to Cavett, saying he had "got very hot at seeing you . . . acquiesce in (if not invite) libels against Lillian Hellman." For the TV host "to sit there without a word of challenge" was "truly shameful," he said.[90]

He also said that his friend was "ten times the lady" Cavett was talking to. Whatever the merits, relevance, or otherwise of that opinion—and to an outsider it sounds as if the words might have been Hellman's own[91]— Hersey's letter also makes explicit that McCarthy's dismissive 1946 verdict on his *Hiroshima*, mentioned in the interview, still rankled him all those years on, even though with Cavett "she seemed to have come up to the edge, at least" of realizing that it "had been a bit silly." In any case, he ungallantly wrote, "I rest easy in the certainty that *Hiroshima* will outlive by many years Mary McC and all her works."

Hiroshima was certainly still alive. Two of Hersey's nonfictional projects in the 1980s were on his early theme of the Japanese and the Second World War. The first involved entirely updating *Hiroshima* by adding a long new section self-explanatorily titled "Aftermath." Again it appeared first in *The New Yorker*,[92] but now he had longer to prepare, including a month in the city and the country that he had championed for forty years.

His 1957 account of the case of William Girard—the GI who had playfully shot dead a Japanese woman—had shown the scorn as well as the compassion he was capable of.[93] Americans abroad were far from being his only theme, but in a sense they had been his life story, his deepest resource. Now, though, he had to subdue the rhetorical power he had brought to the Girard story and, a decade later, to the Algiers Motel scandal. *Hiroshima* had been marked by a style so reserved, so modest in transmitting the narratives of survivors, most of whom were themselves similarly reserved and modest, that there were critics who just didn't get it. Hersey felt bound to write the continuation in a similar voice, but his obligation was still to the protagonists, who had all changed and in very different ways, and behind them to Japanese culture more broadly, which had become brasher, in some respects more confident, and more divided. There were other new considerations. In the immediate wake of the bombing, traumatized Japanese, conscious of being under American rule but also loyal to their country, were disinclined to lay blame. That situation had changed, and vocal criticism of the United States was to be heard alongside attacks on imperial Japan for its bellicosity. But most though not all *hibakusha* were still markedly reluctant to become involved in these disputes. Moving on as best they could seemed preferable, whether for cultural reasons or because keeping going was just about all they could manage, to symbolic acts of "memory." Then again, in a Japan now allied with America, American attitudes and actions were a complex part of the story: forms of reparation, attempts—some of them very clumsy—to atone; attempts, too, still, to keep the lid on. And there was an aspect of the aftermath that consisted, at least potentially, not just of more of the same, but of much more, much worse. *Hiroshima* had described what in comparison with current weaponry was, for all its ghastly novelty, not a very big deal.

The approach is in one way simple: taking his original protagonists one by one, he describes what has happened to each between 1945 and '85, drawing attention to ways in which their lives have gone on being interlinked but not trying to force highly individual developments into any pattern. So as to deal with some of the trans-Pacific and intergenerational complications, he leaves the Reverend Mr. Tanimoto until last. Tanimoto had become the most publicly active, most controversial, in some ways most exploited of the group, both in Japan and in the United States, and the fact that his exploiter was the *Saturday Review*'s Norman Cousins adds salt to Hersey's narrative.[94] It's in this last section, which is structured more fluidly than the others, that he introduces segments of the history of nu-clear proliferation since 1945, as well as the grotesque saga of the "Keloid Girls," and draws together various other painful strands and otherwise loose ends. An effect is that while justice is done to Tanimoto's complicated personal history and he has a climactic place as, from some points of view, the most important character, the others are put in the foreground.

The original cast had not stayed in contact with one another. As Tani-moto touchingly wrote to Hersey before his return, "Since you visited our city for your first time and soon published your book, 'Hiroshima,' we, six of us, tried in enthusiasm to meet each other as many times as possi-ble but, according to change of our own circumstances, we fell in our bad habit of miss of chance."[95] Their stories are, by turns and at once, inspir-ing, depressing, and poetic. As in the original work, Hersey has a perfect ear for words, moments, and scenes that resonate across the pages. In re-tirement, Hatsuyo Nakamura takes up traditional dance. We watch as she and thirty or so other women move formally, heads high, to "a song of celebration of entrance into a house": "May your family flourish / For a thousand generations, / For eight thousand generations."[96] The flourish-ing and otherwise of families is one of the work's themes. When we first met the war widow Nakamura-san (as Hersey now calls her with Japanese correctness), she was digging her three children out of the rubble of their home. By 1985, they are all doing OK. Dr. Fujii and his family, too, have prospered since we saw him gripped by two timbers of his collapsed hos-pital, just keeping his head above the waters of the river the building had fallen into. But as time passes he loses his affection for his wife, becomes stubborn and self-indulgent, and has an accident that leaves him in a veg-etative state. When he dies, his physician son secures an autopsy at the American Atomic Bomb Casualty Commission. Whether or not as a re-sult of radiation, his father's brain had atrophied, his large intestine had expanded, and there was a tumor in his liver. "Then came a sad ending to this hibakusha's story. His family quarrelled over his property, and a mother sued a son."[97]

Not all the protagonists have children to carry on their work or to fight over their inheritance. The badly injured Toshiko Sasaki, buried under the library of the East Asia Tin Works, had been in an arranged engagement, but it fell through, perhaps because of her disabilities and the stigma against *hibakusha*. She becomes a nun, runs an orphanage and then an old people's home, and despite all she has suffered is resolute about not looking back. Her spiritual adviser, Father Kleinsorge, similarly has no family dependents but again is surrounded by a big community of people for whom he cares and who care for him. Christianity played a surprisingly large element in the original book, and the nuns and monks in "Aftermath" continue and develop the motif. They also help articulate a movement away from thoughts specifically about nuclear war and toward a broader understanding of how humans should and shouldn't be governed. If you're going to talk about victims, Sasaki-san increasingly thinks, you have to ask who was ultimately responsible for their victimization—for attacks on Chinese civilians by Japanese troops, for the drafting of American and Japanese men to be killed, for the prostitution of the women whose babies came to her orphanage.

When the book ends, it's with the pathos of Kiyoshi Tanimoto, now in his seventies, eating too much, walking his dog, forgetting things: "His memory, like the world's, was getting spotty." Memory—"cultural memory," commemoration, remembrance, in all their necessity and unreliability—is the right place to stop. And these last pages bring into focus another aspect of the book, closely tied to Hersey's own situation when he wrote it. A lot of time has passed. Father Kleinsorge and Dr. Fujii are dead. All have found the excruciatingly ambiguous effects of radiation hard to distinguish from those of normal aging. If their story has any future life, it's not in themselves for much longer, but in Hersey's work. "Aftermath" is enriched by the writer's dealings with his own situation.

A Jap Is a Jap

Around the time when the updated *Hiroshima* appeared, a civil rights lawyer called John Armor, working in the Library of Congress with an Associated Press photographer, Peter Wright, found a trove of negatives and prints taken by Ansel Adams at the wartime Manzanar Japanese internment camp in Inyo County, California. Hersey agreed to write a text to accompany a selection of the pictures.

As its Hispanic name suggests, Manzanar had once been an apple-growing area, but in 1919 the farms were compulsorily purchased and their water was diverted into the Los Angeles Aqueduct, to serve the city.

The valley became a desert and it was mainly in desert land that the prison camps were established. The first "Nisei" held at Manzanar arrived "voluntarily" in March 1942 after receiving a military notice requesting their resettlement. Subsequently the majority—men, women, children—were compulsorily moved there under armed guard. It was claimed in a booklet given out to them that they were there "for their own protection" but in that case, as one of them asked later, "why did the guns point inward, rather than outward?"[98]

By the time the Adams materials were found, the story of the camps was well known, especially through the work of a historian of U.S. immigration, Roger Daniels. But the pictures themselves were much less familiar. Some of them had been exhibited at Manzanar itself in 1944 and were published as *Born Free and Equal*. As Hersey relates, the topic was intensely controversial then, and some of those who felt too much attention was being paid to it publicly burned this book.

Adams had been invited to the camp by its enlightened second director, Ralph Merritt, who knew his pictures of the nearby Yosemite National Park. For all his celebrity, the photographer worked under restrictive conditions. He was not allowed to take pictures of the guards or their towers, or of any of the fencing. And because the inmates were eager to be understood as useful, productive, and well-integrated, albeit currently excluded members of American society, they not only smile for the camera but also knit for it, read books for it, and grow potatoes for it. The camp's Catholic church and school are featured, as are its pigs and chickens and well-stocked haberdashery store. The prisoners' success in making lives for themselves in the desert, in producing food for other Americans as well as for themselves, ironically led to bitterness outside: Why were these people allowed to do so well? The photographs don't speak of these tensions, and even when the rows of huts are covered with snow, everyone emerging from them looks cheerful and well turned out. Yet in spring, nighttime temperatures in Owens Valley still dropped to freezing; in summer they were often 110 degrees. To a casual eye, then, these images, with their grand backdrop of the Sierra Nevada, differ from the less formal—and censored—pictures of Japanese Americans taken by Dorothea Lange in that they could be taken as presenting internment in a benign, even propagandist way. Hersey supplies a corrective, sardonic context.

About 70 percent of those imprisoned, he points out, had been born in the United States and were therefore citizens, but in the 1942 roundup no distinction was made between them and "enemy aliens" (who by customary international law are liable to such measures in wartime). Each family was given a number and provided with tags to attach to individuals' lapels and to their luggage. A few days were allowed for the liquidation of possessions—businesses, farms, homes, furniture—inevitably at knock-down prices. It was important that Hersey's narrative should not be read through what happened in Europe at the same time, though here—in California!—were blacked-out trains and buses, assembly centers in what had been racetracks and fairgrounds, desolate rows of huts behind wire fences. Aware of the risk, Hersey chooses his words carefully and specifically. They are prophetic:

> Thus began the bitterest national shame of the Second World War for the sweet land of liberty: the mass incarceration, on racial grounds alone, on false evidence of military necessity, and in contempt of their supposedly inalienable rights, of an entire class of American citizens—along with others who were not citizens in their country of choice only because that country had long denied people of their race the right to naturalize . . . How did this slippage in the most precious traditions of a free country come about? Does the Bill of Rights provide a sufficient prophylactic against hysteria and bigotry in a time of national stress? Could the racism underlying these events some day reassert itself? Against the same race? Against another?[99]

His analysis of historians' earlier, much fuller accounts, reinforced by his own research, did not make reassuring reading in 1988, and thirty years later is, if anything, more frightening still. There's the whipping up of xenophobia with exaggerated, in some cases false alarms about attacks from outside and enemy agents within. There are the onslaughts on civic authorities for supposed negligence in the face of what were in fact hoax threats. As claims mounted about the military necessity on the American mainland of measures such as random spot raids, prohibited zones, and, soon, internment, even Hoover of the FBI described the atmosphere as hysterical. General John L. DeWitt, in charge of West Coast defense, reported agitatedly that in 1941, "557 male Japanese less than twenty-five years of age . . . entered West Coast ports." The fact that they were return-ing to their families after periods of schooling in Japan was immaterial. As he said to a press conference, "A Jap is a Jap."

Hersey knew his country too well—knew human beings too well—to lay all this at the door of a few powerful extremists. Racism "has a long claim on the mind of American whites," he wrote before setting out its particular history in the case of Japanese immigrants. By 1942, though, the strongest pressure came from a fear of terrorist action, and although report after report made clear that spot raids on Japanese households had uncovered no military equipment, that investigators had found no treach-erous plans or conspiracies, there were people in Washington, key among them Karl Bendetsen, head of the army's Aliens Division, who were sure they knew better. Local politicians drew enthusiastic audiences with talk of the leftist extremism of members of the Supreme Court and other bod-ies that had shown initial caution about discriminatory measures. And a recommendation by deWitt to Secretary of War Henry Stimson included what in less grim circumstances might have seemed a hilariously circular argument in favor of mass internment: "The very fact that no sabotage has taken place to date is a disturbing and confirming indication that such ac-tion will be taken."[100] Sean Spicer could not have put it better.

As Hersey records, not a single member of either house voted against the internment bill. The program had the support of some of the leading liberals of the day, "even, in his grand offhandedness, Franklin Roosevelt." Liberal attorneys drafted the arguments; liberal Supreme Court justices endorsed them. Time passed and the Pacific war moved toward its grim conclusion. At last, everyone went home, except that in many cases home no longer existed. Even when the ex-prisoners had not sold but had rented their properties or stored their goods, it often proved impossible to recover them. People who had not paid land taxes for the simple reason that the tax demands had not reached them found that their property had been seized.

Extremely slowly, some unfair decisions were reversed. Forty years after the internments began, a congressional commission published its report on the whole sorry affair under the title *Personal Justice Denied*. Five years after that, a program of financial compensation was intro-duced, though only for ex-internees who were still living, not their heirs. Even this measure was opposed by a third of the House. In 1988 President

Reagan signed the Civil Liberties Act. *Manzanar*, with photographs by Ansel Adams and commentary by John Hersey, came out that same year. Hersey's question still hangs in the air: "Could anything like all this happen ever again in the United States of America?" *It Can't Happen Here* is the title of Sinclair Lewis's satirical novel of 1935, imagining America sliding into fascism. It's apt that, half a century after he apprenticed himself to Lewis, and close to the end of his own career, John Hersey should have been thinking along the same lines as his old mentor.

12. A Kind of Daylight in the Mind

JOHN HERSEY spent most of his last winters in Key West and died there of cancer on March 24, 1993, at the age of seventy-eight. The poet Richard Wilbur and his family, along with another very good poet, John Ciardi, and his wife; the Ellisons; and others had bought into a compound, which John and Barbara also joined.[1] Another poet, James Merrill, for many years shared his partner David Jackson's home nearby and became a friend. The compound was on Windsor Lane, in the old section of town: a set of dilapidated houses sold for renovation by a local lawyer. The new occupants shared landscaped grounds full of tropical trees and flowers: "The thump of oranges and avocados on one's roof," Ellison said, "can be quite shocking."[2] To Hersey this retirement place—for all the differences between Key West and the rest of Florida—recalled exotic student days on the Chisholms' yacht *Aras*, and Florida vacations he had been on with his mother and, first, Frances Ann, then Barbara. Mainly, it was an adventure. The Keys had always been something of an artists' colony, not wholly respectable, and while Hersey's neighbors were a mixed bunch, including established Key Westers as well as literary and academic incomers, his new enjoyment of the louche aspects of life both there and on the Vineyard is evident in some short stories he wrote.

As the case of Hellman vs. Truth had shown, Hersey was in some ways more relaxed about his standards these days. CBS's three-hour version of *The Wall* was broadcast in 1982. A coproduction between Time-Life TV and Polish TV, shot in Poland, it not only dispensed with the narrator but treated the stories of individual characters as less important than the fate of the mass.[3] ("One longs for a richer sense of who these characters are," *The New York Times*' reviewer wrote, the "sort of connections that make it possible to truly celebrate their individual triumphs and to mourn their losses.")[4] It was a long way from the strict authorial control Hersey had insisted on, to David Selznick's frustration, thirty years earlier. This easing was accompanied by, and perhaps resulted from, reflections on his whole life and career, some of them public and to that extent themselves representing a shift in attitude. In 1986 he gave an interview to *The Paris Review*—traditionally hospitable to the reminiscences of biography-resistant writers. It was conducted by the novelist Jonathan Dee, a former student of Hersey's, and, like David Sanders's monographs, is respectful of the writer's own version of himself. The same is true of a conversation between Hersey and Kay Bonetti recorded for the National Sound Archive in 1988,[5] though Bonetti elicited some new anecdotes and advanced a probing question: Why is it, exactly, that so good a journalist, and one so overtly invested in truth, has made repeated use of a form she calls "false history"? Hersey doesn't answer the question but it is there. Bonetti also touches on her subject's lifestyle, how settled it seemed by comparison with the bizarreries and wildness of some of his contemporaries. Here even more than in the rest of the interview Hersey chose his words slowly and, while being less than confessional about his first marriage, some of what he said was revealing:

I am myself. I've had two marriages. One didn't work too well, one has worked wonderfully. I have on the whole wanted to live my life in comfort and to be comfortable with myself. I guess I've come to the notion that moderation and some kind of balance work for me . . . There is a price that's paid for self-absorption and self-interest. Among writers, vanity and envy are very powerful emotions and they do cause a lot of havoc. I think perhaps that having seen friends of mine who were writers burned by excesses of these feelings may have helped me at least to try to keep them in hand.

It's interesting that he still thought of himself as having subdued a destructiveness no one detected in him and that is rarely evident in his writing. True, the novels had become increasingly open to forms of sexual turbulence: competition, possessiveness, and jealousy in *The Wall*, *The War Lover*, and *Under the Eye of the Storm*; illicit attraction in *The Marmot Drive* and *My Petition*; and the more dangerous-seeming invasiveness that *The Walnut Door* tries to turn on its head. Hersey is also reckless in a different, political way in *The Algiers Motel Mystery* and *Letter to the Alumni*. Whatever parts of himself he was drawing on in these books, his puritanism encumbers them as fictional elements, and his reticence—surely part of the same apparatus—keeps them largely beyond biographical reach. There was something else, though, that he had always recognized and feared and, with what in the mid-twentieth century came to be called uptightness, tried to control: in another autobiographical statement he mentions "strains of ambition and vanity in my makeup."

The confession is made in a touching essay he circulated in typescript among his family on his seventy-fifth birthday in 1989 and that was later published.[6] Hersey says that although "love for a very small circle of family and friends is what matters most in life," what he really means is "blood" relatives: "those who share the same blood and genes with me," with whom alone "I can unabashedly enjoy shared strengths and forgive shared weaknesses." As for friends, he has had only "a very small number of them," having been "hampered," he says, "by a reserve that is, alas, part of my nature." It sounds painfully close to self-knowledge.

The essay starts, in fact, by saying how difficult self-knowledge is, presenting this as part of the problem of knowledge in itself. The opening sentence, "It is hard to know enough about oneself," is ambiguous: Enough for whom and for what purpose? But if there's a hint of—yes—ambition and vanity in this, it's deflected by the modesty and uncertainty of much that follows, including in several references to religion. Hersey describes himself as a doubter, not an atheist, and a cautious doubter at that. He speaks of the "wonder I feel at the fecundity and variety of nature" as "a kind of worship," and while he regrets being "at a loss to name the object of my devotion" he's without answers, too, for the biggest metaphysical questions: "How account for the primordial void? What happened before the big bang? What is the name and nature of the empty envelope of space into which the universe is said to be expanding?"

Naturally enough, he concludes with some thoughts about death, couched in a series of half-quotations: "Time rides a winged chariot," "Death is my truly mortal enemy," and so on.[7] He talks about this, too, the extent to which literary and biblical texts come to him unbidden, the way they are (in a metaphor he uses a lot here) "in my blood." What's most striking to an outside reader, though, is what isn't included: in particular, the total absence of names. Children, grandchildren, siblings, wives: no one is specifically mentioned—not even Barbara, who for a dozen or more years had been dealing with her own intimations of mortality.[8] Given the alertness to the importance of people's names he showed not so long ago in correspondence with Arthur about his China series,[9] it's all the more noticeable that this valediction is entirely in the first-person singular: "I fear that . . . In my own life, I admire . . . I have tried . . . I have always striven . . . I cling . . . I never cease . . . My skinful of flesh . . . the end of my life." All these and more come in the final paragraphs, leading up to the simultaneously grandiose and empty last stand: "I consider it the bitter, serious task of my old age . . . to make my peace with the great unfairness of human life."

Happily and, it seems, almost without trying, Hersey was simultaneously writing short stories of a new simplicity and lightness: nondidactic, their attention on believable people. With the help of a few much earlier pieces they added up to two collections: *Fling*, published in 1990, and *Key West Tales*, seen through the press by his daughter Brook after he died. Some had recently appeared in little and not-so-little magazines (*Grand Street*, *Atlantic*); a few were completely new. The best stand up in any company. And they have a lot of variety. "Affinities,"[10] about a thief, a bail bondsman, and a peripatetic dog, is charming, funny, and both believable and enjoyably not so. The utterly different story from which *Fling* takes its title is a delicate confection on a melancholy theme. Its situation, an elderly couple and a friend making a tour of the desert states, including a visit to Acoma, lets in Willa Cather and her *Death Comes for the Archbishop* as a recurring, poignantly relevant motif, though one that's treated with brisk irony by the Lillian Hellman–like woman who narrates all but the story's end: "And then, before we had a chance even to imagine Willa in her double-breasted suit on a skinny packhorse, her eyes burning with a fever of perfect sentences, there it was. Acoma."

There's also the bonus of two plainly autobiographical tales. Details including names have been changed, but these pieces are almost as close to life yet as free as James Joyce's short fictions. "God's Typhoon" is about one of Hersey's childhood holidays in Peitaiho, on the northeast coast of China. "The Announcement," where his divorced alter-ego Gordon brings the woman who is to be his second wife to his mother's house for Thanksgiving, is edgy, frank (especially about the difficult brother), full of light tension, yet—like Joyce's family feasts—rich with affection, love, and gratitude. With their simple vividness these fragments, along with parts of "The House on New China Road," make one regret that Hersey never allowed himself to write a full memoir—and also that in fiction he gave so much priority to his longest works.

The stories in *Key West Tales* are equally varied while being unified by their setting and shaped by an alternation between those set in the then present day and historical ones from early colonial times on, between the diary of someone who accompanies Audubon on a bird-watching, bird-slaughtering expedition and a vivid short episode in the career of President Truman, set in his "Little White House." There's a sharp long story of gay middle age and AIDS, excellent on personal dynamics, especially between the dying Billy, his non-lover close friend Paul, and the transvestite nurse Drew, and again between Billy, his father, and his unsparingly sketched stepmother. The latter's "ease with Billy's choice should have been a comfort," the narrator says, "except that she wasn't a woman you could take seriously. She just had a habit of not caring."[11] And among modern pieces like this one, which seem to get down situations close to ones Hersey had seen in the neighborhood, there are some spry imaginative excursions, especially "Fantasy Fest," about a woman meeting her grown-up son for the first time. It is parade week in Key West, and the young man has the idea that both of them should dress up as their fantasies and see if they recognize each other in the results. In the event his mother finds herself at a loss and her son a disappointment ("such an odd-looking little person"),[12] an unfantastic ending that has been prepared with beautiful plausibility. There's much here that points to what Hersey elsewhere achieved more often in journalism than in fiction: a kind of sympathetic insight exemplified in the girl at the Family Service Center in "Piped over the Side": what she says to the naval officers who are about to retire, and also what the last bit of the retirement ceremony can feel like, in all its artifice and bathetic reality.

He had found not only this fictional freedom but also a solid contentment, very different from the stern engagements of the past. He intimated as much both to Kay Bonetti and in "Time's Winged Chariot," and seems to make it explicit in the epigraph to *Antonietta*, the last of his books to appear in his lifetime, dedicated, like *The War Lover* thirty-two years earlier, to Barbara. Below the dedication Hersey quoted the eighteenth-century English essayist Joseph Addison: "Cheerfulness keeps up a kind of daylight in the mind, and fills it with a steady and perpetual serenity."

Serenity hadn't been easy to come by for someone as discontented as Hersey with how the world runs and with how he himself measured up to his own severe standards. For all the material and familial comforts he enjoyed, *Manzanar* shows how little he had come to an accommodation with what still angered him. A few years earlier, anger was the quality he had chosen to single out among those he most valued in Lillian Hellman. Speaking at her funeral in July 1984 he said, "Most of us were startled by it from time to time. Anger was her essence. It was at the center of that passionate temperament. It informed her art . . . Dear Lillian . . . You have given us this anger to remember, and use in a bad world."[13]

Despite what he deprecated as the smallness of his circle of close friends, they turned out in numbers to commemorate him after he himself died. The funeral was on the Vineyard; his ashes are buried in West Chop Village Cemetery. There was also a memorial event in Yale's Battell Chapel, where he had served as a young deacon. Despite his doubts, he was at some level always a Christian: culturally so, of course, and more intimately than that because of the inherited ideas and, with them, the words that have expressed them, that permeated his mind; in his values, too. "Care for the helpless, the forgotten, and the disadvantaged," Howard Lamar said at his memorial, "were always at the center of the imagination of the missionary's son whose work revealed his own missionary sense."[14] But Hersey wasn't sure, and the choices made by those closest to him at these last ceremonies came from diverse intuitions, whether about his humanism, his sheer love of life—of raspberries, fish, osprey—of civic virtue, or of something beyond. His son Martin, by then in his fifties,

some of whose difficulties with living Hersey had vicariously carried, began simply, "I'd like to read from the Bible," and then did so: Psalm 61,
"Hear my cry, O God"; then the bit of St. Paul promising that the trumpet
shall sound, the dead be raised "and we shall be changed." Who can
know? One of the balms of the literary imagination is that certainty comes
by nonrational means. The writer writes something and it is so.

At the end of the ceremony, words gave way to Hersey's first love, music:
to a then-unfinished piece for two violins called *Lost Dreams* that Baird
had been developing as the accompaniment to a work in progress of his
father's, about his violin-playing and his relinquishing it to be a writer.[15]
No one can fully describe music, any more than anyone can explain faith.
His son's work—for example his fusion of Hindu mantra and soul, "My
God Is Real"[16]—often suggests a degree of religious confidence, even
exuberance, beyond anything expressed by his father, but this reflective,
unresolved piece is quite different.

In the printed booklet of the funeral and memorial tributes, the inad-
equacy of musical notation, as of notation of any kind, is exaggerated by
what was presumably a printer's convenience: the two violin parts appear
separately on consecutive spreads—Violin 1's music on pages 52–53, Violin 2's on pages 54–55—rather than together on parallel staves. The effect
is related to what happens in written narrative where simultaneous
events—the impact, say, on different individuals when the bomb explodes
over Hiroshima—can only be related one after another. A reader of the
music, prevented by the separation of the parts from seeing their harmonies, may be frustrated. In the mind's ear, though, and better still on a pair
of violins, matters are different. The two threads follow each other, sometimes catching up, rarely crossing, a steady sequence of semibreves, then
crotchets, then quavers lapping like water on a shore, one equal music.

Sources, References, and Short Titles

The main archive of Hersey papers is at the Beinecke Library, Yale (see pp. 17–19). Some of these bulky materials were originally kept by Grace Hersey, others by John Hersey himself, and were filed in a variety of ways: for example, the author's research materials and drafts by title of book or article; letters roughly by date and source, and/or in alphabetical order of correspondent's surname; or, particularly early correspondence, in a jumble, but often bundled together by approximate date of receipt or (as with, for example, postcards) physical nature. Since arriving at the Beinecke they have not been fully cataloged, though they are consulted quite often by a variety of people. Between visits spread over four years, I often found that the order of documents within folders had changed and that folders themselves—not all of which have identifying numbers—were in new sequences within their boxes. It's worth mentioning, too, that the family correspondence in Box 18 includes some letters from John Hersey's brothers, as well as from himself; and also that drafts of his work are still in the order in which they were acquired by the Beinecke and not of composition. All this makes dependable, precise referencing impossible, so I have confined myself to giving box number, date (when known), and other immediate identifying information (title of work or name of sender, recipient, etc.), which should be enough for any reasonably diligent subsequent researcher.

The Beinecke's own reference numbers are at present YCAL MSS 707 for the bulk of materials (simplified in the footnotes as B for Beinecke) and YCAL MSS 723 for "family papers" (B FP). While the distinction is not meaningful except in terms of how the holdings were acquired, "B Box 2" does not mean the same as "B FP Box 2."

Materials consulted at the Harry Ransom Center, at the University of Texas at Austin, are well ordered and in the footnotes are identified as HRC plus the name of the main archive (Knopf, Selznick, etc.). Similarly for *The New Yorker* archive ("*NY* Archive") at the New York Public Library.

While publication dates are given for articles in newspapers and magazines, page numbers are given only in cases where some particularly detailed point is being made, or when the publication doesn't have an online index or search facility. The following short titles are used for the two journals referred to most often:

NY	*The New Yorker*
NYT[BR]	*New York Times [Book Review]*

In the notes, the following short titles for books by John Hersey are used. Unless otherwise indicated, quotations are from the first U.S. edition, published in New York by Alfred A. Knopf.

A	*Antonietta*, 1991
AMI	*The Algiers Motel Incident*, 1968
AP	*Aspects of the Presidency*, New Haven and New York: Ticknor and Fields, 1980
BA	*A Bell for Adano*, 1944
Blues	*Blues*, 1987
C	*The Call: An American Missionary in China*, 1985
CB	*The Child Buyer: A Novel in the Form of Hearings before the Standing Committee on Education, Welfare, & Public Morality of a certain State Senate, Investigating the conspiracy of Mr. Wissey Jones, with others, to Purchase a Male Child*, 1960
Con	*The Conspiracy*, 1972
Fling	*Fling and Other Stories*, 1990
H	*Hiroshima*, 1946; new edition, 1985, Harmondsworth, UK: Penguin Books, 1986.
HS	*Here to Stay: Studies in Human Tenacity*, 1962
IV	*Into the Valley: A Skirmish of the Marines*, 1943
KWT	*Key West Tales*, 1994
LA	*Letter to the Alumni*, 1970
Lotus	*White Lotus*, 1965
LS	*Life Sketches*, Norwalk, Connecticut: Easton Press, 1989
M	with Ansel Adams, *Manzanar*, Random House, 1988
MB	*Men on Bataan*, 1942
MD	*The Marmot Drive*, 1953
MP	*My Petition for More Space*, 1974

OMW	*Of Men and War*, New York: Scholastic Book Services, 1963
SP	*A Single Pebble*, 1956
TFW	*Too Far to Walk*, 1966
UES	*Under the Eye of the Storm*, 1967
Wall	*The Wall*, 1950
WC	ed., *The Writer's Craft*, 1974
WD	*The Walnut Door*, 1977
WL	*The War Lover*, 1959

The following additional abbreviations are used in the notes:

als	autograph letter signed
cc	carbon copy
tls	typed letter signed
ts	typescript

Notes

Preface: Civic Virtue and Our Present Difficulties

1. The matter became world news once Trump's candidacy took off. See, for example, John Swaine, "How Trump's $50m Golf Club Became $1.4m When It Came Time to Pay Tax," *Guardian*, March 12, 2016, https://www.theguardian.com/us-news/2016/mar/12/donald-trump-briarcliff-manor-golf-course-tax. For pictures of the club's ponds, cascades, clubhouse, residential real estate, and other amenities, see http://www.trumpnationalwestchester.com.

1. A Sentimental Journey

1. The articles, originally titled "The House on New China Road," appeared weekly from May 10, 1982, under the traditional *New Yorker* heading A Reporter at Large.
2. Corporal Philip M. Fetzer to an unknown correspondent, July 24, 1942, B FP Box 2.
3. Anne Frank's *Diary of a Young Girl* eventually appeared from Doubleday in 1952. Hersey's own publisher, Alfred A. Knopf, was among those who rejected the book. See pp. 153 and 274.

4. See pp. 224–27.
5. The "New Journalism" is what Tom Wolfe called it in his 1973 anthology, but it has had many names and has been described in many different ways, few of which continue to seem so new once examples are put alongside comparable work by Mark Twain, say, or the Robert Louis Stevenson of *A Footnote to History: Eight Years of Trouble in Samoa*. Journalists have always brought stylistic color to their work in ways that have resemblances to some of the techniques of fiction. In the 1930s and '40s, both Time-Life and *The New Yorker* encouraged writing of this kind while Wolfe, Hunter S. Thompson, and company were still infants. The issues at stake are essentially ones of degree, not kind. How far do you intensify facts? Is it useful to be a participant in your story? The philosophical dimensions, on the other hand, are complex, involving as they do issues ranging from "authenticity," including whether or not a living person can tell a true story about death (see Mary Mc-Carthy's objection to *Hiroshima*, pp. 144–45.), to an anthropological concern with how far a participant, by the sheer fact of being one, alters the story she is part of.

   In practical terms, each case has to be judged on its merits. The youthful Hersey went too far toward giving an impression that he was present on Bataan (see pp. 64–69). But the autobiographical passages in *The Algiers Motel Incident* (see p. 237) arose from his sense that "invisibility" risks turning into non-accountability, and also that in this impassioned polemic he couldn't pretend to be objective. In his *Paris Review* interview with Jonathan Dee, Hersey gave a diplomatic account of the topic, albeit one that still arguably claims too much novelty for it:

   > I think it is true that I was one of many who began to experiment . . . with ways of using the devices of fiction in journalism. I was certainly not alone in that . . . The important thing that was taking place was that journalists were making it more possible for readers to identify with the figures and the events about which they were writing . . . But eventually two things polluted the so-called New Journalism. The fictional methods tempted some writers to cross the line, touch up their nonfiction—to invent. And then the fictional voice that transferred to journalism became more and more audible . . . so that, in the end, the figure of the journalist became more important than the events being written about.

   (It's worth mentioning, by the way, that Hersey's characteristic reluctance to name living contemporaries in critical contexts may on this occasion have had something to do with the fact that among those once-intrusive journalistic figures was George Plimpton, the editor of the journal in which the interview appeared.)
6. *AMI*, 237.
7. *LA*.
8. Pierson College; see ch. 10.
9. The writer was the radical senior citizen Dwight Macdonald, another Yalie. The occasion was Hersey's antiwar protest in the White House. Michael Wreszin, ed.,

A Moral Temper: The Letters of Dwight Macdonald (Chicago: Ivan R. Dee, 2001), 452.

10. *NY*, May 17, 1982.

11. But see p. 292.

12. In the 1982 articles it is mentioned three times: at the beginning and end of the first installment and as the conclusion of the opening section of the second.

13. Unreferenced quotations hereabouts are from *The New Yorker* articles.

14. For example at Tanglewood in August 1937: JH tls to his parents, Aug. 6, 1937, B FP Box 2.

15. A manuscript book of exercises—"John R. Hersey Violin. Teacher—Mr. Paul Federoffsky"—is in B FP Box 3. Federovsky used the teaching methods developed by the Czech violinist Otakar Ševčik. His handwritten notes for the young American ("At the bow Middle"; "Détaché large") give no indication of the strength of his feelings.

16. *Paris Review*; see p. 288.

17. "Why?," a story written by Hersey at Hotchkiss and published in the school's *Literary Monthly*, January 1932. This and other information about Hersey's academic performance was discovered by a later Hotchkiss alumnus, Nathaniel Sobel, in the course of researching his Yale senior-year essay "Searching for John Hersey" (2012), 15.

18. Founded in 1901, the Kiessling was the first Western restaurant in China, though the missionary-founded Astor Hotel—the country's first Western hotel—predates it by four decades. Both still flourish.

19. Vividly evoked in his story "God's Typhoon," in *Fling*.

20. "John Hersey, The Art of Fiction No. 92," *Paris Review*, Summer–Fall 1986—the magazine's one-hundredth issue. The interview was conducted by his former student, the novelist Jonathan Dee, over a three-day stay with the Herseys at their home on Martha's Vineyard.

21. Arthur was skeptical about this idea, and it seems as though in other ways either Huang Yusheng's memory or John Hersey's understanding, or both, may have been at fault. Hersey reported that the school "became" the university, whereas in fact it continues to this day as a separate entity. I'm grateful to Jiu Peng, a Nanking alumna, for this clarification.

22. The classroom was first housed in the school building itself, where it was visited by, among others, Sasha Su-Ling Welland, who describes it in *A Thousand Miles of Dreams: The Journeys of Two Chinese Sisters* (Lanham, MD: Rowman & Littlefield, 2006), 123–24. In 1998 the classroom was moved to a museum commemorating Zhou and his independently powerful wife, Deng Yingchao, where it can still be seen.

23. Pencil draft to "Dear Friends," from context written by Grace, summarizing her and her husband's work in 1919–21. Letterhead of the North China International Society of Famine Relief, Tientsin, "Sec. R. M. Hersey," B FP Box 2.

24. Letter from an editor at *Asia* magazine, 1982, B Box 63.

25. B Box 63.

26. Dan Chiasson, "Paper Trail: The Material Poetry of Susan Howe," *NY*, Aug. 7 and 14, 2017, 78.

27. "Time's Winged Chariot," see pp. 292*ff*.

28. "As to the rest of the jacket, is it going to be necessary to have a biography of the author? I feel very strongly that the kind of cereal an author eats for breakfast, together with a photo showing him clamped grimly to a pipe—all that is quite irrelevant. All that matters is what the man has written." JH to Harold Strauss about *The Wall*, Oct. 26, 1949, B Box 24.

29. See pp. 212*ff*.

30. Originals or copies of the correspondence are in the Knopf archives, HRC Box 411, and in B Box 25.

31. Sept. 11, 22, 29, 1964, HRC Box 411.

32. Nov. 7, 1964, HRC Box 411. The picture eventually used for *White Lotus*, showing Hersey outdoors in a sweater and open-necked shirt, does seem preferable to the more formal suit-and-tie-in-the-office ones in earlier books.

33. Two examples: He was angry that the Penguin edition of *Hiroshima* failed to follow aspects of the layout used by *The New Yorker*. He wrote to Allen Lane on Nov. 29, 1946, "Is it possible that [your editorial staff] thought the space breaks and the use of heavy initials in the New Yorker version of the story were merely decorative? Did no one read the story? // The New Yorker editors, I must also report, are dismayed at the reflection which this disregard for the contrapuntal structure of the story casts upon them, since the introduction explicitly says that this version, except for spellings, is 'exactly as it appeared in the pages of the New Yorker.'" B Box 36. Again, in 1963, when four of his war articles were to be published as *Of Men and War*, he explained, "All . . . the stories . . . are broken into sections, and in composition these sections should be separated by space breaks. These sections are like chapters, and represent breaks in chronology or in narrative. If possible, I would urge the use of large initial letters." B Box 49.

34. See p. 215.

35. Twayne's United States Authors Series. The book was first published in 1965 and then in an updated version, *John Hersey Revisited*, in 1991. Sanders first wrote to Hersey about his research on May 7, 1962, but was held up initially because when Hersey asked for his publishers' advice, they said they didn't know Sanders. B Box 20.

36. JH als to William Koshland, May 3, 1965, HRC.

37. Talking in a 1988 interview about his change of narrative vantage point in writing *The Wall*, from an omniscient narrator to the person of Levinson, Hersey explicitly elided the earlier narrator with himself: "I, John Hersey, could not have known enough about the experiences of the Warsaw Ghetto, so I decided to turn it over to someone else." Interview with Kay Bonetti for the American Audio Prose Library, 1988.

38. The brothers' correspondence about the articles, along with a complete set of galleys corrected and annotated by Arthur, is in B Box 63.

39. See pp. 231*ff.*

40. Most of Hersey's work was drafted in his easily legible longhand and then typed or, later, word-processed. The manuscript of *Hiroshima* is in pencil on 127 pages of flimsy paper.

41. These papers are currently listed as YCAL MSS 707. A number of other letters remain in the family's possession.

42. JH to his parents from the U.K., 1936–37, B FP Box 2.

2. To Be a Hersey

1. Sept. 27, 1936, B FP Box 2.

2. Some of the bottles, as well as other artifacts and documents from the Law period, are preserved by the town's lively Historical Society, housed in the public library. I'm grateful to the society's chair and archivist, Karen Smith, for giving me a tour of the village and showing me the collection.

3. *Our Village: Briarcliff Manor, N.Y., 1902 to 1952* (privately printed, c. 1952). Copy inscribed by Grace Hersey to her son Rob, B FP Box 3.

4. Nathaniel Sobel, "Searching for John Hersey," 13.

5. Hersey himself was among the mythmakers, and the phrase "towering eccentrics" is his own, used for members of the Hotchkiss faculty, in a funeral oration for the former head, George Van Santvoord, delivered on May 17, 1975. Still, that oration gives a vivid account of its subject, as well as of the speaker's affection for him: "He wanted a man not just to be learned, but rather to be wise, decent, humane, generous, forgiving, and light of heart in heavy days. As to all these traits, he gave us the great gift of his example." Kolowrat, 294–300; reprinted in *LS*, 3–9.

6. *Paris Review*; see p. 301, n. 21.

7. The letters from Hotchkiss are in B Box 18.

8. *Paris Review*; see n. 7, above. This was in 1930, a year after Faulkner's novel appeared. As for the more conventionally social-realist John Galsworthy, Hersey lamented to his parents that "he has written so much."

9. Nathaniel Sobel (see p. 301, n. 17) discovered them in the course of his research at Hotchkiss.

10. Karen M. Sharman, ed., *Glory in Glass: A Celebration of the Briarcliff Congregational Church 1896–1996* (Briarcliff, N.Y.: privately printed, 1996), 31.

11. Hersey from Yale to his parents, n.d., B Box 18.

12. About forty of Hotchkiss's three hundred pupils had free places. In return, they were required to do various menial tasks—cleaning classrooms, waiting on tables—but Hersey, among other scholarship boys, seems to have managed to turn these into a mark of distinction in other pupils' perception as well as his own. Kolowrat, 91–92. Hersey describes himself as a "mishkid" in a 1983 *New Republic* profile of Henry Luce reprinted in *LS*, 27.

13. Sobel, "Searching for John Hersey," 18.

14. The quotation's context was to prove relevant: "He hath shewed thee, O man, what is good; and what doth the Lord require of thee, but to do justly, and to love mercy, and to walk humbly with thy God?" (Micah 6:8, KJV).

15. Sobel, "Searching for John Hersey," 17.

16. "A Life in Writing: John Hersey, 1914–1993," *Yale Alumni Magazine*, October 1993, http://archives.yalealumnimagazine.com/issues/93_10/hersey.html.

17. At Hersey's funeral James Merrill said, "His were largely the older, Platonic virtues—Prudence, Temperance, Justice." *John Hersey* (tributes delivered in Battell Chapel, Yale University, May 15, 1993, and at West Chop Village Cemetery, Vineyard Haven, Mass., June 19, 1993; privately printed, 1993), 45.

18. Sanders, *John Hersey Revisited*, 1991.

19. B Box 18.

20. Hersey told Jonathan Dee that in the period immediately before he went to college he had been practicing between four and six hours a day.

21. B Box 18. He was referring to the then-new murals by the Catalan artist Josep Maria Sert. The work by Diego Rivera, specially commissioned for the new Rockefeller Center, included a panel in which a celebratory portrait of Lenin on one side was counterposed with a depiction of John D. Rockefeller—in his son's words, "drinking martinis with a harlot and various other things that were unflattering to the family." Asked to change the work, the artist said he would rather see it destroyed. In 1934 it was duly chiseled off the wall. Rivera made a reconstruction called *Man, Controller of the Universe*, which is on display at the Palacio de Bellas Artes in Mexico City. Materials related to the episode were exhibited at the Mexican Cultural Institute in Washington, D.C., in 2014; see Allison Keyes, "Destroyed by Rockefellers, Mural Trespassed on Political Vision," NPR, http://www.npr.org/2014/03/09/287745199/destroyed-by-rockefellers-mural-trespassed-on-political-vision, accessed August 4, 2017.

22. This was after it had been bought by the U.S. Navy for wartime use. *NYT*, April 30, 1941.

23. Hersey later expressed a preference for the white "colonial" style exemplified by Dartmouth College, New Hampshire—"altogether indigenous, really New England . . . lovely simple white masses, the sort of buildings Yale should have built . . . throughout." JH tls from Stockbridge, Mass., to his parents, August 6, 1937, BFP Box 2.

24. Renamed Hopper College in 2017 because of John L. Calhoun's role in defending slavery.

25. M. C. Leikind, "Stanhope Bayne-Jones: Physician, Teacher, Soldier, Scientist-Administrator, Friend of Medical Libraries," *Bulletin of the New York Academy of Medicine*, 1972, 48, 584–95. Nannie Bayne-Jones wrote to congratulate Grace Hersey on her son's election to Skull and Bones on May 10, 1935. B Box 18.

26. Zara Kessler, "John Hersey's Yale Education" (Yale senior dissertation, 2012), 13, http://www.library.yale.edu/~nkuhl/YCALStudentWork/Hersey-Kessler.pdf.

Hersey played in 1934 and '35; Ford was assistant coach in 1935 while studying at the law school.

27. *John Hersey* memorial tributes, 9.

28. Nov. 3, 1935, B Box 18.

29. *The Key West Citizen* reported on April 3, 1936, that Hugh J. Chisholm's *Aras* had put in with various of the family on board as well as John R. Hersey and Mrs. Sarah Key. Some van Duzers—connected to the founder of Sarah Lawrence College— were also in the party. Undated letters from JH to his parents, B Box 18.

30. George Curtis Church, who reviewed film for the *News*, was among the significant number of Yale students who joined the intelligence services. A translator of German and an enthusiast of German arts, he spent the Second World War at Bletchley Park.

31. The issue of March 13, 1933, for example, which Hersey coedited, contained four such items, including an interview on the front page with the Spanish soprano Lucrezia Bori, in which she talked about financial pressures confronting the Metropolitan Opera.

32. Japan withdrew from the League of Nations on February 24, 1933. The interview appeared on March 11, a month after Hersey became an associate editor. The story was followed up on March 25 when the former head of the Japanese delegation to the League paid a visit to Yale.

33. Sobel, "Searching for John Hersey," 4. Some of the research material Hersey gathered, together with an unbound carbon copy of the dissertation, is in B Box 3.

34. JH to his parents, Nov. 4, 1934, B Box 18.

35. *Paris Review*; B Box 18. John Hersey had come to know the Luces through Arthur, who had roomed with Henry Luce's son at Hotchkiss.

36. JH to Arthur Hersey, Oct. 11, 1936, B FP Box 2. At his mother's suggestion, he wrote weekly in turn to Arthur, Rob, and his parents, and at home the letters were passed on.

37. JH to Arthur Hersey, Nov. 2, 1936, B FP Box 2.

38. Nov. 14, 1936, B FP Box 2.

39. JH to Arthur, Jan. 31, 1937, B FP Box 2.

40. At the Pye Radio Works. Feb. 4, 1937, B FP Box 2.

41. Oct. 25, 1936, B FP Box 2.

42. Stalin's purges. Jan. 31, 1937. It's interesting that Hersey was so silent about these when he was based in Moscow in 1944–45; see pp. 94*ff.* At Cambridge, he confessed to anti-interventionist sentiments in Europe, saying that he didn't "feel strongly enough about German colonization, or the prevention of same, to want to fight for or against; or even about the Fascist or the Communist, or even, I am ashamed to say, the Democratic ideal, to want to fight about them, either." Feb. 28, 1937, B FP Box 2.

43. Sota also found "the number of foreigners engaged on both sides . . . appalling." Nov. 2, 1936, B FP Box 2.

44. April 18, 1937, B FP Box 2.

45. Jan. 31, 1937, B FP Box 2.
46. JH to his parents, Feb. 6[?], 1937, B Box 18, Folder 9.
47. Jan. 24, 1937, B FP Box 2.
48. Nov. 8, 1936, B FP Box 2.
49. Dec. 7, 1936, B FP Box 2.
50. JH tls from Clare College, Cambridge, to his parents, May 12, 1937, B Box 18.
51. And not flawless. "Blimey" is English English; "gotten" isn't.
52. He mentioned the poor health of Roscoe Senior in a letter to Henry Thirkill, master of Clare, July 22, 1937, B FP Box 2. He had also become impatient with the pace of his studies at Cambridge, where he tried unsuccessfully to persuade the authorities to let him complete his two-year course in eight months (technically, to sit for the second part of the tripos at the end of his first academic year). At the time, his idea was to spend the second year on private study, but the essential impulse seems to have been to get back to the States and, as he put it in a letter to his parents, go "out into the world . . . to properly and permanently fend for myself." Tls from Sinclair Lewis, Aug. 6, 1937.
53. Brendan Gill, *Here at The New Yorker* (New York: Da Capo Press, 1975, 1999 ed.), 67.
54. The notion is Lewis's biographer Mark Schorer's: see below, n. 56. Hersey at the time wrote that the couple "got along beautifully," though there may well have been an element of performing for the young man in this. He innocently told his parents that although the Lewises were "invited out by every one on the map, [they] prefer to stay at home doing cross-word puzzles." JH tls from Stockbridge, Mass., to his parents, Aug. 22, 1937, B FP Box 2.
55. Mark Schorer, *Sinclair Lewis: An American Life* (New York: McGraw-Hill, 1961), 631. With his suspicion of biographies, Hersey was doubtful about Schorer's project but agreed to be interviewed for it and later praised the book. Schorer tls to JH, June 24, 1954, B Box 20, 1952–63, S.
56. Sept. 27, 1937, L[aura] Hobson memo to Henry Luce in response to a prompt from Sinclair Lewis, B Box 19.
57. *LS*, 17. This piece about Lewis was written for the *Yale Review* ("First Job," Spring 1987).
58. In a letter to his parents from Lewis's house he says, "I am throwing together, gradually, notes and sketches for some writing of my own: what an atmosphere for that." B Box 18. Perhaps relatedly there's a sheaf of poems, along with a separate item dated June 27, 1937, in B Box 19, 1937–51, *XYZ*.
59. Aug. 6, 1937, B FP Box 2.
60. It seems that Grace Hegger Lewis had previously asked JH to look over the manuscript but he had declined: "I felt a little shame . . . that I hadn't been able to help you make this fine book . . . I didn't know whether I had the right to exploit those few weeks with Red into any kind of expertising. And I may as well be thoroughly honest: I felt protective of Red; I had no idea you could do such a loving book." (The couple had divorced in 1925.) JH als to GHL, Sept. 5, 1954, Sinclair Lewis papers, HRC.

61. *Paris Review*; see p. 301, n. 21.
62. JH to his parents, Aug. 22, 1937, B FP Box 2.
63. Schorer, *Sinclair Lewis*, 666; *LS*, 23–24.
64. See ch. 11.
65. May 10, 1937, B FP Box 2. Hersey told Jonathan Dee that he owed the job in part to a "twenty-four page essay on how rotten *Time* was," which he submitted when he took the magazine's test for the second time.
66. Robert Elson's official history *Time Inc.: The Intimate History of a Publishing Enterprise*, vol. 1, *1923–41* (New York: Atheneum, 1968–1986), 328, is interesting about the problems faced by managing editors of *Time* as a result of internal competition with *Life*.
67. As far as the magazine was concerned, the gap was filled by other features on related topics, including "Negroes: The U.S. Also Has a Minority Problem," with pictures by Alfred Eisenstaedt among others. Alan Brinkley, *The Publisher: Henry Luce and His American Century* (New York: Vintage, 2011), ch. 8.
68. *LS*, p. 64.
69. Michael Wreszin, *A Rebel in Defense of Tradition: The Life and Politics of Dwight Macdonald* (New York: Basic Books, 1994), 47–49.
70. JH to his parents, Oct. 21, 1937, B FP Box 2.
71. *Time*, May 9, 1938.
72. The more so as conflict spread in the Far East. "U.S. *v.* Japan: The Pacific Problem" was illustrated by a double-page narrative map in *Time* on July 1, 1940, indicating the distance of Pearl Harbor from San Francisco on the one hand and Tokyo on the other, graphically illustrating the closeness in size of the rival fleets and the significance of Japanese bases in the Marshall Islands.
73. As with attitudes to European dictatorships, individual U.S. and British diplomats were far from unanimous. In a signed piece for *Life* on July 15, 1940, Hersey profiled the U.S. ambassador to Japan, Joseph Drew, quoting his concept of "dynamic appeasement." Drew, he wrote, believed that "a gentleman can always get the better of a tough guy by continuing to act like a gentleman."
74. JH to his parents, May 15, 1939, B FP Box 2.
75. *Time*, June 26, 1939.
76. The first alone consists of thirty-nine single-spaced typescript pages.
77. See p. 114 (*NY* piece, March 16, 1946).
78. JH to his parents, May 25–27 [1939], B FP Box 2.
79. Jardine, Matheson, for the Indo-China Steam Navigation Company, to JH, June [n.d.] 1939, B FP Box 2.
80. The episode is vividly recounted in Donald Gillies's biography of the then British ambassador, *Radical Diplomat: The Life of Archibald Clark Kerr, Lord Inverchapel, 1882–1951* (London: I. B. Tauris, 1999), 87ff.
81. *Time*, June 26, 1939.
82. See p. 68.
83. June 21, 1939, B FP Box 2.

84. Ibid.
85. Theodore H. White, *In Search of History: A Personal Adventure* (New York: Harper & Row, 1978), 84.
86. June 21, 1939, BFP Box 2.
87. Ibid.
88. B Box 18.
89. *Time*, Dec. 18, 1939.
90. See p. 50.
91. Brinkley, *The Publisher*, ch. 10.
92. Postmarked Oct. 14, 1939, B Box 18.
93. Sept. 1, 1939, B Box 18.

3. On Top of the Hill

1. *Life*, June 6, 1938.
2. Joseph Junior (b. 1915), and John "Jack" (b. 1917). The other Kennedy boys were younger: Robert (b. 1925) and Edward (b. 1932).
3. Nigel Hamilton, *JFK: Reckless Youth* (New York: Random House, 1992), 250.
4. Telegram from FAC to JFK, Feb. 25, 1939, http://www.jfklibrary.org/Asset -Viewer/Archives/JFKPP-004-138.aspx.
5. Henry McKnight. He worked on the *Herald Tribune* and had helped Hersey get his job with Sinclair Lewis (*LS*, 10).
6. JH to Frances Ann from Moscow, Oct. 21, 1944, B Box 23.
7. Hamilton, *JFK*, 255–87.
8. JH to his parents, Oct. 30, Nov. 18, 1939, Jan. 20, 1940, B Box 18.
9. Lew Powell, "In Charlotte, JFK Suffered Wedding-Bell Blues," *North Carolina Miscellany*, North Carolina Collection, University of North Carolina at Chapel Hill, https://blogs.lib.unc.edu/ncm/index.php/2010/04/27/in-charlotte-jfk-suffered -wedding-bell-blues/.
10. Frances Ann to JH, Jan. 21, n.y., B Box 23.
11. That is, in a copy sold in the United States. A small-format "pony edition" was distributed free to U.S. troops. It contained all the editorial content but no advertising and generally ran to thirty-two pages.
12. *Time*, June 3, 1940.
13. JH to his parents, June 7, 1940, B Box 18.
14. *Time*, July 8, 1940.
15. JH to his parents, July 6, 1940, B Box 18.
16. For example, JH to Theodore White, Feb. 7, 1940, B Box 19, 1937–51, *W*.
17. From Hu Shih at the Chinese embassy, Washington, D.C., Feb. 18, 1941, B Box 19, 1937–51.
18. *Why England Slept* was brought out by Wilfred Funk at the end of July 1940. See Hamilton, *JFK*, 334.

19. JH to his parents, July 13, 1940, B Box 18.

20. JH to his parents, Aug. 12, 1940, B Box 18.

21. JH to his parents, Sept. 20, 1940, B Box 18; *Time* cover story, Sept. 30, 1940.

22. JH to his parents, Nov. 2, 1940, B Box 18; *Time* cover story, Nov. 4, 1940.

23. JH to his parents, Nov. 8, 1940, B Box 18.

24. JH to his parents, April 19, 1941, B Box 18.

25. In view of what happened at Pearl Harbor and Clark Field it was unfortunate that the first item in the issue of December 8 began, "Everything was ready. From Rangoon to Honolulu, every man was at battle station."

26. Headed "If War Should Come He Leads the Army That Would Fight Japan," the article appeared among a host of Christmas advertising near the back of the magazine, on pages 122–139.

27. See, for example, Brinkley, *The Publisher.*

28. *Time*, Dec. 22, 1941.

29. Harold Strauss to JH, Dec. 10, 1941, B Box 34.

30. For example, "How to Tell Japs from the Chinese," *Life*, Dec. 22, 1941. That Christmas issue also encouraged goodwill toward America's Chinese allies with a feature on the Nativity story as painted by Chinese Christian artists. For Hersey's later account of the internment of Japanese Americans, see pp. 282*ff.*

31. Some are now in B Box 34.

32. *Life*, Dec. 8, 1941.

33. *MB*, 23, 52, 105.

34. Ibid., 83.

35. They were later repatriated as part of an exchange of prisoners. The couple had previously been sent to Chungking to work with the newly recruited Theodore S. White. Elson, *The World of Time Inc.*, vol. 2, *1941–1960*, 470.

36. For example, chapter 45, titled ". . . Need of Doctors" (*MB*, 45*ff.*), about the primitive military hospital on Bataan, is taken from a piece published under Melville Jacoby's name in *Life*, Feb. 16, 1942, pp. 13–15. It was also tactless of Hersey to open his battle narrative with an account of the bombing of Luzon copied with minimal alterations from the pages of *Life*, Dec. 22, 1941.

37. Anne Fadiman, "Nothing New Under the Sun," in *Ex Libris: Reflections of a Common Reader* (New York: Farrar, Straus and Giroux, 1998), 109–11 (Penguin ed., 87–88).

38. Jack Stillinger, *Multiple Authorship and the Myth of Solitary Genius* (Oxford: Oxford University Press), 1991.

39. Written permission, if it was given, has proved elusive. A cyclostyle finding aid to the enormous Knopf archives at Austin, Texas, prepared by Rich Oram, reveals that some of the company's pre-1945 correspondence was disposed of in the course of office moves before the papers came to the library. Both the Knopf archives and B Box 34 contain copies of a letter to JH from Harold Strauss (Feb. 2, 1942) about permissions issues raised by Knopf's lawyers, but these are confined to matters concerning the War Department and the letters about individual soldiers, all of

which had been cleared. It seems most likely that Luce had agreed to the project orally before Hersey embarked on it. Still, the room for doubt—whether or not specifically raised with Time-Life by reporters whose work had been used—was enough for someone at Knopf to have decided to include in Hersey's next book, *Into the Valley*, a clear note to the effect that Time-Life had given permission for its material to have been used.

40. Robert Lasseter to JH, March 10, 1942, B Box 34. The sum of money isn't specified in the surviving correspondence.

41. Information given to the author by Anne Fadiman, based on a conversation between her and her mother on Nov. 4, 1996. Knopf's records show that the prepublication advance was in two installments of $250: one on signing, on Feb. 26, 1942, and one on delivery, April 21, 1942. Ten percent went to Hersey's agent, Elizabeth Otis, leaving a balance of $450. It seems that this payment to the Jacobys may have been an afterthought, but it was made while they were in Australia and before Mel Jacoby's death, on April 29, 1942.

42. See p. 48.

43. No. 218. The rent for March 16–31 was $150. Hersey described the holiday in an undated letter to his parents in B Box 18.

44. The other is Frazier Hunt, *MacArthur and the War Against Japan* (New York: Scribner, 1944). D. Clayton James, *The Years of MacArthur*, vol. 2, *1941–1945* (Boston: Houghton Mifflin 1970–85), 418.

45. *MB*, 79.

46. The arguments have subsequently segued into another notion, that of "literary nonfiction." And see p. 300, n. 5.

47. William Manchester, *American Caesar: Douglas MacArthur 1880–1964* (Boston: Little, Brown, 1978), 213, drawing on *MB*, 123. Manchester also describes MacArthur's arrival in Melbourne in the words of "John Hersey, who was there," 272.

48. *Time*, June 1, 1942, 33.

49. Speech by Hersey at a party celebrating the fiftieth anniversary of the founding of Knopf, Oct. 29, 1965, reprinted in *LS*, 188*ff.*

50. Jan. 30, 1943, was the tenth anniversary of Hitler's coming to power, but the defeat—and likely destruction—of Paulus's army had become undeniable and he didn't give a speech.

51. *Life*, Nov. 2, 1942, "Nine Men on a Four-Man Raft."

52. The piece was dated Sept. 30, 1942. For Hersey's awakening to racial issues in the United States, see pp. 213*ff.*

53. JH to David Hulburd, Sept. 9, 1942, B FP Box 2.

54. U.S. Army Center of Military History, *Guadalcanal*, 2003.

55. *IV*, 75. Mailer read *Into the Valley* before going to the Philippines. See J. Michael Lennon, *Norman Mailer: A Double Life* (New York: Simon & Schuster, 2013), 71. Hersey's question runs throughout the later novel but is most specifically discussed between Lieutenant Hearn and General Cummings. The General asks,

"Have you ever wondered, Robert, why we're fighting this war?" Hearn's immediate answer, which he goes on to refine, is: "With all the contradictions, I suppose there's an objective right on our side. That is, in Europe. Over here [in the Pacific], as far as I'm concerned, it's an imperialist toss-up. Either we louse up Asia or Japan does." Norman Mailer, *The Naked and the Dead* (London: Allan Wingate, 1949, 319–20).

56. Alfred Knopf to JH, May 18, 1943, B Box 18, 1937–51, *W*.

57. Dec. 1, 1942, B Box 18.

58. Dec. 1, 1942, B Box 19, 1937–51, *N–O*.

59. Hamilton, *JFK*, 550.

60. With the removedness of someone in the mid-Atlantic, he told Blanche, "I would appreciate your not having it styled, for although some of the punctuation might horrify a conventional stylist, I have tried to mark the speech to fit the cadences of the men as they actually talked, not as they ought to have talked." JH to Blanche Knopf, Aug. 1943, B Box 35.

61. Lieutenant Alan R. Jackson, Navy Department Office of Public Relations, Room 1604, 580 Fifth Avenue, New York, tls to Blanche Knopf, Aug. 3, 1943, B Box 35.

4. Getting Hurt Getting Through

1. *NY*, July 3, 1943.

2. JH to Brendan Gill, Aug. 11, 1943, B Box 35, *N*.

3. *Time* supported the Sicily route. The magazine's cover on May 24, 1943, featured the British admiral "Cunningham of the Mediterranean," whose picture is captioned "Before the Second Front, there are islands to take and a sea to cross." Inside, the "World Battlefronts" feature showed Minorca, Corsica, Sardinia, Crete, and southern France, but the first picture is of Italy as seen from Messina, Sicily. Sicily was the main topic of *Time*'s "World Battlefronts" on June 28.

4. I have drawn particularly on Albert N. Garland and Howard McGaw Smyth's official history of the campaign, *United States Army in World War II: Mediterranean Theater of Operations—Sicily and the Surrender of Italy* (Washington, D.C.: Office of the Chief of Military History, Dept. of the Army, 1965), and Rick Atkinson, *The Day of Battle: The War in Sicily and Italy* (London: Little, Brown, 2007).

5. These materials are in B Boxes 35 and 42.

6. *Life*, Aug. 23, 1943. Most of Time-Life's on-the-spot invasion coverage was by Jack Belden; see, for example, *Time*, July 26, 1943, "Battle of Sicily," in which Amgot also figured.

7. *Paris Review* interview.

8. Published on Dec. 27, 1943, to accompany a thirty-two-page "portfolio" of their work. The artists were Dwight Shepler, Paul Sample, Fletcher Martin, Floyd Davis, Aaron Bohrod, and Mitchell Jamieson. A "strength" of their (for the most part

utterly routine illustrative) work, Hersey reassured readers, is that "these artists are not long-haired, loud-talking aesthetes. They are normal, healthy, peace-loving men."

9. Typescripts of different versions of the Sinarchism piece are in B Box 28. Hersey traced the movement's roots to the Falange in Spain and also claimed that it had effective Nazi and Japanese connections, suggesting that "American soldiers may come back from winning the war in another hemisphere to find it being lost in their own." He was on surer ground with his observations of peasant life in the mesa northwest of Mexico City, and of the impact of racist employment practices in Texas on the movement's recruitment in the U.S. Southwest. His description of its early methods is interesting in relation to the religious sympathies of some of his other writing at this time: "The fifteen original organizers canvassed the countryside for recruits. They went among the poor like Franciscan monks, sharing peasant bread and sleeping on the ground." The bullfighting piece, "The Pass of the Dead One," appeared in *Life* on Jan. 10, 1944.

10. *BA*, 250.

11. Letter dated Feb. 10, 1944, from an unidentified acquaintance of Hersey's named Harold, serving in the Inspection Division of Airforce Materiel Command at Dayton, Ohio, B Box 35. Harold listed other implausibilities before exclaiming, "John, your readers *have* to take good men seriously, or there is no point in a book like 'Adano.'"

12. *Nation*, Feb. 12, 1944.

13. David A. Hollinger, *Protestants Abroad: How Missionaries Tried to Change the World but Changed America* (Princeton, N.J.: Princeton University Press, 2017), p. 50.

14. Willa Cather to Fanny Butcher, April 19, 1945: *A Calendar of Letters of Willa Cather.*

15. *Spectator*, March 11, 1944.

16. Knopf royalty statements, Oct. 31, 1944, April 30, 1945, HRC.

17. At the Cort Theatre from Dec. 6, 1944. Gibbs's review appeared on Dec. 16, 1944. Fredric March, Gibbs wrote, "makes Joppolo a living man, desperately tired, fallible, but always passionately devoted to the interests of the people he has been sent to serve. It is the best performance he has given."

18. "Bastard" and "God-damn" were instanced, and it was suggested that "God" would do as an oath, rather than "Jesus." Oct. 2, 1945, B Box 35, *K*.

19. In 1956 and 1957.

20. This was in 1966; B Box 35. Since Hersey had kept letters Toscani and his wife, Georgia, had sent him at the time of the book's publication (e.g., Dec. 26, 1944, B Box 42) saying how much they enjoyed it and how grateful they were for the boost it had given to Frank's army career, the threat was easily averted. Various other people claimed to see themselves in the book but without seeking compensation, among them a Lieutenant Colonel MacCaffrey, who thought he was Lieutenant Colonel Sartorious. B Box 35.

21. In a foreword for a reissue published in the celebrated Modern Library series in

1945. His editor described it as "perhaps the best introduction ever to appear in a Modern Library book." Nov. 29, 1945, B Box 42.

22. Notes for and drafts of the novella are at the Beinecke. This ts is in B Box 1.

23. Ben Hibbs, editor of *The Saturday Evening Post*, to JH, Nov. 15, 1943, B Box 19, 1937–51, S.

24. See later, pp. 98–99. From correspondence between Hersey and senior people at Time-Life about his prospects in the organization, it's clear that almost as soon as he finished writing *Adano* he was weighing his future there against a full-time freelance writing career. See tls Tom Matthews to JH, Sept. 19, 1943, B Box 19, 1937–51, *M*.

25. Leonard Lyons at the *New York Post* to JH, June 13, 1944, B Box 35.

26. *Life*, May 10, 1943. There was an earlier promotional piece ("The Mighty Midgets Prove Their Worth") in *Time*, March 15, 1943.

27. Hersey had already described what all PT crew members knew: that in these waters and without radar, darkness and the silhouettes of mountains made high-speed navigation exceptionally hazardous.

28. Among the more persuasive accounts is in Nigel Hamilton's *JFK: Reckless Youth* (New York: Random House, 1992), 641. Hersey was interviewed about his own narrative and about other aspects of his relationship with Kennedy by Herbert Parmet in preparation for the latter's *JFK: The Presidency of John F. Kennedy* (New York: Dial Press, 1983). A full transcript of the interview is in B Box 59.

29. JH to Grace Hersey, Feb. 24, 1944, B Box 18; Parmet (see n. 28, above), 9–10.

30. Hamilton, *JFK*, 644–45.

31. April 28, 1944, *NY* Archive Box 406.

32. *NY*, June 17, 1944.

33. JH interviewed by Nigel Hamilton, 1990; Hamilton, *JFK*, 641.

34. Anna Bartlett Warner (1827–1915) was also a novelist. Her house, preserved as a museum, is now part of the Military Academy.

35. Parmet: see n. 28, above.

36. Among other things, Joseph Kennedy was repaying a favor. In 1941, Hersey had helped find someone to sort out his papers—a project that it seems JFK half hoped Hersey might have taken on himself. J. F. Kennedy to JH, Feb. 22, 1941, B Box 19, 1937–51, *K*.

37. Parmet (n. 28, above), 12.

38. As he told Parmet (n. 28, above), he was put off by the way he found he had been labeled by the Kennedy campaign. At a White House dinner, he sat next to one of the president's sisters, Pat Lawford. She said, "John Hersey, John Hersey? There's something bad about you. You were for Nixon?" No, he said; he had supported Adlai Stevenson. "Oh, yes," she replied. "I knew there was something bad about you." B Box 54.

39. Quoted in Atkinson, *Day of Battle*, from *Time*, Aug. 9, 1943.

40. Notes for and drafts of the article are in B Box 28 under the heading "Rangers."

41. Quoted in Atkinson, *Day of Battle*, eliding different moments in Hersey's "The Hills of Nicosia," *Time*, Aug. 9, 1943. Hersey vividly describes how "the blind man lifted

his feet high and put them down wherever they fell. He had none of the cautious grace of men long blind, but struck out with his legs as if angry at the path."

42. For example, in the preface to "Nine Men on a Four-Man Raft": "After they recovered their strength, [the survivors] told me this story of their seven-day voyage on an inflated raft . . . I have put the entire story in the mouth of Lieutenant A. W. Anderson, the copilot, but parts of it came from Lieutenant J. P. Van Hour, the pilot, and other crew members." *OMW*, 61.

43. In the first of these articles, published on Nov. 30, 1942, John Field wrote that Patton "looks ten years younger than his 57 years. He stands more than 6 ft. tall, with broad shoulders, narrow hips, and strong arms and legs. With his piercing eyes, he is capable of defeating any of his junior officers at sharpshooting . . . When he gets the chance, he can still play polo or handball better, or run the 100 yards faster, than most Army graduates fresh out of West Point," etc. The April 12 *Time* cover piece ("His body had always been magnificent and versatile . . . He had always done things the hard way, and the spectacular") ran as part of a "World Battlefronts" feature on the prospects for a European invasion. Patton featured again on *Time*'s July 26 cover, saying, "It makes no difference what part of Europe you kill Germans in."

44. Jack Belden, "Adventure in Sicily," *Life*, Aug. 9, 1943. Cf. *Time*, Aug. 2, 1943.

45. JH cable to David Hulburd, Aug. 3, 1943, B Box 23.

46. *Life*, Aug. 23, 1943.

47. JH to Frances Ann, Aug. 1, 1944, B Box 23.

48. JH to Frances Ann, Aug. 12, 1944, B Box 23.

49. JH to Frances Ann, Nov. 13, 1944, B Box 23.

50. Sanders, *John Hersey Revisited*, 23–24.

51. It's estimated that between 1928 and 1953, twenty-five million people were "repressed" by the Soviet regime: that's to say, executed, imprisoned, forcibly resettled, enslaved, or deported. We know from Hersey's letters home from Cambridge that he was aware of the show trials.

52. Oct. 25, 1944, B Box 23.

53. Ibid.

54. Ibid. Later, *Literaturnaya Gazeta* published an article by Raya Orlova, who had traveled with Hersey to Leningrad and had discussed *Adano* with him. The subject was *The War Lover* (see pp. 199*ff*), which, again, was presented as an indictment of a specifically American kind of militarism. B Box 38.

55. Henry Luce to JH, Nov. 5, 1944, B Box 23.

56. David Hulburd to JH, Nov. 11, 1944, B Box 23. "ET-" is telegraphese for "and."

57. Allen Grover to JH, Nov. 9, 1944, B Box 23.

58. JH cable to Luce, Nov. 7, 1944, and related correspondence, B Box 23.

59. JH to Frances Ann, Nov. 6, 1944, B Box 23. The relationship grew in Hersey's Martha's Vineyard years, from the mid-1960s—in the words of her biographer William Wright—"so that at the time of her death, Hersey was not just one of Hellman's two or three closest friends but as much a part of her family as anyone." William

Wright, *Lillian Hellman: The Image, the Woman* (New York: Simon & Schuster, 1986). The degree of Hellman's celebrity in the Soviet Union and her apparent unconcern about the nature of the regime are a story in themselves.

60. JH to Frances Ann, Nov. 6, 8, 13, 1944, B Box 23.
61. JH to Frances Ann, Dec. 12, 13, 15, 1944, B Box 23.
62. The typescript is in B Box 52. According to a note added by JH, Knopf told him the adviser had said, "This book will neither help nor hurt Hersey's reputation."
63. JH to Frances Ann, Jan. 13, 1945, B Box 23.

5. Tu Lu-men, Chu Chi-erh, and Shi-Taling

1. Clare Boothe Luce became one of Connecticut's senators in 1942.
2. Brinkley, *The Publisher*, ch. 10.
3. Tony Judt, *Postwar: A History of Europe Since 1945* (2005; paperback edition, London: Pimlico, 2007), 6.
4. "Henry Luce's China Dream," *New Republic*, May 2, 1983. *LS*, 29.
5. Sanders, *John Hersey Revisited*, 13.
6. "The Communization of Crow Village," *NY*, May 18, 1946.
7. Dec. 13, 1944, B Box 23.
8. Nov. 27, 1944, B Box 23.
9. Elson, *The World of Time Inc.*, vol. 2, *1941–1960*, 100–110.
10. *LS*, 38.
11. Hersey to Luce, Nov. 14, 1944, B Box 23.
12. *LS*, 38–39.
13. Victor Grosz; see *Life*, April 5, 1945. The article followed *Life*'s famous picture spread on the "Big Three" at Yalta.
14. Those, that is, who wanted to have information in the first place. Lillian Hellman said she was not a journalist "and didn't wish to report on the war." This was fortunate in a way, since even she wasn't allowed to ask any questions. Dorothy Gallagher, *Lillian Hellman: An Imperious Life* (New Haven and London: Yale University Press, 2014), ch. 9, "The Incurious Tourist."
15. Anne Applebaum, *Gulag: A History* (London: Allen Lane, 2003), 441.
16. *HS*, 189–239.
17. *HS*, "Prefatory Note," viii.
18. He was sixty-seven. A short obituary appeared in the *NYT* on March 20, 1945.
19. By Twentieth Century Fox, June 21, 1945.
20. Sanders, *John Hersey Revisited*, 11; *Paris Review* interview.
21. Elson, *The World of Time Inc.*, vol. 2, *1941–1960*, 107, n. 15.
22. Michael D. Gordin gives a close account of the logistical as well as strategic preparations involved in *Five Days in August: How World War II Became a Nuclear War* (Princeton and Oxford: Princeton University Press, 2007).
23. Bill Lawrence to JH, May 5, 1945, B Box 19, 1937–51, *L*.

24. *Life*, July 30, 1945. The subhead read, "The Jap air force has turned itself into a suicide weapon . . . Its weirdly trained pilots seek glory in death . . . They cannot win
the war but do great damage." The conference attended by Margaret Mead was organized by the Institute of Pacific Relations, Dec. 16–17, 1944. B Box 28.

25. Bill Lawrence to JH, "Guam / 25 July 1945," B Box 19, 1937–51, *L*.

26. *New York Times*, Sept. 13, 1945. The article was by the science reporter William
Laurence, not to be confused with Hersey's *NYT* friend Bill Lawrence. For another
reporter's version of the situation, see p. 135.

27. David G. McCullough, *Truman* (New York: Simon & Schuster, 1992), pt. 3, ch. 10,
"Summer of Decision."

28. The film, which celebrates the military acknowledgment of bombardiers as equal
to pilots in combat significance and rank, is memorable for its boisterous theme
music, "Song of the U.S. Bombardiers" ("Bomb, bomb, bomb . . .").

29. "Joe Is Home Now," *Life*, July 3, 1944.

30. *HS*, 141.

31. This was against the rules of patient confidentiality, so at the hospital's request
Hersey disguised the fact in his narrative. B Box 28.

32. Dick [Lauterbach] to JH, June 15, 1945: "I wasn't surprised to hear you'd parted
with H. Luce & Co. I could sense in Moscow that you were deeply unhappy about
the coloring of the news." B Box 19, 1937–51, *L*.

33. *NY*, Nov. 3, 1945.

34. See pp. 192–93. *Life* used the opportunity the novel provided to publish Kessel's
pictures of the voyage for the first time on June 11, 1956. A photo feature by him on
the city of Peiping (Beijing) appeared on April 29, 1946.

35. *Life*, June 3, 1946. Some of this went into his story "Why Were You Sent Out Here?,"
Atlantic, Oct. 1989, reprinted in *Fling*.

36. "Letter from Shanghai," *NY*, Feb. 9, 1946.

37. *NY*, March 16, 1946.

38. See p. 47.

39. *NY*, May 4, 1946.

40. March 8, n.y., B Box 23.

41. Wertenbaker to JH, undated cable, B Box 29.

42. "Two Weeks' Water Away," *NY*, May 18, 1946, May 25, 1946. The title refers to the
distance by sea between China and the United States, as explained by Hersey to
some of the Chinese.

43. "The Happy, Happy Beggar," *NY*, May 11, 1946. The Yangtze flows through
I-ch'ang.

44. *John Hersey*, memorial tributes, 16.

45. Walter Morse to *NY*, April 28, 1947, B Box 26.

46. B Box 29.

47. "The Communization of Crow Village," Reporter at Large, *NY*, July 27, 1946.

48. May 21, 1946, B Box 37.

49. B Box 29.

50. "Red Pepper Village." A Chinese mile, or "li," is a traditional unit of distance, once variable but now standardized as 500 meters. The area of severe blast damage at Hiroshima was 8.5 kilometers (5.25 miles) in circumference, or 17 Chinese miles; the area of total destruction was about half that.

51. John Ciardi, "Massive Retaliation," in Edward M Cifelli, ed., *The Collected Poems of John Ciardi* (University of Arkansas Press, 1997), 220.

52. The hymn "Lead, Kindly Light" began as a part-autobiographical poem about Newman's being stuck in a boat becalmed in the straits between Corsica and Sardinia. (Since Ciardi was a Catholic, it's relevant that on this trip Newman, then an Anglican priest but later a preeminent Catholic convert and cardinal, visited Rome for the first time.)

53. See, for example, Mary McCarthy's criticism, pp. 144*ff*.

54. *Manzanar*.

6. Pyramid, Sun, and Cube

1. Aug. 31, 1946, B Box 36.

2. Janet Flanner tls "Rome September 20" to "My dear Ross and Shawn," *NY* Archive Box 50. Flanner compared the piece to "[Mathew] Brady's photographs from the Civil War. One of the first records of how people really looked in war. Printing it as you did, alone and concentrated, was . . . the best thing you could have done in the world, today."

3. The poem, called "Beinecke Library," was published in *Provinces* (New York: Ecco Press, 1991).

4. For Hersey's own account of the Japanese internment, see pp. 282*ff*.

5. W. G. Sebald, *On the Natural History of Destruction* (London: Hamish Hamilton, 1999), 24–26.

6. Oct. 3, 1946, B Box 36.

7. For ecclesiastical purposes at the time, the Hiroshima region was administered by the Jesuits on behalf of the Catholic Church—hence their seemingly disproportionate role in these events.

8. "Aftermath," 1985; see pp. 280*ff*.

9. Mary McCarthy got him completely wrong about this. Her criticisms (see pp. 144–45) included the notion that he treated the bomb "journalistically, in terms of measurable destruction" and that this was "in a sense, to deny its existence." But it's the U.S. authorities who are shown as doing this.

10. "Postscript" by Kiyoshi Tanimoto, sent to JH by Father Kleinsorge, B Box 37.

11. B Box 37.

12. The bank is now used as an exhibition space. For information on the safe makers, see "Herring-Hall-Marvin Safe Co.," Butler County (OH) Place Names, compiled by Jim Blount, https://sites.google.com/a/lanepl.org/butler/home/h/herring-hall-marvin-safe-co.

13. *H*, 106.

14. Wilfred Burchett, *Shadows of Hiroshima* (London: Verso and New Left Books, 1983).

15. B Box 29.

16. See pp. 280*ff.*

17. Hersey made a few changes in the manuscript, most of which involved adding descriptive detail. The only thing that gave him trouble was the title, which went from "EVENTS AT HIROSHIMA" to "ADVENTURES AT . . ." and "SOME EXPERIENCES AT . . ." before finally settling as "HIROSHIMA." "THE 'ORIGINAL CHILD' BOMB" was also considered. B Box 2.

18. I have silently corrected some Latin plant names mistyped in the original document.

19. *H*, 91.

20. In a much-misunderstood passage of *Heart of Darkness* the narrator says that as a boy he had thought of Africa as "a blank space of delightful mystery—a white patch [on a map] to dream gloriously over." Conrad, *Works*, Cambridge Edition: Owen Knowles, ed., *Youth, Heart of Darkness, The End of the Tether* (Cambridge: Cambridge University Press, 2010), 48.

21. *Life*, March 25, July 1, July 15, Aug. 12, Oct. 7, 1946. The event was also mentioned in other articles, for example *Life*, April 15, 1946.

22. The phrase was used by the journalist W. L. White in an article for the *Saturday Review of Literature*, Oct. 16, 1946, B Box 19.

23. Hersey wrote to her from his in-laws' home in Blowing Rock, North Carolina, telling the story: "The response has been wonderful. Quite a number of newspapers, British, Belgian and Swiss ones among them, have asked for permission to reprint the entire article. The American Broadcasting Company is going to read it . . . All these things the New Yorker and I favor, because what we want is the greatest possible number of readers, so that people will have the greatest possible understanding of what it's like to be under attack by atomic bombs." Sept. 4, 1946, B Box 18.

24. *Newsweek*, Sept. 9, 1946.

25. It was a running joke that Time-Life was a chapter of Skull and Bones. A tap on the shoulder is the society's traditional way of conveying an invitation to those chosen.

26. Memo to William Shawn from [William] McGuire, Aug. 30, 1946, *NY* Archive, NYPL.

27. Because the magazine had sold out, facsimiles were printed for Einstein. He had them circulated with a covering letter, dated Sept. 6, 1946, B Box 36:

> Dear Friend:
>
> I am enclosing for your attention a special facsimile reprint of the August 31st issue of *The New Yorker* magazine. This issue was devoted wholly to an article by John Hersey, the distinguished war-correspondent, based on weeks of careful interviews with citizens of Hiroshima who survived the atomic bomb.

I believe that Mr. Hersey has given a true picture of the appalling effect on human beings in a modern community subjected to the unprecedented destruction achieved by the explosion in their midst of one atomic bomb. And this picture has implications for the future of mankind which must deeply concern all responsible men and women. Faithfully yours,

A. Einstein

28. *Time*, Sep. 9, 1946, 50, "The Press."

29. The *New Yorker* Archive contains a sanguine letter from Hersey to Shawn about this, dated Aug. 1, 1946. The two magazines divided equally Hersey's expenses of $3,455.63. "They'll be galled at paying half of the Japan expenses," Hersey wrote, "but you're paying half the more costly expenses for the five or six weeks when I was working [*sic*] the village outside Peiping (and gathering background that made it possible to do the Kalgan village story quickly and cheaply....)." *NY* Archive Box 50. Full details of the deal are in B Box 28.

30. See, for example, B Box 39, especially correspondence between Hersey and the *New Yorker* accountant Harvey Truax, Dec. 20, 1946, Jan. 10, 1947, *NY* Archive Box 1315.

31. HRC Knopf Box 5.5; Feb. 5, 1947, B Box 24.

32. Letters from Yoko Matsuoka, for example, June 8, 1948, B Box 19, 1937–51, *M*.

33. B Box 32.

34. In October 1949. HRC Knopf Box 5.5. For financial comparisons, see http://www.measuringworth.com.

35. For Hersey's short stories, see pp. 290*ff.* "The Woman Who Took Gold Intravenously" and "In Touch" both appeared in *Cosmopolitan* in 1947. In the same year, Cyril Connolly asked Hersey for something for his magazine *Horizon* but seems to have rejected "Do You Like It Here?" B Box 28.

36. "A Short Wait," *NY*, June 14, 1947.

37. *NY*, Jan. 17, 24, 31, 1948.

38. *Politics*, Nov. 1946, p. 367, http://www.americainclass.org/wp-content/uploads/2013/03/mccarthy_onhiroshima.pdf, accessed Aug. 17, 2016.

39. Hersey never forgot this visceral attack and was reminded of it decades later when McCarthy quarreled with his friend Lillian Hellman. See pp. 279–80.

40. The paradoxes are as old, as various, as simple, and as complicated as storytelling itself. Truth matters so much that one of the standard claims of fiction is that its inventions are true. Yet strangeness is so compelling that we often want it more than truth—we are drawn to things "stranger than fiction." Part of both cravings, for the true and for the new, is a need to be told about terrible things: as a way of arming ourselves against them, perhaps, or to assuage feelings of guilt by imaginatively encountering evils much worse than we have committed, or to remind ourselves to do better. The more terrible the stories, the higher we esteem them. McCarthy's point, that those who really know the worst truths about the most terrible things do not survive to tell their stories, was badly put but is important. "I

only am escaped alone to tell thee," a biblical messenger tells Job, and if the repetition of "only . . . alone" reinforces the story's urgency, it also helps undermine its own truth-claim: if no one else escaped (which in this case itself turns out to be false), how can the tale's details be verified? (In the book of Job 1:15, four people come individually to Job to describe the slaughter and/or abduction of Job's family, servants, and/or livestock. Each story is different, not least about who or what brought the event to pass: the Sabeans according to the first; divine fire according to the second; the Chaldeans, the next says; a hurricane, the next. What all have in common is the speaker's sense of being the unique survivor.)

Most artists, and those who believe in the value of artists' work, make a claim that answers the witness problem but at the cost of forfeiting "authenticity." One way or another, it's said, whether through imagination or representational skill, artists can communicate truth more powerfully than other people—perhaps even more powerfully (though artists themselves are naturally cautious about claiming this) than people with empirical knowledge. Even if the claim doesn't go this far, it's clear that to deny imaginative access to literal truths would be to prevent the imaginative retelling of factual events in subsequent eras. In any case, speaking practically, writers often admit to having invented before they researched.

41. See, for example, Michael Yavenditti, "John Hersey and the American Conscience," *Pacific Historical Review* 43 (1974): 48.

42. Alfred Knopf to JH, Sept. 19, 1946, HRC Knopf Box 5.5. Hersey replied to Knopf, "I thought I had been at great pains to keep the tone of guilt about using the bomb at a minimum . . . But for the Germans, maybe."

43. For example at Washington and Jefferson College, where his fellow honorees included Senator J. William Fulbright and the literary scholar Christian Gauss. Cutting dated Oct. 26, 1846, B Box 19 W.

44. Circular from the War Department, Oct. 10, 1945, B Box 19.

45. Yoko Matsuoka, later McClain, was then in her early twenties. She lived in Tokyo throughout the war and translated for the Americans during the occupation, including for Hersey while he was in Japan. Soon after the *New Yorker* issue containing *Hiroshima* appeared, she wrote proposing herself as its translator and agent there. She subsequently studied and taught in the United States. April n.d., 1946, B Box 24; Sept. 17, 1946, B Box 19.

46. See the letter from "Berry," below: "When Nora Wain [the *Saturday Evening Post*'s Tokyo correspondent from 1947 to 1951] was received by MacArthur when she first arrived the Great Man told her that if she were, in her stay in Japan, 'to write just one book as fine as Hiroshima,' her stay would have been a success. He described Hiroshima, on several occasions in his talks with her, as the finest piece of writing done so far on Japan . . . as 'great' and 'superior' and 'classic.'"

47. This letter, dated Feb. 19, n.y. [1949?], is in B Box 37, which also contains one to Hersey from William Koshland at Knopf dated Feb. 9, 1949, drawing attention to MacArthur's claim. Two days later, an officious communication was sent by GHQ

about the legalities of passing on yen earnings. The cuts are referred to in an earlier letter from Yoko Matsuoka dated Oct. 20, 1948. Other correspondence about this is to be found in B Box 24.

48. Yoko Matsuoka to Hersey, Feb. 19, 1947, B Box 24.
49. July 7, 1948, B Box 24.
50. T. Aijima from Hosei University Press to JH, May 13, 1949, B Box 37.

7. Listening to the Dead

1. Nov. 20, 1947, B Box 37.
2. See p. 160.
3. Unidentified newspaper cuttings in B Box 19, 1937–51, *E* and *F*.
4. May 19, 1947, *NY* Archive Box 50.
5. On Turkey Hill Road. B Box 24.
6. *AP*, 3.
7. See E. J. Kahn, Jr., "The Children's Friend," an article on Dr. Seuss (Theodor Seuss Geisel), *NY*, Dec. 17, 1960.
8. For example, in 1948, JH to Grace Hersey, March 7, May 10, July 16, Nov. 12; in 1949, July 5, Aug. 2, Sept. 5, B Box 18.
9. JH to Grace Hersey, Feb. 5, 1953, B Box 18.
10. March 14, 1946, B Box 23.
11. Correspondence about the magazine appears in B Boxes 18 and 19, 1937–51, *S*.
12. "A Fable South of Cancer"; see Sanders, *John Hersey Revisited*, 35–36.
13. "Slightly out of Focus." The article appeared in September 1947 and was reprinted in *LS*, 143f.
14. Arnold Rampersad, *Ralph Ellison: A Biography* (New York: Knopf, 2007), 216. '47 paid ten cents a word, and the excerpt was 5,600 words long, so this was the most Ellison had ever received for a story. The magazine asked for some cuts: "The tattoo of the American flag above the white woman's crotch seemed excessive." Also deleted was "the erection which projected from" the biggest of the black boys in response to her.
15. "Is a man of any use against an avalanche?" Hersey wrote. "What can an ordinary citizen do against what he believes to be a trend towards war? Can he do anything but defend himself with tremendously thick battlements of apathy? Higher up on the mountain, right now, there are sounds of boulders sliding: what should one man do alone?" B Box 29, *M*.
16. *Collier's*, March 29, April 5, 12, 1947. By his own standards somewhat thin, though it has interesting things to say about Marshall's failure to support the liberals in China, the profile hasn't been reprinted. In being about someone who "had a very high code, and . . . always lived up to it," it is among Hersey's many attempts to depict moral heroes.
17. Blue pencil note on a carbon copy of a letter from Harold Ross to [Gustave] Lobrano,

Jan. 10, 1947. See also a more decisive memo from Roger Angell, Jan. 19, 1947, and Shawn's diplomatic letter to JH of Feb. 9, 1959, *NY* Archive Box 50.

18. See p. 144.

19. He resumed the attack as soon as *The Wall* was finished, with topics including killings of and by police in prohibition Kentucky and a radioactive "Bikini cloud" supposedly floating around the world. Harold Ross to JH, July 5, 1949, B Box 19, 1937–51, S.

20. JH to Grace Hersey, Feb. 2, 1948, B Box 18.

21. Hersey's notes fill B Box 49.

22. He sent a book on the subject with his thank-you letter. Aug. 31, 1948, B Box 36.

23. By an academic psychologist, David Boder, in 1946.

24. JH to Grace Hersey, Feb. 5, 1949, B Box 18.

25. The text of the talk, "How THE WALL Came to be Written," delivered on Dec. 13, 1949, is in B Box 32.

26. This is a huge debate, ably summarized by, among many others, Anna Richardson in "The Ethical Limitations of Holocaust Literary Representation," https://www .gla.ac.uk/media/media_41171_en.pdf, accessed April 20, 2017.

27. The various versions are in B Boxes 3, 35, 36, and 43.

28. Dec. 9, 1948, B Box 24.

29. Leslie Fiedler in particular—see pp. 166*ff.*

30. Hersey's different versions of the process are the same in terms of fact but differ in interpretation. In the last of them, an unpublished 1984 talk titled "The Need for Memory," he introduces more-sophisticated ideas about narrative point of view, and Sanders gives special credit to these as products of mature reflection (Sanders, *John Hersey Revisited*, 26). But Hersey's immediate concerns at Knopf's 1949 sales meeting were surely truer to the experience he had just been through, and these are what I draw on here.

31. Cc (almost certainly from Pat Knopf), Nov. 28, 1949, HRC Knopf Box 49.5.

32. The book had appeared in Dutch in 1947. Knopf's reader in this case was a Mrs. Ernest Wiener. Her report, dated July 17, 1950, describes the "unusual circumstances" in which the diary was written but doesn't mention the author's fate. The narrative makes "very dull reading," she says. "Even if the work had come to light five years ago, when the subject was timely, I don't see that there would have been a chance for it." Thanks to the initiative of Judith Jones (see p. 273), Doubleday took the gamble in 1952. HRC Knopf.

33. See discussion of Hersey's *The War Lover*, pp. 199*ff.*

34. The group had the code name Oyneg Shabes (Sabbath Delight).

35. I draw here on Samuel D. Kassow's introduction to *Warsaw Ghetto Oyneg Shabes-Ringelblum Archive, Catalogue and Guide*, ed. Robert Moses Shapiro and Tadeusz Epzstein (Bloomington, IN, 2009).

36. New York: Roy Publishers. Kassow mentions a later, fuller edition (New York: Duell, Sloan and Pearce, 1946).

37. Kassow, introduction to *Warsaw Ghetto*, notes 2, 24, 39.

38. Among them Joseph Kermish, ed., *To Live with Honor and Die with Honor: Selected Documents from the Warsaw Ghetto Underground Archives Oyneg Shabbath* (Jerusalem: Yad Vashem, 1986).

39. See n. 36, above.

40. *Wall*, 556–60.

41. Ibid., 579–81.

42. Ibid., 582.

43. Ibid., 547.

44. "Universality" is itself, of course, a fraught term in this context. The Nazi extermination program, though not restricted to Jews, was overwhelmingly targeted against them. And whether or not "universality" denies this specificity, it clearly invites one to look beyond it—or even to overlook it. Concern about whether a movie version of *The Wall* might be "too Jewish" in appeal was one of the issues that bothered David Selznick—see p. 162.

45. Personal letter from Gollancz, Nov. 23, 1949, and earlier letter from Laurence Pollinger at Pearn, Pollinger and Higham to Elizabeth Otis, Nov. 2, 1949, B Box 27. Victor Gollancz's publication of *Adano* had been predictably held up by postwar paper shortages in the U.K. Hamish Hamilton claimed unfair dealing, saying he had wanted to do the book but hadn't offered because of the paper situation, and was "disgusted" that Gollancz, having secured the rights, held up publication "by two years." B Box 19, 1937–51, *H*.

46. JH to Grace Hersey, Dec. 30, 1949, B Box 18.

47. James Thurber to JH, Jan. 28, 1950, B Box 19, 1937–51, *T*. Hamilton had been Thurber's U.K. publisher since 1943.

48. Polish producer Lazar Wechsler. See p. 164.

49. *Herald Tribune*, Feb. 26, 1950.

50. When Gerald Reitlinger's history *The Final Solution* appeared in 1953, Max Beloff wrote in the *Jewish Chronicle* that although there was ample evidence of the existence of Hitler's death camps, "public opinion outside Jewry nowhere accepts the fact." Quoted in Hilary Spurling, *Anthony Powell* (London: Hamish Hamilton, 2017), 322.

51. *NY*, March 4, 1950.

52. I wish I had known about this essay in 1991, when Kazin, whose work I admire and with whom I was lucky enough to have become friendly, to my astonishment took the line that Martin Amis should not have written *Time's Arrow*, a novel about Auschwitz, "because he wasn't there." I produced the usual counterarguments, especially that fiction simply couldn't exist under such conditions, and teased Alfred that, anyway, by his own admission he hadn't read the book he deplored: What would Professor Kazin have said to a student who took such a stance? But he was unteasable, testily unpersuadable.

53. Cables from J. E. Fontaine and John T. Howard, both March 9, 1950, Selznick Archive, HRC.

54. JH to Selznick, June 26, 1950, HRC Selznick.

55. Selznick internal memo to Dan O'Shea, Feb. 27, 1950, HRC Selznick.
56. *Morning Faces*. O'Shea, May 23, 1950, HRC Selznick.
57. For example, Selznick memo to Earl Beaman, Nov. 16, 1950, HRC Selznick.
58. Selznick to Louis Stone, June 20, 1950, HRC Selznick.
59. A copy of this letter is in B Box 27.
60. See Smithsonian Folkways, *Songs from* The Wall: *The Play About the Warsaw Ghetto Uprising: Ghetto, Partisan, Folk and Love Songs*, http://www.folkways.si .edu/songs-from-the-wall-the-play-about-the-warsaw-ghetto-uprising-ghetto -partisan-folk-and-love-songs/drama-judaica/album/smithsonian, accessed February 1, 2016. The stage text was published under Hersey's and Lampell's joint names by Random House in 1961. For casting and other details, see "John Hersey," Internet Broadway Database, https://www.ibdb.com/broadway-cast-staff/john -hersey-10012.
61. Philip Roth is among those who found Selznick's version of Hemingway's novel "embarrassing." *New Republic*, Feb. 17, 1958.
62. *NYT*, Oct. 12, 1960. *The New Yorker*'s John McCarten didn't share Taubman's admiration, though he found Yvonne Mitchell "authoritative . . . even when the lines Mr. Lampell has provided are too literary to be entirely plausible." *NY*, Oct. 22, 1960. Neither reviewer mentioned the music.
63. See pp. 179*ff*.
64. For a history of the magazine and its place in post–World War II U.S. culture and politics, see Benjamin Balint, *Running Commentary: The Contentious Magazine That Transformed the Jewish Left into the Neoconservative Right* (New York: Public Affairs, 2010). Balint doesn't mention the small saga about *The Wall*; the relevant papers are in the *Commentary* archives at HRC Box 131.5.
65. The son of an Edinburgh rabbi, Daiches had worked for the British Information Service in Washington during World War II. At the time of his Hersey review, his books included *Literature and Society* (1938).
66. *Commentary*, October 1950.
67. "Straddling the Wall," in Leslie Fiedler, *Collected Essays*, vol. 2 (New York: Stein and Day, 1971), 36–40.
68. Fiedler acknowledged in his letter that Kristol had done his best to mollify him about the original decision, but he argued that a magazine had an obligation to publish what it had commissioned and said that generally he sensed that it was becoming "more and more difficult for [him] to get on with *Commentary*." Feb. 27, 1950, *Commentary* Archive, HRC 131.5.
69. Fiedler wrote to Kristol, "I hope you'll understand & forgive my using some of your remarks, more or less distorted, in the mouth of the *Kibbitzer*."
70. Individuals are identifiable from their initials with the help of Benjamin Balint's history of the magazine; see n. 65, above. A weary note to Kristol from the editor in chief, Elliot Cohen, says that the magazine "will have to come to some decision on this." It's unclear whether or not Cohen was behind the second rejection—indeed, whether or not any such decision was ever firmly taken.

71. Publicity for Hamish Hamilton's U.K. edition. To Hamilton's disappointment, it sold only seventeen thousand copies, though he said this was "a remarkable performance for a 15/- [fifteen-shilling] novel in present conditions here." Jamie Hamilton to JH, Jan. 8, 1951, B Box 24.

72. Martha Gellhorn tls to "Mr. Hersey," May 5, [1950], B Box 36.

73. J. Michael Lennon, ed., *Selected Letters of Norman Mailer* (New York: Random House), 244.

74. Sept. 14, 1950, B Box 36.

75. June 20, 1950, B Box 19, 1937–51.

76. April 24, 1951, B Box 19, 1937–51.

77. B Box 19, 1937–51, *K*.

78. In 1949. B Box 19.

79. In 1952. B Box 27.

8. Mr. Straight Arrow

1. June 1951, B Box 32.

2. See Geoffrey M. Kabaservice, *The Guardians: Kingman Brewster, His Circle, and the Rise of the Liberal Establishment* (New York: Holt, 2004), 138–39.

3. David McCullough, *Truman*, ch. 16, "Commander in Chief."

4. "A Day at Saratoga," *NY*, Jan. 3, 1948; *LS*, 166.

5. *AP*, 6.

6. July 16, 1945, McCullough, *Truman*, ch. 10, "Summer of Decision."

7. At a secret meeting on April 25, 1945.

8. This meeting, on June 18, 1945, discussed every means except the still-secret A-bomb.

9. G.E.M. Anscombe, "Mr. Truman's Degree," Oxford, 1958.

10. *AP*, 54.

11. Ibid., 4.

12. Stephen Spender, "The Truly Great," *Collected Poems 1928–53* (London: Faber & Faber, 1955).

13. For book publication in *AP*, Hersey wrote a foreword from which some of the information here is drawn.

14. Technically, the war was between North and South Korea, but within days the United Nations, in the form of an American unit, had intervened on behalf of the South, and General MacArthur had taken command of that country's defense. The North Korean army was Soviet trained and equipped, and many of its troops had fought in the Chinese Civil War under Mao. China itself became directly involved in October 1950.

15. *AP*, 27. A successful UN offensive the previous month had taken American troops across the thirty-eighth parallel into North Korea and, by definition, toward the Chinese border. China retaliated in two waves starting in late October. A UN offensive

across the entire front, Operation Home By Christmas, collided with the second Chinese wave and was driven back in what became the longest retreat in U.S. history.

16. In the magazine serialization, this was the first installment; the meeting came second.

17. In his preface to *Plutarch's Lives, Translated from the Greek by Several Hands*, 1683.

18. See pp. 266*ff.*

19. April 13, 1951. I'm grateful to Leo Robson for drawing this letter to my attention.

20. *AP*, ix.

21. April 21, 1949, B Box 19.

22. Christopher Bigsby, *Arthur Miller*, vol. 2 (London: Weidenfeld & Nicolson, 2011), 279. The apartment was the journalist Jack Goodman's.

23. *AP*, 136–38.

24. See pp. 188, 190.

25. See, by contrast, his article on the next Israeli generation, pp. 264*ff.*

26. Amos 9:15.

27. JH to William Koshland at Knopf, Dec. 4, 1953, Oct. 15, 1954, Dec. 7, 1954, Knopf, HRC Knopf 130.6.

28. July 26, 1958, HRC Knopf.

29. JH to Grace Hersey, Sept. 5, 1950, B Box 18.

30. See pp. 276*ff.*

31. See pp. 192*ff.*

32. Nov. 11, 1954, and n.d., B Box 19, 1952–63, *G.*

33. "Surely the provocation to drink that was faced by Melville, James, Twain, and other leading figures of the nineteenth century was as great as any we face today," Gill mused, "but none of them drank too much and most of us do. It is a mystery." *Here at The New Yorker* (New York: Da Capo Press, 1975,1995 ed.), 260.

34. *John Hersey*, memorial tributes, 39–41.

35. JH to Grace Hersey, June 14, 1953, B Box 18.

36. JH to Grace Hersey, Aug. 12, Sept. 16, 1954. The magazine was *Home and Garden*.

37. Draft B Box 18.

38. JH from the Algonquin Hotel to Grace Hersey, Feb. 19, 1957, B Box 18.

39. In his article about Hungary; see p. 191.

40. Hersey also wrote the foreword for a pictorial biography of Stevenson. See Porter McKeever, *Adlai Stevenson: His Life and Legacy* (New York: Morrow, 1989), 210; and John Bartlow Martin, *Adlai Stevenson of Illinois* (Garden City, N.Y.: Doubleday, 1976), 622.

41. Hersey himself regretted that Stevenson's lack of "the common touch" made him unable "to reach all levels of society." Jean H. Baker, *The Stevensons: A Biography of an American Family* (New York: Norton, 1996), 320.

42. JH to Alfred Knopf, Dec. 3, 1953, HRC Knopf 130.6.

43. Guy E. Snavely of USIA to JH, Sept. 21, 1954, B Box 19, 1952–63, *S.*

44. JH to his parents, Sept. 27, 1936, B FP Box 2. Conant, he added, was "very gracious, very young, very tired."

45. These journeys were recounted to his mother, for example, in a letter from the Hilton Hotel, Albuquerque, Feb. 24, 1915, B Box 18.

46. Interview with Kay Bonetti for the American Audio Prose Library, 1988.

47. *CB*; see pp. 205*ff*. Two novels, in fact; the Stradivarius prompted *Antonietta*; see p. 277*ff*.

48. Kissinger's letter was sent on Jan. 10, 1957, B Box 20, 1952–63, *R*. Hersey became a trustee of Putney School, Vermont, in 1953.

49. JH to Grace Hersey, Oct. 16, 1956, B Box 18; see also B Box 56, and David Sanders, *John Hersey Revisited*, 37.

50. July 11, 1956. *The Papers of Adlai Stevenson*, vol. 6, *Toward a New America, 1955–57*, ed. Walter Johnson (Boston: Little, Brown, 1976), 167–68. *The War Lover* appeared without any apparent delay in 1959.

51. *Papers of Adlai Stevenson*. Hersey evidently accepted the invitation, since his letter to his mother about his involvement (n. 49, above) is dated mid-October.

52. The schedule is described in Rampersad, *Ralph Ellison*, 433, n. 14, 327–29.

53. A poorly censored copy of a letter dated Oct. 11, 1956, to the founding director of the FBI, J. Edgar Hoover, reached Arthur Schlesinger, who forwarded it to Hersey. The letter claimed that as presidential candidate, Adlai Stevenson had surrounded himself with pro-Communist speechwriters, naming Hersey, Schlesinger, and J. K. Galbraith. The main charges made against Hersey were that he had been a trustee of the Institute of Pacific Relations, which had been accused by a Senate judiciary committee of being "a vehicle for Kremlin policies"; that he had been "in contact with" unnamed Soviet and Chinese Communist agents; that he had "supported the convicted reds in Hollywood who were jailed for refusing to testify"; and that he had attended a Moscow event held to discuss his "contribution to 'literature.'" B Box 23, *S*. In 1959, when colleagues in Eastern Europe sent him unsolicited materials, their letters were held up by the FBI: June 11, 1959, B Box 19, 1952–63, *B*.

54. Describing a former Nazi military base at Traiskirchen, south of Vienna, that was turned into a refugee camp, Hersey mentions "a huge waste of furniture that had once been requisitioned for military use and was supposed to be awaiting return to its myriad owners." Who these owners had been and for what reason and by what processes their furniture had been "requisitioned" are among the questions the article glides over. *HS*, 68–69.

55. *MD*, 107.

56. *SP*, 102.

57. See Sanders, *John Hersey Revisited*, 43.

58. Ibid., 48.

59. "I wrote a long compendium—hotels, motor courts, where to buy ranch pants for Blanche, what to see, etc., etc. I wrote to Newt Drury about him." Drury was director of the National Parks Service of the Department of the Interior. ("Alfred A. Knopf," privately printed 1952, reprinted in *LS*, 188–205.)

60. "Over the Mad River," *NY*, Nov. 17, 1955, reprinted in *LS*, 254–81.

61. "A Game on a Hill," *NY*, Dec. 7, 1957.

62. See pp. 127*ff.*

63. Clinton in private to Strobe Talbott during the 1996 Moscow summit, as reported by Evan Osnos, David Remnick, and Joshua Yaffa, "Active Measures," *NY*, March 6, 2017.

64. *NYT*, June 4, 1958.

65. For this and other information here, I have drawn on Brook Hersey's memorial tribute to her mother, "Barbara Hersey: July 17, 1919–August 17, 2007," given in Key West.

66. Gardner Botsford, interviewed by Linda H. Davis for her biography *Chas Addams: A Cartoonist's Life* (New York: Random House, 2006), 106.

67. Hersey later recounted the occasion in lightly fictionalized form as "The Announcement," *Fling*, 81–101. It appears there as a Thanksgiving dinner, but his letters suggest that the first visit he and Barbara made together to Briarcliff was for Grace's birthday: March 3, 1958, B Box 18.

68. Dec. 6, 1959, B Box 20, *S*.

9. Those Breakthroughs I Yearn For

1. See pp. 236*ff.*

2. See p. 70.

3. *WL*, 382.

4. Ibid., 28.

5. See below, n. 7.

6. *WL*, 156.

7. Snowden's death haunts Yossarian as Lynch's does Boman, in both cases forming a recurring element in the narrative (though Hersey doesn't attempt the remorseless unpeeling of the story that gives *Catch-22* part of its structure, as well as its tragic center). But the eventual revelation of what passed between Yossarian and Snowden is anticipated, in Boman's case, by the death of Max.

8. March 3, 1958, B Box 38.

9. April 11, 1958, B Box 38.

10. An exception among reviewers was the editor of *Air Force Magazine*, Captain Frank W. Andersen, a former literary academic who read the novel as a "preachy" attack on war rather than an attempt to understand its attractions, and who wasn't convinced by the characters. Andersen was sensitive, though, to the fact that Boman is young and that the book is about an enforced, exceptionally painful phase in his development. *Air Force Magazine*, Dec. 1959, B Box 38.

11. From Irwin and Marian Shaw in Paris, Nov. 5, 1959, B Box 20.

12. A translation of the review is in B Box 38.

13. The characteristically voluminous relevant memos and correspondence are in the Selznick Archive, HRC.

14. In *The Wall* and *Adano*. These details—for the year 1958—come from correspondence with the McIntosh & Otis agency, B Box 27.

15. In 1958 the latter included republication of his Kennedy article "Survivor" and an Urdu version of *Adano* transmitted by the BBC World Service.

16. But see the new last part of *Hiroshima*, pp. 280*ff.*, and *Manzanar*, pp. 282*ff.*

17. There must, though, have been black servants at Frances Ann's family's home in Blowing Rock, and the Cannons, who had been growing cotton in the South since the early eighteenth century, could not originally have done so without slaves.

18. Especially in his article about Private John Daniel Rame, "The Brilliant Jughead," *NY*, July 28, 1945.

19. "Intelligence, Choice and Consent," in the Woodrow Wilson Foundation series *Education in the Nation's Service: A Series of Articles on American Education Today*, 1959. The article was reprinted as "Janet Train" in *LS*, 206–28.

20. The phrase was used by Wilson in his inaugural address as president of Princeton University, October 1902. He became president of the United States eleven years later.

21. March 5, 1959, from Tom Mendenhall, master of Berkeley College, Yale, inviting him to be Hoyt lecturer; April 18, 1959, regarding the arrangements. Letters concerning JH's interests in education include those from Agnes Meyer on behalf of the National Committee for the Support of Public Schools. For the Yale committee, see Tom Mendenhall from Smith College. These are in B Box 20, 1952–63.

22. A similar but more circumscribed hope would be expressed by Eleanor Roosevelt in her posthumously published *Tomorrow Is Now* (1963): "With proper education . . . we may justly anticipate that the life of the next generation will be richer, more peaceful, more rewarding than any we have ever known."

23. *New Republic*, Oct. 10, 1960.

24. March 24, 1961, Nov. 1, 1967. BBC Radio's Third Programme, as it was then called, broadcast its version on May 15, 1962. B Boxes 27 and 39.

25. Feb. 2, 1960, B Box 18.

26. In her memorial tribute, Brook Hersey describes how her mother's ability to make friends and connect with people helped her father, "more reserved by nature, to have a rich social life."

27. Jan. 25, 1960, B Box 18.

28. Nov. 1, 1960, B Box 19.

29. For example, April 19, 1964, from Arthur Hersey to JH, B Box 18.

30. JH to Grace Hersey, Feb. 17, 1964, B Box 18. Six years earlier he had cracked a vertebra: JH als to Morris Leopold Ernst (founder of the American Civil Liberties Union), Nov. 10, 1958, HRC.

31. June 5, 11, 26, July 25, Aug. 29, 1963, B Box 20, *N–O*.

32. Sept. 18, 1962, B Box 20, 1952–63.

33. Syracuse, his parents' university, had made a similar request in 1963: Box 20, 1963–66, S. In 1964, in response to the Library of Congress, Hersey half offered the manuscripts of *Men on Bataan* and *Into the Valley*, but learning that other

materials had gone to Yale, the library took the view that it was best to keep everything in one place. B Box 20, 1963–66, L.

34. May 14, 1964, B Box 20, 1963–66, W.

35. In the United States at that time copyright lasted twenty-eight years from the date of publication, as compared with the much more favorable Western European period of the duration of the author's life plus fifty years. B Box 20, 1952–63, S, various letters May–June 1962; letter from Lewis Mumford Feb. 8, 1963, B Box. 20, 1952–63, M. The administration's response was less than he hoped for—indeed Hersey described it as "a slap in the face." He was more accustomed, these days, to the responsive tone taken by Adlai Stevenson, who had assured him a few years earlier that he thought he was achieving some results in his dealings with the Soviet authorities over copyright in U.S. works. Nov. 28, 1958, B Box 20, 1952–63, S.

36. Feb. 5, 1963, Barney Rosset of Grove Press, B Box 20, 1952–63, R. Originally published in France in 1934, the book had been reissued by Grove Press in 1961. Lawsuits were brought against it in twenty-one states. Though procedurally very different, the situation in terms of social morality replicated that in Great Britain a few years earlier over D. H. Lawrence's *Lady Chatterley's Lover*.

37. June 28, 1963, B Box 20, 1952–63, XYZ.

38. See ch. 10, "The Master."

39. New York: Scholastic Books, 1963. The other items were about Guadalcanal, "Nine Men on a Four-Man Raft" (see pp. 69–70), "*Borie*'s Last Battle," and "Front Seats at Sea War."

40. "For one brief shining moment there was Camelot," White wrote in *Life*, Dec. 6, 1963, two weeks after the assassination.

41. Jan. 10, 1964, B Box 20.

42. In spring 1965.

43. "Our Romance with Poverty," *American Scholar* 33, no. 4 (Autumn 1964): 530.

44. Ibid., 525.

45. Ibid., 526.

46. Ibid., 531.

47. Author's note accompanying a reprint of the *Post* article in *LS*, 282. Here the article is headed "Varsell Pleas," the pseudonym that Hersey gave at the time to Norman Clark. In the *Post* the heading was "To Whom a Vote Is Worth a Life, " *Saturday Evening Post*, Sept. 26, 1964.

48. For 1964 he declared earnings of $68,836.65 before paying commissions, professional expenses, and other exempt items. Box 32. The comparative figures are drawn from U.S. Bureau of the Census, Current Population Reports, Series P-60, No. 51, "Income of Families and Persons in the United States: Census—1963," https://www2.census.gov/prod2/popscan/p60-043.pdf, accessed Dec. 6, 2016.

49. *Life*, Sept. 4, 1964.

50. It is included in the Library of America's anthology *Reporting Civil Rights: Part Two, American Journalism 1963–1973*, ed. Clayborne Carson (2003), 197*ff*.

51. *LS*, 284–85.

52. Ibid., 288.
53. Ibid., 304.
54. Along with Rachel in *The Wall*, Hester in *The Marmot Drive*, Daphne in *The War Lover*, and later Elaine in *The Walnut Door*.
55. Sanders, *John Hersey Revisited*, 65.
56. *Lotus*, 56, 70.
57. Ibid. 210. Earlier (actually later, chronologically speaking, but it's in the prologue, so it sets the tone), White Lotus tells us this:

> Yes, I have come to take fear of open cruelty for granted, I have learned how to stifle that fear, to push it down. But it is harder for me to deal with covert cruelty, implicit cruelty—with the massively threatening conditions of life that the yellows have imposed on us: the oppressive fitness, in the yellow scheme of things, of the conversion of the Peking cattle pens to a jail, where white men waited for capricious sentences with equanimity, betting on cricket fights; the rage and hunger that drove young men in Up-from-the-Sea [Shanghai] to become "sweepers," stabbing rice bags on street carts and brushing up the spilled rice on the dung-dusty pavement and racing off with it. It is the generality of our existence that has filled me with a dread I don't know how to subdue. Not the specific bamboo blow, but rather the great accumulation of affronts, the taking of their total for granted, even as the conditions of life "improve"—this is what is intolerable, because this seems to us whites to get worse, not better.

It's obvious what doesn't work here, and not difficult to show how it can be made to sound right—for example by changing some details so that it becomes what it actually is: a civil rights speech by a white American. "Yes, the Negro has come to take fear of open cruelty for granted, he has learned how to stifle that fear, to push it down. But it is harder for him to deal with covert cruelty, implicit cruelty—with the massively threatening conditions of life that we Whites have imposed on him," etc.

58. Ibid., 670.
59. Dogtooth's story of Peace's rebellion and White Lotus's memories of it. *Lotus*, 622.
60. Hersey used the 1952 edition. Named after a great African American educator, John Hope Franklin was a contemporary of Ralph Ellison (like him, from Oklahoma) who, having come up through a segregated school and Fisk, historically a black university, went to Harvard in the late 1930s, majored in history, and became prominent in Phi Beta Kappa. When the United States entered the Second World War, Franklin tried to enlist but was rejected on racial grounds. The first black person to hold a major American chair of history, he was visiting professor of American history and institutions at Cambridge (England) in 1962 and taught at Chicago from 1964: a tumultuous time to have gone there.
61. A pirated edition appeared in Taiwan in 1970.
62. Sanders himself and also, mentioned by him, Nancy Lyman Huse and Samuel B. Girgus; see Sanders, *John Hersey Revisited*, 70–71, 114.

63. *TLS*, July 8, 1965.
64. Knopf to JH, Feb. 5, 1956, HRC Knopf 411.2.
65. O'Hara quoted by JH in letter to Alfred Knopf, Feb. 3, 1965, HRC Knopf 411.2.
66. JH to Alfred Knopf; see n. 65, above.
67. JH to Alfred Knopf, May 7, 1965, HRC Knopf 411.2. The review began, "It's too bad about John Hersey . . . He longed to write great novels that would endure for centuries; he has written magnificent volumes of journalism that make the Book of the Month Club." *Time*, Jan. 29, 1965.
68. In an exchange about the reception of *The Marmot Drive*, for example, Strauss volunteered various retrospective criticisms of how Hersey handled Hester's boyfriend Eben: "It is not so much that he is a weak character as that he is weakly drawn . . . Perhaps it is [this], and the consequent misconception of Hester's relationship to him, that led so many reviewers to misunderstand Hester's behavior." Dec. 21, 1953, HRC Knopf 86.2.
69. JH's als reply Dec. 23, 1953, to Harold Strauss's letter, n. 68, above, HRC Knopf 86.2.
70. Alfred Knopf note on memo from William K[oshland], Aug. 8, 1958, HRC Knopf 86.2.
71. Letter from JH to Sam Girgus, Feb. 8, 1972, quoted in a letter from JH to Nancy Lyman Huse, Oct. 27, 1973, B Box 22, 1970–73, *HIJ*. Girgus later became an academic specializing in American literature and popular culture.
72. To Nancy Lyman Huse; see n. 71, above. It's worth pointing out that his books were always accessible in public libraries—often prominently displayed by librarians who had read and liked them. And he was one of the few serious authors whose works, in his case especially *A Single Pebble*, were often recommended as suitable for book reports in middle schools and high schools.
73. David Bromwich suggests (private communication) that *Too Far to Walk* may have been influenced by John Updike's 1963 college novel *The Centaur*, which also involves a male adolescent hero in a story that, while essentially realistic, has "overlays of myth." Updike was another Knopf author. *The Centaur* won the National Book Award.
74. *TFW*, 243.

10. The Master

1. This chapter draws on Geoffrey M. Kabaservice, *The Guardians: Kingman Brewster, His Circle, and the Rise of the Liberal Establishment* (New York: Holt, 2004); and on Kessler, "John Hersey's Yale Education."
2. Program for the White House Festival of the Arts, June 14, 1965, B Box 32.
3. See p. 229.
4. Don McKinney of *The Saturday Evening Post* to JH, June 8, 1965, B Box 20, 1963–66, S. The magazine wanted an on-the-spot article about "the American fighting man."

5. The word "master," or (Latin) *magister*, for the head of a school or college, was common in the Renaissance and survives at Oxbridge but in 2016 was discontinued at Yale, after a similar decision at Harvard.

6. Kessler, "John Hersey's Yale Education."

7. G. S. Mustin to Kingman Brewster, June 21, 1965, Beinecke KBR, Box 204, quoted by Kessler, "John Hersey's Yale Education," 28. For Mustin's career, see, for example, his coauthored article "Prevention of Corrosion in Naval Aircraft," *Corrosion* 7, no. 11 (November 1951), http://corrosionjournal.org/doi/abs/10.5006/0010 -9312-7.11.377?code=nace-prem-site.

8. Hand-corrected typescript of installation address, B Box 21, 1963–66, *Y*. It's worth noting that while Kingman Brewster defended critics of the war on his staff as well as among the student body, he himself remained neutral on the issue. When Coffin reproached him with this, he explained his reasoning persuasively: "I have not had a confident notion about what I would do tomorrow morning at nine o'clock if I had responsibility for U.S. policy. Until I do have such a confident notion, I do not find it appealing simply to say that war is horrible or that peace is desirable." Kabaservice, *The Guardians*, 258.

9. *Shadow and Act*, 1964.

10. The aide-mémoire is dated December 8, 1965. B Box 45. The chair of English at the time was Maynard Mack, a great scholar, a conservative, and—as it proved— flexible enough to commission Hersey, a decade later, to edit a book of essays on Ellison for an academic series he ran.

11. See *WC*, 267–82.

12. Sept. 12, 1966, B Box 21, 1963–66.

13. Kessler, "John Hersey's Yale Education."

14. "I know already, by the way, that I'm going to be able to carry on my own work full-steam here; I have a well-protected upstairs study and long mornings (8 a.m.-12:30) at my desk with no interruptions at all." JH als to Harold Strauss, Sept. 27, 1965, HRC Knopf.

15. In the same letter, n. 14, above, JH told Harold Strauss he would be delivering the typescript of the novel "in a day or two" and expressed his concern that people might think it was about his Yale students.

16. *The War Lover* is retrospectively told by the copilot, whereas *Under the Eye* has a third-person narrator.

17. *UES*, 182.

18. Ibid., 161.

19. It was a widely held view, but, as in many other parts of the world, the most lasting aspects of the renewal were highways.

20. Kabaservice, *The Guardians*, 250.

21. Nov. 18, 1965, B Box 25.

22. Dec. 1, 1965, B Box 27.

23. Hellman's thirty-year relationship with Dashiell Hammett, to call which difficult would be like calling the labors of Hercules trying, ended with his death in

1961. Peter Feibleman, who had sent Hellman a letter when he was an abused ten-year-old, and first met her in his teens, was at another low point in his life when he went to the Vineyard at her invitation. He became an increasingly frequent visitor and, after her death in 1984, inherited the house she had built in 1961–62 in the grounds of the large place she and Hammett had shared. Oddly, neither Feibleman nor Hellman is mentioned in the other's entry in Wikipedia, at least at this writing, but he produced a tender, fluid account of the relationship: *Lilly: Reminiscences of Lillian Hellman* (New York: Morrow, 1988). The book's occasional preciousness is part of, and generally counterweighed by, its often comical, sometimes grim truth—in the literary sense of truth, that is.

24. JH to Grace Hersey, June 24, 1966, B Box 18.

25. JH als from 231 Park St., New Haven, to Blanche Knopf, June 3, 1966, HRC Knopf.

26. JH to Grace Hersey, July 20, 1966, B Box 18.

27. Schlesinger to JH, March 7, 1967, B Box 21, 1966–69, S.

28. Kabaservice, *The Guardians*, 350.

29. Ibid., 314–15.

30. *AMI*, 160.

31. Joseph A. Califano, Jr., *The Triumph and Tragedy of Lyndon Johnson: The White House Years* (College Station: Texas A&M University Press, 2000), 219.

32. Correspondence between JH and Kurt Luedtke of the *Detroit Free Press* from February 1968 sets out possible terms of "a joint effort that would have mutual benefits to us, to you [Hersey] and to the community." The proposal was for a manuscript of 25,000 to 35,000 words to be published first in magazine format in a run of about 650,000 copies, but possibly as soon as twenty-four hours afterward elsewhere. The correspondence goes into the details of legal responsibility and format, but the main obstacle seems to have been that the *Free Press* people were unwilling to commit in advance to beginning the story on the entire front page. "Use of the full Page 1," they argued reasonably enough, "implies that the only news event in the world on the day we publish was the Algiers story. Our readers just won't stand for that; I doubt they should, frankly." B Box 45.

33. Hersey actually puts it more complicatedly in a passage whose logic is not strong: "The uses of invisibility—as Ralph Ellison has made so vividly and painfully clear—an inability or unwillingness to see the particularity of one's fellow man, and with it a crucial indifference as to whether one is seen truly as oneself—these uses of not-seeing and of not-being-seen are of the essence of racism." *AMI*, 30.

34. *AMI*, 34.

35. *FT*, Oct. 31, 1968.

36. Introduction to *AMI*, 1998 ed. (see n. 44, below), xix.

37. *AMI*, 334.

38. For a later, less impressionistic examination of the case, see Sidney Fine, *Violence in the Model City: The Cavanagh Administration, Race Relations, and the Detroit Riot of 1967* (Ann Arbor: Michigan University Press, 1988), 271–90.

39. *AMI*, 66.

40. Ibid., 345.

41. Horace Manges of Weil, Gotshal & Manges tls to Norman Lippitt of Boesky & Lippitt, July 8, 1968, B Box 47. Manges didn't mention, but must have noticed, that it was in the interests of Lippitt's own reputation that the book should be muffled. Lippitt's chances of securing an acquittal had in any case been greatly enhanced by a decision to move the case out of Detroit to a largely white area of Michigan, on the pretext of protecting the white defendants from black prejudice.

42. The John Hersey Foundation, of which he was not a director, supported educational and other social projects aimed at reducing racial conflict, especially in the New Haven area. Kessler, "John Hersey's Yale Education," 38.

43. Robert A. Terrell to JH, Oct. 18, 1968, B Box 45.

44. Baltimore and London: Johns Hopkins University Press, 1998, with a new introduction by Thomas J. Sugrue.

45. July 6, 1968, B Box 45.

46. September 1968, B Box 46.

47. *AMI*, 373-78.

48. *Saturday Review of Literature*, July 6, 1968.

49. One half-deranged black man did fire a pistol from a Detroit rooftop and was shot by police. No other evidence of anything like sniping was ever found. *AMI*, 338-39, ch. 40 "Snipers: The Myth."

50. Kabaservice, *The Guardians*, 402.

51. Brook Hersey's description of her mother at Pierson applies equally well to her father.

52. Kabaservice, *The Guardians*, 302.

53. See p. 300, n. 5.

54. *AMI*, 31-32.

55. See, for example, Kessler, "John Hersey's Yale Education," p. 304, n. 27.

56. *LA*, 29.

57. It is found in Jewish as well as Christian theology and is among the themes of Hersey's *The Wall*.

58. *LA*, 88-89.

59. JH circular letter to "Dear Piersonite," June 1969, B Box 21, 1966-69, *HIJ*.

60. *Yale Alumni Magazine*, October 1970.

61. *LA*, 77.

62. In the *Yale Daily News* itself, Richard Fuchs wrote: "His analysis of the purity, depth and future of youth's commitment to change is, I am afraid, somewhat naive . . . Violent radicals will have to forego [sic] their violence, conservative alumni will have to forego their conservatism, blacks will have to forego their suspicion of whites." Oct. 6, 1970.

63. Private communication.

64. *LA*, 137.

65. Name illegible, Oct. 11, 1970, B Box 21, 1966–69.

66. Roy Sussman in Mill Valley, California, to JH, Aug. 19, 1970; John Miller in Quang Nam Province, Vietnam, to JH, Aug. 21, 1970, loc. cit.

67. Oct. 3, 1970, loc. cit.

68. Feb. 24, 1971, loc. cit.

11. Sweet Land of Liberty

1. *Con*, 133–34.

2. No. 420.

3. JH cc ts April 17, 1970, requesting an interest-free loan of $60,000 to be repaid over ten years and explaining why it was a financially fair idea; William Koshland's positive response, Jan. 4, 1971. B Box 25. (Hersey's argument was that because his earnings from Knopf were, by mutual agreement, "spread forward," Knopf was always sitting on large sums of money that were essentially his own: in the late 1960s, on average $220,000 per year, an increase of $175,000 since the 1950s.)

4. George de Mare to JH, Nov. 23, 1960, B Box 19, 1952–63, D. De Mare's novel *The Empire* was published in 1956.

5. This was early in 1966. Drawing heavily on the impressions of one of Hellman's students, Ralph Penner, Carl Rollyson gives a detailed account of her semester at Pierson in *Lillian Hellman: Her Legend and Her Legacy* (New York: St. Martin's Press, 1988), 423–29. Penner was intrigued by Hersey's friendship with her: "She was a very brusque, tough individual. He was a very contemplative, sensitive and caring person. And he let you know that the moment you met him."

6. But Warren's 1946 novel *All the King's Men* was originally planned as a verse play, and there's his "tale in verse and voices," *Brother to Dragons* (1953).

7. May 6, 1972, B Box 54.

8. "When I called you," Hersey wrote to Culler on Nov. 19, 1972, "I did not mean to be nominating myself for Robert Penn Warren's professorship as it falls free; I simply would like to teach another departmental course beside the one I now teach." Nov. 19, 1972, B Box 54.

9. Yale "is very sticky about positions on the regular faculty for non Ph.D.s," Hersey wrote from Rome to Daniel Stern. "There is an opening for the rest of us in seminars originating and taught in the residential colleges . . . [but these] pay very badly." Daniel Stern papers, HRC, May 6, 1971.

10. The program was established in 1971 by Charles Twitchell Davis. Among the early appointees was Henry Louis Gates, Jr.

11. African Americanists apart, they included the poet-critic John Hollander, the eighteenth-century scholars Ronald Paulson and Patricia Meyer Spacks, and the Shakespearean G. K. Hunter.

12. Course details are given by Zara Kessler in "John Hersey's Yale Education," 47*ff*. She also describes entry procedures, names some of the alumni, and quotes from their comments.

13. Jackson Diehl in Kessler, "John Hersey's Yale Education," 49.

14. Bernardine Connelly in *John Hersey*, memorial tributes, 13–14.

15. Other journalists included David Lauter, Ruth Marcus, and Jane Mayer. Among the fiction writers were Jonathan Dee, Jean Diehl, and Eileen Pollack.

16. Notes made by Hersey for his course "The Craft of Writing," B Box 38, quoted by Kessler, "John Hersey's Yale Education," 48.

17. *John Hersey*, memorial tributes, 40.

18. Elizabeth Otis to JH, June 19, 1970, B Box 27. Her author John Steinbeck died in 1968.

19. He retired in 1974 and died of a heart attack the following year.

20. Shawn to JH, c/o Elizabeth Otis, Aug. 3, 1972, turning down "Bridge over Dry Creek Bed," B Box 27.

21. The review, by Susan Lardner, called the book "slapdash." *NY* Archive Box 1511, Sept. 30, 1968. The decision about *The Conspiracy* is recorded in *NY* Archive Box 855.

22. "A Game on a Hill" (see pp. 194*ff*.) appeared on Dec. 7, 1957. For Hersey's influence on Mailer's novel, see p. 310, n. 55.

23. Nov. 2, 1966, B Box 21.

24. Text copied in tls from JH to Nancy Lyman Huse, B Box 22, 1970–73.

25. There's a letter in the Hersey archive from Mailer's publisher, Rinehart & Co., inviting him to read (and, implicitly, provide a publicity quote for) *The Naked and the Dead*—written, the letter says, "by a man of twenty-five by the name of Norman Mailer who saw service in the Philippines and Japan . . . as a rifleman in a reconnaissance platoon." The folder doesn't contain Hersey's response, if any. Feb. 4, 1948, B Box 19, 1937–51, *P–Q*.

26. Fadiman was a judge for the Book of the Month Club, which made *The Conspiracy* one of its choices. The quotation comes from an article by him included as a flyer in members' copies.

27. B Box 25, 1970–73.

28. Peter De Vries to JH, Nov. 15, 1970, B Box 22, 1970–73, *D*.

29. These numbers come from a table prepared for Hersey by Knopf dated Sept. 11, 1964, B Box 25.

30. List dated April 15, 1959, HRC Knopf.

31. April 9, 1975, B Box 25. Green had joined Knopf in 1964, after the Random House takeover.

32. Ginzburg's *Ti ho sposato per allegria* (1964) was made into a film in Italian in 1967. An earlier translation, by Jane House, had been given an airing at the City University of New York in 1969; see http://www.janehouseprods.com/Jane_House_Produc tions/2002-03_files/Program-Ginzburg.pdf. The text of Hersey's version is in B Box 57. See also Sheldon Kleinman (managing director) tls to JH detailing the terms of

JH's agreement with Yale Rep., Jan. 24, 1972; and Natalia Ginzburg tls to JH with suggestions about how to translate certain phrases, Jan. 27, 1972, both in B Box 54.

33. He told David Sanders (1989) that this was one of his prompts for writing the book.

34. T. A. Shippey, *TLS*, May 16, 1975. The "column of citizens four abreast" in which the narrator of *MP* stands "stretches back along Church Street to the corner of Elm and around toward Orange and out of sight," *MP*, 3–4. Topographical details are even more precise and vivid in the *WD*.

35. Granville Hicks in the *NYT* called it a "readable little novel." Sept. 22, 1974. For the *TLS*, see n. 34.

36. *Paris Review* interview.

37. The later novel is *Antonietta*; see pp. 277*ff.*

38. *WD*, 118.

39. "First principle: *Plywood sucks*," wrote Harold Beaver in the *TLS*. "Second law: *Veneer is Nixonian: all cover-up.*"

40. Gene Lyons, *NYTBR*, Sunday, Sept. 18, 1977. The book was reviewed for the daily *Times* by Christopher Lehmann-Haupt, who also said he couldn't believe Hersey "ever had real people in mind," October 3, 1977.

41. *WC*, 6.

42. In a letter to a teacher there dated October 27, 1973, he expressed some concerns about what he saw as a change in its ethos. JH to Nancy Lyman Huse; see p. 337, n. 24, above. A representative of John Hersey High School spoke with gratitude at his memorial service at Yale in May 1993: *John Hersey*, memorial tributes, 28–30.

43. For example, a paper given at MIT's Wiesner Colloquium, May 21, 1980, on the continuing relevance of C. P. Snow's *The Two Cultures* (1959).

44. In August 1975. B Box 59.

45. August 7, 1972. The article generated considerable correspondence, first in the forum's journal, August–September 1972, and then in response to reprints in *Briefcase*, the journal of the National Legal Aid and Defender Association, and *Intellectual Digest* (both November 1972).

46. Other members of the committee included the MIT president Jerome Wiesner, the *New York Review of Books* editor Robert Silvers, and several prominent arts figures, including Leonard Bernstein, Paul Newman, and Mike Nichols. See William Wright, *Lillian Hellman: The Image, the Woman* (New York: Simon & Schuster, 1986), 337. The Watergate meeting was held in Martha's Vineyard in July 1973. Hersey joined the board of the Committee Against Government Secrecy that September. B Box 54.

47. JH manuscript draft letter, Jan. 16, 1971, to H. I. Romnes, B Box 22, 1970–73.

48. See, for example, a letter to JH from Congresswoman Ella Grasso, Aug. 23, 1974, agreeing with his resistance to immunity for Nixon. B Box 22, 1974–81.

49. Correspondence about the visit is in B Box 59.

50. "Successors," *NY*, Dec. 16, 1974, reprinted in *LS*, 329–66.

51. *LS*, 329.

52. Ibid., 353.

53. Ibid., 356.

54. Ibid., 332.

55. *AP*, 141, foreword to the Ford section. Apart from this addition, the text that appears in *AP* is identical to the *NYT* version.

56. Ibid., 145.

57. Ibid., 169.

58. Walter Isaacson, *Kissinger: A Biography* (New York: Simon & Schuster, 1992), ch. 28, "The Magic Is Gone: Setbacks in the Sinai and Southeast Asia."

59. *AP*, 228.

60. Ibid., 177.

61. Cousins had been at the magazine since 1942, for much of that time as its editor in chief.

62. JH to Norman Cousins, Jan. 7, 1977, B Box 44.

63. *NYT*, Nov. 24, 1976.

64. Shirley Hazzard to JH, Nov. 29, 1976, B Box 44. In addition to being a novelist, Hazzard had worked at the UN Secretariat.

65. Some time earlier he had begun relearning Chinese, his hopes of returning to Tianjin having been raised by Nixon's 1972 visit. (Information from Brook Hersey.)

66. See pp. 3*ff.*

67. See pp. 282*ff.*

68. *Call*, 17.

69. In *The Writer's Craft* he includes a passage of Tolstoy that, in turn, draws on the Russian painter Karl Briullov. Hersey summarizes the point being made as "the mystery of the 'infinitely minute degrees'—of pitch, of tone, of timing, of intensity, of truth—that separate art from all that is not art." *WC*, 25.

70. Judith Jones tls to JH, May 18, 1981, B Box 25.

71. *Paris Review* interview. *Fling* is dedicated to Judith Jones.

72. *Call*, 346.

73. *NYRB*, May 30, 1985.

74. In his notes at the back of the novel, Hersey acknowledges "with gratitude, most valuable encouragement and guidance, from the inception of this work, from John K. Fairbank."

75. Brook Hersey, "Barbara Hersey: July 17, 1919–August 17, 2007"—memorial tribute given at Key West.

76. *John Hersey*, memorial tributes, 47–48.

77. *Fling*, 5. See pp. 290*ff.*

78. Interview with Kay Bonetti for the American Audio Prose Library, 1988. Hersey repaid Hartt by giving the college's commencement address in 1957. B Box 32. Yet when, later on, Baird gave him a violin for Christmas, he "never opened the case": *Paris Review* interview.

79. *New Republic*, May 2, 1983.

80. *NYTBR*, May 10, 1987.

81. He did so on Dec. 4, 1987. The tribute was published in the Academy's *Proceedings*,

Second Series, no. 38, 1987, and like the other articles mentioned in this paragraph was collected in *LS*.

82. "Critic at Large," *NY*, July 18, 1988.

83. *NYT*, July 22, 24, 1988.

84. JH tls to Singer, May 16, 1983, Dvorah Telushkin Collection, HRC.

85. JH correspondence with Mailer, Feb. 11, April 20, June 10, 1984, Mailer Collection, HRC.

86. The MacDowell Medal, presented at the MacDowell Colony, New Hampshire, Aug. 15, 1976. Hersey's speech is reprinted in *Life Sketches*. *The Conspiracy* is dedicated to Hellman.

87. Feibleman, *Lilly*, 257.

88. The story has been told often. The women were old rivals, and McCarthy was among those who had given up Communism while Hellman hung on to it. A relevant aspect, rarely stressed, is the fact that Hellman's last stage play, the doomed *My Mother, My Father, and Me,* appeared in the same year, 1963, as Mary McCarthy's highly successful *The Group*, which stayed on the *New York Times* bestseller list for the next two years. In 1964, interviewed by *The Paris Review*, Hellman said that "in fiction, [Miss McCarthy] is a lady writer, a lady magazine writer." Quoted by Feibleman, *Lilly*, 284.

89. *An Unfinished Woman*, 1969; *Pentimento*, 1973; *Scoundrel Time*, 1976.

90. JH to Dick Cavett, Jan. 26, 1980, B Box 22, 1974–81, C.

91. Hellman had phoned Hersey at the end of the show to suggest that they should both sue. Wright, *Lillian Hellman*, 386.

92. *NY*, July 15, 1985. Apart from a small amount of introductory material to each section, "reminding" readers who the characters were and where the original story had left them in 1946, the text is identical to the one published, along with the earlier parts, in book form.

93. See pp. 195*ff.*

94. See pp. 270*ff.*

95. B Box 63.

96. *H*, 129.

97. Ibid., 173.

98. *Manzanar*, xii.

99. *M*, 11.

100. Ibid., 44.

12. A Kind of Daylight in the Mind

1. Information partly from Brook Hersey, partly from Wright, *Lillian Hellman*, 352. Lillian Hellman visited and put down a deposit on one of the apartments, but decided instead to continue spending her winters in Los Angeles.

2. Rampersad, *Ralph Ellison*.

3. The screenplay was by Millard Lampell, author of the very different stage version (see p. 165). Directed by Robert Markowitz, it starred Lisa Eichhorn as Rachel Apt and Tom Conti as Dolek Berson. Never released in movie theaters, this version of *The Wall* went unmentioned by *The New Yorker* and wasn't helped by appearing in the same year as Alan Parker's identically titled documentary about Pink Floyd. More recently it has been overshadowed by Jan Komasa's 2014 Polish documentary *Warsaw Uprising*, made entirely from contemporary footage.

4. Tony Schwartz, *NYT*, Feb. 16, 1982.

5. Interview with Kay Bonetti.

6. "Time's Winged Chariot." The text appears in Clifton Fadiman, ed., *Living Philosophies: The Reflections of Some Eminent Men and Women of Our Time* (New York: Doubleday, 1990), 16–22.

7. Time's winged chariot appears most famously in Andrew Marvell's poem "To His Coy Mistress." Saint Paul talks about death as "the last enemy" in his First Epistle to the Corinthians 15:26.

8. Soon after the couple bought the Key West property, Barbara Hersey underwent surgery and chemotherapy for breast cancer. She also developed rheumatoid arthritis and from then until her death was regularly in pain.

9. See pp. 150*ff.*

10. "Affinities" first appeared in 1987 in *Shenandoah*, edited by the Southern writer R. T. Smith.

11. *KWT*, 23.

12. Ibid., 153.

13. The funeral was held in Martha's Vineyard on July 23, 1984.

14. *John Hersey* memorial tributes.

15. The work was first performed at the Woodstock Bookfest on March 24, 2018, the twenty-fifth anniversary of Hersey's death. The violinists were Katherine Hannauer and Laura Hackstein. Hersey's words were read by the novelist Colm Toíbín. https://hudsonvalleyone.com/2018/03/15/a-father-a-son-and-a-collaboration-25-years-in-the-making/.

16. Baird Hersey and Prana with Krishna Das, https://www.youtube.com/watch?v=3oA7Sneut3w, accessed Oct. 5, 2017, lyrics at https://www.musixmatch.com/lyrics/Baird-Hersey-PRANA-with-Krishna-Das/My-God-Is-Real.

Acknowledgments

This is a study of John Hersey's career, not a full biography. My interest in his work was sharpened in 1992 when I taught a course at Princeton on international literature set in the Second World War, which was subsequently offered in changing forms over a period of twenty years at the University of Warwick. The course was popular, and the reactions of students helped shape my own. In informal polls, *Hiroshima* was always voted one of the most powerful of the texts studied. Primo Levi's *If This Is a Man* and Anne Frank's *Diary of a Young Girl* were among the others, and in connection with them, as well as with Hersey's novel *The Wall*, I'm glad to acknowledge the influence of Yosef Hayim Yerushalmi and his wonderful book *Zakhor: Jewish History and Jewish Memory* (1982).

Useful information is contained in the two versions of a book by David Sanders published in a series for students: *John Hersey* (1965) and *John Hersey Revisited* (1991). Sanders had Hersey's personal help and tends to take the writer's fiction at his own valuation, whereas an argument of the present study is that Hersey's "literary nonfiction"— broadly, his journalistic and biographical work—most deserves readers' attention. This isn't controversial; it is what most contemporary critics thought, as well as Hersey's best editors. But Sanders did a service to readers by describing and contextualizing his fiction so sympathetically. As for what he ignores, it would be good if a publisher commissioned a new selection of Hersey's articles, many of which have never been reprinted.

The notes give details of the main works I've drawn on, including two well-researched

Yale student projects that deserve additional mention here: Zara Kessler's "John Hersey's Yale Education" and Nathaniel Sobel's "Searching for John Hersey." In the course of his preparations, Sobel unearthed, among other things, Hersey's school records.

At the outset I was fortunate in having the support of a two-year Leverhulme Emeritus Research Fellowship and one-month fellowships at Yale's Beinecke Library and at the Harry Ransom Research Center in Austin, Texas. These grants helped pay for a modest amount of research assistance from the meticulous Andrina Tran at Yale. At the Ransom Center, Phillip Fry and Virginia T. Seymour checked some references for me. Nancy F. Lyon, Sandra Markham, and Molly Schwartzburg at the Beinecke; Richard Oram and Rick Watson at the Ransom Center; Kate Jacobs at Hotchkiss School; Barbara Michael and Abby Lester at Sarah Lawrence College; and Kyle R. Triplett, librarian of the Brooke Russell Astor Reading Room for Rare Books and Manuscripts at the New York Public Library, all gave expert assistance.

Nick Bunnin and Katie Lee introduced me to helpful contacts in and to do with China, and I'm especially grateful to Jiangxi Zhangjin, who encouraged Jiu Peng, Moxi Zhang, and Li Zhanjing to accompany me on a couple of enjoyable Hersey-related expeditions in Tianjin. David Hollinger allowed me to read an absorbing draft of a relevant chapter of his book *Protestants Abroad: How Missionaries Tried to Change the World but Changed America* (2017). Karen Sharman, of the Briarcliff Manor Historical Society, showed me the society's museum and archive, gave me a vivid guided tour of the village and its Congregational church, and introduced me to other knowledgeable residents of the Herseys' U.S. hometown. As a result of conversations about Hiroshima with Elizabeth Chappell and her friend Tomoko Nakamura, I was fortunate enough to be shown around that city by Ken Tanimoto, son of a key figure in Hersey's *Hiroshima*. I won't forget standing with him at the place from which on August 6, 1945, his father ferried desperate injured people across the Kyobashi-gawa River, away from the flames.

Friends old and new have been generous with their hospitality and time. Isabel Fonseca and Martin Amis put me up several times in Brooklyn. The novelist Jonathan Dee, a former student of Hersey's and his interlocutor in a *Paris Review* interview, talked to me informatively. On Martha's Vineyard, Rose Styron had me to stay, took me to see the Herseys' former summer home, and showed me the writer's grave. In addition, Peter Blegvad, Irene Brendel, Jung Chang, Anne Fadiman, Roy Foster, Kate Nouri Hughes, James Koester, SSJE, Lynn Freedman, Caroline Raphael, Leo Robson, Laura Roosevelt, and Ileene Smith all helped in a variety of ways.

A draft was completed at the Fondazione Bogliasco, Liguria. I'm more than grateful for the time my wife and I spent there in the spring of 2017 and for the stimulating company of our fellow residents: Carla Guelfenbein, James Longenbach, Tess Martin, Helen O'Leary, Antonio Ramos, Neil and the late Wendy Rolnick, Joanna Scott, and Cori Thomas. Gianni Biaggi de Blasys and Laura Harrison were indulgent hosts, and Ivana Folle, Valeria Soave, and Claudia Martínez del Hoyo were among those who simplified all aspects of work and life at the Villa dei Pini.

I'm particularly grateful to Edmund Fawcett, who brought to bear on a late draft his expertise both as a historian of political thought and as a former Washington correspondent and literary editor of *The Economist*. Earlier on, individual parts were read and commented on by two other friends, Paul Freedman and David Bromwich, both long-serving professors at Yale. Successive versions were read by Hersey's literary executor, Brook Hersey. While she has helped in a number of ways, not least in giving permission for her father's words to be quoted, Ms. Hersey has also been faithful to what she believes was his wish that no biography of him should be written. Though the book does not have her formal approval, it has benefited from her comments. Whatever errors remain are, of course, my own.

Some parts appeared first in *The Times Literary Supplement*, and I'm grateful to the editors concerned, Peter Stothard and Stig Abell.

John Davey, former editor in chief of Basil Blackwell, died while I was revising the book. He was my first publisher, and without his reckless encouragement, I don't know how I would have got started all those years ago. Farrar, Straus and Giroux first brought out something of mine in the United States in 1988, and I would like to acknowledge the warm friendship and professional support of the late Roger Straus and of Peggy Miller and Jonathan Galassi.

Despite the demands of her own work, my wife, Maria Alvarez, has managed to live with the book from its outset, has read parts of it at various stages, and has made discriminating but always constructive comments. This isn't, though, why it is dedicated to her.

JT, LONDON, MARCH 2018

Index